For Reference

Not to be taken from this room

EUROPEAN POLITICAL FACTS
1918–73

EUROPEAN POLITICAL FACTS 1918–73

Chris Cook and John Paxton

Facts On File
119 West 57th Street, New York, N.Y. 10019

First published in the United Kingdom 1975 by
THE MACMILLAN PRESS LTD

Reissued in the United States 1978 by
FACTS ON FILE INC.
New York

Library of Congress Cataloging in Publication Data

Cook, Chris, 1945–
  European political facts, 1918–73.

  Reprint of the ed. published by Macmillan, London.
  Includes index.
  1. Europe – Politics and government – 1918–1945.
  2. Europe – Politics and government – 1945–
  3. International agencies. I. Paxton, John, joint
author. II. Title.
  [JN12.C64 1078]   320.9'4'05   77-28298
  ISBN 0-87196-377-9

CONTENTS

PREFACE

As European countries move closer together for political, economic, social and cultural co-operation, there is an increasing need for readily accessible facts concerning the recent history of these countries. We have made this our prime aim in compiling *European Political Facts, 1918–73*.

Our coverage is from the Atlantic to the Urals and in adopting this broad, outward-looking concept of Europe we have, naturally, encountered considerable editorial difficulties. The general aim is comparability between countries. This was not always easy to achieve and in some cases impossible, particularly for comparisons between 'East' and 'West' Europe.

Nineteen-eighteen is a watershed between an old and a new Europe and the editors felt that this was a realistic starting point although some facts are given for earlier years where these are pertinent. Space naturally limits the data which can be presented for 35 countries covering a span of 56 years.

We are grateful to many people and organizations for their help and advice. In the first place we should like to acknowledge our debt to David Butler, who was a pathfinder with his highly successful *British Political Facts* (Butler and Freeman, Macmillan).

Gratitude also goes to Sheila Fairfield for hours of work digging for facts; to Brian Hunter for tremendous help on eastern European countries; and to Stephen Brooks for his meticulous work on defence matters.

We have to thank Eve Beadle and Virginia Walker for excellent typing and sharp eyes for inconsistencies. We must also thank Mary Barker, Eve Beadle and Alison Johnson for their very great help with proof reading.

But some error and inconsistency can still appear in a work of this kind and the editors are solely responsible. We do ask readers to alert us if they spot error, and constructive and informed criticism will be welcome for future editions.

Chris Cook
July 1974   John Paxton

1 INTERNATIONAL ORGANIZATIONS

THE UNITED NATIONS

The United Nations is an association of states which have pledged themselves, through signing the Charter, to maintain international peace and security and to co-operate in establishing political, economic and social conditions under which this task can be securely achieved. Nothing contained in the Charter authorizes the organization to intervene in matters which are essentially within the domestic jurisdiction of any state.

The United Nations Charter originated from proposals agreed upon at discussions held at Dumbarton Oaks (Washington, DC) between the USSR, US and UK from 21 Aug to 28 Sep, and between US, UK and China from 29 Sep to 7 Oct 44. These proposals were laid before the United Nations Conference on International Organization, held at San Francisco from 25 Apr to 26 June 45, and (after amendments had been made to the original proposals) the Charter of the United Nations was signed on 26 June 45 by the delegates of 50 countries. Ratification of all the signatures had been received by 31 Dec 45.

The United Nations formally came into existence on 24 Oct 45, with the deposit of the requisite number of ratifications of the Charter with the US Department of State. The official languages of the United Nations are Chinese, English, French, Russian and Spanish; the working languages are English, French and (in the General Assembly) Spanish and Russian.

The headquarters of the United Nations is in New York City, USA.

Membership. Membership is open to all peace-loving states whose admission will be effected by the General Assembly upon recommendation of the Security Council.

The Principal Organs of the United Nations are: 1. The General Assembly 2. The Security Council 3. The Economic and Social Council 4. The Trusteeship Council 5. The International Court of Justice 6. The Secretariat.

1. THE GENERAL ASSEMBLY consists of all the members of the United Nations. Each member is entitled to be represented at its meetings by five

delegates and five alternate delegates, but has only one vote. The General Assembly meets regularly once a year, commencing on the 3rd Tuesday in September; the session normally lasts until mid-December and is resumed for some weeks in the new year if this is required. Special sessions may be convoked by the Secretary-General if requested by the Security Council, by a majority of the members of the United Nations or by one member concurred with by the majority of the members. The General Assembly elects its President for each session.

The first regular session was held in London from 10 Jan to 14 Feb and in New York from 23 Oct to 16 Dec 46.

Special sessions have been held, on Palestine, in 1947, 1948, 1963 and 1967; emergency sessions on the Middle East and on Hungary in 1956, on Lebanon in 1958, on the Congo in 1960, on South West Africa and the Middle East in 1967.

The work of the General Assembly is divided between six Main Committees and the Special Political Committee, on each of which every member has the right to be represented by one delegate. I. Political Security. II. Economic and Financial. III. Social, Humanitarian and Cultural. IV. Trust and Non-Self-Governing Territories. V. Administrative and Budgetary. VI. Legal.

In addition there is a General Committee charged with the task of co-ordinating the proceedings of the Assembly and its Committees; and a Credentials Committee which verifies the credentials of the delegates. The General Committee consists of 25 members, comprising the President of the General Assembly, its 17 Vice-Presidents and the Chairmen of the seven Main Committees. The Credentials Committee consists of nine members, elected at the beginning of each session of the General Assembly. The Assembly has two standing committees – an Advisory Committee on Administrative and Budgetary Questions and a Committee on Contributions. The General Assembly establishes subsidiary and *ad hoc* bodies when necessary to deal with specific matters. These include: Special Committee on Peace-Keeping Operations (33 members), Commission on Human Rights (32 members), Advisory Committee on the UN Emergency Force (7 members), Commission for the unification and rehabilitation of Korea (7 members), Committee on the peaceful uses of outer space (28 members), Conciliation Commission for Palestine (3 members), Conference of the Committee on Disarmament (26 members), International Law Commission (25 members), Scientific Committee on the effects of atomic radiation (15 members), Special Committee on the implementation of the declaration on the granting of independence to colonial countries and peoples (24 members), Special Committee on the policies of Apartheid of the Government of the Republic of South Africa (11 members), UN High Commissioner for Refugees, UN Relief and Works Agency for Palestine Refugees in the Near East, Peace Observation Commission (14 members), UN Commission on International Trade Law (29

2

members), UN Commission on International Trade Law (29 members) and Committee on the Peaceful Uses of Sea-bed and Ocean Floor Beyond the Limits of National Jurisdiction (91 members), Preparatory Committee on the Human Environment Conference, Stockholm, 1972 (27 members), Preparatory Committee on the Second Development Decade (27 members).

The General Assembly may discuss any matters within the scope of the Charter, and, with the exception of any situation or dispute on the agenda of the Security Council, may make recommendations on any such questions or matters. For decisions on important questions a two-thirds majority is required, on other questions a simple majority of members present and voting. In addition, the Assembly at its fifth session, in 1950, decided that if the Security Council, because of lack of unanimity of the permanent members, fails to exercise its primary responsibility for the maintenance of international peace and security in any case where there appears to be a threat to the peace, breach of the peace or act of aggression, the General Assembly shall consider the matter immediately with a view to making appropriate recommendations to members for collective measures, including in the case of a breach of the peace or act of aggression the use of armed force when necessary, to maintain or restore international peace and security.

The General Assembly receives and considers reports from the other organs of the United Nations, including the Security Council. The Secretary-General makes an annual report to it on the work of the organization.

2. THE SECURITY COUNCIL consists of 15 members, each of which has one representative and one vote. There are five permanent and ten non-permanent members elected for a two-year term by a two-thirds majority of the General Assembly. Retiring members are not eligible for immediate re-election. Any other member of the United Nations will be invited to participate without vote in the discussion of questions specially affecting its interests.

The Security Council bears the primary responsibility for the maintenance of peace and security. It is also responsible for the functions of the UN in trust territories classed as 'strategic areas'. Decisions on procedural questions are made by an affirmative vote of nine members. On all other matters the affirmative vote of nine members must include the concurring votes of all permanent members (in practice, however, an abstention by a permanent member is not considered a veto), subject to the provision that when the Security Council is considering methods for the peaceful settlement of a dispute, parties to the dispute abstain from voting.

For the maintenance of international peace and security the Security Council can, in accordance with special agreements to be concluded, call on armed forces, assistance and facilities of the member states. It is assisted by a Military Staff Committee consisting of the Chiefs of Staff of the permanent members of the Security Council or their representatives.

The Presidency of the Security Council is held for one month in rotation by the member states in the English alphabetical order of their names.

The Security Council functions continuously. Its members are permanently represented at the seat of the organization, but it may meet at any place that will best facilitate its work.

The Council has two standing committees, of Experts and on the Admission of New Members. In addition, from time to time, it establishes *ad hoc* committees and commissions such as the Truce Supervision Organization in Palestine. It has also appointed a Representative for India and Pakistan.

Permanent Members: China, France, USSR, UK, USA.

Non-Permanent Members: Guinea, India, Panama, Sudan, Yugoslavia (until 31 Dec 73); Australia, Austria, Indonesia, Kenya, Peru (until 31 Dec 74).

3. THE ECONOMIC AND SOCIAL COUNCIL is responsible under the General Assembly for carrying out the functions of the United Nations with regard to international economic, social, cultural, educational, health and related matters. By Jan 63, 14 specialized inter-governmental agencies working in these fields had been brought into relationship with the United Nations. The Economic and Social Council may also make arrangements for consultation with international non-governmental organizations and, after consultation with the member concerned, with national organizations; by Dec 65, 141 non-governmental organizations had been granted consultative status and a further 219 were on the register.

The Economic and Social Council consists of one delegate each of 27 member states elected by a two-thirds majority of the General Assembly. Nine are elected each year for a three-year term. Retiring members are eligible for immediate re-election. Each member has one vote. Decisions are made by a majority of the members present and voting.

The Council nominally holds two sessions a year, and special sessions may be held if required. The President is elected for one year and is eligible for immediate re-election.

The Economic and Social Council has the following commissions:

Regional Economic Commissions: ECE (Economic Commission for Europe); ECAFE (Economic Commission for Asia and the Far East. Bangkok); ECLA (Economic Commission for Latin America. Santiago, Chile); ECA (Economic Commission for Africa. Addis Ababa). These Commissions have been established to enable the nations of the major regions of the world to co-operate on common problems and also to produce economic information.

(1) Six Functional Statistical Commissions with sub-commission on Statistical Sampling; (2) Commission on Human Rights, with sub-commission on

4

Prevention of Discrimination and Protection of Minorities; (3) Social Development Commission; (4) Commission on the Status of Women; (5) Commission on Narcotic Drugs; (6) Population Commission; (7–10) Four regional Economic Commissions for Europe, Asia and the Far East, Latin America, Africa.

The Economic and Social Council has the following standing committees: The Economic Committee, Social Committee, Co-ordination Committee, Committee on Non-Governmental Organizations, Interim Committee on Programme of Conferences, Committee for Industrial Development, Advisory Committee on the Application of Science and Technology to Development, Committee on Housing, Building and Planning.

Other special bodies are the Permanent Central Opium Board, the Drug Supervisory Body, the Interim Co-ordinating Committee for International Commodity Arrangements and the Administrative Committee on Co-ordination to ensure (1) the most effective implementation of the agreements entered into between the United Nations and the specialized agencies and (2) co-ordination of activities.

Membership: Haiti, Hungary, Lebanon, Madagascar, Malaysia, New Zealand, Niger, USA, Zaïre (until 31 Dec 73); Bolivia, Burundi, Chile, China, Finland, Japan, Poland, USSR, UK (until 31 Dec 74); Algeria, Brazil, France, Mali, Mongolia, Netherlands, Spain, Trinidad and Tobago, Uganda (until 31 Dec 74).

4. THE TRUSTEESHIP COUNCIL. The Charter provides for an international trusteeship system to safeguard the interests of the inhabitants of territories which are not yet fully self-governing and which may be placed thereunder by individual trusteeship agreements. These are called trust territories. By 1968 all, except two, trust territories had become independent or joined independent countries.

The Trusteeship Council consists of the two members administering trust territories: Australia, USA: the permanent members of the Security Council that are not administering trust territories: China, France, USSR and UK. Decisions of the Council are made by a majority of the members present and voting, each member having one vote. The Council holds one regular session each year, and special sessions if required.

5. THE INTERNATIONAL COURT OF JUSTICE was created by an international treaty, the State of the Court, which forms an integral part of the United Nations Charter. All members of the United Nations are *ipso facto* parties to the Statute of the Court.

The Court is composed of independent judges, elected regardless of their nationality, who possess the qualifications required in their countries for appointment to the highest judicial offices, or are jurisconsuls of recognized competence in international law. There are 15 judges, no two of whom may be nationals of the same state. They are elected by the Security Council and the General Assembly of the United Nations sitting independently. Candidates are chosen from a list of persons nominated by the national groups in the Permanent Court of Arbitration established by the Hague Conventions of 1899 and 1907. In the case of members of the United Nations not represented in the Permanent Court of Arbitration, candidates are nominated by national groups appointed for the purpose by their governments. The judges are elected for a nine-year term and are eligible for immediate re-election. When engaged on business of the Court, they enjoy diplomatic privileges and immunities.

The Court elects its own President and Vice-Presidents for three years and remains permanently in session, except for judicial vacations. The full court of 15 judges normally sits, but a quorum of nine judges is sufficient to constitute the Court. It may form chambers of three or more judges for dealing with particular categories of cases, and forms annually a chamber of five judges to hear and determine, at the request of the parties, cases by summary procedures.

Competence and Jurisdiction. Only states may be parties in cases before the Court, which is open to the states parties to its Statute. The conditions under which the Court will be open to other states are laid down by the Security Council. The Court exercises its jurisdiction in all cases which the parties refer to it and in all matters provided for in the Charter, or in treaties and conventions in force. Disputes concerning the jurisdiction of the Court are settled by the Court's own decision.

The Court may apply in its decision: (a) international conventions; (b) international custom; (c) the general principles of law recognized by civilized nations; and (d) as subsidiary means for the determination of the rules of law, judicial decisions and the teachings of highly qualified publicists. If the parties agree, the Court may decide a case *ex aequo et bono.* The Court may also give an advisory opinion on any legal question to any organ of the United Nations or its agencies.

Procedure. The official languages of the Court are French and English. At the request of any party the Court will authorize the use of another language by this party. All questions are decided by a majority of the judges present. If the votes are equal, the President has a casting vote. The judgment is final and without appeal, but a revision may be applied for within ten years from the date of the judgment on the ground of a new decisive factor. Unless otherwise decided by the Court, each party bears its own costs.

Judges. The judges of the Court, elected by the Security Council and the General Assembly, are as follows: (1) To serve until 5 Feb 76: Fouad

Ammoun (Lebanon), Cesar Bengzon (Philippines), Sture Petren (Sweden), Manfred Lachs (Poland), Charles D. Onyeama (Nigeria). (2) To serve until 5 Feb 79: Frederico de Castro (Spain), Louis Ignacio-Pinto (Dahomey), C. Dillard (USA), Eduardo Jiménez de Aréchaga (Uruguay), Platon D. Morozov (USSR). (3) To serve until 5 Feb 82: André Gros (France), Isaac Forster (Senegal), Sir Humphrey Waldock (UK), Nagendra Singh (India), José Maria Ruda (Argentina).

'National' Judges. If there is no judge on the bench of the nationality of the parties to the dispute, each party has the right to choose a judge. Such judges shall take part in the decision on terms of complete equality with their colleagues.

The Court has its seat at The Hague, but may sit and exercise its functions elsewhere whenever it considers this desirable. The expenses of the Court are borne by the United Nations.

Registrar: Stanislas Aquarone (Australia).

6. THE SECRETARIAT is composed of the Secretary-General, who is the chief administrative officer of the organization, and an international staff appointed by him under regulations established by the General Assembly. However, the Secretary-General, the High Commissioner for Refugees and the Managing Director of the Fund are appointed by the General Assembly. The first Secretary-General was Trygve Lie (Norway), 1946–53; the second, Dag Hammarskjöld (Sweden), 1953–61; the third, U Thant (Burma), 1961–71.

The Secretary-General acts as chief administrative officer in all meetings of the General Assembly, the Security Council, the Economic and Social Council and the Trusteeship Council.

Secretaries-General:

Trygve Lie (Norway)	1 Feb 46 – 10 Apr 53
Dag Hammarskjöld (Sweden)	10 Apr 53 – 17 Sep 61
U Thant (Burma)[1]	3 Nov 61 – 31 Dec 71
Kurt Waldheim (Austria)	1 Jan 72 –

The Secretary-General is assisted by 11 Under-Secretaries-General and 5 Assistant Secretaries-General.

The UN DEVELOPMENT PROGRAMME, created on 22 Nov 65, is an amalgamation of the programme of Technical Assistance and the Special Fund. *Administrator*: Rudolph Peterson (USA).

---

[1] Acting Secretary-General 1961–2.

AGENCIES IN RELATIONSHIP WITH THE UN
(as in 1973)

	IAEA	ILO	FAO	UNESCO	WHO	BANK &	FUND	ICAO	UPU	ITU	WMO	IFC	IMCO	GATT
Albania	*	–	–	*	*	–	–	*	*	*	–	–	–	–
Austria	*	*	*	*	*	*	*	*	*	*	*	*	–	*
Belgium	*	*	*	*	*	*	*	*	*	*	*	*	*	*
Bulgaria	*	*	*	*	*	–	*	*	*	*	–	–	*	–
Byelorussia	*	*	–	*	*	–	–	*	*	*	–	–	–	–
Czechoslovakia	*	*	*	*	*	–	*	*	*	*	–	*	*	*
Denmark	*	*	*	*	*	*	*	*	*	*	*	*	*	*
Finland	*	*	*	*	*	*	*	*	*	*	*	*	*	*
France	*	*	*	*	*	*	*	*	*	*	*	*	*	*
Germany (East)	–	*	–	*	*	–	–	*	*	*	–	*	–	–
Germany (West)	*	*	*	*	*	*	*	*	*	*	*	*	*	*
Greece	*	*	*	*	*	*	*	*	*	*	*	*	*	*
Hungary	*	*	*	*	*	–	*	*	*	*	–	–	*	–
Iceland	*	*	*	*	*	*	*	*	*	*	*	*	*	*
Irish Rep.	*	*	*	*	*	*	*	*	*	*	*	*	*	*
Italy	*	*	*	*	*	*	*	*	*	*	*	*	*	*
Liechtenstein	*	–	–	–	–	–	–	*	*	–	–	–	–	–
Luxembourg	*	*	*	*	*	*	*	*	*	*	*	*	–	*
Malta	–	*	*	*	*	–	*	*	*	–	–	–	*	*
Monaco	*	–	–	*	*	–	–	*	*	–	–	–	–	–
Netherlands	*	*	*	*	*	*	*	*	*	*	*	*	*	*
Norway	*	*	*	*	*	*	*	*	*	*	*	*	*	*
Poland	*	*	*	*	*	–	*	*	*	*	–	–	*	*
Portugal	*	*	*	–	*	*	*	*	*	*	*	*	–	*
Romania	*	*	*	*	*	*	*	*	*	*	–	–	*	*
San Marino	–	–	–	–	–	–	–	–	–	*	–	–	–	–
Spain	*	*	*	*	*	*	*	*	*	*	*	*	*	*
Sweden	*	*	*	*	*	*	*	*	*	*	*	*	*	*
Switzerland	*	*	*	*	*	–	*	*	*	*	–	–	*	*
Turkey	*	*	*	*	*	*	*	*	*	*	*	*	*	*
Ukraine	*	*	–	*	*	–	–	*	*	*	–	–	–	–
USSR	*	*	–	*	*	–	*	*	*	*	–	–	*	–
UK	*	*	*	*	*	*	*	*	*	*	*	*	*	*
Vatican	*	–	–	–	–	–	–	*	*	–	–	–	–	–
Yugoslavia	*	*	*	*	*	*	*	*	*	*	*	*	*	*

UPU members also include: French Overseas Territories; Netherlands Antilles and Surinam; Portuguese Overseas Provinces; Spanish territories in Africa; UK overseas territories.

ITU members also include French Overseas Territories; Portuguese Overseas Provinces; Spanish territories in Africa; UK protectorates and overseas territories.

WMO members also include British Caribbean Territories; French Polynesia; French Somaliland; Hong Kong; Mauritius; Netherlands Antilles and Surinam; New Caledonia; Portuguese East and West Africa; Spanish territories in Africa.

The UN CONFERENCE ON TRADE AND DEVELOPMENT was established by the General Assembly on 30 Dec 64. It comprises those states which are members of the UN, its specialized agencies or the International Atomic Energy Agency. Its permanent organ, the Trade and Development Board (55 members), meets twice a year. Its four subsidiary organs meet annually; these are the Committees on Commodities, Manufactures, Shipping, and Invisibles and Financing Related to Trade. The first UNCTAD was held in Geneva in 1964, the second in New Delhi in 1968 and the third in Santiago (Chile) 1972.

Secretary-General: Manuel Perez Guerrero (Venezuela, Mar 69–31 Mar 72).

Headquarters: Geneva, Switzerland.

The UN DEVELOPMENT ORGANIZATION (UNIDO) has worked as an autonomous body with the UN to promote industrialization and co-ordinate activities undertaken by the UN family in this field since 1967. Principal body is the 45-member Industrial Development Board, which formulates UNIDO's policy and its programme of activities. UNIDO tries to help the urgent need of developing countries to accelerate their promotional and operational activities and supports them by relevant studies and research.

Executive Director: Ibrahim H. Abdel-Rahman.

Headquarters: Rathausplatz 2, Vienna, Austria.

THE LEAGUE OF NATIONS

The League of Nations formally came into existence on 10 Jan 20, through the coming into force at that date of the Treaty of Versailles. The two official languages of the League were English and French. The seat of the League was Geneva, Switzerland.

The League of Nations was an association of states which had pledged themselves, through signing the Covenant (*i.e.* the constitution of the League) not to go to war before submitting their disputes with each other, or states not members of the League, to arbitration or enquiry and a delay of from three to nine months. Furthermore, any state violating this pledge was automatically in a state of outlawry with the other states, which were bound to sever all economic and political relations with the defaulting state.

Secretaries-General of the League:

Sir Eric Drummond [E of Perth] (Britain)	1919–32
Joseph Avenol (France)	1933–40

On Joseph Avenol's resignation, 26 July 40, Sean Lester (Irish Republic) became Acting Secretary-General.

Membership. The following European States joined the League on the dates given below:

Albania[1]	16 Dec 20
Austria	16 Dec 20
Belgium	10 Jan 20
Bulgaria	16 Dec 20
Czechoslovakia	10 Jan 20
Denmark	8 Mar 20
Estonia[1]	22 Sep 21
Finland	16 Dec 20
France	10 Jan 20
Germany	8 Sep 26
Greece	30 Mar 20
Hungary	18 Sep 22
Irish Free State	10 Sep 23
Italy	10 Jan 20
Latvia[1]	22 Sep 21
Lithuania[1]	22 Sep 21
Luxembourg	16 Dec 20
Netherlands	9 Mar 20
Norway	5 Mar 20
Poland	10 Jan 20
Portugal	8 Apr 20
Romania	8 Apr 20
Spain	10 Jan 20
Sweden	9 Mar 20
Switzerland	8 Mar 20
Turkey	18 July 32
USSR	18 Sep 34
UK	10 Jan 20
Yugoslavia	10 Feb 20

[1] Made declarations putting the protection of their national minorities under League auspices as a condition of their entry into the League.

The following European states withdrew from the League: Spain on 8 Sep 26, Germany on 21 Oct 33, Italy on 11 Dec 37, and Hungary on 11 Apr 39, announced their withdrawal from the League; according to Art. 1, par. 3, of the Covenant the notice of withdrawal only came into force two years after it had been given. On 22 Mar 28, Spain resolved to continue a member of the League.

Austria ceased to be a member after her annexation by Germany in Mar 38.

The League was formally dissolved in 1946, but in practice it had not met since 1939.

THE ORGANS OF THE LEAGUE

The Primary Organs of the League were: 1. The Council, 2. The Assembly, 3. The Secretariat, 4. The Permanent Court of International Justice (at The Hague).

1. THE COUNCIL was originally composed of four permanent members (the British Empire, France, Italy and Japan) and four non-permanent members to be elected every year by a majority of the Assembly. The first non-permanent members, appointed by the Peace Conference and named in the Covenant before the first Assembly met, were Belgium, Brazil, Greece and Spain. With the approval of the majority of the Assembly, the Council was able to appoint new permanent and non-permanent members. At the Assembly of Sep 26 Germany was admitted to the League and given a permanent seat on the Council. At the same time the number of non-permanent seats, already increased to six in 1922, was further increased to nine, the period of office to be three years. In order to institute the new system of rotation, three were elected for one year, three for two years, and three for three years, so that at all subsequent Assemblies three members retired instead of nine at once. Furthermore, the rule was established that a retiring member was ineligible for re-election for three years unless specially declared re-eligible. The number of members elected after being declared re-eligible could not exceed three. Hitherto the only states to secure a declaration of re-eligibility had been Poland and Spain. Both countries applied for re-eligibility in 1937, but neither of them obtained the necessary majority for re-election during the 18th Assembly, Sep 37. China re-entered the Council in 1936 as a result of such a declaration. Owing to complaints that a number of members of the League were in practice unable to enter the Council, a tenth non-permanent seat was created for three years in 1933, and in 1936 this seat was continued in existence for another three years and an eleventh non-permanent seat created for three years (*i.e.* till 1939). Any member of the League not represented on the Council was invited to send a representative to sit on it at any meetings at which matters especially affecting it were being discussed. A similar invitation could be extended to states not members of the League.

The Council met on the 3rd Monday in January, the 2nd Monday in May, and just before and after the Assembly in September.

2. THE ASSEMBLY. Every state member of the League was entitled to be represented by a delegation to the Assembly composed of not more than three delegates and three substitute delegates, but it had only one vote. It met at the seat of the League (Geneva) on the second or, in certain circumstances, the first Monday in September. It could meet at other places than Geneva; extraordinary sessions could be called to deal with urgent matters.

The President was elected at the first meeting of the session, and held office for the duration of the session.

The Assembly divided itself into the following seven principal committees, on each of which every state member of the League had the right to be represented by one delegate:

I. Juridical.
II. Technical Organizations.
III. Disarmament.
IV. Budget and Staff.
V. Social Questions.
VI. Political Questions and admission of New Members.
VII. As an experiment, the General Committee of the 19th Assembly decided to set up a Seventh Committee to deal with questions of Health, Opium and Intellectual Co-operation.

The decisions of the Assembly had to be voted unanimously, except where the Covenant or the Peace Treaties provided otherwise. As a general principle decisions on questions of procedure were voted by majority, or in some cases by a two-thirds majority.

3. THE SECRETARIAT was a permanent organ composed of the Secretary-General and a number of officials selected from among citizens of all member states and from the United States of America. The Secretary-General, who took office in July 33, was M. Joseph Avenol (French). The other officials were appointed by the Secretary-General with the approval of the Council.

The Under-Secretaries-General as from 1 Feb 37 were:

Mr Sean Lester (Irish Republic) Deputy Secretary-General
Mr F. Walters (UK)
M Vladimir Sokoline (USSR) as from 20 Feb 37
M Podesta Costa (Argentine) as from Jan 38

4. PERMANENT COURT OF INTERNATIONAL JUSTICE. The Permanent Court at the Hague was created by an international treaty, the Statute of the Court, which was drafted in 1920 by a committee appointed by the Council of the League of Nations and revised in 1929 with amendments which came into force in 1936. The revised Statutes adopted at the 10th Assembly provided for 15 judges for the Court, and stipulated that the Court should remain permanently in Session except for such holidays as it may decide. The judges were elected jointly by the Council and the Assembly of the League for a term of nine years.

On the dissolution of the League of Nations and the establishment of the United Nations Organization, the Court was superseded by the International court of Justice.

The Secondary Organs of the League were:

(a) The Technical Organizations
1. Economic and Financial
2. Health
3. Communications and Transit
(b) Advisory Committees
1. Military, Naval and Air Commission
2. Commission of Enquiry for European Union
3. Mandates Commission
4. Opium Committee
5. Social Committee
6. Committee of Experts on Slavery
(c) Committees of Intellectual Co-operation
(d) International Institutes
1. Institute of Intellectual Co-operation (Paris)
2. Institute of Private Law (Rome)
(e) Administrative Organization
    High Commissioner for Free City of Danzig

INTERNATIONAL LABOUR ORGANIZATION

The ILO was constituted in 1919 as an autonomous organization of the League of Nations. Its aim is to improve labour conditions through international action. Membership of the League carried with it membership of the Organization. When the League was dissolved the Organization was recognized as a specialized agency of the UN.

At its inception the ILO consisted of the International Labour Conference, meeting at least once a year, and the International Labour Office controlled by a governing body composed of 16 Government representatives, 8 employers' representatives and 8 workers' representatives. The decision of the Conference took the form of Draft Conventions or Recommendations. A draft Convention obliged the state concerned to approach the competent authority and ask for action. If action was taken, the member state was obliged to communicate the formal ratification of the Convention to the Secretary-General of the League. A Recommendation, if acted upon, did not require formal ratification, but the Secretary-General was informed of the action taken.

The ILO held 24 sessions between 1919 and 1939, adopted 63 Draft Conventions and 56 Recommendations; 134 ratifications were recommended to the competent authorities for action, 51 were authorized by the competent authorities, 837 were actually deposited with the Secretary-General of the League.

The following bodies assisted the work of the ILO:

The Joint Maritime Commission
The Correspondence Committee on Social Insurance
The Permanent Agricultural Committee
The Correspondence Committee on Industrial Hygiene
The Committee of Experts on Native Labour
The Committee of Experts on the Application of Conventions
The Advisory Committee on Salaried Employees
The Correspondence Committee on Accident Prevention
The Correspondence Committee on Women's Work
The Committee of Statistical Experts
The Advisory Committee on Management
The Advisory Committee of Correspondents on Workers' Spare Time
The Correspondence Committee on Unemployment Insurance and Placing
The Migration Committee
The Committee of Experts on Safety in Coalmines
The Committee of Experts on Rights of Performers as regards Broadcasting
The International Tripartite Committee on the Textile Industry

EUROPEAN TRADE UNION CONFEDERATION

The ETUC was formally established in Feb 73 with some 29m. members from 14 EEC and EFTA countries (Austria, Belgium, Denmark, Finland, France, West Germany, Iceland, Italy, Luxembourg, Netherlands, Norway, Sweden, Switzerland, UK) and the proscribed *Unión General de Trabajadores* of Spain.

INTERNATIONAL CONFEDERATION OF FREE TRADE UNIONS

The ICFTU was founded in London in 1949. The amended constitution provides for co-operation with the UN and the ILO and for regional organizations to promote trade unionism, especially in developing countries.

The Congress of the Confederation meets every three years and elects the Executive Board of 29 members nominated on an area basis for a three-year period; the Board meets at least twice a year. There are joint committees with the International Trade Secretariat. Main member groups, 1970: British Trades Union Congress, 9·1m.; Deutscher Gewerkschaftsbund, 6·5m.; confederazione Italiana Sindacati Lavoratori, 2·4m.; Swedish Landsorganisationen, 1·6m.; Österreichischer Gewerkschaftsbund, 1·5m.; French Confédération Générale du Travail Force Ouvrière, 0·5m.

WORLD FEDERATION OF TRADE UNIONS

The WFTU was established in 1945, representing trade-union organizations in more than 50 countries, Communist and non-Communist (excluding Germany and Japan). In Jan 1949 the British, Netherlands and US trade unions withdrew from WFTU, and by 1951 all non-Communist unions had left, as had the Yugoslavian Federation.

The Congress meets every four years. In between, the governing body is the General Council of 134 members which meets once a year at least. In between meetings of the General Council WFTU is controlled by the Bureau, consisting of the President, the General Secretary and members from different continents, the total number being decided at each Congress. The Bureau is elected by the General Council.

Main member groups in 1969: Soviet All-Union Central Council of Trade Unions, 86m.; East German Free German Trade Union Federation, 7·3m.; Polish Central Council of Trade Unions, 6·9m.; Czechoslovak Central Council of Trade Unions, 5·4m.; Italian General Confederation of Labour, 3·5m.; Romanian General Confederation of Labour, 3·2m.; the Hungarian Central Council of Trade Unions, 2·8m.; French Confederation of Labour, 2m.

WORLD CONFEDERATION OF LABOUR

The International Federation of Christian Trade Unions was established in 1920 as a mainly Catholic organization; it ceased to exist in 1940 through Fascist and Nazi suppression, most of its members being Italian or German. It was reconstituted in 1945 and renamed World Confederation of Labour in 1968. Its policy is based on the papal encyclicals *Rerum novarum* (1891) and *Quadragesino anno* (1931), but it claims some Protestant members in Europe.

The Christian International is federative, leaving wide discretion to the autonomy of its constituent unions. Its governing body is Congress, which meets every three years. The General Council, meeting at least once a year, is composed according to the proportion of membership of Congress. Congress elects the Executive Committee of at least 12 members which appoints the Secretary-General.

Main member groups in 1970: Confederation of Christian Trade Unions of Belgium, 1m.; French Democratic Confederation of Labour, 0·7m.; Netherlands Catholic Workers Movement, 0·4m.

EUROPEAN MOVEMENT

The European Movement was founded in Paris in 1947. In 1948 it convened the Congress of Europe at the Hague, the recommendations of which led to the creation of the Council of Europe. The Movement aims to inform public opinion and study the problems of European union. Member associations:

Association Européenne des Enseignants
Centre d'Action Européenne Fédéraliste
Conseil des Communes d'Europe
European League for Economic Co-operation
Mouvement Libéral pour l'Europe Unie
Mouvement Gauche Européenne
Nouvelles Équipes Internationales
Union de Résistants pour une Europe Unie

There are national councils in: Austria, Belgium, Denmark, France, Germany (West), Greece, Ireland, Italy, Luxembourg, the Netherlands, Norway, Sweden, Switzerland, Turkey, UK.

There are national committees in exile for: Albania, Bulgaria, Czechoslovakia, Estonia, Hungary, Latvia, Lithuania, Poland, Romania, Spain, Yugoslavia.

There are 75 representatives on the Council and 20 on the executive Bureau.

ORGANIZATION FOR ECONOMIC CO-OPERATION AND DEVELOPMENT (OECD)

On 30 Sep 61 the Organization for European Economic Co-operation (OEEC) was replaced by the Organization for Economic Co-operation and Development. The change of title marks the Organization's altered status and functions: with the accession of Canada and USA as full members it ceased to be a purely European body; while at the same time it added development aid to the list of its other activities. The member countries are now Australia, Austria, Belgium, Canada, Denmark, Finland, France, West Germany, Greece, Iceland, Irish Republic, Italy, Japan, Luxembourg, the Netherlands, Norway, Portugal, Spain, Sweden, Switzerland, Turkey, UK and USA. New Zealand and Yugoslavia participate in certain of the Organization's activities and have been given special status for these associations.

Chairman of the Council (*ministerial*): Gregorio Lopez Bravo (Spain)
Chairman of the Council (*official level*): The Secretary-General
Chairman of the Executive Committee: Belgium
Secretary-General: Emile Van Lennep (Netherlands)
Headquarters: Château de la Muette, 2, rue André Pascal, Paris (16 ᵉ)

The aims of the reconstituted Organization, as defined in the convention signed on 14 Dec 60, are as follows: (a) to achieve the highest sustainable economic growth and employment and a rising standard of living in member countries, while maintaining financial stability, and thus to contribute to the development of the world economy; (b) to contribute to sound economic expansion in member as well as non-member countries in the process of economic development; and (c) to contribute to the expansion of world trade on a multilateral, non-discriminatory basis in accordance with international obligations. Responsibility for the achievement of these aims has been vested in the Economic Policy Committee, the Development Aid Committee and the Trade Committee. The second of these is made up of representatives of all the 16 principal capital-exporting member countries, together with the Commission of the European Communities. Other committees deal with economic and development review; the environment; technical co-operation; payments; invisible transactions; insurance; fiscal matters; agriculture; fisheries; education; science policy; manpower and social affairs; energy, industry, gas, tourism, maritime transport, etc. Two of the purely European aspects of OEEC have been retained: the European Nuclear Energy Agency and the European Monetary Agreement with its Board of Management.

An OECD Development Centre began work in 1963. In 1968 a Centre for Educational Research and Innovation was set up.

NORTH ATLANTIC TREATY ORGANIZATION (NATO)

On 28 Apr 48 the Canadian Secretary of State for External Affairs broached the idea of a 'security league' of the free nations, in extension of the Brussels Treaty of 17 Mar 48. The United States Senate, on 11 June, recommended 'the association of the United States with such regional and other collective arrangements as are based on continuous self-help and mutual aid, and as affect its national security'. Detailed proposals were subsequently worked out between the Brussels Treaty powers, the USA and Canada.

On 4 Apr 49 the foreign ministers of Belgium, Canada, Denmark, France, Iceland, Italy, Luxembourg, the Netherlands, Norway, Portugal, the UK and the USA met in Washington and signed a treaty, the first article of which read as follows:

'The parties undertake, as set forth in the Charter of the United Nations, to settle any international disputes in which they may be involved by peaceful means in such a manner that international peace and security and justice are not endangered, and to refrain in their international relations from the threat or use of force in any manner inconsistent with the purposes of the United Nations.'

17

The Treaty came into force on 24 Aug 49. Greece and Turkey were admitted as parties to the Treaty in 1951 (effective Feb 52), the Federal Republic of Germany in Oct 54 (effective 5 May 55).

As reorganized by the Council at its session in Lisbon in Feb 52, the structure of NATO is as follows:

The *Council*, the principal body of the organization, 'charged with the responsibility of considering all matters concerning the implementation of the provisions of the Treaty', incorporates the Council and the Defence Committee originally envisaged. The Council is a Council of Governments, on which NATO nations are normally represented by their Minister for Foreign Affairs and/or the Minister of Defence, or by other competent Ministers, especially those responsible for financial and economic affairs. The council normally meets at ministerial level two or three times a year.

Each member government appoints a *Permanent Representative* to represent it on the Council when its ministerial representatives are not present. Each Permanent Representative also heads a national delegation of advisers and experts. The Permanent Representatives meet once or twice a week and can be called together at short notice at any time.

In carrying out its role, the Council is assisted by a number of committees, some of a permanent nature, some temporary. Like the Council, the membership of each committee is made up of national representatives. They study .questions submitted to them by the Council for recommendation. The work of the committees has a direct bearing on the activities of the International Secretariat.

The Political Committee, charged with preparing the political agenda for the Council, dates from 1957 as does the Economic Committee, which studies and reports to the Council on economic issues of special interest to the Alliance. In 1963 a Defence Planning Committee was established as the civilian co-ordinating body for the defence plans of member countries. Since France's withdrawal from NATO military organizations, this committee is composed of the Permanent Representatives of the 14 countries which take part in NATO's integrated common defence. Like the Council, it also meets at ministerial level. And at the Ministerial meeting in Dec 66 two bodies for nuclear planning were established: the Nuclear Defence Affairs Committee and a Nuclear Planning Group of 7–8 members.

Among other important committees are: the Science Committee and the Infrastructure Committee, whose varied tasks are directly linked to fundamental and applied research; the Senior Civil Emergency Planning Committee; the Committee for European Airspace Co-ordination; the Committee for Pipelines; the Committee for Information and Cultural Relations; and the Civil and Military Budget Committees, who carefully supervise the expenditures of NATO funds for the maintenance of the International Secretariat and military headquarters. In Nov 69 the Council established a Committee on the

Challenges of Modern Society to consider problems of the human environment. This new committee examines methods of improving the exchange of views and experience among the Allied countries in the task of creating a better environment for their societies.

More recently, the old Armaments Committee has been replaced by the Conference of National Armaments Directors.

Headquarters: 1110 Brussels, Belgium.

Secretary-General: Joseph Luns (Italy), appointed Oct 71.

The Secretary-General takes the chair at all Council meetings, except at the opening and closing of Ministerial sessions, when he gives way to the Council President. The office of President is held annually by the Foreign Minister of one of the Treaty countries.

The *Military Committee* is composed of the Chiefs of Staff or their representatives of all the member countries except France, which in 1966 withdrew from the Military Committee while remaining a member of the Council. (Iceland, having no military establishment, may be represented by a civilian.) It meets at Chiefs of Staff level two or three times a year as required, but remains in permanent session at the level of military representatives and is assisted by an integrated *international military staff*. It provides general policy guidance of a military nature to the Council.

In Dec 50 the Council approved the establishment of an integrated force for the defence of Western Europe under a Supreme Headquarters Allied Powers, Europe (SHAPE). General Eisenhower was the first Supreme Allied Commander Europe (SACEUR); he was succeeded by Generals Ridgway (1 June 52), Alfred M. Gruenther (11 July 53), Lauris Norstad (20 Nov 56), Lyman L. Lemnitzer (1 Jan 63) and Andrew J. Goodpaster (1 July 69); Deputies: Field-Marshal Lord Montgomery, 1950–8; Gen Sir Richard Gale, 1958–60; Gen. Sir Hugh Stockwell, GCB, KBE, DSO, 1960–3; Marshal of the Royal Air Force Sir Thomas Pike, GCB, CBE, DFC, 1964-7; Gen Sir Robert Bray, KCB, CBE, DSO, 1967-70; Gen Sir Desmond Fitzpatrick, DSO, MBE, MC, 1970–.

The *European Command* covers the land area from the North Cape to the Mediterranean and from the Atlantic to the eastern border of Turkey, excluding the UK and Portugal, the defence of which does not fall under any one major NATO Command.

The *Atlantic Command* extends from the North Pole to the Tropic of Cancer and from the coastal waters of North America to those of Europe and Africa, but excludes the Channel and the British Isles. The Supreme Allied Commander Atlantic (SACLANT), Adm Charles K. Duncan (USN), is an operational rather than an administrative commander, and, unlike SACEUR, has no forces permanently attached to his command in peace-time.

The *Channel Command* covers the English Channel and the southern North Sea. The Allied C- in-C Channel is Adm Sir Edward Ashanore.

The *Canada-US Regional Planning Group*, which covers the North American area, develops and recommends to the Military Committee plans for the defence of this area. It meets alternately in Washington and Ottawa.

WESTERN EUROPEAN UNION

On 17 Mar 48 a 50-year treaty 'for collaboration in economic, social and cultural matters and for collective self-defence' was signed in Brussels by the Foreign Ministers of the UK, France, the Netherlands, Belgium and Luxembourg.

On 20 Dec 50 the Western Union defence organization was merged with the North Atlantic Treaty command.

After the rejection by France of the European Defence Community on 30 Aug 54 a conference was held in London from 28 Sep to 3 Oct 54, attended by Belgium, Canada, France, Federal Germany, Italy, the Netherlands, Luxembourg, the UK and the USA, at which it was decided to invite the Federal Republic of Germany and Italy to accede to the Brussels Treaty, to end the occupation of Western Germany and to invite the latter to accede to the North Atlantic Treaty; the Federal Republic agreed that it would voluntarily limit its arms production, and provision was made for the setting up of an agency to control the armaments of the seven Brussels Treaty powers; the UK undertook not to withdraw from the Continent her four divisions and the Tactical Air Force assigned to the Supreme Allied Commander against the wishes of a majority, *i.e.* four, of the Brussels Treaty powers, except in the event of an acute overseas emergency.

At a Conference of Ministers held in Paris from 20 to 23 Oct 54 these decisions were put into effect. The Union was formally inaugurated on 6 May 55.

The *Council of WEU* consists of the Foreign Ministers of the seven powers or their representatives. An *Assembly*, composed of the WEU delegates to the Consultative Assembly of the Council of Europe, meets twice a year, usually in Paris. An *Agency for the Control of Armaments* and a *Standing Armaments Committee* have been set up in Paris. The social and cultural activities were transferred to the Council of Europe on 1 June 60.

After the breakdown of the negotiations for Britain's entry into the Common Market in 1963 the six EEC countries proposed to the UK that the WEU Council (the Six and the UK) should meet every three months 'to take stock of the political and economic situation in Europe'. The UK welcomed this proposal, and regular meetings took place.

Headquarters: 9 Grosvenor Place, London, SW1.

Secretary-General: Georges Heisbourg.

COUNCIL OF EUROPE

In 1948 the 'Congress of Europe', bringing together at The Hague nearly 1,000 influential Europeans from 26 countries, called for the creation of a united Europe, including a European Assembly. This proposal, examined first by the Ministerial Council of the Brussels Treaty Organization, then by a conference of ambassadors, was at the origin of the Council of Europe. The Statute of the Council was signed at London on 5 May 49 and came into force two months later. The founder members were Belgium, Denmark, France, the Irish Republic, Italy, Luxembourg, the Netherlands, Norway, Sweden and the United Kingdom. Turkey and Greece joined in 1949, Iceland in 1950, the Federal Republic of Germany in 1951 (having been an associate since 1950), Austria in 1956, Cyprus in 1961, Switzerland in 1963, Malta in 1965.

Membership is limited to European states which 'accept the principles of the rule of law and of the enjoyment by all persons within (their) jurisdiction of human rights and fundamental freedoms'. The Statute provides for both withdrawal (Art 7) and suspension (Arts 8 and 9). Greece withdrew from the Council in Dec 69.

Structure. Under the Statute two organs were set up: an inter-governmental *Committee of* (Foreign) *Ministers* with powers of decision and of recommendation to governments, and an inter-parliamentary deliberative body, the *Consultative Assembly* – both of which are served by the Secretariat. In addition, a large number of committees of experts have been established, two of them, the Council for Cultural Co-operation and the Committee on Legal Co-operation, having a measure of autonomy; on municipal matters the Committee of Ministers receives recommendations from the European Local Authorities Conference.

The Committee of Ministers meets usually twice a year, their deputies ten times a year.

The Consultative Assembly normally consists of 140 persons elected or appointed by their national parliaments (Austria 6, Belgium 7, Cyprus 3, Denmark 5, France 18, Germany 18, Iceland 3, Irish Republic 4, Italy 18, Luxembourg 3, Malta 3, Netherlands 7, Norway 5, Sweden 6, Switzerland 6, Turkey 10, UK 18); it meets for three-week-long sessions every year. For domestic reasons Cyprus is not at present represented in the Assembly. The work of the Assembly is prepared by parliamentary committees.

The *Joint Committee*, consisting of the Committee of Ministers and representatives of the Assembly, harmonizes relations between the two organs.

Under the European Convention of 1950 a special structure has been established for the protection of human rights. A *European Commission* investigates alleged violations of the Convention submitted to it either by

21

states or, in some cases, by individuals. Its findings can then be examined by the *European Court of Human Rights* (set up in 1959), whose obligatory jurisdiction has been recognized by 11 states, or by the Committee of Ministers, empowered to take binding decisions by two-thirds majority vote.

For questions of national refugees and over-population, a Special Representative has been appointed, responsible to the governments collectively.

Aims and Achievements. Art 1 of the Statute states that the Council's aim is 'to achieve a greater unity between its members for the purpose of safeguarding and realizing the ideals and principles which are their common heritage and facilitating their economic and social progress'; 'this aim shall be pursued ... by discussion of questions of common concern and by agreements and common action'. The only limitation is provided by Art 1 (d), which excludes 'matters relating to national defence'.

It has been the task of the Assembly to propose action to bring European countries closer together, to keep under constant review the progress made and to voice the views of European public opinion on the main political and economic questions of the day. The Ministers' role is to translate the Assembly's recommendations into action, particularly as regards lowering the barriers between the European countries, harmonizing their legislation or introducing where possible common European laws, abolishing discrimination on grounds of nationality and undertaking certain tasks on a joint European basis.

In May 1966 the Committee of Ministers approved a programme, designed to streamline the activities of the Council of Europe. It comprises projects for co-operation between member governments in economic, legal, social, public health, environmental and educational and scientific matters; and is to be reviewed every year.

Over 70 conventions have been concluded, covering such matters as social security, patents, extradition, medical treatment, training of nurses, equivalence of degrees and diplomas, innkeepers' liability, compulsory motor insurance, the protection of television broadcasts, adoption of children, transportation of animals and *au pair* replacement. A *Social Charter* sets out the social and economic rights which all member governments agree to guarantee to their citizens.

The official languages are English and French.

Chairman of the Committee of Ministers: (held in rotation).

President of the Consultative Assembly: Giuseppe Vedovato (Italy).

President of the European Court of Human Rights: Henri Rolin (Belgium).

President of the European Commission of Human Rights: James E. S. Fawcett (UK).

Secretary-General: Lujo Tončić-Sorinj (Austria).

Headquarters: Maison de l'Europe, Strasbourg, France.

EUROPEAN COMMUNITIES

Six countries of Western Europe – Belgium, France, Federal Germany, Italy, Luxembourg and the Netherlands – have established three communities with the aims of gradually integrating their economies and of moving towards political unity: the European Coal and Steel Community (ECSC), the European Economic Community (EEC) and the European Atomic Energy Community (EAEC or EURATOM).

Up to 1 July 67 the three communities, though legally separate under their constituent treaties, had some institutions in common. On that date they merged their three executives in one Commission of the European Communities and also their three councils. This was the first step towards the complete merger of the three communities under a new single treaty.

On 30 June 70 membership negotiations began between the Six and UK, Denmark, Irish Republic and Norway. On 22 Jan 72 those 4 countries signed the Treaty of Accession to the Community. In Nov 72 a Norwegian referendum rejected entry, but on 1 Jan 73 UK, Irish Republic and Denmark became full members.

The COMMISSION consists of 13 members appointed by the member states to serve for four years, the President and 5 Vice-Presidents serve for two years, but who act independently in the interests of the Community as a whole. Its task is the implementation of the Treaties, and in this it has the right of both initiative and execution: it proposes to the Council of Ministers the methods by which the aims of the Treaties can be achieved, and is then responsible for carrying them through.

President: François-Xavier Ortoli.
Address: 200, rue de la Loi, Brussels, 1040.

The COUNCIL OF MINISTERS consists of Ministers from the 9 national governments and represents the national as opposed to the Community interests. It is the body which has the power of decision in the Community. Under the Treaties many of its decisions are taken to be by qualified majority vote; since the 'Luxembourg Compromise' of 1966 majority voting has been used for minor matters only.

Address: 2 rue Ravenstein, Brussels, 1.

The EUROPEAN PARLIAMENT consists of 198 members delegated by the 9 national Parliaments. The EEC Treaty provides for the direct election of its members, and arrangements for this are now under discussion between the Council and the Parliament. It has to be consulted over the annual budgets of the three Communities and a wide range of other matters. It can dismiss the

Commission on a motion of censure approved by a two-thirds majority. As part of the decision in 1970 to provide the Community with its own independent financial resources, the Parliament has been given more control over the administrative budget consisting of non-mandatory expenditure, *i.e.*, expenditure not arising directly from the Treaty or from regulations made under it.

President: Cornelius Berkhouwer.

Address: Centre Européen du Kirchberg, Luxembourg.

The COURT OF JUSTICE is composed of nine judges, is responsible for the adjudication of disputes arising out of the application of the treaties, and its findings are enforceable in all member countries.

President: Robert Lecourt.

Address: 12, rue de la Côte-d'Eich, Luxembourg.

The ECONOMIC AND SOCIAL COMMITTEE, common to the EEC and EURATOM, has an advisory role and consists of 144 representatives, employers, trade unions, consumers, etc. The CONSULTATIVE COMMITTEE, of 84 members, performs a similar role for the ECSC.

EUROPEAN ECONOMIC COMMUNITY

(EEC or COMMON MARKET)

The EEC came into being on 1 Jan 58, based on the treaty signed in Rome on 25 Mar 57, by Belgium, France, Germany, Luxembourg, Italy and the Netherlands. The UK, the Irish Republic and Denmark became members on 1 Jan 73.

The Customs Union. The Treaty required the achievement of a complete customs union between the six countries over a transitional period of 12 to 115 years. This was achieved 18 months ahead of the 12-year schedule when, on 1 July 68, customs duties on trade between the Six were removed. The customs tariffs of the 3 new member countries will be phased out by stages, ending on 1 July 77. The first reduction of 20% took place on 1 Apr 73. The last alignment on the common external tariff was also made at the same time; it is based upon the average of the national tariffs, less a reduction of 20% on some items negotiated in the Dillon-Round tariff-cut talks in GATT and the first two-fifths of the tariff cuts agreed under the Kennedy-Round.

The Economic Union. Work is progressing on common transport and external trade policies and the co-ordination of financial, commercial, economic and social policies. The Treaty forbids agreements or practices which restrict, prevent or distort free competition, and firms now have to submit such agreements to the Commission, except in cases where Community regulations have exempted certain types of agreement.

At the Paris 'summit' of Oct 72 the Nine affirmed the aim of economic and monetary union by the end of 1980 and to increase their collabor tion in the fields of scientific research and advanced technology. The summit also declared the resolve to set up, by 3 July 73, an action programme which will be the basis of a community environment policy.

The Common Agricultural Policy (CAP). The basic features of a common policy in agriculture were first adopted in Jan 62. The aims are greater efficiency in production, stable market conditions, a fair return for farmers and reasonable prices for consumers. The two essential principles are common price levels and the replacement of national systems of protection by a Community system whose most characteristic feature is a system of variable levies on imports of certain farm products. The common marketing arrangements for all major items were operative by July 68. Management committees of national experts advise the Commission on the various products. A European Guidance and Guarantee Fund has also been established to finance the common policy. Various measures have been introduced at a Community level to help the modernization of farms and to assist older farmers who wish to give up farming their land. The 3 new member countries will gradually be integrated into the CAP during a 5-year period ending on 1 July 77.

Community Resources. Originally the EEC budget was financed entirely from direct contributions by member states. An independent revenue system for the Community is now being phased which will ultimately comprise 90% of all food-import levies, 90% of import duties and the product of up to 1 percentage point of the value-added taxes imposed by the member states.

External Relations. In 1961, UK, the Irish Republic, Norway and Denmark opened negotiations for membership but these were broken off at the insistence of France in 1963. A fresh attempt in 1967 failed for the same reason.

After the retirement of President de Gaulle, and particularly after The Hague 'summit' meeting of the Six, it became clear that renewed efforts might succeed and on 30 June 70 successful negotiations began. The basis of the agreement was that the principles of the 1957 treaty remain intact and the great majority of the regulations made in it will continue to apply to the new Community of Nine.

Greece and Turkey are associated with the Community, with a view to eventual full membership when their economies have become strong enough to allow them to compete on the Community market. Since the Greek *coup d'état* in Apr 67 the Association Agreement has been 'frozen' and no further steps towards a customs union taken. An Association Agreement with Malta was signed in Dec 70 and with Cyprus in Dec 72.

Association of 18 African ex-colonies, now fully sovereign and independent, was renewed for a further 5 years by a convention signed at Yaounde in 1963. This gives the 18 free entry to the EEC market and provides access to a special European Development Fund – additional to national aid – to which the Six allotted nearly $1,400m. for the years 1958–69. The Convention, renewed in 1969, for the years 1970–75, provided for another $1,000m. in aid grants and loans. Developing Commonwealth countries have been offered special trade agreements or association agreements similar to those between the present Community and its associated countries in Africa. Trade agreements with Israel, Lebanon, Egypt, Spain and Yugoslavia are in operation, and negotiations are in progress with Jordan. Regular contacts have been maintained between the community and Latin-American countries with a view to future agreements. In the Paris 'summit' of Oct 72 the enlarged community reaffirmed its determination to follow a common commercial policy towards Eastern Europe with effect from 1 Jan 73.

As a first step towards the creation of a political union, the Six agreed, in 1970, to hold twice-yearly consultations on foreign policy; the first meeting of foreign ministers was held in Nov 70.

EUROPEAN COAL AND STEEL COMMUNITY

The ECSC came into being on 10 Aug 52 following the ratification of a treaty signed in Paris on 18 Apr 51. The original suggestion for it was made in the Schuman Plan on 9 May 50, which proposed the pooling of Franco-German coal and steel production in a Community open to other Western European countries as a first step towards a United States of Europe. UK, the Irish Republic and Denmark joined the ECSC on 1 Jan 73.

Until 1 July 67 the *High Authority* was the executive body of the ECSC and consisted of eight members appointed by the Six governments plus one co-opted member. After the merger of the Executives its power passed to the single European Commission which is now responsible for the execution of the ECSC Treaty.

The Common Market for Coal and Steel. A common market for coal, iron ore and scrap was established on 10 Feb 53, for steel on 1 May 53 and for special steels on 1 Aug 54. A harmonized external tariff on steel is now at around 9%. Rules for fair competition have been established; currency restrictions, the dual-pricing system (under which prices for export and home-consumed coal and steel varied) and discriminatory transport rates based upon nationality have been abolished within the Community.

26

To meet the changing circumstances in the two industries, and especially to ensure that the contraction of the coal industry occurs without social or economic dislocation, the High Authority had by Apr 70 granted readaption aid to 408,100 workers, most of them coalminers, at a cost of $155m., matched by an equivalent amount from the governments; it had also spent $112m. on research.

A Common Energy Policy. Of the various forms of energy, coal falls within the competence of the ECSC, nuclear energy within that of EURATOM, and all others within that of the EEC. The first effective steps towards a common energy policy for the Community were taken when a Protocol of Agreement on Energy was signed by the three Communities in Apr 64. In Dec 68 the single commission published guidelines for a common energy policy.

EUROPEAN ATOMIC ENERGY COMMUNITY (EURATOM)

EURATOM came into being on 1 Jan 58 following the ratification of a treaty signed in Rome on 25 Mar 57. Its task is to promote a common effort between its six members in the development of nuclear energy for peaceful purposes.

The execution of the treaty now rests with the *European Commission*, which is advised by a *Scientific and Technical Committee* (27 members) and the *Economic and Social Committee* (144 members). Major decisions are taken by the *Council of Ministers*, which is common also to the EEC.

EUROPEAN FREE TRADE ASSOCIATION (EFTA)

On 31 Dec 72 the UK and Denmark formally left EFTA to join the EEC, leaving EFTA with 6 member countries: Austria, Iceland, Norway, Portugal, Sweden and Switzerland. A seventh country, Finland, is an associate member. The Stockholm Convention establishing the Association entered into force on 3 May 60 and Finland became associated on 27 Mar 61. Iceland joined EFTA on 1 Mar 70 and was immediately granted duty-free entry for industrial goods exported to EFTA countries, while being given 10 years to abolish her own existing protective duties.

When the Association was created it had three objectives: to achieve free trade in industrial products between member countries, to assist in the creation of a single market embracing the countries of Western Europe, and to contribute to the expansion of world trade in general.

The first objective was achieved on 31 Dec 66, when virtually all inter-EFTA tariffs were removed. This was three years earlier than originally planned. Finland removed her remaining EFTA tariffs a year later on 31 Dec 67.

The fulfilment of the second aim was secured on 22 Jan 72 when the UK and Denmark signed the Treaty of Accession to the EEC whereby they became members of the enlarged Community from 1 Jan 73. On 22 Jul 72 5 other EFTA countries, Austria, Iceland, Portugal, Sweden and Switzerland signed Free Trade Agreements with the EEC. It is expected that a similar agreement negotiated with Finland will be signed during 1973. Norway whose intention of joining the EEC was reversed following a referendum is also expected to sign an agreement with the enlarged community, thus providing arrangements for eventual free trade in industrial goods among 16 Western European countries.

The third objective was to contribute to the expansion of world trade. EFTA has succeeded in this in two ways: between 1960 and 1971, EFTA total purchases from the rest of the world rose from $24,147m. to $55,833m. (131%). EFTA sales to the rest of the world rose by 148%.

EFTA tariff treatment applies to those industrial products which are of EFTA origin, and these are traded freely between member countries. Each EFTA country remains free, however, to impose its own rates of duty on products entering from outside the EFTA area.

Generally, agricultural products do not come under the provisions for free trade, but bilateral agreements have been negotiated to increase trade in these products.

The operation of the Convention is the responsibility of a Council assisted by a small secretariat. Each EFTA country holds the chairmanship of the Council for six months.

Secretary-General: Bengt Rabaeus.

Headquarters: 9–11 Rue de Varembe 1211 Geneva 20, Switzerland.

COUNCIL FOR MUTUAL ECONOMIC ASSISTANCE

Membership. Founder members, in 1949, were USSR, Bulgaria, Czechoslovakia, Hungary, Poland, Romania. Later admissions were Albania (1949; ceased participation 1961), Cuba (1972), East Germany (1950), Mongolia (1962). Since 1964 Yugoslavia has enjoyed associated status with limited participation. Observers are China, North Korea, North Vietnam.

The Charter consists of a preamble and 17 articles.

Extracts from the *Charter*:[1]

Article 1 *Aims and Principles*: '(1) The purpose of the Council is to facilitate, by uniting and coordinating the efforts of its member countries, the planned development of the national economy, acceleration of economic and technical progress in these countries, a rise in the level of industrializa-

[1] In the language of the official English version.

tion in countries with less developed industries, uninterrupted growth of labour productivity and a steady advance of the welfare of the peoples. (2) The Council is based on the principles of the sovereign equality of all member countries.'

Article 2 *Membership* 'open to other countries which subscribe to the purposes and principles of the Council'.

Article 3 *Functions and Powers* to (a) 'organize all-round . . . cooperation of member countries in the most rational use of natural resources and acceleration of the development of their productive forces' (b) 'foster the improvement of the international socialist division of labour by coordinating national economic development plans, and the specialization and cooperation of production in member countries' (d) to 'assist in . . . carrying out joint measures for the development of industry and agriculture . . . transport . . . principal capital investments . . . [and] trade'.

Article 4 *Recommendations and Decisions* '. . . shall be adopted only with the consent of the interested member countries'.

The Structure. The supreme authority is the *Session* of all members held (usually annually) in members' capitals in rotation. All members must be present, and decisions must be unanimous. The *Executive Committee* is made up of one representative from each member state of deputy premier rank. It meets at least once every three months and has a *Bureau for Common Questions of Economic Planning.*

The administrative organ is the *Secretariat.*

The *Secretariat*: Prospekt Kalinina, 56, Moscow, G-205.

The *Secretary*: N. V. Faddeev.

There is a *Committee for Co-operation in the Field of Planning* and a *Committee for Scientific and Technical Co-operation.*

There are *Permanent Commissions* on Economic Questions; Statistics; Foreign Trade; Currency and Finance; Electricity; Peaceful Uses of Atomic Energy; Geology; Coal Industry; Oil and Gas Industry; Chemical Industry; Iron and Steel Industry; Non-Ferrous Metals Industry; Engineering Industry; Radio Engineering and Electronics Industries; Light Industry; Food Industry; Agriculture; Construction; Transport; Posts and Telecommunications; Standardization. There is an *Institute of Standardization* and two *Standing Conferences* of Water Conservation Authorities, and of Freight and Shipping Organizations. The latter has a Chartering Co-ordination Bureau.

The *International Bank for Economic Co-operation* was founded in 1963 with a capital of 300m. roubles and started operating on 1 Jan 64. It undertakes multilateral settlements in 'transferable roubles'[1] and advances credits to finance trading and other operations. The transferable rouble is a unit of account: gold content 0.9874 12 grammes.

---

[1] *i.e.* used for intra COMECON clearing accounts only.

29

The *International Investments Bank* was founded in 1970 and went into operation on 1 Jan 71 with a capital of 1,000m. roubles (70% transferable and 30% convertible or in gold). In 1971 it financed 16 engineering, transport and chemical projects.

Stages of Development: COMECON was founded in Jan 49, partly in response to such Western initiatives as the Marshall Plan, and ostensibly to promote economic development through the joint utilization and co-ordination of resources. In its early years, however, member states were dominated by the Stalinist drive to autarky and the Council remained a façade functioning merely as a registration agency for bilateral foreign trade and credit agreements. The mid-1950s brought the first attempts to reduce the parallelism in member states' economies, and the Council began to function as a discussion centre for long-term plan co-ordination, a process perhaps hastened by the signature of the Treaty of Rome in 1957.

In 1962 Khrushchev, with the support of the more industrialized members (Czechoslovakia, East Germany, Poland) attempted to convert COMECON from a trade organization into a supra-national authority under which member states' economies would be integrated according to the 'international socialist division of labour'.

Integration plans failed at this stage, partly owing to domestic developments in the USSR (dismissal of Khrushchev), and partly owing to the obstructionist attitude of Romania, who objected to the status of non-industrialized raw-material producer.

In the aftermath of the USSR's invasion of Czechoslovakia renewed Soviet pressure in 1969 for integration encountered rather less intransigence.[1]

Present Trends: The *Comprehensive Programme* foresees increased international co-operation with no lessening of respect for national sovereignty. No supra-national authority is envisaged.

Long-term plans are to be co-ordinated and capital investments harmonized. An additional form of trade is envisaged in non-quota goods which need not be balanced bilaterally but counted in total trade for clearing purposes. Standardization and specialization of production have begun. Long-term aims include the establishment of arbitration organs with powers to settle disputes, and strengthening the transferable rouble to full convertibility.

[1] Romania refused to adhere to the International Investments Bank when it was first mooted in 1970 but joined eventually in 1971. Her trade within COMECON was scheduled to increase after 1972. Hungary and Poland propounded a view that a free trade area with preferential tariffs should be formed and individual currencies should ultimately be made convertible.

BIBLIOGRAPHY

Aubrey, H. G., *Atlantic Economic Co-operation: The OECD*. New York, 1967
Caillot, J., *Le C.A.E.N.* Paris, 1971
Diebold, W., *The Schuman Plan: A Study in Economic Co-operation, 1950-59*. New York, 1959
Levinson, C., *International Trade Unionism*. London, 1972
Mellor, R. E. H., *COMECON: A Challenge to the West*. New York, 1971
Palmer, M., and others, *European Unity: A Survey of European Organizations*. London, 1968
Robertson, A. H., *European Institutions, Co-operation, Integration, Unification*. London, 1966
Shaeffer, H. W., *Comecon and Politics of Integration*. London and New York, 1972
Thant, U, *Towards World Peace*. New York, 1964
Walters, F. P., *A History of the League of Nations*. 2 vols. London, 1952
Survey of C.M.E.A. activities. Moscow, annual
Basic Principles of International Socialist Division of Labour. Moscow, 1962

2 HEADS OF STATE

ALBANIA

Declared independent 1912, invaded by Austria in 1916. Italian C.-in-C. in Albania proclaims independence again on 3 June 17. A provisional republican government ruled until 1921, followed by government under a Council of Regents until Jan 25, when Albania was proclaimed a Republic.

PRESIDENT

Ahmed Beg Zogu   31 Jan 25–30 Aug 28
Albania was proclaimed a monarchy on 1 Sep 28 and the President became King Zog I.

KING

Zog I, m. Countess Geraldine Apponyi   1 Sep 28–13 Apr 49
                                  (formally deposed *in absentia* 2 Jan 46)
Victor Emmanuel III of Italy (*see* Italy)   14 Apr 39–30 Nov 43
                                  (reigned following Italian invasion until
                                  Italian cabinet nullified his Albanian title)
Between 1 Dec 43 and 1 Dec 45 there were provisional governments with no head of state. The Republic was proclaimed 12 Jan 46.

PRESIDENT

Dr Omer Nishani   13 Jan 46–24 July 53
Maj.-Gen. Haxhi Lleshi   24 July 53–

AUSTRIA

The Republic was proclaimed on 12 Nov 18.

PRESIDENT

Dr X. Seits   12 Nov 18–9 Nov 20
          (President of the National Assembly and stood in for a head of state)
Dr M. Hainisch   9 Dec 20–4 Dec 28
Dr W. Miklas   5 Dec 28–13 Mar 38

Austria was incorporated into the German Reich on 12 Mar 38. For 1938–45 *see* Germany. A provisional government was installed on liberation, 28 Apr 45.

PRESIDENT

Dr K. Renner	20 Dec 45–31 Dec 50
Dr T. Körner	27 May 51–4 Jan 57
Dr A. Schärf	5 May 57–28 Feb 65
F. Jonas	23 May 65–

BELGIUM

KING

Albert, m. Elizabeth of Bavaria, succeeded his uncle
Leopold II   17 Dec 09–17 Feb 34
Leopold III, m. (i) Astrid of Sweden (ii) Mlle Lilian Baels,
succeeded his father   23 Feb 34–20 Sep 44
Regency   21 Sep 44–21 July 50
Leopold III   22 July 50–16 July 51 (abdic.)
Baudouin, m. Fabiola de Mora y Aragón,
succeeded his father   17 July 51–

BULGARIA

KING

Ferdinand (elected), m. (i) Marie Louise of Parma
(ii) Eleonore of Reuss Köstritz   7 July 87–4 Oct 18 (abdic.)
Boris III, m. Giovanña of Savoy,
succeeded his father   4 Oct 18–28 Aug 43
Simeon II, succeeded his father   28 Aug 43–8 Sep 46
On 8 Sep 46 a plebiscite ended the monarchy and established a Republic, which was proclaimed on 15 Sep, but had no head of state until the new constitution came into force on 4 Dec 47.

PRESIDENT (Chairman of the Praesidium)

Dr M. Netchev	9 Dec 47–27 May 50
Gen. G. Damianov	27 May 50–27 Nov 58
D. Ganev	30 Nov 58–20 Apr 64
G. Traikov	23 Apr 64–
T. Zhivok	7 Jul 71–

CYPRUS

From 1918 until 1959 Cyprus was a British dependency; for heads of state *see* United Kingdom. An independent Republic came into being on 16 Aug 60, the President having been previously elected.

PRESIDENT

Archbishop Makarios   14 Dec 59–

CZECHOSLOVAKIA

An independent state was founded on 14 Nov 18, formed from four provinces of the Austrian Empire: Bohemia, Moravia, Silesia, Slovakia. (Hungarian Slovakia and Ruthenia joined the Czechoslovak state in 1920.)

PRESIDENT

Tomas G. Masaryk	14 Nov 18–13 Dec 35
Dr Edvard Beneš	18 Dec 35–4 Oct 38
Dr Emil Hácha	1 Dec 38–1 June 45

Dr Beneš continued as President of the Czech government in exile after Czechoslovakia was proclaimed a German protectorate on 16 Mar 39. He returned to Prague in 1945. (Slovakia: *see* separate entry.)

PRESIDENT

Dr Edvard Beneš	2 June 45–7 June 48
K. Gottwald	14 June 48–14 Mar 53
A. Zápotecký	21 Mar 53–13 Nov 57
A. Novotný	19 Nov 57–22 Mar 68
Gen. L. Svoboda	30 Mar 68–

DENMARK

KING

Christian X, m. Alexandrine of Mecklenburg, succeeded his father
  Frederick VIII   14 May 12–20 Apr 47
Frederick IX, m. Ingrid of Sweden,
  succeeded his father   20 Apr 47–14 Jan 72

QUEEN

Margrethe II, m. Henri de Morpezat,
  succeeded her father   14 Jan 72–

ESTONIA

Proclaimed an independent state 24 Feb 18. The constitution came into force on 20 Dec 20, with a provisional government in power. On formation of the cabinet in 23 the Prime Minister was given powers of head of state.

PRIME MINISTER AND HEAD OF THE STATE

I. Kukk	25 Nov 23–15 Dec 24
M. Jaakson	16 Dec 24–14 Dec 25
J. Teemant	15 Dec 25–8 Dec 27
M. Toenisson	9 Dec 27–3 Dec 28
A. Rei	4 Dec 28–8 July 29
O. Strandmann	9 July 29–11 Feb 31
C. Paets	12 Feb 31–20 Feb 32
J. Teemant	21 Feb 32–31 Oct 32
C. Paets	1 Nov 32–26 Apr 33

A new constitution, setting up the office of President, was adopted on 3 Oct 34. Constantin Paets was appointed President.

The USSR incorporated Estonia as a member on 7 Aug 40.

FINLAND

Proclaimed independent on 6 Dec 17, and a Regent installed. Republican constitution came into force on 14 June 19.

PRESIDENT

Prof K. J. Ståhlberg	1 Aug 19–15 Feb 25
Dr L. Relander	16 Feb 25–15 Feb 31
Dr P. E. Svinhufvud	16 Feb 31–14 Feb 37
K. Kallio	15 Feb 37–30 Nov 40
Dr R. Ryti	19 Dec 40–4 Aug 44
Field-Marshal Mannerheim	4 Aug 44–9 Mar 45
J. Paasikivi	9 Mar 45–15 Feb 56
Dr U. Kekkonen	15 Feb 56–

FRANCE

PRESIDENT OF THE REPUBLIC

R. Poincaré	17 Jan 13–17 Jan 20
P. Deschanel	17 Jan 20–23 Sep 20
A. Millerand	23 Sep 20–10 June 24
G. Doumergue	13 June 24–31 May 31
P. Doumer	31 May 31–7 May 32
A. Lebrun	10 May 32–11 July 40

Marshal Pétain on 11 July 40 took over the powers of President and added them to his own as Prime Minister. He then appointed a Chief of State.

CHIEF OF STATE

Adm. Darlan	10 Feb 41–16 Nov 42
P. Laval	17 Nov 42–12 May 45 (left France)

A Government of National Unity was formed on 1 Dec 45, with Gen. Charles de Gaulle as head of state. He resigned on 2 Feb 46. A new constitution came into force on 24 Dec 46 (Fourth Republic).

PRESIDENT OF THE REPUBLIC

V. Auriol	16 Jan 47–23 Dec 43
R. Coty	24 Dec 53–5 Oct 58

A new constitution came into force on 5 Oct 58 (Fifth Republic).

PRESIDENT OF THE REPUBLIC

Gen. C. de Gaulle	21 Dec 58–28 Apr 69
G. Pompidou	15 June 69–

GEORGIA

Proclaimed an independent state 26 May 18.

PRESIDENT

N. Jordania	26 May 18–

Georgia was occupied by Soviet forces in 1921, and became a member of the USSR.

GERMANY

The Republic was proclaimed on the abdication of Kaiser Wilhelm II, on 9 Nov 18.

PRESIDENT

Friedrich Ebert	11 Feb 19–28 Feb 25
P. von Hindenburg	26 Apr 25–2 Aug 34

CHANCELLOR AND FÜHRER

Adolf Hitler	2 Aug 34–30 Apr 45
Adm. C. Doenitz	30 Apr 45–5 June 45

All power was transferred to the Allied Control Council on the surrender of Germany at the end of World War II on 5 June 45. The constitution of the Federal Republic of Germany came into force on 21 Sep 49.

PRESIDENT

Dr T. Heuss	12 Sep 49–1 July 59
Dr H. Lübke	1 July 59–5 Mar 69
Dr G. Heinemann	5 Mar 69–

The constitution of the German Democratic Republic came into force on 7 Oct 49.

PRESIDENT

Wilhelm Pieck	11 Oct 49–7 Sep 60

The office of President was replaced by the Council of State on 12 Sep 60.

CHAIRMAN OF THE COUNCIL OF STATE

Walter Ulbricht	12 Sep 60–1 Aug 73
Willi Stoph	3 Oct 73–

GREECE

KING

Alexandros, succeeded on the expulsion of his father, Konstantinos	12 June 17–25 Oct 20
Konstantinos XII, m. Sophia of Prussia. Recalled by plebiscite to succeed his son	5 Dec 20–27 Sep 22 (abdic.)
Gëorgios II, m. Elizabeth of Romania, succeeded his father	27 Sep 22–18 Dec 23 (expelled)

A Republic was established by plebiscite on 13 Apr 24.

PROVISIONAL PRESIDENT

Adm. Konduriotis	20 Dec 23–18 Mar 26

DICTATOR

Gen. Pangalos	18 Mar 26–22 Aug 26

PROVISIONAL PRESIDENT (reappointed)

Adm. Konduriotis	4 Dec 26–14 Dec 29

PRESIDENT

A. Zaimis	14 Dec 29–3 Nov 35

By a plebiscite on 3 Nov 35 the Republic ended and the monarchy was restored.

KING

Gëorgios II, returned.	25 Nov 35–1 Apr 47

Paul I, m. Frederika Louise of Brunswick,
 succeeded his brother   1 Apr 47–6 Mar 64
Konstantinos XIII, m. Anne-Marie of Denmark,
 succeeded his father   6 Mar 64–1 June 73

The King handed over his powers to a Regent on 13 Dec 67 and left Greece. The monarchy was declared abolished on 1 June 73.

PROVISIONAL PRESIDENT

G. Papadopoulos   1 June 73–25 Nov 73

PRESIDENT

Lieut.-Gen. P. Ghizikis   25 Nov 73–

HUNGARY

An independent Republic was proclaimed on 16 Nov 18.

PROVISIONAL PRESIDENT

Count M. Károlyi   16 Nov 18–22 Mar 19

The Soviet Hungarian Republic was proclaimed by Béla Kun's government on 22 Mar 19, and was followed by a counter-revolutionary régime under Admiral Horthy. In Jan 20 Hungary was proclaimed a monarchy.

REGENT

Adm. M. von Nagybánya Horthy   1 Mar 20–16 Oct 45

A Regency Council was appointed after Horthy's resignation and ruled until the setting up of the Provisional National Government on 24 Dec 45. A new republican constitution came into force on 1 Feb 46.

PRESIDENT

Dr Z. Tildy   1 Feb 46–30 July 48
A. Szakasits   3 Aug 48–24 Apr 50
S. Rónai   8 May 50–1 Aug 52

CHAIRMAN OF THE PRAESIDIUM

I. M. Dobi   1 Aug 52–14 Apr 67

CHAIRMAN OF THE PRESIDING COUNCIL

P. Losonczi   14 Apr 67–

ICELAND

A sovereign state came into being on 1 Dec 18, still acknowledging the Danish King as head.

KING

Christian X (*see* Denmark)　　　　　　　1 Dec 18–24 May 44

The link with the crown was ended and a republic came into being on 17 June 44.

PRESIDENT

Sveinn Björnssen	17 June 44–24 Jan 52
Ásgeir Ásgeirsson	1 July 52–1 Aug 68
Kristján Eldjárn	1 Aug 68–

IRISH REPUBLIC

By the Irish Free State Agreement Act of 1922 Ireland obtained the status of a self-governing Dominion, still recognizing the British sovereign as head of state.

KING

George V (*see* United Kingdom)
Edward VIII (*see* United Kingdom)
George VI (*see* United Kingdom)

The constitution of the Irish Free State as an independent sovereign state came into force on 29 Dec 37.

PRESIDENT

Dubhglas de hIde (Dr Douglas Hyde)	25 June 38–24 June 45
S. T. Ô Ceallaigh (S. T. O'Kelly)	25 June 45–24 June 59
Éamon de Valéra	25 June 59–24 June 73
Erskine Childers	25 June 73–

ITALY

KING

Victor Emmanual III, m. Elena of Montenegro, succeeded his father Umberto	29 July 00–9 May 46 (abdic.)
Umberto II, succeeded his father	9 May 46–13 June 46 (abdic.)

(On 30 Mar 38 King Victor Emmanual gave unlimited powers to Benito Mussolini to hold in time of war and in the name of the King. Mussolini resigned these powers on 25 July 43.)
A Republic was proclaimed on 18 June 46.

PRESIDENT

L. Einaudi	10 May 48–29 Apr 55
G. Gronchi	29 Apr 55–6 May 62

A. Segni   6 May 62–28 Dec 64
G. Saragat   28 Dec 64–29 Dec 71
G. Leone   29 Dec 71–

LATVIA

Proclaimed a sovereign state on 18 Nov 18.

PRESIDENT
J. Tschakste   18 Nov 18–8 Apr 27
G. Zemgals   8 Apr 27–8 Apr 30
A. Kviesis   9 Apr 30–11 Apr 36
K. Ulmanis   12 Apr 36–21 July 40

The USSR agreed to accept Latvia on 6 Aug 40.

LIECHTENSTEIN

PRINCE
John II, succeeded his father   12 Nov 58–11 Feb 29
Francis I, succeeded his brother   11 Feb 29–25 Aug 38
Francis Joseph II, m. Countess Gina von Wilczek,
    succeeded his great uncle   25 Aug 38–

LITHUANIA

Proclaimed an independent state 16 Feb 18
Constituent assembly elected an acting president on 15 Apr 20.

ACTING PRESIDENT
A. Stulginskis   15 Apr 20–8 June 26

PRESIDENT
Dr Grinius   8 June 26–19 Dec 26
M. Smetona   19 Dec 26–30 June 40

On 21 July 40 Lithuania voted to become a member of the USSR.

LUXEMBOURG

GRAND-DUCHESS
Marie-Adelaide, succeeded her father
    Grand Duke Willem   26 June 12–15 Jan 19 (abdic.)

Charlotte, m. Felix of Bourbon Parma, succeeded
  her sister   15 Jan 19–12 Nov 64 (abdic.)

GRAND DUKE

Jean, m. Joséphine Charlotte of Belgium,
  succeeded his mother   12 Nov 64–

MALTA

An independent member of the Commonwealth acknowledging the British
sovereign as head of state. *See* United Kingdom.

MONACO

PRINCE

Albert, m. (i) Lady Mary Douglas Hamilton,
  (ii) Alice, Dowager Duchess de Richelieu,
  succeeded his father   10 Sep 1889–26 June 22
Louis II, succeeded his father   26 June 22–9 May 49
Rainier III, m. Miss Grace Kelly, succeeded
  his grandfather   9 May 49–

THE NETHERLANDS

QUEEN

Wilhelmina, m. Henry of Mecklenburg Schwerin,
  succeeded her father   23 Nov 1890–4 Sep 48 (abdic.)
Juliana, m. Bernhard of Lippe-Besterfeld,
  succeeded her mother   4 Nov 48–

NORWAY

KING

Haakon VII, formerly Prince Carl of Denmark,
  m. Maud of Great Britain, elected to
  the throne   18 Nov 05–21 Sep 57
Olav V, m. Märtha of Sweden, succeeded
  his father   21 Sep 57–

41

POLAND

Independent state proclaimed on 5 Nov 18.

PRESIDENT

J. Pilsudski	11 Nov 18–9 Dec 22
Gabriel Narutowicz	9 Dec 22–16 Dec 22 (assassinated)
S. Wojciechowski	20 Dec 22–15 May 26
I. Moscicki	1 June 26–29 Mar 39

On 29 Mar 39 the German occupation of Poland began.

PRESIDENT, HEAD OF THE POLISH GOVERNMENT IN EXILE

W. Raczkiewicz	30 Sep 39–28 June 45

PRESIDENT

Boleslaw Bierut	28 June 45–21 July 52

On 22 July 52 a new constitution replaced the office of President with a Council of State.

PRESIDENT OF THE COUNCIL OF STATE

A. Zawadski	20 Nov 52–7 Aug 64
E. Ochab	12 Aug 64–8 Apr 68
Marshal M. Spychalski	10 Apr 68–23 Dec 70
J. Cyrankiewicz	23 Dec 70–28 Mar 72
H. Jabloński	28 Mar 72–

PORTUGAL

PRESIDENT

Dr S. Paes	28 Apr 18–14 Dec 18 (assassinated)
João Antunes	16 Dec 18–5 Oct 19
Dr A. de Almeida	5 Oct 19–5 Oct 23
M. T. Gomes	5 Oct 23–11 Dec 25
Dr B. L. Machado Guimarâes	11 Dec 25–1 June 26

A provisional government was in power from 1 June 26 until 29 Nov 26.

PRESIDENT

Marshal A. O. F. Carmona	29 Nov 26–18 Apr 51
Marshal F. H. C. Lopes	22 July 51–9 Aug 58
Rear-Adm. A. de D. R. Tomás	9 Aug 58–

ROMANIA

KING

Ferdinand I, m. Marie of Saxe-Coburg and Gotha, succeeded his uncle	11 Oct 14–21 July 27

Mihai (Michael) I, succeeded his grandfather since his father
  Carol had renounced his rights   21 July 27–8 June 30
Carol II, m. Helen of Greece, succeeded his son by
  act of parliament   8 June 30–6 Sep 40 (abdic.)
Mihai I, proclaimed on abdication of his father.   6 Sep 40–30 Dec 47 (abdic.)

As a result of a plebiscite a Republic was established and the King abdicated.

PRESIDENT OF THE PRAESIDIUM

C. I. Parhon   13 Apr 48–23 Jan 52
Dr P. Groza   2 June 52–7 Jan 58
I. G. Maurer   11 Jan 58–21 Mar 61
G. Gheorghiu-Dej   21 Mar 61–19 Mar 65
C. Stoica   22 Mar 65–9 Dec 67
N. Ceauçescu   9 Dec 67–

SAN MARINO

No titular head of state; co-regents are annually elected.

SLOVAKIA

Declared an independent country 14 Mar 39.

PRESIDENT

Dr J. Tiso   26 Oct 39–1 Apr 45

Slovakia was re-incorporated with Czechoslovakia in Apr 45.

SPAIN

KING

Alphonso XIII, m. Victoria Eugenie Battenberg,
  succeeded his father at his birth   17 May 1886–14 Apr 31 (abdic.)

A Republic proclaimed on 14 Apr 31.

PRESIDENT

N. A. Zamora y Torres   10 Dec 31–7 Apr 36
M. Azaña   10 May 36–4 Mar 39

CHIEF OF THE STATE

Gen. Francisco Franco   9 Aug 39–

SWEDEN

KING

Gustaf V, m. Victoria of Baden, succeeded his father
  Oscar II   8 Dec 07–29 Oct 50
Gustaf VI Adolf, m. (i) Margaret Victoria of Connaught,
  (ii) Lady Louise Mountbatten, succeeded his father   29 Oct 50–16 Sep 73
Carl XVI Gustaf, succeeded his grandfather   16 Sep 73–

SWITZERLAND

PRESIDENTS (elected for an annual term)

Year	President	Year	President
1918	Dr F. Ludwig	1946	Karl Kobelt
1919	Gustave Ador	1947	
1920	Giuseppe Motta	1948	Enrico Celio
1921	Edmund Schulthess	1949	Ernst Nobs
1922	Dr Robert Haab	1950	Max Petitpierre
1923	Karl Scheurer	1951	Eduard von Steiger
1924	Dr Ernest Chuard	1952	Karl Kobelt
1925	Dr Jean M. Musy	1953	Philipp Etter
1926	Henri Häberlin	1954	Rudolphe Rubattel
1927	Giuseppe Motta	1955	Max Petitpierre
1928	Edmund Schulthess	1956	Markus Feldmann
1929	Dr Robert Haab	1957	Hans Streuli
1930	Dr Jean M. Musy	1958	Thomas Holenstein
1931	Dr Henri Häberlin	1959	Paul Chaudet
1932	Dr Giuseppe Motta	1960	Max Petitpierre
1933	Dr Edmund Schulthess	1961	Friedrich Trangott Wahlen
1934	Dr Marcel Pilet-Golaz	1962	Paul Chaudet
1935	Rudolf Minger	1963	Willy Spühler
1936	Dr Albert Meyer	1964	Ludwig von Moos
1937	Dr Giuseppe Motta	1965	Hanspeter Tschudi
1938	Dr Johannes Baumann	1966	Hans Schattner
1939	Philipp Etter	1967	Roger Bonvin
1940	Dr Marcel Pilet-Golaz	1968	Willy Spühler
1941	Dr Ernst Wetter	1969	Ludwig von Moos
1942	Philipp Etter	1970	Hanspeter Tschudi
1943	Enrico Celio	1971	Rudolf Guägi
1944	Walter Stampfi	1972	Nello Celio
1945	Eduard von Steiger	1973	

TURKEY

SULTAN

Mohammed V, succeeded his brother	27 Apr 09–3 July 18
Mohammed VI, suceeded his brother	3 July 18–1 Nov 22

The office of Sultan was abolished on 1 Nov 22 and only that of Caliph (held by the Sultans) retained, to be filled by election from the Osman princes.

CALIPH

Prince Abdul Medjid	17 Nov 22–2 Mar 24

A republic was proclaimed on 29 Oct 23.

PRESIDENT

M. Kemal Atatürk	29 Oct 23–10 Nov 38
I. Inönü	11 Noy 38–21 May 50
C. Bayar	22 May 50–27 May 60
C. Gursel	26 Oct 61–27 Mar 66
Cevdet Sunay	28 Mar 66–

USSR

Constitution for the Federal Republic adopted on 10 July 18, by a government which took office on 8 Nov 17.

PRESIDENT OF THE COUNCIL OF PEOPLE'S COMMISSARS

V. I. Ulianov-Lenin	8 Nov 17–29 Dec 22

A new constitution of 30 Dec 22 replaced this office by a Central Executive Committee with four chairmen.
A new constitution came into force on 5 Dec 36 establishing the office of Chairman of the Praesidium of the Supreme Soviet of the USSR, as head of state.

CHAIRMAN

M. I. Kalinin	5 Dec 36–27 July 46
N. M. Shvernik	19 Mar 46–6 Mar 53
Marshal K. E. Voroshilov	6 Mar 53–7 May 60
L. I. Brezhnev	7 May 60–15 July 64
A. I. Mikoyan	15 July 64–9 Dec 65
N. V. Podgorny	9 Dec 65–

UNITED KINGDOM

KING

George V, m. Victoria Mary of Teck, succeeded his father
Edward VII   6 May 10–20 Jan 36
Edward VIII, succeeded his father   20 Jan 36–10 Dec 36 (abdic.)
George VI, m. Lady Elizabeth Bowes-Lyon, succeeded on the
abdication of his brother   10 Dec 36–6 Feb 52

QUEEN

Elizabeth II, m. Philip of Greece, succeeded her
father   6 Feb 52–

VATICAN

SUPREME PONTIFF

Benedict XV	3 Sep 14–22 Jan 22
Pius XI	6 Mar 22–13 Feb 39
Pius XII	2 Mar 39–9 Oct 58
John XXIII	28 Oct 58–3 June 63
Paul VI	21 June 63–

YUGOSLAVIA

The state was founded on 29 Dec 18 as the Serb, Croat and Slovene State (Montenegro joined on 1 Mar 21). The name was changed to Yugoslavia on 3 Oct 29.

KING

Peter I, m. Zorka of Montenegro, elected king   2 June 03–6 Aug 21
Alexander I, m. Marie of Romania, succeeded his
father   6 Aug 21–9 Oct 34 (assassinated)
Peter II, succeeded his father   9 Oct 34–29 Nov 45 (abdic.)

On 29 Nov 45 King Peter abdicated and a Republic was proclaimed.

PRESIDENT OF THE PRESIDIUM

Dr I. Ribar   2 Dec 45–13 Jan 53

PRESIDENT OF THE REPUBLIC

Marshal J. Broz-Tito   14 Jan 53–

3 PARLIAMENTS

ALBANIA

From 1920 until the Italian invasion Albania had a parliamentary system of government with a single elected chamber, but neither under the Republic nor under the monarchy did this function effectively. Under the Republic formed in 1946 there has been one chamber, the People's Assembly, elected on universal suffrage of all over 18, and sitting for a four-year term. The Assembly elects its Presidium and Council of Ministers. The Chairman of the Presidium is also the head of the state, and the Chairman of the Council of Ministers the Prime Minister. The Assembly, the Council and the Presidium operate on the Soviet pattern; the Assembly sits for short sessions, the Presidium more or less permanently, although the Assembly must meet twice a year. The Assembly has one member for each 8,000 voters. The Presidium has a chairman and three deputy chairmen, a secretary and ten members. The initiation and passing of legislation, and the exercise of legislative and executive power is the same as in the Soviet Union.

AUSTRIA

On 12 Nov 18 the Austrian members of the Austro-Hungarian imperial Reichsrat, having constituted themselves the German National Assembly, declared that Austria was a Republic. The following January a Constituent Assembly was elected as supreme authority for the purposes of framing a new constitution which came into operation in Nov 20. The Assembly had one chamber and was elected on universal adult suffrage. The new constitution provided for a bi-cameral federal legislature. The National Council was elected by proportional representation for four years, and could be adjourned only by its own decision. It could be summoned immediately on the request of at least a quarter of its members, or of the government. The Federal Council was elected by the Provincial Diets, having representatives from each province who sat for the length of term of their Diet. The Federal Council could initiate bills through the government; a bill passed by the National Council would be passed to the Federal Council and, if amended by them, reconsidered by the National Council and passable by a majority in that house. The Federal Council had no power to amend estimates.

The President was elected by both houses in joint session, for four years; his duties were mainly ceremonial and symbolic and all acts of government were the responsibility of ministers. The ministers were elected by the National Council on a motion submitted by its Principal Committee, and were not allowed to continue as Council members, if they were, or to become Council members while in office. Legislature and Executive were widely separate. The government suspended parliament in 1933 and in 1934 dissolved the Socialist Party: after strong reaction a new constitution, with socialist leanings, was brought in in 1935, but parliament worked with increasing difficulty until the integration with Germany in 1938, when it virtually ceased to operate.

A constitution similar to that of 1920 was restored in 1945. The state has now a Nationalrat with 165 deputies elected on the original suffrage and a Bundesrat of 50 deputies elected by the Provincial Diets. Bills must pass both houses. The National Council sits for four years; two regular sessions are convened each year in spring and autumn, and an extraordinary session may be held if the government or one third of the members of either house demand it. The Federal Council has representatives of the provinces according to size, with not more than twelve and not less than three members for each; the members are not necessarily members of the Provincial Diets, but they must be eligible to be so.

Bills may be initiated by either house or by the government but must be presented in the National Council. There is provision also for the popular initiative; every proposal signed by 200,000 Länder voters or half the voters in each of the three Länder must be submitted to the National Council. The National Council may also request a referendum on a bill which it has assented to. All bills go secondly to the Federal Council which may object to them within eight weeks; the bill becomes law if the National Council reaffirms it with half its members present.

BELGIUM

Belgium is a constitutional monarchy with two legislative chambers, the Chamber of Representatives and the Senate. The King shares legislative powers with the two chambers and exercises the executive power in conjunction with his ministers; he may not act alone. He appoints ministers from among members of parliament, and sanctions laws. The chamber of Representatives consists of 212 members – the maximum number is one for every 40,000 inhabitants – elected on proportional representation for four year terms. Members must be at least 25. The Senate members must be at least 40 and are elected as follows: one member for every 200,000 inhabitants, elected by the provincial councils on proportional representation; half the number of Chamber deputies elected by the same electorate. Since 1965 there have been 106 directly-elected members and 48 provincial members. Constitutionally the Chamber and the Senate have equal powers; bills may be introduced in both houses and must pass both before being signed by the King. Traditionally the legislature possessed considerable control over the cabinet, since all legislation passes through a strong committee system in both houses. In the years between the two world wars particularly this provided stability when political life was disrupted by Fleming-Walloon or Catholic-Protestant differences.

In Oct 21 the length of service for members of the Senate was reduced from eight years to four, and the franchise was extended to all men over 21, together with women who were war-widows or war-sufferers. Before 1921 there was a system of plural votes on grounds of property or income. The franchise was extended to women in 1948.

Senate and Chamber meet annually in October (November until 1921) and must sit for at least forty days. The government, through the King, has power to dissolve either chamber separately or both chambers at once. In the latter case a new election must take place within forty days and a meeting of the Chambers within two months; no adjournment for longer than one month may be made without the consent of both Chambers.

Money bills originate in the Chamber of Representatives. There is also a strong subsidiary body – the Court of Accounts – with members appointed by the Chamber with authority to control all treasury work and all provision for revenue and expenditure. By an Act 23 Dec 46 a Council of State was also set up, with separate sections for legislation and administration on constitutional matters.

BULGARIA

The constitution of 1879 was still in operation in 1918, after amendment in 1911. The legislature was a single chamber, the National Assembly (Sobranje). Members were elected by universal manhood suffrage; one member for every 20,000 inhabitants. All literate men over 30 were eligible to sit, except for soldiers, clergy and those deprived of civil rights. The term was four years, but the Assembly could be dissolved at any time by the King, and elections held within two months. There was a second, but not permanent, chamber, the Grand Sobranje; this had twice the membership of the Sobranje but was elected only for special purposes. It sat to decide questions on territory, changes to the constitution or the succession to the throne. Both houses were elected on proportional representation. Laws passed by the National Assembly required the assent of the King, who might himself initiate legislation through his ministers. After 1911 the King might also make treaties with foreign powers without having the Assembly's consent; he might also issue regulations and take emergency measures in time of danger, although it was the cabinet who assumed responsibility for such measures. Cabinet members were chosen by the King. They were required to countersign royal acts and were responsible both to the King and to the Assembly.

In Oct 37 an electoral law fixed the number of Sobranje members at 160 (it had previously had 227) and the size of constituencies to at least 20,000 electors, comprising all men and all married women over 21.

A Republic was proclaimed in Sep 46 and a new constitution drawn up in Dec 47. This provided for a parliament on the Russian model, except that there was only one assembly, as before, consisting of deputies elected by secret, direct and universal suffrage of all inhabitants over 18, one deputy for every 30,000 – later every 20,000 – inhabitants. The Assembly elected its Presidium of chairman, two deputy chairmen, secretary and 15 members; this is the most powerful organ of the state. There is also a Council of Ministers elected by the National Assembly. The relation of the three bodies to each other is on the Russian pattern.

CZECHOSLOVAKIA

The constitution of the Republic was put into operation in 1920. It provided for a two-chamber parliament, the National Parliament, which consisted of a Chamber of Deputies and a Senate, elected on proportional representation by all citizens over 21. The Chamber was elected for six years and had 300 deputies; the Senate sat for eight years and had 150 members. Legislation might be introduced by the government or by either of the chambers. Bills passed by the deputies were passed to the Senate for consideration. A bill rejected by the Senate could still become law if passed again with an absolute majority by the deputies. If the Senate rejected it by a three-quarters majority then it required a three-fifths majority to pass in the Chamber. A bill initiated in the Senate died if it was dismissed twice by an absolute majority in the Chamber. Bills relating to money and defence could only be initiated by the deputies. The legislature had no strong control over the government; if the National Parliament rejected a government bill the government could still decide (unanimously) to put the bill to a referendum, provided it was not an amendment to the constitution.

The President (Dr Masaryk) was in fact elected for life, but the constitution provided that in future the President would be elected by the National Parliament for a seven-year term. His election would need the attendance of an absolute majority of the parliament and a three-fifths majority of votes. He was to be head of state, but the government would be responsible for the exercise of his powers. He could not declare war without parliamentary approval. He could dissolve both chambers, but not during the last six months of his presidency. He might return a bill to parliament with his observations on it, when it could only be carried if an absolute majority of all members adhered to it.

The parliament did not operate effectively after Czechoslovakia became a German Protectorate in 1939.

A new constitution of June 48 provided for a single-chamber National Assembly with 300 members elected for six years. In 1953 a Presidium on the Soviet model was set up, with a Chairman (Prime Minister) and ten deputies; later in the same year the number of deputies was reduced to four and the Presidium considerably reduced in power. In 1969 the state became a federation; the new Federal Assembly consists of the Chamber of Nations, with 75 Czech and 75 Slovak delegates elected by the National Councils of the Czechs and Slovaks, and the Chamber of the People which has 200 deputies elected by national suffrage.

DENMARK

The constitutional Charter of 1915 provided that the legislative power should be held by the King and the Rigsdag (parliament) jointly, and that the executive power be held by the King and exercised through his ministers, although he could not declare war or sign a peace treaty without parliament's consent. There were two chambers: the Folketing (lower house) had 149 members, 117 of them elected by proportional representation and 31 additional seats divided among parties who had insufficient votes to win any. It sat for a four-year term but might be dissolved by the King. There was no specific ruling that the ministers who formed the King's Council of State and who were appointed and dismissed by him, were responsible to the Folketing in the parliamentary sense. The King normally presided over the Council of State; he had the right to object to its decisions and to re-introduce the matter at a future meeting. In his absence the Prime Minister presided. The Landsting had 78 members indirectly elected and sat for a term of eight years; those members elected in the Landsting electoral districts sat for four years, when there was a further election for half of their number; members elected by the former Landsting sat for the whole eight years; there were 56 members elected in the districts and 19 by the Landsting. Parliament was obliged to meet annually in October. Ministers had access to both houses but could only vote in the chamber of which they were members.

The constitutional Charter of June 1953 abolished the Landsting. The Folketing remained with 179 members, 135 of them elected in the districts, and 40 additional seats. The Council of State continued to operate as a cabinet, ministers being individually and collectively responsible to the Folketing for their actions. The legislative power is still the joint prerogative of the Queen and the Folketing, and the executive power is still vested in the Queen acting through her ministers.

Any member may initiate a bill. Bills are approved or not after three readings. If one-third of members request it, a bill that has been passed may be subject to a referendum. A bill that is to be subject to referendum may be withdrawn within five weeks of its being passed. The referendum is held and its result acted upon in accordance with the Prime Minister's decision.

ESTONIA

The Constitutional Assembly of 1918 formulated a constitution which came into force in 1920. This provided for a republican state with a State Assembly elected by all citizens over 25, by proportional representation, and sitting for three years.

The Assembly had 100 members, and elected its own chairman and officers from among them. The Assembly appointed a government responsible to it and consisting of the head of state and his ministers. The executive prepared the budget and submitted it to the Assembly for approval. Bills passed in the Assembly might remain unpromulgated for two months if one-third of the Assembly demanded it; within that period a referendum could be demanded, or the bill's adoption recommended, by 25,000 citizens entitled to vote.

A second constitution was framed in 1934 and a third in 1938, when the main changes were made. A President was to be popularly elected for a term of six years. Parliament had two chambers, the first having 80 members directly elected by the national electorate for a five-year term. The second – the State Council – had 40 members all over 40 years of age and elected by organizations and public bodies. The Prime Minister, no longer head of state, was chosen by the President and formed his own cabinet which was responsible to parliament. He did not automatically resign on a vote of no confidence; it was the President's decision whether the cabinet should be dismissed or parliament dissolved. Since 1940 Estonia has been a constituent republic of the USSR.

FINLAND

The constitutional law of 1919 provided for a republican state with a President and a single-chamber parliament. The President is elected indirectly for a six-year term. He ratifies or withholds consent to new law, dissolves the Diet and orders new elections and conducts foreign affairs. In all this he must act through his ministers, who are individually and collectively responsible to the Diet, and must take all his decisions in meetings of the cabinet. He has a strong veto power on legislation, and if he does not give the necessary approval within three months the bill dies. In this event, if the new Diet accepts the bill exactly as it was after new elections, it becomes valid without his assent.

Every citizen entitled to vote is eligible to be a member of the Diet, which has 200 members and is elected by proportional representation for a four-year term (originally a three-year term). The house meets annually for at least 120 days after which it determines the date of its own rising. The President, as embodying the supreme executive power, initiates legislation by introducing bills into the Diet; the Diet with the President has power to propose a new law or to repeal or amend an existing one. New bills are drafted by the Council of State (cabinet), and may be passed for opinion to the Supreme Court or Supreme Administrative Court. Bills adopted by the house are submitted to the President. The Council of State has no fixed size but consists of as many ministers as are necessary, and always includes a Chancellor of Justice and a deputy who have the right to assist at all sessions of the Council of State and of tribunals and public departments, with free access to their minutes. These may not be members of the Diet. There is a strong system of Diet committees which must be constituted within five days of the opening of a session. Standing committees are the Committees on Fundamental Laws, Laws, Foreign Affairs, Finance and a Bank Committee. The Grand Committee must also be established within the same period, having 45 members elected by the Diet. No member of the government may be a committee member. The Grand Committee serves as a body to consider bills which have had their first reading and previously been passed to one of the specialist committees for opinion. The opinion of the Grand Committee is heard at the second reading.

FRANCE

The Third Republic kept the constitution of 1875 until it ended in 1940. This provided for two chambers, a Chamber of Deputies and a Senate. The Chamber of 26 members was elected for four years by manhood suffrage on proportional representation. The Senate had 314 members elected for nine years, one third retiring every three. Both houses assembled annually in January, and were obliged to remain in session for at least five months of the twelve. Bills could be presented in both houses either by the government or by private members, except financial bills which were solely the concern of the deputies. There was also a Council of State presided over by the Minister of Justice and other members all appointed by the President. It gave opinion on any question of administration put to it by the government.

The President was a symbolic head of state, theoretically with many powers but in practice not exercising them. He had the right to dissolve the Chamber, but did not use it after 1877; the suspensory veto over acts of parliament was never used. His role in lawmaking and the determination of policy was controlled by the cabinet.

The government's executive power lay with the ministers who were not necessarily members of either house and were chosen by the President in conjunction with the Prime Minister. They were responsible to both houses and were obliged to countersign (individually) every act of the President. Political dissension between many small parties made for weakness in the executive which had on several occasions to be offset by a grant of special powers made by parliament to the ministers. Special powers to proceed by decree for budgetary and taxation measures were granted in 1926; special powers were also granted in 1934, 1935, 1937 and 1938 and over a hundred decrees issued. Similarly ministers seldom felt strong enough to ask for a dissolution and election on the defeat of a measure; they normally resigned. Between 1870 and 1934 France had 88 ministries with an average life of less than nine months.

The constitution for the Fourth Republic was submitted to the vote in 1946. The Senate was replaced by the Council of the Republic as a purely advisory body, the Chamber by the National Assembly as the legislative body. The executive had limited power to dissolve parliament, and popular sovereignty was invested in the referendum. In 1954, by a constitutional amendment, the Council of the Republic had some power restored to it as a delaying body, with power to hold up National Assembly action in public matters for 108 days. It could also initiate bills and pass them to the National Assembly. The Assembly then had 627 members, 544 of them from Metropolitan France, elected all at the same time for a five-year term. The position of the President was similar to that under the Third Republic, except that the President of the Council of Ministers (Prime Minister) had taken over some of his powers, principally the power to propose legislation to parliament and to issue edicts to supplement the law. The programme of the cabinet had to be approved by public vote by an absolute majority of the National Assembly before the Council of Ministers could be appointed. Once appointed they were responsible to the Assembly but not to the Council of the Republic. The Prime Minister in theory had considerable powers; he assured the execution of all national laws, directed the armed forces and appointed most civil and military officials. In practice, however, he spent much of his time trying to maintain a cohesive executive when no one party was ever strong enough to govern alone.

Under the Fifth Republic the President is head of the government as well as head of state. He can dissolve parliament, negotiate treaties and deal with emergencies without counter-signature. He appoints (rather than formally nominating) the Prime Minister. He is indirectly elected for a seven-year term, but there is no bar to re-election. He may submit matters to the Constitutional

54

Council for opinion, ask parliament to reconsider bills, give ruling on proposals to submit bills to referendum. Before acting outright in an emergency he must consult both executive and legislature, but he is not bound to their advice. Nor is he bound to accept the resignation of the government if the National Assembly has caused it to resign. The National Assembly now has 552 members – 465 from Metropolitan France – and neither the Prime Minister nor any of the cabinet are allowed to hold seats in it. The Council of the Republic continues as the Senate, and all bills go to it. Both houses sit for about five months of the year, which is shorter than previously. The number of private members' bills is considerably fewer – an average of 2,000 a year under the Fourth Republic, 200 a year under the Fifth – and the programme of the National Assembly is determined by the government and not by the house. The Senate now has 283 members for Metropolitan France and 19 others.

EAST GERMANY

The People's Chamber is the only legislative body. It was formed from the previous People's Council as a constituent body at the same time as the formation of the Federal Republic in Bonn. On 7 Oct 49 the Chamber enacted a constitution for the Democratic Republic. A new constitution was approved by referendum on 6 Apr 68.

The Chamber has 500 deputies who are directly elected for four years. It assures the enforcement of its own laws and decisions and lays down the principles to which the Council of State, the Council of Ministers, the National Defence Council, the Supreme Court and the Procurator General should adhere. No one can limit the rights of the Chamber. It can hold plebiscites, declare a state of defence when necessary, and approve and terminates state treaties. In between its sessions it authorizes the Council of State to fulfil all tasks resulting from the Chamber's laws and decisions. The Council is elected for four years. It deals with bills to be submitted to the Chamber and submits them for discussion by the Chamber's committees; it convenes the Chamber either on request or on its own initiative; it issues decrees and decisions with the force of law; it has power to interpret existing law; it issues the writs for elections; its Chairman represents the Republic in international relations. (The Council was formed to replace the office of President abolished in 1960.) The Council is an organ of the Chamber and responsible to it.

The Council of Ministers is also an organ of the Chamber and elected by it. Its Chairman is proposed to the Chamber by the Chairman of the Council of State. It functions collectively in the exercise of executive power; from within its ranks it appoints a Presidium; the Chairman of the Council is also the Chairman of the Presidium. The Chamber reaches decisions by majority vote.

Bills may be presented by the deputies of the parties or mass organizations represented, by the committees of the Chamber, the Council of State, the Council of Ministers or by the Confederation of Free German Trade Unions. The bill's conformity with the constitution is examined by the Council of State; the bill is then discussed in committee and comments submitted to the Chamber in plenary session. Drafts of basic laws, prior to their being passed, are submitted to the electorate for discussion.

The Chamber can be dissolved before the end of its electoral term only on its own decision taken on a two-thirds majority. After the end of an electoral term the Council of Ministers and the Council of State continue their work until the new Chamber elects new Councils.

WEST GERMANY

Parliament consists of the Federal Diet (Bundestag) elected on universal, direct and secret elections for four years, and the Federal Council (Bundesrat) which is composed of members of governments of the Länder. The Bundestag has 496 members and 22 non-voting members for Berlin.

Elections for a new Bundestag take place in the last three months of its term, or in the case of its dissolution after not more than 60 days. The new house meets not more than 30 days after election. The President of the Bundestag may convene the house at any time and must do so if asked by one-third of its members or by the Federal President or Federal Chancellor.

Meetings are public, but the public may be excluded. Members of the Bundesrat or of the government have free access to the Bundestag meetings and committee meetings and must be heard at any time; the same is true of Bundestag members at meetings of the Bundesrat, and either house may demand the presence of any member of the Federal Government.

The governments of the Länder appoint and recall those of their members who make up the Bundesrat, or they may appoint other members to represent them. Each Land has at least three votes; Länder with over 2m. inhabitants have four, those with over 6m. have five. Each Land has as many members as it has votes, and the votes may only be given as a block. The government has an obligation to keep the Bundesrat informed of the conduct of Federal affairs.

Bills are introduced in the Bundestag either by the government or by members of either house. Government bills go to the Bundesrat first, and the house must give an opinion within three weeks. A bill adopted in the Bundestag then goes to the Bundesrat, which may within two weeks demand a joint committee to consider it. Bills altering or adding to the constitution require Bundesrat approval before they may be passed; such bills need a two-thirds majority in both houses. For other bills the Bundesrat has a power of veto, but even then a veto adopted by a majority of Bundesrat votes may be rejected by a majority of Bundestag votes. There is provision for a state of legislative emergency for a bill which the Bundestag has rejected despite the government declaring it urgent, or a bill which has been put forward with a request for a vote of confidence.

The Federal Chancellor is elected by the Bundestag on the proposal of the Federal President. Ministers are appointed and dismissed by the President on the Chancellor's proposal. The Chancellor determines and assumes responsibility for general policy, and within that policy the ministers run their own departments on their own responsibility. The President is elected by indirect vote for a five-year term; immediate re-election is allowed once. His orders and instructions require countersignature by the Chancellor or by a minister.

The constitution of 1919 had set up a similar bi-cameral parliament; the differences in its operation were that the votes of any one state in the then Reichsrat did not have to be cast as a block vote; the government had wider powers of dissolution and special ordinance to counter the power of the Bundestag; the President's powers were extensive, and his term was seven years. It was he who initiated orders and decrees, although they had still to be countersigned. He appointed all national officials; he decided the sessions and dissolutions of the Reichstag; he ordered referenda. Without consulting the government or the legislature he could, in time of danger, suspend the national authorities and appoint a national commissioner in their place, employ the armed forces and suspend certain fundamental rights. By 1932 his emergency powers had been used 233 times, the Reichstag having the right to repeal any measures taken when the emergency was over.

(Note: the constitution of 1919 provided for popular election of the President. In fact President Ebert was elected by the Constituent Assembly itself, and Adolf Hitler assumed the Presidency by incorporating it with his own office of Chancellor. Paul von Hindenburg was the only popularly-elected President.)

By the law of 14 July 33 all political parties except the National Socialist German Workers' Party were declared illegal; the Reichstag did not operate normally from that date. Its meetings became shorter until they were limited to sessions of two or three days, and it met infrequently. It remained virtually dead until 1949.

GREECE[1]

The constitution of 1911 continued in force until 1925 when it was replaced temporarily by a new one; this was abandoned in 1935 and the original re-instated although some parts of the second constitution were substituted for some of the original clauses later in the year. The constitution of 1952 further

---

[1] On 1 June 73 a Republic was declared and the monarchy abolished.

amended that of 1911, and remained in force until 1968 when a new one was adopted after a referendum. All of them except that of 1925 have provided for a single-chamber parliament, the House of Representatives.

The House has at least 150 members elected by direct universal suffrage for four years. It meets annually in October for each regular session, which must be for at least three months. It sits in public but the public may be excluded, if the majority of members so decide. It shares with the King or his Regent the legislative power and the right of proposing laws; this second right the King or the Regent exercises through his ministers. Their countersignature is necessary for all his acts, and through them his executive power is exercised. If no minister consents to sign the decrees dismissing an entire ministry and appointing a new one, they may be signed by the President of the new ministry whom the King has appointed. He may suspend the work of a session once only; he may dissolve the house, but the decree of dissolution must include the convocation of the electors within 45 days and of the new house within three months. He has no power to delay the operation of the law. A bill is at first accompanied by an explanatory report and sent to a committee of the house; it is brought in for discussion when the committee has reported, or when the time allowed for such report has elapsed. No proposal is considered accepted unless it has been discussed and voted on twice at separate sittings. A bill can be passed in one sitting provided the committee to which it was submitted has agreed, and provided less than twenty representatives object before the close of the debate. Ministers have free access to debates and may demand a hearing at any time; they vote only if they are members. They are individually responsible to the House, and no order from the King can release them from their responsibility.

The 1925 Republican constitution provided for a Senate as well as a Chamber of Representatives, and a President. The President was elected for five years by both houses in joint session. The Chamber had between 200 and 300 directly-elected members and the Senate 120 members indirectly elected. The ministers were responsible to both houses for the actions of the executive, *i.e.* the President. Bills could be introduced by members of both houses and by the government; the Senate had power to delay legislation but the Chamber could pass a bill by majority vote over the Senate's opposition after three months or earlier at a joint session if the Senate requested one. The budget was initiated in the Chamber and the Senate was obliged to pronounce on it within one month. The President required ministerial countersignature for all his acts.

HUNGARY

The first permanent Parliament set up after the end of the Austro-Hungarian monarchy was the National Assembly of 1920. The head of the state was

Admiral Horthy who held the title of Regent; he had power of suspensive veto over laws passed by the Assembly and power to dissolve the house provided a newly elected Assembly met within 90 days. When the Assembly ended in 1922 a law was passed by government decree (*i.e.* by the Regent's ministers) making the 200 seats in rural constituencies subject to open and not secret voting. Men over 24 who had completed the course at elementary school, and women over 30 with certain qualifications received the vote. The government's supporters were returned in strength, but the working of parliament became disorderly and difficult. In 1924 the government was granted extraordinary powers for a two-year period of reconstruction.

In 1926 a second chamber was formed, comprising male members of the former reigning house, elected representatives of hereditary members of the former Upper House, about 50 members elected by town and county municipalities, about 31 members as religious representatives, about 40 members elected by institutions and organizations and some life members appointed by the head of the state. It ceased functioning after 1944. In 1937 the Regent was made no longer responsible to parliament. In 1938 the number of deputies in the Assembly was increased from 245 to 260. The Assembly proclaimed a Republic in 1946. In 1949 a further – Communist – constitution was set up with parliament electing a Presidium on the Soviet model; the Presidium is in continual session and has power to dissolve government bodies and to annul legislation. The Assembly has 349 deputies, and since 1967 more than one candidate has been allowed to stand for election in each constituency. Members are elected for four years. The Assembly also elects a Council of Ministers with a chairman as Prime Minister. The relationship between Assembly, Council and Presidium is on the Soviet model.

ICELAND

The constitution in force in 1918 was based on the Charter of 1814. Executive power belonged to the King (who was King of both Denmark and Iceland as two separate sovereign states) and was exercised through ministers responsible to him and to parliament (the Althing). The legislative power rested conjointly with the Althing and the King. The Althing had 40 members, 34 of them elected by universal suffrage in constituencies and the remaining 6 elected for the whole country on proportional representation. The 34 sat for 6 years, the rest for 12. The Althing had an Upper House of 14 members – *i.e.* the 6 described above and 8 others elected by the whole Althing from among the 34. The remaining 26 members formed the Lower House. The Althing met every other year in July, and could not sit for longer than four weeks without royal sanction. Ministers had free access to both houses, but could only vote in the house of which they were members. Budget bills had to be introduced in the Lower House, but all other bills could be introduced in either. If the houses could not agree on a bill they assembled in common sitting and the decision was by a two-thirds majority except in the case of a budget bill, for which a simple majority was enough.

In the Charter of 1920 and its amendments of 1934 some alterations were made to the composition of the Althing: the number of members had not to exceed 49, of whom 38 were elected from the constituencies, each electing candidates by simple majority except for the capital which elected 6 on proportional representation. Not more than 11 supplementary seats were distributed among parties having insufficient seats in proportion to their electors. The Upper House was composed of one-third of Althing members elected by both houses in common sitting. The Althing met every year. Budget bills must be laid before both houses in joint session. The republic was proclaimed in 1944 and a President elected to exercise executive power through the ministers. He serves for four years.

IRISH REPUBLIC

There are two houses in the Irish parliament, the House of Representatives (Dáil) and the Senate. The House has 144 members elected by universal adult suffrage. The Senate has 60 members of whom 11 are nominated by the Prime Minister, 6 elected by the universities and 43 elected by a college from representatives of the public services and interests. The President is elected for a seven-year term and may be re-elected for consecutive terms. The constitution in force is that of 1937. The constitution formed by Dáil Eireann in 1919 was a temporary one, not intended as a permanent basis for a fully operating government. It provided for a chairman for the Dáil, a Prime Minister and other ministers; it defined the competence of the Dáil and made provision for audit and budgeting. The constitution of the Irish Free State in 1922 provided for a constitutional monarchy with responsible government by a cabinet of ministers. In order to restrict the power of the executive there was also provision for referendum and popular initiative, and for the direct election by the Dáil of ministers who were not Dáil members or members of the cabinet. All these measures, however, had lapsed or been removed within five years.

Note: The 1937 constitution did not declare a Republic. It provided instead for a continuation of the arrangements made at the abdication of Edward VIII, when the mention of the Crown was removed from the previous constitution and an ordinary statute (The Executive Authority (External Relations) Act) put in its place to provide an organ for the state in the conduct of its external affairs. In 1948 it was therefore possible to create the Republic by ordinary legislation and not by changing the constitution. The President appoints the Prime Minister on the nomination of the Dáil, and the other ministers on the nomination of the Prime Minister, with the previous approval of the Dáil. The Prime Minister holds office until he chooses to resign, in which case the government is deemed also to have resigned, until he loses majority support or until he himself secures dissolution by asking the President. Appointment to the government is distinct from appointment to a department. Members of the government may include members of the Senate (but in practice have only done so twice). There is provision for ministers without portfolio.

Bills are proposed mainly by the government in planned legislative programmes. There is provision for private members' bills, but few are initiated. The Senate has power to delay legislation while the Dáil reconsiders its previous decision. Bills can be discussed at parliamentary party meetings either between their preparation and presentation to the house, or between presentation and second reading.

There may be no amendment to the constitution without a referendum, though this was possible before 1930.

ITALY

Italy is a Republic, with a President and a parliament consisting of a Chamber of Deputies and a Senate. The Chamber is elected for five years by direct and universal suffrage with one deputy for every 80,000 inhabitants. The Senate is elected for six years with at least six senators for each Region – one for every 200,000 inhabitants – except for the Valle d'Aosta which has only one. The President can nominate five senators for life, and may himself become a senator for life upon retiring from the Presidency.

Parliament may be dissolved by the President. A cabinet need resign only on a motivated motion of censure.

A joint session of Chamber and Senate is needed to elect a President, with an additional three delegates from each Regional Council (one from the Valle d'Aosta). The presidential term is seven years.

The Republic was established in 1946, following a referendum on 2 June and the consequent abdication of King Umberto II on 13 June. The republican constitution came into force on 1 Jan 48.

The constitution prior to 1948 was an expansion of the Statuto fondamentale del Regno of 1848. The executive power belonged to the sovereign and was exercised through responsible ministers; legislative power rested in King and parliament, which consisted of a Senate and a lower chamber. This latter was the Chamber of Deputies until 1938; it was elected by universal adult male suffrage for five years with one deputy for every 71,000 of the population. The King had power to dissolve it at any time provided he ordered new elections and convoked a new meeting within four months. In 1938 the

Chamber was replaced by the Chamber of Fasci and Corporations which had first met in 1929. Membership of this consisted of the Duce and the members of the Grand Fascist Council, a third body whose approval was needed for all constitutional measures and which consisted of original members of the Fascist Party on its coming to power, who were appointed for an indefinite period, ministers and other dignitaries appointed for the duration of their terms of office and other members appointed for three years by the Duce. The Duce as Prime Minister was responsible to the King.

Suffrage in 1919 was by proportional representation. In 1923 this was replaced by a system of election in fifteen constituencies, with two-thirds of seats allotted to whichever party gained at least 25% of total votes. In 1925 there was a further alteration introducing single-member constituencies, by-elections and suffrage for all over 25. Parliament, however, did not function normally after the Fascist ministry took power in 1922, as the Fascists were the only effective party.

LATVIA

The constitution came into force in 1922 and provided for a repulican state with a single house of parliament (the Saeima). The house had 100 representatives directly elected on universal adult suffrage by proportional representation for a term of three years. The house elected the state President by absolute majority for a three-year term. The President chose the Prime Minister, who appointed the cabinet. The cabinet was responsible to the house. The President had the right to dissolve parliament only after the proposal to dissolve it had been voted on and confirmed by the electorate. If he did not obtain this confirmation he was obliged to resign. In 1934 the parliament was disbanded and a government set up which combined executive and legislative power in the former Council of Ministers. This government was led by the former Prime Minister Karlis Ulmanis. He combined his office with that of President in 1936. Since 1940 Latvia has been a constituent republic of the USSR.

LIECHTENSTEIN

The constitution of 1921 provides for a Diet of 15 members in one house, elected on universal suffrage and proportional representation. They sit for four years. The Prince convokes, closes and dissolves the Diet, and may adjourn it for three months provided the adjournment is announced before the full Diet. Convocation may be demanded by 400 citizens, and dissolution decided by plebiscite on the demand of 600. The Diet supervises the entire administration of the state. Bills may be initiated by the Diet, the Prince acting through the government, and the citizens (400 or three communes). To be valid a law must be passed by an absolute majority of at least two-thirds of members. If the

Diet rejects a bill submitted to it by popular initiative, it is obliged to submit the bill to referendum, when it can be passed by the citizens even if the Diet disagrees. The government is appointed by the Prince with the approval of the Diet; he acts through them, but all his actions must be countersigned and it is his ministers who are responsible.

LITHUANIA

The constitution was adopted in 1922 and provided for a single-chamber parliament elected for three years by universal suffrage and proportional representation. Elections for a new house had to take place before the expiration of the previous term. The President of the Republic was elected by parliament for three years and by absolute majority; he could run for two successive terms but no third term without a break. He appointed the Prime Minister, and confirmed the ministers chosen by him, and also appointed the State Comptrollers (with auditing powers), but all bodies appointed could only function with the confidence of the house. He had power to return a bill to the house for reconsideration within twenty-one days of the passage; but was then bound to accept it if it was passed again by an absolute majority. His power of delay could be cancelled by a declaration of urgency by the house. He presided at and took part in cabinet meetings.

Any amendment to the constitution could be brought forward by the house, the government, or 50,000 citizens, but needed a three-fifths majority of the total number of deputies for adoption. After that a referendum could be demanded on it. Ministers had individual and collective responsibility.

In 1926 the democratic system was brought to an end by political confusion. Further constitutional changes were made in 1928 and 1938 on authoritarian lines. By 1938 a dictatorship had been established and the house was no longer operating normally. In 1940 Lithuania became a constituent republic of the USSR.

LUXEMBOURG

The constitution of 1868 was amended in 1919, 1948 and 1956. In 1919 it was decided that sovereign power was vested in the people and that deputies to the single Chamber of Deputies were to be elected on universal suffrage by the list system of proportional representation. The Chamber of Deputies had 48 members in 1919. They were elected for a six-year term, half of them being re-elected every three years. The head of state shared legislative power with the Chamber and exercised the executive power through the cabinet. The constitution allowed the sovereign to organize the government. The sovereign also chose the 15 members of the permanent Council of State who served for life. The Council discussed proposed legislation and was obliged to give an opinion on any matter referred to it by the sovereign or the representatives of the law.

In 1956 the term of office for deputies was altered to five years.

The Grand Duke names and dismisses the government, which must consist of at least three members who may not be members of the Chamber, and who are responsible collectively and individually.

Bills are passed after two readings with an interval of three months approved by an absolute majority.

MONACO

Executive power is vested in the Prince, the Minister of State who represents him, and the Council. The Minister directs all administration and presides over the Council with the casting vote. The Council consists of three members named by the Prince (members for the Interior, Finance and Public Works). The Council takes its decisions after deliberation and prepares drafts and ordinances for the Prince's consideration. Legislative power is vested in the Prince and the National Council which is voted in for eighteen years on universal suffrage. The Assembly of the National Council chooses a Bureau, with President and Vice-President. The Assembly sits for two sessions a year, each of 15 days at most; the Prince may convoke and dissolve it. He communicates with the Assembly through the Minister of State, who, together with the councillors, may attend at his own wish and must attend when asked. The initiative rests with the Prince, but the National Council may submit draft proposals to him and ask him to initiate them. The National Council controls the budget, which is submitted to it by the Council, and has sole right to levy direct taxation.

THE NETHERLANDS

The parliament consists of two chambers. The Upper House has had 75 members since 1956, prior to which it had 50. They are elected by members of the Provincial States. The Second Chamber has had 150 deputies since 1956 (100 before that) and they are directly elected on universal suffrage and proportional representation. The Second Chamber shares legislative power with the sovereign, who has power to dissolve both chambers provided elections take place within 40 days and the new house or houses be convoked within three months.

The Upper House is elected for six years, and half the members retire every three years. The Lower House members are elected for four years.

Bills are proposed either by the Sovereign, acting through responsible ministers, or by a member of the Lower House. The Upper House has power only to approve or reject them without amendment; the houses must ultimately agree. Ministers and Secretaries of State attend sessions of both houses either at their own or parliament's wish, but they may not be members of either house. The constitution can only be revised if the bill for its revision is passed and confirmed again by a second parliament after the dissolution of the first.

The constitutional amendments of 1922 provided that the Upper House should be elected for six years and not for nine as formerly. Until 1922 the right to declare war and to conclude and ratify treaties with foreign powers was a royal power, exercised in conjunction with the cabinet. Since then, the exercise of these powers has depended on previous parliamentary sanction. The constitution allows considerable royal initiative, but in practice the operation of the cabinet system has set this aside. There is also a Council of State of not more than 16 members which sits as an advisory body on all legislative matters and is consulted by the Crown, the government or parliament.

NORWAY

Norway's constitution dates from 1814; although there have been amendments since, the nature of the Storting (Parliament) is virtually the same as then provided. The state is a constitutional monarchy; in default of male heirs the King proposes a successor to parliament which have the right to select another. The King also has power of veto which may be exercised twice; a bill which passes three parliaments formed by three elections becomes law without his assent.

Parliament assembles in October every year for a session of no fixed duration. Once the house is assembled it divides in two by electing one-quarter of its members to form the Lagting or Upper House; the remaining three-quarters forming the Odelsting or Lower House. There is a president nominated for each house and for the joint house. Most questions are decided by the joint house, but legislation must be considered by both houses separately. If they disagree, then the bill must be decided by parliament as a whole and the decision taken on a two-thirds majority (of voters, not of total membership). The same majority is needed for constitutional amendments.

The executive is represented by the Crown acting through the Prime Minister and cabinet of 14 ministers. The ministers attend sessions of parliament and take part in discussions, but they do not vote. They do initiate bills.

There is a strong committee system through which all proposed legislation must pass before submission to the house. All bills are proposed in the Odelsting, and if accepted are sent to the Lagting. The Lagting may either approve a bill as it stands or reject it as it stands and give its reasons. If rejected it is returned to the Odelsting which will send it once more, either in an amended or original form, to the Lagting. If still rejected the joint session must take place to pass it.

The Crown has no power of dissolution, nor can it summon parliament to meet. The dates of meeting are decided by parliament itself. Election is direct, by all citizens over 20 and by proportional representation. The 150 members are elected for a three-year term.

POLAND

The constitution of the Republic came into operation in 1920. The legislature consisted of a Diet and a Senate. Diet members were elected on universal suffrage for a five-year term. The Senate was elected on universal suffrage of all citizens over 30 and by proportional representation in the provincial districts. It sat also for five years.

National minorities represented 20% of Diet membership.

The Diet had the power of initiating legislation, and had to submit every bill it passed to the Senate. The Senate was obliged to refer a bill back within 30 days if it was suggesting amendments; otherwise the bill was promulgated. If the Diet accepted the Senate's amendments by a simple majority or rejected them by a majority of eleven-twentieths, the bill was passed in the form it left the Diet for the second time.

A President was elected by parliament as a whole for a term of seven years. His position was largely symbolic and his actions required the consent of parliament. He might dissolve the Diet if he had the consent of the Senate, but the Senate in so consenting determined its own dissolution. He exercised the executive power through a council of ministers responsible to the Diet.

There was also a Supreme Court of Control which made independent and judicious survey of the government's provincial administration. Its president was a minister, not a member of the Council of Ministers but responsible to the Diet.

The constitution could only be amended by a two-thirds majority of at least half the number of deputies and senators fixed by law. It might be revised once every 25 years by simple majority of a joint session.

The constitution of 1935 made radical changes in the office of President and the composition of the houses. The working of the original Diet was frequently disrupted by party differences; now there were to be no political parties in the Diet or the Senate. The Senate was to have one-third of its 96 Senators nominated by the President of the Republic and the remaining two-thirds elected by colleges.

The President was chosen by referendum from two candidates, one elected by the two houses together and the other nominated by the retiring President. He could now exercise without countersignature his right to nominate and dismiss the Prime Minister and the Inspector-General of the armed forces, to nominate judges and senators, and to dissolve the Diet and the Senate before the end of their term. If the Diet and the Senate demanded the dismissal of a minister or of the cabinet, the President might concur or dissolve the houses.

The present constitution was adopted in 1952. There is now one chamber which sits for four years and is elected by all citizens over 18. It elects, on the Russian pattern, a Council of Ministers with a Chairman as Prime Minister, and a Council of State composed of a Chairman, a Secretary and 14 members, which sits in almost permanent session and exercises the power of a Presidium.

PORTUGAL

By the republican constitution of 1911, legislative power was given to a Congress with a Chamber of Deputies and a Senate. There were 164 deputies elected for three years by male suffrage. The Senate had 71 members elected by electoral colleges formed from the Municipal Councils, and sat for six years with half the number retiring every three years. The Chamber of Deputies had priority in the discussion of financial bills, bills promoted by the government and of those relating to the armed forces. The Senate might amend or reject, but both houses had to agree, by joint session if necessary, before a bill could be promulgated by the President.

The President was elected by joint session of both houses for a four-year term. He had no power of veto but did have power of dissolution after consulting the cabinet. The cabinet was responsible for his acts. For the period of the first constitution the cabinet was extremely weak owing to differences between numerous small parties. Its power to advise dissolution was used frequently and both houses were dissolved for long periods.

The constitution of 1933 is still in force. It provided for a President directly elected by citizens with literacy or financial qualifications. The National Assembly was to have one chamber with 90 deputies elected for four years by direct suffrage. There was to be a Privy Council of ten members to assist the President. In practice one party took over the National Assembly and has retained control. In 1959 the constitution was amended to provide for indirect election of the President by an electoral college made up of members of the National Assembly and of the Corporative Chamber. On 25 Apr 74 the Government was overthrown and a Junta of National Salvation installed. The dissolution of the National Assembly and of the Council of State followed.

ROMANIA

The constitution of 1866 continued in force with amendments until 1923. It provided for a monarchy acting through responsible ministers, and a two-chamber parliament. The Chamber of Deputies was elected by three classes of electors whose franchise depended on property and educational qualifications. The Senate was elected by two classes with property qualifications higher than those required for electors to the Chamber. By the 1923 constitution the King's powers were defined as those of a constitutional monarch, sharing legislative power with the Chamber and the Senate. All three had the right of initiating measures.

The Chamber of Deputies was elected in universal suffrage by all over 21, by proportional representation and compulsory ballot. The Senate was composed of elected and *ex officio* members, some elected on a similar system to members of the Chamber, some by electoral colleges of local councillors with one senator for each Department (the largest local government unit), and some by members of Chambers of Commerce, institutes of Agriculture and Commerce etc., and by the universities. The *ex officio* members included church officials, members of learned institutions, former political and parliamentary figures. All bills, initiated by either the chamber or the King, passed before a Legislative Council which gave help in drafting and co-ordinating measures. It was consulted in all cases except those concerning the budget. The King had power of suspensive veto. A constitution was adopted in 1938 which introduced Senate members nominated by the King, equal in number to those elected. Senators sat for nine years and deputies for six, and the election of deputies was now by all citizens of 30 years and over engaged in manual work, agriculture, commerce, industry or intellectual work. Senators were elected by the same professions, but the age limit was 40. In 1939 the Principal Council and the Grand Council were instituted, to elect eight representatives from each of three classes – agriculturists, free professions and workers. The Principal Council would have executive power and the Grand Council would be an advisory body. By that time the parliament had been in dissolution for over a year, having been dissolved in December 1937. In December 1947 the state became a republic. A new constitution was passed in 1948 providing for one chamber, the Grand National Assembly, which is elected for four years with one deputy for every 40,000 inhabitants. This body sits in short sessions twice a year. It elects a Presidium which sits almost permanently and to which its legislative powers are delegated. The Presidium has a chairman, who is head of state, four vice-chairmen, a secretary and 22 members. There is also a Council of Ministers, but all ministerial policies are shaped by deliberative collegiate bodies of which the minister is chairman. The Council of Ministers and the Presidium (or Council of State) relate to the Assembly as on the Russian pattern.

SPAIN

Spain was a constitutional monarchy until the system was virtually set aside by the military *coup d'état* under General Primo de Rivera in 1923. The constitution had provided for legislative power being exercised by the parliament of two chambers and the King; both chambers were equal in authority, and ministers were responsible to them. Parliamentary life was frequently disrupted and always weakened by political confusion, and no single strong authority emerged.

The military and civil dictatorships which followed abolished the parliament temporarily together with the post of Prime Minister and other Ministries except War and Foreign Affairs. In 1925 a civilian cabinet was restored, but the parliament was still in dissolution.

The constitution of 1931 provided a single-chamber parliament, Congress, and a republican state under a President. The Congress was elected for four years by universal suffrage on proportional representation. Electors and deputies had to be over 23. Executive power was exercised through the cabinet and the Prime Minister. After two parliaments each lasting approximately two years, and a third of six months, a totalitarian government was set up under General Franco. The 'organic law' of this government was published in 1936 and consolidated in 1966. Executive power is held by the head of state and by a Prime Minister whom he appoints from a list of three candidates chosen by the Council of the Realm. The Prime Minister serves for five years; he may be removed earlier on the advice of the Council but not on the advice of the Cortes (Parliament). The head of state directs affairs through the Council of Ministers. There is also the Council of the Realm, which has 16 members of which ten are elected by the Cortes, and a chairman who is also President of the Cortes. The National Council has one elected councillor for each province, 40 councillors appointed by the head of state, 12 elected by the Cortes, six appointed by the Prime Minister and a Secretary-General appointed by the head of state. Its function is to watch over political life, in particular to foster the principles of the National Movement. The Cortes is the supreme organ of popular participation. Its function is the preparation and passing of laws, which is done through commissions and through plenary session. The Commissions are arranged and appointed by the President of the Cortes in agreement with the government. President and government also arrange their agenda. Laws once passed are sent to the head of state who may within one month return them to the Cortes for fresh deliberation. The Cortes consists of members of the government; national councillors; presidents of the supreme court of justice, the council of the realm, the supreme military tribunal, the court of exchequer and the national economic council; 150 representatives of trade unions; representatives of municipalities and provincial councils elected by their respective corporations; 100 deputies (2 from each province) elected by the heads of families; 30 representatives of universities, learned societies, chambers of commerce.

SWEDEN

Since 1971 the Swedish Diet has consisted of one chamber. It has 350 members directly elected by universal suffrage for three years. All over 19 have the vote, and proportional representation is used in 28 constituencies from which 310 members are elected. The remaining 40 seats are distributed to parties receiving at least 4% of votes.

Executive power is with the King, who exercises it through the Council of State with the Prime Minister at its head. All members of the Council of State are responsible for the acts of the government. The ministries prepare bills for the Diet, issue general directives and make higher appointments but do not as a rule take individual administrative decisions. This is done by central boards, whose organization depends on the appropriations granted by the Diet. The King in Council may ask the advice of the boards, but is not bound to follow it. All members of the Council of State are also members of parliament.

Until 1971 there were two chambers, the Upper and Lower Houses. The Upper House had members elected by proportional representation, candidates being chosen on property or income qualifications. They sat for eight years and were elected by members of county councils, the electors of Stockholm and five other large towns. The Lower House had 230 members elected by proportional representation. In 1921 women were given the franchise like men at the age of 23. Also in 1921 the two houses gained the right to appoint their own speakers, with an elected substitute to take his place if necessary. Formerly speakers were appointed by the King. In the same year the King's prerogative of consulting a private committee on important questions of foreign relations was modified; a Foreign Affairs Committee was set up consisting of 16 members from each house and appointed by the parliament, and the King was bound to take its advice. All foreign agreements of importance were submitted to parliament for ratification.

Bills passed by the houses passed through a strong committee system which provided opinion on all except finance bills. If the houses disagreed on any bill, the matter would go to each house separately; the houses would then sit together and decide by majority. Both houses had equal powers in framing laws.

SWITZERLAND

The constitution is that of 1874, and under it the highest authority is vested in the electorate. This consisted of all male citizens over 20 until 1971 when the franchise was extended to women. The electorate has power through referendum to vote on amendments to or revision of the constitution. Referenda are also held on laws and international treaties if 30,000 voters or eight cantons request them, and the electorate can also initiate constitutional amendments if 50,000 voters support the initiative. The legislature consists of two chambers, the Council of States and the National Council. The Council of States has 44 members chosen and paid by the 22 cantons; election procedures depend on which canton they represent. The National Council has 200 councillors directly elected for four years in proportion to the population of the cantons, with at least one member for each canton or half-canton. Members are paid not by the cantons but from federal funds.

Laws to be submitted to popular vote must have been agreed by both chambers. The chief executive authority lies with the Bundesrat or Federal Council. It has seven members elected from seven different cantons by a joint session of both chambers. It sits for a four-year term. The members must not hold any other office in the cantons or the Confederation. The President of the Federal Council is the President of the Confederation. He and his vice-president are first magistrates of the state. They are elected by a Federal Assembly for one year only. The seven members of the Council act as ministers and heads of the seven administrative departments.

Bills can be introduced in parliament by a member, by either of the houses or by the Federal Council.

TURKEY

In Apr 20 the Grand National Assembly declared itself the sole sovereign representative of the nation, and repudiated the authority of the Sultan and the old parliament at Constantinople. The Assembly consisted of one chamber and every citizen over 18 voted for its members, who had to be at least 30. Members sat for two years then (from 1924) for four years. The house sat annually and could not be in recess for more than four months of the year. Special sessions could be convened at the request of one-fifth of the members, the President of the Council or the President of the Republic. The Assembly was responsible for preparing, framing and passing laws, concluding conventions and treaties of peace, making declarations of war, examining and ratifying laws presented to it by the Commission on the Budget, coining money and administering punishment and pardon. A law passed by the Assembly was passed to the President of the Republic. He might return it for further consideration within ten days, but the Assembly could override his objections and re-vote the law. On bills concerning the budget or the constitution there was no power of veto. The President was elected by the Assembly for its own term, and might be re-elected. All his acts required countersignature by the President of the Council and the minister concerned. The President appointed the President of the Council (Prime Minister) who in turn designated members of his council from among members of the Assembly. Within a week of his appointment he was obliged to offer a programme and ask for a vote of confidence. Ministers were collectively and individually responsible to the Assembly.

There was also a Council of State from among suitably qualified men by the Assembly. This gave advice on legislation.

In 1934 the age for the franchise was altered to 23 and the age for deputies to 31.

In 1937 the principles of the Republican People's Party were incorporated into the constitution; from then on only this party was active in parliament, although there were independent members. Opposition parties came into being again in 1945. The Grand National Assembly was dissolved by the military *coup d'état* of 1960. A further constitution was framed in 1961.

This provided for a seven-year term for the President, who might not be re-elected. He was to be elected by joint session of two houses, the National Assembly and the Senate, which has 150 members directly elected, 15 nominated by the President and 18 life senators. Laws are only initiated by the Assembly and the Council of Ministers. Bills are debated first in the Assembly and then referred to the Senate. If the houses do not agree on the bill, the decision is made by a joint committee which prepares another draft for submission to the Assembly. The Assembly must then accept either this draft or the one previously passed to the Senate, or the one amended by the Senate. If the Senate has amended by absolute majority, the Assembly can only revert to its unamended draft, also by absolute majority. Any bill which the Assembly rejects but the Senate adopts is returned to the Assembly for review.

USSR

The Union of Soviet Socialist Republics was formally constituted on 6 July 23. The central executive power was the Council of the Union together with the Council of Nationalities, the latter being composed of five representatives from each of the autonomous and Allied republics and one representative from each of the autonomous regions. The supreme authority, however, lay with the Central Executive Committee which was elected by the Congress of Soviets of the Union. This was the source of all legislation and its decrees and resolutions were sovereign. Between its sessions authority was exercised by the Presidium, which was self-electing and nearly identical in membership with the Presidium of the Russian Socialist Federal Soviet Republic. The Central Executive Committee met infrequently and for short terms; the power of the Presidium was therefore considerable. By 1926 the Executive Committee numbered about 300 and met three times a year. The Presidium prepared the order of business and executed the resolutions passed, being itself in almost continuous session.

The Central Executive Committee also elected the Council of People's Commissars. Originally this had greater power than the Presidium and acted as a cabinet of ministers responsible for departments, but by 1923 its power as a body had been considerably weakened. The Presidium had power to ratify or to stay the executions of the Council's resolutions, to be a court of appeal for any Commissar against the Council as a whole, and to require quarterly reports of all proceedings and instructions of the Council.

A new constitution was formed on 5 Dec 36 and is still in force. Under it there still exists the Council (or 'Soviet') of the Union and the Soviet of Nationalities, forming the two chambers of the Supreme Soviet; their legislative rights are equal; they are elected for a term of four years, the Soviet of the Union by citizens of the USSR on the basis of one deputy for every 300,000 inhabitants, the Soviet of Nationalities by citizens voting by Union and Autonomous Republics, Autonomous Regions and National Areas. The latter Soviet has 32 deputies from each Union Republic, 11 from each Autonomous Republic, 5 from each Autonomous Region and 1 from each National area. The Council of Ministers (previously called People's Commissars) is appointed by the Supreme Soviet. It is the highest executive and administrative organ but has no legislative power. It executes laws already made and co-ordinates departmental administration. The Chairman of the Council is equivalent to a Prime Minister. It has two First Deputy Chairmen with no departmental responsibility, and four vice-chairmen of whom one has a departmental responsibility. It is itself responsible to the Supreme Soviet or to the Presidium when the Soviet is not in session.

The Presidium of the Supreme Soviet has 33 members including a chairman (the President of the USSR), 15 vice-chairmen, 16 members and a secretary. It is the practice to elect the chairmen of the presidia of the Union Soviets from among the vice-chairmen. Members of the Council of Ministers may not be elected to the Presidium. The Presidium convenes the sessions of the Supreme Soviet, dissolves it in the event of a deadlock and arranges new elections. It has the power to conduct referenda, to rescind the decisions and orders of the Council of Ministers if they are not in accordance with the law or constitution. The Presidium itself is empowered to interpret the law and constitution. Ministers are appointed and removed by the Presidium, but normally at the instance of the Council of Ministers. The Presidium commands the armed forces and has the power to declare war.

UNITED KINGDOM

Parliament has two houses, the House of Lords and the House of Commons. The Commons are elected directly by universal adult suffrage for a five-year term. The Lords is composed of hereditary peers and peeresses, those on whom peerages have been conferred for life, 2 archbishops and 24 bishops.

No English or Scottish peer may sit in the Commons unless he has disclaimed his title for life; Irish peers may sit.

The executive power lies nominally with the Crown, but in fact is exercised through the cabinet of responsible ministers, headed by the Prime Minister who recommends the appointment of other ministers. Ministers are members of either house.

In 1918 the House of Lords was as it had been reorganized by the Parliament Act of 1911. Bills certified by the Speaker of the House of Commons as money bills were to receive the royal assent one month after being sent to the House of Lords, whether the Lords had approved them or not. Any other public bill (except for one extending the life of parliament) passed by the Commons in three successive sessions and rejected by the Lords was to receive the royal assent nevertheless, provided two years had elapsed between the second reading in the first session of the Commons and the third reading in the third session. The 1949 Parliament Act reduced the delaying powers of the upper house to two sessions and one year. In 1958 the parliamentary balance of the house was improved by the introduction of peerages given for life to men and women by the Sovereign on the advice of the Prime Minister. Opposition party leaders are able to convey their own recommendations for peerages through the Prime Minister to the Queen.

Parliament sits from September or October to the same time of the following year, with a summer recess beginning in July. During adjournments the Speaker or the Lord Chancellor may give notice of an earlier meeting if it is in the national interest. All sessions end by prorogation, and all bills not passed by then lapse. Bills (including private members' bills) may originate in either House unless they deal with finance or representation when they are introduced in the Commons. Until 1939 private members generally had precedence for bills and motions on some 22 days in each session, of which some 13 days would be Fridays and shorter than other working days. Since 1967 private members have had precedence on 20 Fridays in each session. The United Kingdom has no written constitution.

YUGOSLAVIA

The supreme organ of government is the Federal Assembly. It has five chambers: Federal, Economic, Education and Culture, Social Welfare and Health, Organizational-Political. Each chamber has 120 deputies, and the Federal chamber has also 70 members delegated by the 6 republics and 2 autonomous provinces; they sit as a Chamber of Nationalities and are concerned with the rights of different peoples within the state. Members of all assemblies are elected for four years, with half their number renewed every two years. No-one can be elected successively as a member of the same chamber or of the Federal Executive Council.

The Federal Chamber elects the Federal Executive Council from among its deputies. The Council is the Assembly's political executive organ, and comprises a President, 2 Vice-Presidents and 14 members.

The Federal Assembly elects the President of the Republic at a joint meeting of all the chambers and also elects the presidents and vice-presidents of the Assembly. The original constitution of the Serb, Croat and Slovene State in 1920 provided for a constitutional monarchy. The Crown and the parliament had legislative authority, and the Crown and the ministers executive authority. The Crown had no power to refuse to proclaim any law which had been passed by the Assembly, and the opening, prorogation or dissolution of the house required countersignature by a minister. There was one house composed of 313 deputies elected for four years by universal male adult suffrage on proportional representation. Bills went before a system of commissions after they had been introduced and before detailed debate; parties often represented racial minorities and had little in common, so that cabinets were often weak and without support and discussion of legislation inadequate. Ministers were subject both to the King and to the Assembly, and their decree-making powers were subject to Assembly control.

A state of emergency led to the suspension of the parliamentary system in 1929. A new constitution in 1931 introduced a second chamber, the Senate, which had members elected for six years with half their number renewed every three years. The King might nominate as many Senators as were elected; the right of election to the Senate was reserved to members of the Chamber of Deputies and Provincial Chambers and to Burgomasters, provided they were over 40. There was one senator elected for every 300,000 inhabitants. Members of the Chamber of Deputies were elected by all males over 21.

The Republic was established in 1945. The constitution framed in 1953 provided for a parliament similar to the present one, save that the Assembly had two houses, the Federal Council and the Council of Producers, the latter being composed of one deputy for every 70,000 of the active population – that is, all engaged in production, transport and commerce. The houses sat separately except for joint sessions to elect officers, including the President of the Republic.

BIBLIOGRAPHY

Andrews, W. G. (ed.), *European Political Institutions: A Comparative Government Reader.* Princeton, 1962
Charney, J. P., *Le Suffrage politique en France.* Paris, 1965
Dahl, R. A., *The Government and Politics of Ireland.* OUP, 1971
Kyriakides, S., *Cyprus: Constitutionalism and Crisis Government.* U. of Pennsylvania Press, 1968
Senelle, R., *A Survey of Political and Administrative Development in Belgium.* Brussels, 1961
Weil, G. L., *The Benelux Nations.* New York, 1970

4 MINISTERS

ALBANIA

Turham Pasha was Prime Minister from 1918-20. S. Delvin, 1920 and in Dec 20 H. Prishtina was P.M. for a few days. P. Evangheli, July-Dec 21; X. Ypi, Dec 21-Dec 22. A. Zogu (later King Zog) Dec 22-Feb 24; S. Verlaci, Feb 24-June 24; F. Noli, Jun-Dec 24; K. Kotta, Dec 24-Mar 30.

Date of taking office	Prime Minister	Foreign Minister	Finance Minister
12 Jan 33	P. Evangheli	X. Vila	A. Dibra

In Apr 39 Italy invaded Albania and in June the office of Foreign Minister was abolished.

Date of taking office	Prime Minister	Foreign Minister	Finance Minister
12 Apr 39	S. Verlazi	X. Dino	
3 Dec 41	M. Kruja		
19 Jan 43	E. Libohova		
13 Feb 43	M. Bushati		
12 May 43	E. Libohova		
2 Dec 45	E. Hoxha	N. Miskane	
24 Mar 46		E. Hoxha	
		Gen. M. Shehu	
24 July 53		B. Shtylla	T. Jakova
20 July 54	Gen. M. Shehu		A. Kellezi
4 June 56			A. Verli
18 Mar 66		N. Nase	

AUSTRIA

Date of taking office	Prime Minister	Foreign Minister	Finance Minister
12 Nov 18	Dr K. Renner	Dr K. Renner	R. Reisch
25 June 20	Dr M. Mayr	Dr M. Mayr	Dr F. Grimm
21 June 21	J. Schober	Baron Hennet	Dr A. Gurtler
31 May 22	Dr I. Seipel	Dr A. Grunberger	Dr V. Kienbock
17 Nov 24	Dr K. Ramek	Dr H. Mataja	Dr J. Ahrer
15 Jan 26	Dr I. Seipel	Dr I. Seipel	Dr V. Kienbock
3 May 29	M. Streeruwitz		
26 Sep 29	J. Schober	J. Schober	O. Juch
25 Sep 30	M. Vaugoin		
3 Dec 30	O. Ender		
20 June 31	K. Buresch		

AUSTRIA (*continued*)

Date of taking office	Prime Minister	Foreign Minister	Finance Minister
29 Jan 32		K. Buresch	E. Weidenhoffer
20 May 32	E. Dollfuss	E. Dollfuss	
10 May 33			K. Buresch
30 July 34	K. Schuschnigg	E. Berger-Waldenegg	
18 Oct 35			L. Draxler
3 Nov 36		G. Schmidt	H. Neumayer
13 Mar 38	A. Seyss Inquart	W. Wolf	
25 May 38			M. Fischbock

Note: The cabinet was limited in size after the union with the German Third Reich. The Foreign Ministry was carried on in Berlin by the German Foreign Minister. The Seyss Inquart cabinet was dissolved on the Allied occupation of Austria, and a provisional government under Dr K. Renner took office on 28 Apr 1945.

Date of taking office	Prime Minister	Foreign Minister	Finance Minister
18 Dec 45	Dr L. Figl	Dr L. Figl	G. Zimmerman
1 May 46		K. Gruber	
7 Nov 49			E. Margaretha
23 Jan 52			R. Kamitz
2 Apr 53	J. Raab		
25 Nov 53		L. Figl	
16 July 59		B. Kreisky	
9 June 60		E. Heilingsetzer	
11 Apr 61	A. Gorbach	B. Kreisky	J. Klaus
27 Mar 63			F. Korinek
2 Apr 64	J. Klaus		W. Schmitz
18 Apr 66		L. Toncic-Sorinj	
18 Jan 68		K. Waldheim	S. Koren
21 Apr 70	B. Kreisky	R. Kirschlager	H. Androsch

BELGIUM

Date of taking office	Prime Minister	Foreign Minister	Finance Minister
21 Nov 18	L. Delacroix	P. Hyams	L. Delacroix
20 Nov 20	H. Carton de Wiart	H. Jaspar	G. Theunis
14 Dec 21	G. Theunis		
13 May 25	M. van de Vijvere		
17 June 25	Viscomte Poullet	E. Vandervelde	Baron Houtart
22 Nov 27		P. Hyams	
24 Nov 29	L. Delacroix		

77

(continued

BELGIUM (continued)

Date of taking office	Prime Minister	Foreign Minister	Finance Minister
6 June 31	J. Renkin	P. Hyams	
19 Feb 32			J. Renkin
23 Oct 32	Ct. de Brocqueville		H. Jaspar
12 June 34		H. Jaspar	M. Sap
25 Mar 35	P. van Zeeland	P. van Zeeland	M. L. Gérard
13 June 36		P. H. Spaak	H. de Man
24 Nov 37	P. E. Janson		
9 Mar 38			M. Merlot (ad interim)
1 May 38			M. Soudan
15 May 38	P. H. Spaak		M. L. Gérard
3 Dec 38			A. Jannsen
21 Jan 39		P. E. Janson	
20 Feb 39	H. Pierlot	E. Soudan	C. Gutt
18 Apr 39		H. Pierlot	
4 Sep 39		P. H. Spaak	
11 Feb 45	A. van Acker		G. Eyskens
31 Mar 46			F. de Vogel
19 Mar 47	P. H. Spaak		G. Eyskens
10 Aug 49	G. Eyskens	P. van Zeeland	H. Liebaert
8 June 50	J. Duvieusart		J. van Houtte
15 Aug 50	J. Pholien		
15 Jan 52	J. van Houtte		Baron Janssen
22 Apr 54	A. van Acker	P. H. Spaak	H. Liebaert
11 May 57		V. Larock	
25 June 58	G. Eyskens	P. Wigny	J. van Houtte
25 Apr 61	T. Lefevre	P. H. Spaak	A. Dequae
28 July 65	P. Harmel		G. Eyskens
20 Mar 66	P. van den Boeynants	P. Harmel	R. Henrion
18 June 68	G. Eyskens		Baron J. Snoy et d'Oppuers
20 Jan 72			A. Vlerick
22 Jan 73	E. Le Burton	R. van Elslande	W. de Clercq

BULGARIA

Date of taking office	Prime Minister	Foreign Minister	Finance Minister
14 Oct 19	A. S. Stamboliiski	A. S. Stamboliiski	R. Daskalov
11 Jan 22			M. Turlakov
10 Feb 23			P. Yanev

Note: Premier Stamboliiski was killed during the *coup d'état* of 9 June 23

BULGARIA (*continued*)

Date of taking office	Prime Minister	Foreign Minister	Finance Minister
9 June 23	A. Tsankov	K. Kaltov	P. Todorov
1 Jan 25	A. Lyapchev	A. Burov	V. Mollov
12 Oct 31	N. Mushanov	N. Mushanov	S. Stefanov
19 May 34	K. Georgiev	K. Georgiev	P. Todorov
			(*coup d'état*)
24 May 34		K. Batalov	
22 Jan 35	Gen. P. Zlatev		M. Kalandarov
			(*coup d'état*)
21 Apr 35	P. M. Toshev	G. Kyoseivanov	M. Ryaskov
			(*coup d'état*)
23 Nov 35	G. Kyoseivanov		K. Gunev
38			D. Bozhilov
16 Feb 40	B. Filov	I. Popov	
11 Apr 42		B. Filov	
9 Sep 43	D. Bozhilov	S. Kirov	
10 Oct 43		D. Shishmanov	
1 June 44	I. Bagryanov	I. Bagryanov	D. Savov
12 June 44		P. Draganov	
2 Sep 44	K. Muraviev	P. Stainov	A. Girginov
9 Sep 44	K. Georgiev		P. Stoyanov
31 Mar 46		G. Kulishev	I. Stefanov
22 Nov 46	G. Dimitrov	K. Georgiev	
11 Dec 47		V. Kolarov	
21 July 49	V. Kolarov		
6 Aug 49		V. Poptomov	P. Kunin
8 Oct 49			K. Lazarov
1 Feb 50	V. Chervenkov		
27 May 50		M. Neichev	
17 Apr 56	A. Yugov		
18 Aug 56		K. Lukanov	
19 Nov 62	T. Zhivkov		
27 Nov 62		I. Bashev	D. Popov
8 July 71	S. Todorov		
16 Dec 71		P. Mladenov	

CZECHOSLOVAKIA

Date of taking office	Prime Minister	Foreign Minister	Finance Minister
14 Nov 18	K. Kramař (provisional government)		
8 July 19	V. Tusar	E. Beneš	K. Sontag
15 Sep 20	J. Černý		M. Hanošek
26 Sep 21	E. Beneš		A. Novák
8 Oct 22	A. Švehla		T. Becka
18 Mar 26	J. Černý		K. Engliš
12 Oct 26	A. Švehla		
13 Oct 27	Mgr. J. Šrámek		
1 Feb 29	J. Udrzal		B. Vlasek
8 Dec 29			K. Engliš
16 Apr 31			K. Trapl
29 Oct 32	M. Malypetr		
18 Dec 35		M. Hodža	
29 Feb 36	M. Hodža	K. Krofta	E. Franke
21 July 37			J. Kalfus
22 Sep 38	Gen. J. Syrový		
4 Oct 38		F. Chvalkovský	
30 Nov 38	R. Beran		

Note: The Ministry of Foreign Affairs was dissolved by the Reich Protectorate, 18 Mar 39.

27 Apr 39	Gen. A. Eliáš	—	

Note: A government in exile was set up in London following the German invasion.

24 July 40	Mgr. J. Šrámek	J. Masaryk	E. Outrata
27 Oct 41			L. Feierabend
6 Nov 45	Z. Fierlinger		V. Šrobár
2 July 46	K. Gottwald		J. Dolansky
15 June 48	A. Zápotocký	V. Clementis	
14 Mar 50		V. Široký	
31 Jan 53		V. David	
21 Mar 53	V. Široký		J. Kabes
15 Sep 53			J. Duris
22 Sep 63	J. Lenárt		R. Dvořák
11 Nov 65			B. Sucharda
1 Apr 68	O. Černík	J. Hajek	
19 Sep 68		O. Černík	

CZECHOSLOVAKIA (*continued*)

Note: On 31 Dec 68 Czechoslovakia became a federation, with separate governments for the Czech Socialist Republic and the Slovak Socialist Republic. Details below are for the central, federal, government:

1 Jan 69	O. Černík	J. Marko	B. Sucharda
3 Jan 71	L. Štrougal		R. Rohliček
9 Dec 71		B. Chnoupek	

DENMARK

Date of taking office	Prime Minister	Foreign Minister	Finance Minister
4 May 20	N. Neergard	E. Scavenius	N. Neergard
9 Oct 22		C. M. T. Cold	
23 Apr 24	T. Stauning	C. P. O. G. Moltke	C. V. Bramsnaes
29 Apr 29		P. Munch	
			H. P. Hansen
4 Nov 35			V. Buhl
		E. Scavenius	
4 May 42	V. Buhl		
16 July 42			M. Andersen
9 Nov 42	E. Scavenius		J. Koefoed
8 Nov 45	K. Kristensen	G. Rasmussen	T. Kristensen
13 Nov 47	H. Hedtoft		H. C. Hansen
30 Oct 50	E. Erikson	O. B. Kraft	T. Kristensen
30 Sep 53	H. Hedtoft	H. C. Hansen	V. Kampmann
29 Jan 55	H. C. Hansen		
9 Oct 58		J. O. Krag	
19 Feb 60	V. Kampmann		
1 Mar 60			K. Philip
5 Sep 61			H. R. Knudsen
3 Sep 62	J. O. Krag	P. Haekkerup	
9 Nov 62			P. Hansen
24 Aug 65			H. Grünbaum
28 Nov 66		J. O. Krag	
1 Oct 67		H. Tabor	
1 Feb 68	H. T. I. Baunsgard	P. Hartling	P. Moller
17 Mar 71			E. Ninn-Hansen
9 Oct 71	J. O. Krag	K. B. Andersen	H. Grünbaum
5 Oct 72	A. Jørgensen		

FINLAND

Date of taking office	Prime Minister	Foreign Minister	Finance Minister
26 Nov 18	L. Ingman	C. Enckell	
18 Apr 19	K. Castren		
18 Aug 19	J. Vennola		
15 Mar 20	M. Erich	E. R. W. Holsti	M. Wartiowaara
1 Mar 21	J. Vennola		R. Ryti
14 Nov 22	K. Kallio	J. Vennola	
18 Jan 24	A. K. Kajander	C. Enckell	H. M. J. Relander
22 Nov 24	L. Ingman	H. Procopé	Y. Pulkkinen
1 Jan 26	K. Kallio	E. N. Setälä	K. Järvinen
13 Dec 26	V. Tanner	V. Voionmaa	A. Ryoma
27 Dec 28	O. Hantere	H. Procopé	H. M. J. Relander
16 Aug 29	K. Kallio		T. H. Reinekka
20 Mar 31	J. Sunila	M. Yrsjö-Koskinen	K. Järvinen
14 Dec 32	T. M. Kivimaki	A. V. Hackzell	H. J. M. Relander
12 Mar 37	A. K. Kajander	E. R. W. Holsti	V. Tanner
16 Nov 38		V. Voionmaa	
13 Dec 38		E. Erkko	
2 Dec 39	R. Ryti	V. Tanner	M. Pekkala
27 Mar 40		R. Witting	
4 Jan 41	J. W. Rangell		M. Pekkala and J. Koivosto (*Joint Ministry*)
May 42			V. Tanner
4 Mar 43	E. Linkomies	H. Ramsay	
8 Aug 44	A. Hackzell	C. Enckell	M. Hiltonen
21 Sep 44	U. Castren		
11 Nov 44	J. Paasikivi		M. Helo
9 Apr 45			S. Tuomija
25 Mar 46	M. Pekkala		R. Törngren
29 July 48	K. A. Fagerholm		O. Hiltunen
18 Mar 50	U. Kekkonen	A. Gartz	V. J. Sukselainen
17 Jan 51			O. Hiltunen
20 Sep 51		S. Tuomioja	V. J. Rantala
9 July 53		R. Törngren	
16 Nov 53	S. Tuomioja		T. Junnila
5 May 54	R. Törngren	U. Kekkonen	V. J. Sukselainen
20 Oct 54	U. Kekkonen	J. Virolainen	P. Tervo
17 Feb 56	K. A. Fagerholm	R. Törngren	A. Simonen
27 May 57	V. J. Sukselainen	J. Virolainen	N. Meinander

FINLAND (*continued*)

Date of taking office	Prime Minister	Foreign Minister	Finance Minister
2 July 57			M. Miettunen
29 Nov 57	R. von Feiandt	P. J. Hynninen	L. Hietanen
26 Apr 58	R. Kuuskoski		M. I. O. Nurmela
29 Aug 58	K. A. Fagerholm	J. Virolainen	P. Hetemäki
13 Jan 59	V. J. Sukselainen	R. Törngren	W. Sarjala
19 June 59		A. Karjalainen	
14 July 61	M. Miettunen		
13 Apr 62	A. Karjalainen		
18 Dec 63	R. R. Lehto	J. Hallama	E. J. Rekola
12 Sep 64	J. Virolainen	A. Karjalainen	E. Kaitila
27 May 66	K. R. Passio		M. Koivisto
29 Dec 67			E. Raunio
22 Mar 68	M. Koivisto		
14 May 68	T. Aura	V. Leskinen	P. Hetemäki
15 July 70	A. Karjalainen		C. O. Tallgren
29 Oct 71	T. Aura	O. Mattila	P. Hetemäki
25 Feb 72	R. Passio	K. Sorsa	M. Koivisto
4 Sep 72	K. Sorsa	A. Karjalainen	J. Virolainen
			E. Niskanen

FRANCE

Date of taking office	Prime Minister	Foreign Minister	Finance Minister
20 Jan 20	A. Millerand	A. Millerand	F. Marsal
20 Oct 20	M. Leygues		
16 Jan 21	M. A. Briand	M. A. Briand	P. Doumer
15 Jan 22	R. Poincaré	R. Poincaré	M. de Lasteyrie
9 June 24	F. Marsal		
14 June 24	E. Herriot	E. Herriot	E. Clementel
16 May 25	M. Painlevé		
23 Nov 25	M. A. Briand		
23 Aug 26	R. Poincaré	M. A. Briand	R. Poincaré
11 Nov 28			H. Cheron
27 July 29	A. Briand		
2 Nov 29	A. Tardieu	A. Briand	P. Reynaud
13 Dec 30	M. Steeg		
27 Jan 31	P. Laval	A. Briand	P.-E.Flandin
14 Jan 32		P. Laval	
20 Feb 32	A. Tardieu	A. Tardieu	
3 June 32	E. Herriot	E. Herriot	M. Germain-Martin

(continued

FRANCE (*continued*)

Date of taking office	Prime Minister	Foreign Minister	Finance Minister
18 Dec 32	J. Paul-Boncour	J. Paul-Boncour	H. Cheron
31 Jan 33	E. Daladier		G. Bonnet
26 Oct 33	A. Sarraut		
26 Nov 33	C. Chautemps		
30 Jan 34	E. Daladier	E. Daladier	F. Piétri
4 Feb 34			P. Marchandeau
9 Feb 34	G. Doumergue	Louis Barthou	M. Germain-Martin
13 Oct 34		P. Laval	
8 Nov 34	P.-E. Flandin		
1 June 35	F. Bouisson		J. Caillaux
7 June 35	P. Laval		
24 Jan 36	A. Sarraut	P.-E. Flandin	
5 June 36	L. Blum	Y. Delbos	V. Auriol
22 June 37	C. Chautemps		G. Bonnet
18 Jan 38			P. Marchandeau
13 Mar 38	L. Blum	J. Paul-Boncour	L. Blum
10 Apr 38	E. Daladier	G. Bonnet	P. Marchandeau
2 Nov 38			P. Reynaud
21 Mar 40	P. Reynaud	P. Reynaud	L. Lamoureux
18 May 40		E. Daladier	
5 June 40		P. Reynaud	Y. Bouthilier
16 June 40	Marshal P. Pétain	P. Baudouin	
24 Oct 40		P. Laval	
14 Dec 40		P.-E. Flandin	
10 Feb 41		Adm. F. Darlan	
18 Apr 42	P. Laval	P. Laval	P. Cathala
10 Sep 44	Gen. C. de Gaulle	G. Bidault	R. Pleven
29 Jan 46	F. Gouin		A. Philip
24 June 46	G. Bidault		R. Schuman
16 Dec 46	L. Blum	L. Blum	A. Philip
22 Jan 47	P. Ramadier	G. Bidault	R. Schuman
24 Nov 47	R. Schuman		R. Mayer
26 July 48	A. Marie	R. Schuman	P. Reynaud
5 Sep 48	R. Schuman		C. Pineau
12 Sep 48	H. Queuille		H. Queuille
12 Jan 49			M. Petsche
28 Oct 49	G. Bidault		
2 July 50	H. Queuille		
12 July 50	R. Pleven		
10 Mar 51	H. Queuille		
11 Aug 51	R. Pleven		R. Mayer

FRANCE (*continued*)

Date of taking office	Prime Minister	Foreign Minister	Finance Minister
20 Jan 52	E. Faure		E. Faure
8 Mar 52	A. Pinay		A. Pinay
8 Jan 53	R. Mayer	G. Bidault	M. Bourgès-Mauoury
28 June 53	J. Laniel		E. Faure
19 June 54	P. Mendès-France	P. Mendès-France	E. Faure
23 Feb 55	E. Faure	A. Pinay	P. Pfimlin
31 Jan 56	G. Mollet	C. Pineau	P. Ramadier
5 Nov 57	F. Gaillard		P. Pfimlin
8 Jan 59	M. Debré	M. Couve de Murville	A. Pinay
May 59			M. Baumgartner
15 Apr 62	G. Pompidou		V. Giscard d'Estaing
9 Jan 66			M. Debré
12 July 68	M. Couve de Murville	M. Debré	F. Ortoli
22 June 69	J. Chaban-Delmas	M. Schumann	V. Giscard d'Estaing
6 July 72	P. Messmer		
5 Apr 73		M. Jobert	J. Fontanet

GERMANY

Date of taking office	Prime Minister	Foreign Minister	Finance Minister
13 Feb 19	P. Scheidemann	V. von Brockdorff-Rantzau	E. Schiffer
21 June 19	G. Bauer		M. Erzberger
28 Mar 20	H. Müller	Dr A. Köster	J. Wirth
25 June 20	C. Fehrenbach	W. Simons	
10 May 21	J. Wirth		A. Hermes
31 Jan 22		W. Rathenau	
22 Nov 22	W. Cuno	H. von Rosenberg	
13 Aug 23	G. Stresemann	G. Stresemann	
30 Nov 23	W. Marx		H. Luther
15 Jan 25	H. Luther		O. von Schleiben
19 Jan 26			H. Reinhold
17 May 26	W. Marx		H. Kohler
28 June 28	H. Müller		R. Hilferding
1 Apr 30	H. Brüning	J. Curtius	H. R. Dietrich
9 Oct 31		H. Brüning	

Note: The Brüning government was dismissed on 30 May 32.

(*continued*

GERMANY (*continued*)

Date of taking office	Prime Minister	Foreign Minister	Finance Minister
2 June 32	F. von Papen	K. von Neurath	L. E. Schwerin von Krosigk
4 Nov 32	K. von Schleicher		
30 Jan 33	A. Hitler		
5 Feb 38		J. von Ribbentrop	
30 Apr 45	C. Doenitz		

Note: Admiral Doenitz surrendered his powers to the allied occupation forces on 5 June 45.

WEST GERMANY

Date of taking office	Prime Minister	Foreign Minister	Finance Minister
20 Sep 49	K. Adenauer		F. Schäffer
13 Mar 51		K. Adenauer	
6 June 55		H. von Brentano	
24 Oct 57			F. Etzel
14 Nov 61		G. Schröder	H. Starke
11 Dec 62			R. Dahlgrün
17 Oct 63	L. Erhard		
1 Dec 66	K. Kiesinger	W. Brandt	F. J. Strauss
21 Oct 69	W. Brandt	W. Scheel	A. Möller
13 May 71			K. Schiller
7 Jul 72			H. Schmidt

EAST GERMANY

Date of taking office	Prime Minister	Foreign Minister	Finance Minister
15 Nov 50	O. Grotewohl	G. Dertinger	H. Loch
15 Jan 53		A. Ackermann	
1 Oct 53		L. Bolz	
24 Nov 55			W. Rumpf
24 Sep 64	W. Stoph		
24 June 65		O. Winzer	
13 July 67			S. Bohm
3 Oct 73	H. Sindermann		

GREECE

Date of taking office	Prime Minister	Foreign Minister	Finance Minister
27 June 17	E. K. Venizelos	N. Politis	M. Negropontis
1 Apr 21	D. Gounaris	J. Baltazzi	M. Protopapadakis
26 Nov 22	Col. Gonotas	A. Alexandris	M. Kofinas
11 Mar 24	M. Papanastasiou	M. Papanastasiou	M. Papanastasiou
7 Oct 24	A. Michalakopoulos	A. Michalakopoulos	C. Gotsis
25 Oct 25	T. Rangalos	L. R. Canacaris	T. Rangalos
4 Dec 26	A. Zaimis	A. Michalakopoulos	C. Gotsis
19 July 28	E. Venizelos	A. Karapanos	G. Maris
23 Dec 30		A. Michalakopoulos	
23 Apr 32			K. Varvaressos
26 May 32	M. Papanastasiou	M. Papanastasiou	
5 June 32	E. Venizelos	A. Michalakopoulos	
3 Nov 32	P. Tsaldaris	J. Rallys	P. Tsaldaris
13 Jan 33	E. Venizelos	A. Michalakopoulos	M. Kaphantaris
6 Mar 33	Gen. Othonais (ad interim)		
10 Mar 33	P. Tsaldaris	D. Maximos	S. Loverdos
5 Mar 35		P. Tsaldaris	G. Pesmazoglou
9 Oct 35	Gen. Kondylis	J. Theotokis	Gen. Kondylis
30 Nov 35	C. Demerdjis	C. Demerdjis	M. Mandjavinos
15 Mar 36			G. Mantzarinos
21 Jan 37	J. Metaxas	J. Metaxas	P. Rediadis
11 Feb 37			M. Apostolides
29 Jan 41	A. Korizis		
21 Apr 41	E. Tsouderos	E. Tsouderos	E. Tsouderos
30 Sep 41			K. Varvaressos
13 Apr 44	S. Venizelis	S. Venizelis	M. Manzadones
26 Apr 44	G. Papandreou	G. Papandreou	
8 June 44			P. Kanellopoulos
31 Aug 44			A. Svolos
3 Jan 45	Gen. Plastiras	J. Sophianopoulos	G. Sideris
8 Apr 45	Adm. Voulgaris		G. Mantzarinos
11 Aug 45		I. Politis	
17 Oct 45	Archp Danaskires		
1 Nov 45	P. Kanellopoulos	P. Kanellopoulos	Prof. Cassimatis
21 Nov 45	T. Sofoulis	J. Sophianopoulos	M. Mylonas
29 Jan 46		C. Rendis	
4 Apr 46	M. Poulitsas	C. Tsaldaris	S. Stephanopoulos
17 Apr 46	C. Tsaldaris		D. Helmis

(continued

GREECE (*continued*)

Date of taking office	Prime Minister	Foreign Minister	Finance Minister
27 Jan 47	D. Maximos		
29 Aug 47	C. Tsaldaris		
7 Sep 47	T. Sofoulis		
30 June 49	A. Diomedes		
6 Jan 50	J. Theotokis	P. Pipinellis	G. Mantzarinos
23 Mar 50	S. Venizelis	S. Venizelis	M. Zaimis
15 Apr 50	Gen. Plastiras	Gen. Plastiras	G. Kartalis
13 Sep 50	S. Venizelis	S. Venizelis	S. Castopoulos
2 Feb 51			G. Mavros
8 Aug 51		I. Politis	
27 Oct 51	Gen. Plastiras	S. Venizelis	C. Evelpidis
19 Nov 52	A. Papagos	S. Stephanopoulos	C. Papayannis
15 Dec 54			D. Eftaxias
6 Oct 55	C. Karamanlis	S. Theotokis	A. Apostolides
29 Feb 56			C. Thiraios
27 May 56		G. Averoff	
5 Mar 58	M. Georgakoloulos	G. Pesmajogiou	M. Mestikopoulos
17 May 58	C. Karamanlis	E. Averoff	C. Papaconstantinou
4 Nov 61			S. Theotokis
19 June 63	P. Pipinelis	P. Pipinelis	
8 Nov 63	G. Papandreou	S. Venizelos	C. Mitsotakis
30 Dec 63	J. Paraskevopoulos	C. Xanthopoulos-Palamos	
18 Feb 64	G. Papandreou	S. Kostopoulos	C. Mitsotakis
20 July 65	G. Athanasiadis-Novas	G. Melas	S. Allamanis
20 Aug 65	E. Tsirimokos	E. Tsirimokos	
17 Sep 65	S. Stephanopoulos		G. Melas
11 Apr 66		S. Stephanopoulous	
11 May 66		I. Toumbas	
22 Dec 66	I. Paraskevopoulos	P. Economou-Gouras	P. Stergiotis
3 Apr 67	P. Kanellopoulos	P. Kanellopoulos	C. Papaconstantinou
21 Apr 67	C. Kollios	P. Economou-Gouras	A. Adroutsopoulos
2 Nov 67		C. Kollios	
20 Nov 67		P. Pipinelis	
13 Dec 67	G. Papadopoulos		
1 Jan 70		G. Papadopoulos	
26 Aug 71			I. Koulis
8 Oct 73	S. Markezinis	C. Xanthopoulos-Palamos	
25 Nov 73	A. Androutsopoulos	S. Tetenes	A. Androutsopoulos

88

HUNGARY

Date of taking office	Prime Minister	Foreign Minister	Finance Minister
14 Mar 20	A. Simonyi-Semadam	Ct P. Teleki	Baron F. Korányi
14 Apr 21	Ct I. Bethlen	Ct D. Banffy	M. Hegedűs
1 Jan 22			T. Kállay
17 June 22		G. Daruvary	
1 June 24		T. Scitovsky	J. Bud
1 Nov 25		L. Valkó	
5 Sep 28			A. Wekerle
1 Oct 29	Ct J. Károlyi	Ct J. Károlyi	
22 Aug 31	G. Károlyi	L. Valkó	Ct J. Károlyi
1 Dec 31			Baron F. Korányi
1 Oct 32	G. Gömbös	K. Kánya	B. Imrédy
8 Jan 35			T. Fabinyi
12 Oct 36	K. Dáranyi		
9 Mar 38			L. Reményi-Schneller
13 May 38	B. Imrédy		
28 Nov 38		B. Imrédy	
10 Dec 38		Ct S. Csáky	
16 Feb 39	Ct P. Teleki		
15 Feb 41		L. Bárdossy	
5 Apr 41	L. Bárdossy		
10 Mar 42	I. Kállay		
23 Mar 44	D. Sztójay	D. Sztójay	
29 Aug 44	Gen. Lakatos	Fd.-Marshal Henvey	
16 Oct 44	F. Szálasi	Baron Keményi	
21 Dec 44	Gen. B. Miklos	J. Gyöngyösy	I. Vásáry
10 July 45			M. Ottványi
15 Nov 45	Z. Tildy		F. Gordon
5 Feb 46	F. Nagy		L. Dinnyés
13 Mar 47			M. Nyárády
31 May 47	L. Dinnyés	M. Mihalyti	
23 Sep 47		E. Molnár	
5 Aug 48		L. Rajk	
9 Dec 48	I. Dobi		E. Gerő
10 June 49		G. Kállai	I. Kossa
24 Feb 50			K. Olt
13 May 51		K. Kiss	
14 Aug 52	M. Rákosi		
16 Nov 52		E. Molnár	
4 July 53	I. Nagy	J. Boldoczky	

(continued

HUNGARY (*continued*)

Date of taking office	Prime Minister	Foreign Minister	Finance Minister
18 Apr 55	A. Hegedüs		
30 July 56		I. Horváth	
24 Oct 56	I. Nagy		
4 Nov 56	J. Kádár		I. Kossa
9 May 57			I. Antos
27 Jan 58	F. Münnich		
16 Feb 58		E. Sík	
16 Jan 60			R. Nyers
13 Sep 61	J. Kádár	J. Péter	
27 Nov 63			M. Timar
28 June 65	G. Kállai		
14 Apr 67	J. Fock		P. Vályi
13 May 71			L. Faluvégi

ICELAND

Date of taking office	Prime Minister	Foreign Minister	Finance Minister
25 Feb 20	J. Magnusson		N. Gudmundsson
15 Mar 22	S. Egers		M. Jonsson
22 Mar 24	J. Magnusson		J. Thorlaksson
28 Feb 27	T. Thorhallsson		N. J. Kristjansson
			E. Arnarson
20 Oct 31			A. Asgeirsson
3 June 32	A. Asgeirsson		
29 July 34	H. Jonasson		E. Jonsson
17 Apr 39			J. Moller
18 Nov 41		O. Thors	
		S. Stefansson	
16 May 42	O. Thors		
16 Dec 42	B. Thordarson	V. Thor	B. Olafsson
1 Oct 44	O. Thors	O. Thors	P. Magnusson
4 Feb 47	S. J. Stefansson	B. Benediktsson	J. T. Josefsson
14 Mar 50	S. Steinthorsson		E. Jonsson
13 Sep 53	O. Thors	K. Gudmundsson	
24 July 56	H. Jonasson	G. I. Gudmundsson	
20 Dec 58	E. Jonsson		G. I. Gudmundsson
20 Nov 59	O. Thors		G. Thorodssen
14 Nov 63	B. Benediktsson		

90

ICELAND (*continued*)

Date of taking office	Prime Minister	Foreign Minister	Finance Minister
1 Sep 65		E. Jonsson	
10 July 70	J. Hafstein		
10 Oct 70			M. Jonsson
14 July 71	O. Johannesson	E. Agustsson	H. Sigurdsson

IRISH REPUBLIC

16 Jan 22   Provisional government: Finance and General Minister Michael Collins,
Foreign Affairs Minister Gavan Duffy.

Date of taking office	Prime Minister	Foreign Minister	Finance Minister
6 Dec 22	W. Cosgrave	D. Fitzgerald	W. Cosgrave
			E. Blythe
		P. MacGilligan	
9 Mar 32	E. de Valera	E. de Valera	S. MacEntee
27 Sep 39			S. T. O'Kelly
9 June 44			F. Aiken
18 Dec 48	J. A. Costello	S. MacBride	P. MacGilligan
30 May 51	E. de Valera	P. Aiken	A. MacEntee
2 June 54	J. A. Costello	L. Cosgrave	G. Sweetman
20 Mar 57	E. de Valera	F. Aiken	J. Ryan
23 June 59	S. Lemass		
21 Apr 65			J. Lynch
9 Nov 66	J. Lynch		
10 Nov 66			C. Haughey
2 July 69		P. Hillery	
8 May 70			G. Colley
14 Mar 73	L. Cosgrave	G. FitzGerald	R. Ryan

ITALY

Date of taking office	Prime Minister	Foreign Minister	Finance Minister
21 June 19	F. Nitti	V. Scialoja	G. de Nava
15 June 20	G. Gioletti	Ct Sforza	F. Tedesco
25 Feb 22	L. Faeta	Dr C. Schauzer	G. Bertone
30 Oct 22	B. Mussolini	B. Mussolini	A. de Stefani

91

(continued

ITALY (*continued*)

Date of taking office	Prime Minister	Foreign Minister	Finance Minister
30 Aug 25			Ct G. Volpi
1 Jan 29			A. Mosconi
12 Sep 29		D. Grandi	
20 July 32		B. Mussolini	G. Jung
24 Jan 35			Ct P. Thaon de Reval
9 June 36		Ct G. C. de Cortellezzo	
6 Feb 43		B. Mussolini	Baron G. Acerbo
25 July 43	Marshal Badoglio	Baron Guariglea	D. Bartolini
9 June 44	I. Bonomi		M. Siglienti
10 Dec 45		A. de Gaspari	M. Presenti
19 June 45	F. Parri		M. Scoccimaro
4 Dec 45	A. de Gasperi		
17 Oct 46		P. Nenni	
30 May 47		Ct Sforza	G. Pella
23 May 48			E. Vanoni
16 July 53		A. de Gaspari	
17 Aug 53	G. Pella	G. Pella	
18 Jan 54	A. Fanfani	A. Piccione	A. Zoli
10 Feb 54	M. Scelba		R. Tremelloni
18 Sep 54		G. Martino	
6 July 55	A. Segni		G. Andreotti
20 May 57	A. Zoli	G. Pella	
19 June 58	A. Fanfani	A. Fanfani	L. Preti
16 Feb 59	A. Segni		P. E. Taviani
25 Mar 60	F. Tambroni	A. Segni	G. Trabucchi
26 July 60	A. Fanfani		
29 May 62		A. Piccione	
21 June 63	G. Leone		M. Martinelli
4 Dec 63	A. Moro	G. Saragat	R. Tremelloni
6 Mar 65		A. Fanfani	
23 Feb 66			L. Preti
24 June 68	G. Leone	G. Medici	M. F. Aggradi
12 Dec 68	M. Rumor	P. Nenni	O. Reale
5 Aug 69		A. Moro	G. Bosco
27 Mar 70			L. Preti
6 Aug 70	E. Colombo		
15 Feb 72	G. Andreotti		G. Pella
26 Jun 72		G. Medici	A. Valsecchi
8 Jul 73	M. Rumor	A. Moro	E. Colombo

LUXEMBOURG

Date of taking office	Prime Minister	Foreign Minister	Finance Minister
1 Apr 21	E. Reuter		A. Neyens
1 Mar 25	P. Pruom		A. Schmit
1 July 26	J. Bech		M. Clemang
1 Aug 26			P. Dupong
5 Nov 37	P. Dupong	J. Bech	

Note: On 15 Aug 40 the government was declared void by the German forces of occupation. A government in exile continued in London.

29 Dec 53	J. Bech		P. Werner
1 Jan 58	P. Frieden		
25 Feb 59	P. Werner	E. Schauss	
15 July 64		P. Werner	
23 Dec 67		P. Gregoire	
29 Jan 69		G. Thorn	

MALTA

Date of taking office	Prime Minister	Foreign Minister	Finance Minister
4 Nov 47	Dr P. Boffa		
1 Jan 50			A. Colombo
26 Sep 50	E. Mizzi		F. Azzopardi
20 Dec 50	B. Olivier		
11 Mar 55	D. Mintoff		D. Mintoff

Note: Mr Mintoff resigned in Apr 58 and the constitution was suspended.

5 Mar 62	B. Olivier		G. Felice
21 June 71	D. Mintoff	D. Mintoff	J. Abela

THE NETHERLANDS

Date of taking office	Prime Minister	Foreign Minister	Finance Minister
9 Sep 18	C. J. M. R. de Beerenbroeck	H. A. van Karnebeek	S. de Vries
28 July 21			D. J. de Geer
11 Aug 23			H. Colijn
31 July 25	H. Colijn		

(continued

THE NETHERLANDS (*continued*)

Date of taking office	Prime Minister	Foreign Minister	Finance Minister
8 Mar 26	D. J. de Geer		D. J. de Geer
30 Mar 27		F. B. van Blokland	
10 Aug 29	C. J. M. R. de Beerenbroeck		
24 May 33	H. Colijn	A. C. D. de Graeff	P. J. Oud
23 June 37		H. Colijn	J. A. de Wilde
14 Sep 37		J. A. N. Patijn	
21 May 39			H. Colijn
10 Aug 39	D. J. de Geer	E. N. van Kleffens	D. J. de Geer
4 Sep 40	P. S. Gerbrandy		J. I. M. Welter
23 Nov 41			J. W. Albarda
15 Sep 42			J. van den Broek
24 Feb 45			G. W. M. Huysmans
23 June 45	W. Schermerhorn		P. Lieftinck
26 Feb 46		J. H. van Royen	
13 July 46	L. J. M. Beel	C. G. W. H. Baron van Boetzelaer van Ooterhuit	
7 Aug 48	W. Drees	D. U. Stikker	
1 Sep 52		J. W. Beyen J. M. A. H. Luns *Joint Ministry*	J. A. van der Kieft
12 Oct 56			H. J. Hofstra
22 Dec 58	L. Beel	J. M. A. H. Luns	J. Zijlstra
19 May 59	J. E. de Quay		
24 July 63	V. G. M. Marijunen		J. H. Witteveen
12 Apr 65	J. Cals		A. Vondeling
22 Nov 66	J. Zijlstra		J. Zijilstra
3 Apr 67	P. J. S. de Jong		H. J. Witteveen
6 July 71	B. W. Biesheuvel	W. K. N. Schmelzer	R. J. Nelissen
11 May 73	J. den Uyl	M. van der Stoel	W. F. Duisenberg

NORWAY

Date of taking office	Prime Minister	Foreign Minister	Finance Minister
20 Feb 19	G. Knudsen	N. C. Ihlen	A. Omholt
21 June 20	O. B. Halvorsen	C. F. Michelet	E. H. Bull
22 June 21	O. A. Blehr	A. C. Raested	O. A. Blehr
5 Mar 23	O. Halvorsen	C. F. Michelet	A. Berge

NORWAY (*continued*)

Date of taking office	Prime Minister	Foreign Minister	Finance Minister
1 May 23	A. Berge		
7 July 24	J. L. Mowinckel	J. L. Mowinckel	A. Holmboe
4 Mar 26	I. Lykke	I. Lykke	F. L. Konow
13 Feb 28	J. L. Mowinckel	J. L. Mowinckel	P. Lund
12 May 31	N. Kolstad	B. Bradland	F. Sundby
15 Mar 32	J. Hundseid		
27 Feb 33	J. L. Mowinckel	J. L. Mowinckel	P. Lund
14 Nov 34			G. Jan
19 Mar 35	J. Nygaardsvold	H. Kont	A. Indreboe
			K. Bergsvik
30 June 39			O. F. Torp
21 Feb 41		T. H. Lie	

Note: the government in exile continued in London.

1 Mar 42			P. Hartmann
24 June 45	E. Gerhardsen		G. Jahn
1 Nov 45			E. Brofoss
1 Nov 47			O. Meisdalshagen
16 Nov 51	O. F. Torp		T. Bratteli
21 Jan 55	E. Gerhardsen		M. Lid
1 Mar 57			T. Bratteli
23 Apr 60			P. J. Bjerve
23 Jan 63			A. Cappelen
27 Aug 63	J. Lyng	E. Wikborg	D.Varvik
24 Sep 63	E. Gerhardsen	H. Lange	A. Cappelen
12 Oct 65	P. Borten	J. Lyng	O. Myrvoll
22 May 70		S. Stray	
13 Mar 71	T. Bratteli	A. Cappelen	R. Christiansen
7 Oct 72	L. Korvald		
18 Oct 72		D. Vårvik	J. Norbom
16 Oct 73	T. Bratteli	K. Frydenlund	P. Kleppe

POLAND

Date of taking office	Prime Minister	Foreign Minister	Finance Minister
19 Jan 19	I. Paderwski, provisional government.		
14 Dec 19	L. Skulski	S. Patek	W. Grabski
24 June 20	W. Grabski		
24 July 20	W. Witos	Prince Sapieha	J. K. Steczkowski

(continued

POLAND (*continued*)

Date of taking office	Prime Minister	Foreign Minister	Finance Minister
23 Sep 21	A. Ponikowski	K. Skirmunt	J. Michalski
28 June 22	M. Sliwinski		
31 July 22	M. Nowacki		
16 Dec 22	W. Sikorski	Ct A. Skrzyński	W. Grabski
28 May 23	W. Witos		
19 Dec 23	W. Grabski	Ct M. Zamoyski	
		Ct A. Skrzyński	
29 Nov 25	Ct A. Skrzyński		J. Zdziechowski
9 June 26	K. Bartel		
2 Oct 26	J. Piłsudski	A. Zaleski	G. Czechowicz
18 Oct 28	K. Bartel		M. Grodyński
14 Apr 29	K. Świtalski		
29 Dec 29	K. Bartel		
1 Apr 30	W. Sławek		I. Matuszewski
25 Aug 30	J. Piłsudski		
4 Dec 30	W. Sławek		
29 Dec 30	K. Bartel		
27 May 31	A. Prystor		J. Piłsudski
7 Sep 32			Z. Zawadzki
2 Nov 32		J. Beck	
10 May 33	J. Jędrzejewicz		
13 May 34	L. Kozłowski		
28 Mar 35	W. Sławek		
12 Oct 35	M. Kosciałkowski-Zyndram		E. Kwiatkowski
16 May 36	F. S. Składkowski		
20 Sep 39	W. Sikorski	A. Zaleski	A. Koc

Note: The government in exile continued in Paris and later in London.

Date	Prime Minister	Foreign Minister	Finance Minister
1 Jan 41			H. Strasburger
28 Aug 41		Ct E. Raczyński	
14 July 43	S. Mikołajczyk	T. Romer	L. Grosfeld
30 Nov 44	T. Arciszewski	A. Tarnowski	J. Kwapiński
28 June 45	E. Osobka-Morawski	W. Rzymowski	K. Dąbrowski
6 Feb 47	J. Cyrankiewicz	Z. Modzelewski	
17 Mar 51		S. Skrzeszewski	
20 Nov 52	B. Bierut		
19 Mar 54	J. Cyrankiewicz		
27 Apr 56		A. Rapacki	
27 Jan 57			T. Dietrich
16 Nov 60			J. Albrecht
15 July 68			S. Majewski

POLAND (*continued*)

Date of taking office	Prime Minister	Foreign Minister	Finance Minister
22 Dec 68		S. Jędrychowski	
28 June 69			J. Trendota
23 Dec 70	P. Jaroszewicz		
22 Dec 71		S. Olszowski	S. Jędrychowski

PORTUGAL

Date of taking office	Prime Minister	Foreign Minister	Finance Minister
12 Mar 20	A. N. Bapista	X. da Silva	P. Lopes
2 Mar 21	B. Machado	D. Pereira	A. M. da Silva
9 Feb 22	A. M da Silva	M. Barbosa-Magalhaes	M. Puero
1 Jan 23		D. Pereira	V. Guimarães
18 Dec 23	A. de Castro		A. de Castro
15 Feb 25	V. Guimarães	P. Martins	V. Guimarães
18 Dec 25	A. M. da Silva	V. Borges	A. M. Guedes
9 July 26	A. O. de F. Carmona	A. M. de B. Rodrigues	J. J. S. de Cordes
10 Nov 28	J. V. de Freitas	M. C. Q. Meireles	A. de O. Salazar
20 Jan 30	D. de Oliveira	F. A. Branco	
5 July 32	A. de O. Salazar	C. de S. Mendes	
11 Apr 33		J. C. da Mata	
23 Oct 34		A. de M. Guimarães	
18 Jan 36		A. R. Monteiro	
		A. de O. Salazar	
28 Aug 40			J. P. da C. L. Lumbrales
4 Feb 47		J. C. da Mata	
1 Aug 50		P. A. V. Cunha	A. A. de Oliveira
8 July 55			A. M. P. Barbosa
13 Aug 58		M. G. N. D. Matias	
3 May 61		A. M. G. F. Nogueira	
13 June 65			U. C. de A. Cortes
17 Aug 68			J. A. D. Rosas
26 Sep 68	M. J. das N. A. Caetano		
1 Apr 69		M. J. das N. A. Caetano	
14 Jan 70		H. M. de M. d'E. Patricio	
11 Aug 72			A. C. A. Dias

ROMANIA

Date of taking office	Prime Minister	Foreign Minister	Finance Minister
16 Mar 20	Gen. A. Averescu	D. Zamsirescu	C. Argetoianu
21 June 20		T. Ionescu	M. Titulesco
19 Jan 22	I. Brătianu	I. Duca	V. Brătianu
30 Mar 26	Gen. A. Averescu	M. Mitilineu	I. Lapedatu
27 Mar 27			Gen. A. Averescu
24 Nov 27	V. Brătianu	N. Titulescu	V. Brătianu
11 Nov 28	J. Maniu	G. Mironescu	M. Popovici
Jun 30			M. Manoilescu
19 Apr 31	N. Iorga	C. Argetoianu	C. Argetoianu
		Prince D. Ghica	Prince D. Ghica
6 June 32	A. Vaida-Voevod	G. Mironescu	
11 Aug 32		A. Vaida-Voevod	G. Mironescu
8 Oct 32		N. Titulescu	
19 Oct 32	J. Maniu		V. Madgearu
14 Jan 33	A. Vaida-Voevod		
14 Nov 33	I. Duca		D. Brătianu
29 Dec 33	C. Angelescu		
3 Jan 34	G. Tatarescu		
5 Jan 35			V. Slăvescu
4 Feb 35			V. Antonescu
30 Aug 36		V. Antonescu	M. Cancicov
28 Dec 37	O. Goga	I. Micescu	E. Savu
11 Feb 38	M. Cristea	G. Tatarescu	M. Cancicov
30 Mar 38		N. Petrescu-Comnen	
21 Dec 38		G. Gafencu	
1 Feb 39			M. Constantinescu
6 Mar 39	M. Calinescu		
21 Sep 39	Gen. Argeseanu		
28 Sep 39	C. Argetoianu		
24 Nov 39	G. Tatarescu		
2 June 40		I. Gigurtu	
4 July 40	I. Gigurtu	M. Manoilescu	E. Savu
3 Sep 40	I. Antonescu		
15 Sep 40		M. Sturdza	G. Cretzianu
1 Dec 40		I. Antonescu	
27 Jan 41			N. Stoenescu
16 Oct 42			A. Neagu
24 Aug 44	C. Sănătescu	G. Niculescu-Buzeşti	G. Potopeanu
2 Dec 44	N. Radescu	C. Vişoianu	M. Romniceanu

ROMANIA (*continued*)

Date of taking office	Prime Minister	Foreign Minister	Finance Minister
6 Mar 45	P. Groza	G. Tatarescu	D. Alimănişteanu
29 Nov 46			A. Alexandrini
7 Nov 47		A. Pauker	V. Luca
9 Mar 52			D. Petrescu
2 June 52	G. Gheorghiu-Dej		
5 July 52		S. Bughici	
2 Oct 55	C. Stoica	G. Preoteasa	M. Manescu
14 July 57		I. G. Maurer	
11 Jan 58		A. Bunaciu	
21 Mar 61	I. G. Maurer	C. Manescu	A. Vijoli
13 July 68			V. Pirvu
19 Aug 69			F. Dŭmitrescu
13 Oct 72		G. Macovescu	

SPAIN

Date of taking office	Prime Minister	Foreign Minister	Finance Minister
5 May 20	M. Dato	Marquis de Lema	D. Pascual
13 Mar 21	M. Allendesalazar		M. Arguelles
8 Mar 22	S. Guerra	F. Prida	M. Bergamin
7 Dec 22	Marquis de Alhucemas	S. Alba	J. M. Pedregal
3 Dec 25	Primo de Rivera	M. Yanguas	M. Calvo-Sotelo
27 Feb 27		P. de Rivera	
1 Jan 30	Gen. Berenguer	Duke of Alba	M. Arguelles
1 Apr 31	A. Zamora	A. Lervoux	I. Prieto
16 Dec 31	M. Azaňa y Diaz	L. Z. Escolano	J. C. Romeu
1 Mar 33	A. L. Garcia	L. P. Romero	M. M. Ramon
4 Oct 34		J. J. R. Garcia	
19 Feb 36	M. Azaňa y Diaz	A. Barcia y Trelles	G. F. Lopez
4 Sep 36	F. L. Caballero	J. A. del Vaijo	J. Negrín
17 May 37	J. Negrín	J. Giralt	

A military rebellion under General Francisco Franco forced the civil war of 1936-9. With the surrender of Madrid in Mar 39 the Loyalist government fled to France and a corporate state was set up under Franco's dictatorship.

1 Feb 38	F. Franco	Count de Jornada	M. Amado
10 Aug 39		J. B. Atienza	J. L. Lopez
17 Oct 40		R. S. Súñer	*(continued*

99

SPAIN (*continued*)

Date of taking office	Prime Minister	Foreign Minister	Finance Minister
20 May 41			J. B. Burin
3 Sep 42		F. Gomez-Jordana	
11 Aug 44		J. F. de Lequerica	
21 July 45		A. M. Artajo	
1 Mar 52		F. Gomez y de Llano	
1 Feb 57		F. M. Castialla y Maiz	M. Navarro Rubio
7 July 65			J. J. Espinoza
29 Oct 69		G. L. Bravo de Costro	A. M. Luque
9 Jun 73	Adm. L. Carrero Blanco		
11 Jun 73		L. López Rodó	A. Barrera de Irimo
1 Jan 74	C. Arias Navarro		

SWEDEN

Date of taking office	Prime Minister	Foreign Minister	Finance Minister

SWITZERLAND

The Federal Council has an active Vice-President elected for one year, and seven members each responsible for a department, elected for four years.

	Vice-President	Foreign Affairs	Finance
1935	A. Meyer	G. Motta	A. Meyer
1936	G. Motta		
1937	J. Baumann		
1938	P. Etter		
1939	M. Pilet-Golaz		E. Wetter
1940	H. Obrecht	M. Pilet-Golaz	
1941	P. Etter		
1942	E. Celio		
1943	W. Stampfli		
1944	M. Pilet-Golaz		E. Nobs
1945	K. Koblet	M. Petitpierre	
1946	P. Etter		
1947	E. Celio		
1948	E. Nobs		
1949	M. Petitpierre		
1950	E. von Steiger		
1951	K. Koblet		
1952	P. Etter		M. Webber
1953	R. Rubattel		
1954	J. Escher		H. Streuli
1955	M. Feldmann		
1956	H. Streuli		
1957	T. Holenstein		
1958	P. Chaudet		
1959	G. Lepovi		
1960	F. Traugott Wahlen		J. Bourgknecht
1961	P. Chaudet		
1962	J. Bourgknecht	F. Traugott Wahlen	
1963	L. van Moos		R. Bonvin
1964	H. P. Schudi		
1965	H. Schaffner		
1966	R. Bonvin	W. Spuhler	
1967	W. Spuhler		
1968	L. van Moos		N. Celio
1969	H. P. Schudi		
1970	R. Gnagi	P. Grabner	
1971	N. Celio		
1972	R. Bonvin		
1973	E. Brugger		G.-A. Chevellaz

TURKEY

Date of taking office	Prime Minister	Foreign Minister	Finance Minister
5 Apr 20	(*Grand Vizier*) Damad Ferid Pasha	Damad Ferid Pasha	Reshai Bey
21 Oct 20	(*Grand Vizier*) Tewfik Pasha	Sefa Bey	Abdullah Bey
		Izzet Pasha	Nuzhet Bey

20 Jan 21   New constitution established a Council of Commissioners instead of a cabinet.

1 Feb 23	(*President*) Reouf Bey	Ismet Pasha	Abdul Halik Bey
30 Oct 23	Ismet Pasha		
4 Mar 25		Tevfik Rustu Bey	
			Hassan Bey
			Abdul Halik Bey
2 Nov 27			S. Saracoglu
28 Sep 30			Abdul Halik Bey
1 May 31			Fuad Agrali
1 Mar 35	Ismet Inönü		
13 Oct 37	J. Bayar		
12 Nov 38		S. Saracoglu	
27 Jan 39	R. Saydam		
11 Mar 43	S. Saracoglu	N. Menemencioglu	
15 June 44		S. Saracoglu	
14 Sep 44		H. Saka	N. E. Sumer
7 Aug 46	R. Peker		H. Nazmikismir
9 Sep 47	H. Saka	N. Sadak	
11 June 48			S. Adalan
16 Jan 49	S. Gunaltay		I. Aksal
22 May 50	A. Menderes	F. Koprulu	H. Ayan
10 Mar 51			H. Polatkan
15 Apr 55		A. Menderes	
9 Dec 55		F. Koprulu	N. Okmen
20 June 56		E. Menderes	
30 Nov 56			H. Polatkan
25 Nov 57		F. R. Zorlu	
28 May 60	C. Gursel	S. Sarpa	E. Alican
24 Dec 60			K. Kurdas
20 Nov 61	I. Inönü		S. Inan
25 June 62		F. C. Erkin	F. Melen
21 Feb 65	S. H. Urguplu	H. Isik	I. Gursan
27 Oct 65	S. Demirel	I. S. Caglayangil	

TURKEY (*continued*)

Date of taking office	Prime Minister	Foreign Minister	Finance Minister
12 Nov 66			C. Bilgehan
3 Nov 69			M. Erez
1 Mar 71	N. Erim	O. Olcay	S. N. Ergin
22 May 72	F. Melen	U. H. Bayülken	S. Özbek
15 Apr 73	N. Talû	U. H. Bayiilken	S. T. Müftüoglu

USSR

Date of taking office	Prime Minister	Foreign Minister	Finance Minister
8 Nov 17	V. I. Lenin	G. V. Chicherin	N. N. Krestinskii
1 Dec 22			G. Y. Sokolnikov
1 Jan 24	A. I. Rykov		
1 Mar 26			N. P. Bryukhanov
1 Jan 31	V. M. Molotov	M. M. Litvinov	G. F. Grinko
1 Aug 37			V. Y. Chubar

Ministers were called People's Commissars until 1946.

19 Jan 38			A. G. Zverev
3 May 39		V. M. Molotov	
7 May 41	J. V. Stalin		
17 Feb 48			A. N. Kosygin
28 Dec 48			A. G. Zverev
4 Mar 49		A. Y. Vyshinski	
6 Mar 53	G. M. Malenkov	V. M. Molotov	
9 Dec 55	N. A. Bulganin		
1 June 56		D. T. Shepilov	
15 Feb 57		A. A. Gromyko	
31 Mar 58	N. S. Khrushchev		
16 May 60			V. F. Garbuzov
15 Oct 64	A. N. Kosygin		

UNITED KINGDOM

Date of taking office	Prime Minister	Foreign Minister	Finance Minister
6 Dec 16	D. Lloyd George		
10 Dec 16		A. Balfour	A. Bonar Law

(continued

UNITED KINGDOM (*continued*)

Date of taking office	Prime Minister	Foreign Minister	Finance Minister
10 Jan 19			A. Chamberlain
23 Oct 19		Lord Curzon	
1 Apr 21			Sir R. Horne
23 Oct 22	A. Bonar Law		
24 Oct 22			S. Baldwin
22 May 23	S. Baldwin		
27 Aug 23			N. Chamberlain
22 Jan 24	J. R. MacDonald	J. R. MacDonald	P. Snowden
4 Nov 24	S. Baldwin		
6 Nov 24		Sir A. Chamberlain	W. Churchill
5 June 29	J. R. MacDonald		
7 June 29		A. Henderson	P. Snowden
25 Aug 31		Marquis of Reading	
5 Nov 31		Sir J. Simon	N. Chamberlain
7 June 35	S. Baldwin	Sir S. Hoare	
22 Dec 35		A. Eden	
28 May 37	N. Chamberlain		Sir J. Simon
21 Feb 38		Viscount Halifax	
10 May 40	W. Churchill		
12 May 40			Sir K. Wood
22 Dec 40		A. Eden	
24 Sep 43			Sir J. Anderson
26 July 45	C. Attlee		
27 July 45		E. Bevin	H. Dalton
13 Nov 47			Sir S. Cripps
19 Oct 50			H. Gaitskell
9 Mar 51		H. Morrison	
26 Oct 51	Sir W. Churchill	Sir A. Eden	R. Butler
6 Apr 55	Sir A. Eden		
7 Apr 55		H. Macmillan	
20 Dec 55		S. Lloyd	H. Macmillan
10 Jan 57	H. Macmillan		
13 Jan 57			P. Thorneycroft
6 Jan 58			D. Heathcoat Amory
27 July 60		Lord Home	S. Lloyd
13 July 62			R. Maudling
18 Oct 63	Sir A. Douglas-Home		
20 Oct 63		R. Butler	
16 Oct 64	H. Wilson	P. Gordon Walker	J. Callaghan

UNITED KINGDOM (*continued*)

Date of taking office	Prime Minister	Foreign Minister	Finance Minister
22 Jan 65		M. Stewart	
11 Aug 66		G. Brown	
30 Nov 67			R. Jenkins
16 Mar 68		M. Stewart	
19 June 70	E. Heath		
20 June 70		Sir A. Douglas-Home	I. Macleod
25 July 70			A. Barber
4 Mar 74	H. Wilson	J. Callaghan	D. Healey

YUGOSLAVIA

Date of taking office	Prime Minister	Foreign Minister	Finance Minister
19 Feb 21	S. Protić	M. Trumbitch	V. Janković
24 Dec 21	N. Pashić	M. Nintchić	K. Kumanudi
3 Dec 22			M. Stojadinović
8 Apr 26	N. Uzunović		N. Uzunović
1 Feb 27		N. Peritch	B. Narković
23 Feb 28	V. Vukitčević	V. Marinković	
6 Jan 29	Gen. P. Zivković		S. Svrljuga
4 Apr 32	V. Marinković		M. Georgević
11 July 32	M. Serškie	B. Jevtić	
27 Jan 34	N. Uzonivić		
Dec 34	B. Jević		
24 June 35	M. Stojadinović	M. Stojadinović	D. Letica
5 Feb 39	D. Cvetković	A. C. Marković	V. Juričić
26 Aug 39			J. Šutej
27 Mar 41	Gen. D. Simović	M. Nintchić	

In 1941 the Axis powers occupied Yugoslavia. A government-in-exile was established in London in June 1941 and eventually moved to Cairo.

11 Jan 42	S. Jovanović		
Jun 43	M. Trifimović		
10 Aug 43	B. Purić		I. Cicin-Sain
7 Mar 45	Marshal J. B. Tito	I. Subasić	S. Zejević
2 Feb 46		S. Simić	
6 May 48			D. Radosavljević
31 Aug 48		E. Kardelj	
1 Nov 51			M. Popović
14 Jan 53		K. Popović	R. Nedelković
1 Jan 54			N. Bozinović
1 Jan 57			A. Humo
1 Jan 59			N. Minćov

(continued

YUGOSLAVIA (*continued*)

Date of taking office	Prime Minister	Foreign Minister	Finance Minister
1 Jan 63			K. Gligorov
29 June 63	P. Stambolić		
23 Apr 65		M. Nikezić	
18 May 67	M. Spiljak		J. Smole
28 Apr 69		M. Tepavac	
17 May 69	M. Ribičić		
30 July 71	D. Bijedić		
5 Dec 72	M. Minich		

BIBLIOGRAPHY

Berkeley, H. J., *The Power of the Prime Minister*. London, 1968
Brandt, W., *My Road to Berlin*. London, 1960
Brecht, A., and Glaser, C., *The Art and Technique of Administration in German Ministries*. Harvard Univ. Press, 1940
Brook-Shepherd, G., *Dollfuss*. London, 1961
Fischer, L., *The Life of Lenin*. London, 1965
Heidenheimer, A. J., *Adenauer and the CDU*. The Hague, 1960
Howard, A., and West, R., *The Making of the Prime Minister*. London, 1965
King, A. S., *The British Prime Minister, A. Reader*. London, 1969
Rose, R., *People in Politics*. London, 1970
Schuschnigg, K., *Dreimal Osterreich*. Vienna, 1937
Sheridan, R., *K. von Schuschnigg, A Tribute*. London, 1942
Spaak, P. H., *The Continuing Battle – Memoirs of a European 1936–66*. London, 1971
Williams, E. F., *A Pattern of Rulers*. London, 1965

5 ELECTIONS

ALBANIA

In Mar 1920 the Lushnjë congress elected a National Assembly and a Senate. Political parties began to emerge: a group known as 'liberals' and one known as 'conservatives'.

Elections were held on 4 Feb 21 to a National Assembly of 77 deputies and a Senate of 18 (6 of whom were appointed). Alternate governments were formed by the conservative feudalistic Progressive Party and the People's Party which itself split into a right-wing faction headed by A. Zogu and a liberal faction (becoming a Democratic party) headed by Bishop Fan Noli.

At the elections of Dec 23, 40 Progressive and 35 People's Party candidates were returned, together with 20 independents. Fan Noli left the People's Party to form an opposition and seized power on 17 June 24. His government itself split into Radical and National Democrats, and Zogu seized power again in Dec 24.

By a new constitution of Feb 25 a bicameral National Assembly was set up with deputies elected every three years and a partly-elected Senate. The President was to be elected by the National Assembly for a seven-year period. In the 1925 elections opposition groups were not permitted to stand and complete victory went to the Zogists. Zogu became President.

By a new constitution of 1 Sep 28 the Senate was abolished and a National Assembly of 56 set up. Political parties were forbidden and elections were indirect and on a limited suffrage. Government-nominated candidates were presented to the electors for approval. Albania became a monarchy and Zogu its king under the name Zog I. The elections of 1932 and 1937 were held under these conditions.

On 2 Dec 45 elections were held for a new People's Assembly. 82 candidates stood on the single Democratic Front list for 82 seats. 89·9% of electorate voted, and 93·16% of votes cast were for the Democratic Front.

At the elections of 28 May 50 the electorate was 641,241, the turn-out 99·43% of whom 98·18% voted for the 121 deputies (1 per 10,000). Turn-out in the elections since (30 May 54; 1 June 58; 3 June 62; 11 July 66; 20 Sep 70) has never been less than 99% and reached (it was claimed) 100% in 1970. One deputy represents 8,000 electors. Elections are held every four years.

Some parties are referred to by initials. *See* Chapter 6, 'Political Parties', for full names.

AUSTRIA

Voting procedures. Direct secret proportional elections in multi-member constituencies. Tyrol and Vorarlberg provinces had compulsory voting by law from 1919, Styria from 1949. Universal adult suffrage for all over 20 (over 21 in 1930 and 1945).

	Electorate	Valid votes	Votes per party		Seats	% of electorate	% of votes
1919	3,554,242	2,973,454	SDP	1,211,814	69	34·1	40·7
			CSP	1,068,382	63	30·0	36·0
			Grossdeutsche Partei	545,938	24	15·4	18·4
1920	3,752,212	2,980,328	CSP	1,245,531	85	33·2	41·8
			SDP	1,072,709	69	28·6	36·0
			GdVP	514,127	28	13·7	17·2
1923	3,849,484	3,312,606	CSP	1,490,876	82	38·7	45·0
			SDP	1,311,870	68	34·1	39·6
			GdVP	422,600	15	11·0	12·8
1927	4,119,626	3,641,526	CSP } GdVP }	1,756,761[1]	73 12	42·6	41·4 6·8
			SDP	1,539,635	71	37·4	42·3
1930	4,121,282	3,687,082	SDP	1,516,913	72	36·8	41·1
			CSP	1,314,468	66	31·9	35·6
			NWbLb	427,962	19	10·4	11·6
1945	3,449,605	3,217,354	OVP	1,602,227	85	46·4	49·8
			SPO	1,434,898	76	41·6	44·6
			KPO	174,257	4	5·0	5·4
1949	4,391,815	4,193,733	OVP	1,846,581	77	42·0	44·0
			SPO	1,623,524	67	37·0	38·7
			FPO } WdU }	489,213[1]	16	11·1	11·7
1953	4,586,870	4,318,688	SPO	1,818,517	73	39·6	42·1
			OVP	1,781,777	74	38·8	41·2
			FPO } WdU }	472,866[1]	14	10·3	10·9
1956	4,614,464	4,351,908	OVP	1,999,989	82	43·3	46·1
			SPO	1,873,292	74	40·6	43·0
			FPO } WdU }	283,749[1]	6	6·1	6·5
1959	4,696,633	4,362,856	SPO	1,953,935	78	41·6	44·8
			OVP	1,928,043	79	41·0	44·2
			FPO	336,110	8	7·1	7·7
1962	4,805,351	4,456,131	OVP	2,024,501	81	42·1	45·4
			SPO	1,960,685	76	40·8	44·0
			FPO	313,895	8	6·5	7·0

[1] Two-party front

	Electorate	Valid votes	Votes per party		Seats	% of electorate	% of votes
1966	4,886,534	4,531,864	OVP	2,191,128	85	44·8	48·4
			SPO	1,928,922	74	39·5	42·6
			FPO	242,599	6	5·0	5·3
1970	5,045,841	4,588,961	OVP	2,051,012	79	40·6	44·7
			SPO	2,221,981	81	44·0	48·4
			FPO	253,425	5	5·0	5·5
1971	4,984,448	4,556,990˙	OVP	1,964,713	80	39·4	43·1
			SPO	2,280,168	93	45·7	50·0
			FPO	248,473	10	5·0	5·5

BELGIUM

Voting procedures. Proportional representation in single-member constituencies. Vote for all males over 25 for the Chamber of Representatives and over 30 for the Senate, until the constitutional revision of 1920–1 set the electoral age at 21. Women received the right to vote in 1948.

	Electorate	Valid votes	Votes per party		Seats	% of electorate	% of votes
1919	2,102,710	1,762,141	Catholics	645,462	71	30·69	36·62
			Socialists	645,075	70	30·67	36·60
			Liberals	310,853	34	14·78	17·64
1921	2,226,797	1,931,842	Catholics	715,041	69	32·11	37·01
			Socialists	672,445	68	30·19	34·80
			Liberals	343,929	33	15·44	17·80
1925	2,346,096	2,079,920	Socialists	820,116	78	34·95	39·43
			Catholics	751,058	75	32·01	36·11
			Liberals	304,467	23	12·97	14·64
1929	2,497,446	2,230,069	Socialists	803,347	70	32·16	36·02
			Catholics	788,914	71	31·58	35·37
			Liberals	369,114	28	14·77	16·55
1932	2,555,743	2,335,192	Catholics	899,887	79	35·21	38·55
			Socialists	866,817	73	33·91	37·11
			Liberals	333,567	24	13·05	14·28
1936	2,652,707	2,362,454	Socialists	758,485	70	28·59	32·10
			Catholics	653,717	61	24·64	27·67
			Liberals	292,972	23	11·04	12·40
			Rexistes	271,491	21	10·23	11·49
1939	2,667,341	2,338,437	Catholics	764,843	73	28·67	32·73
			Socialists	705,969	64	26·46	30·18
			Liberals	401,991	33	15·07	17·19

	Electorate	Valid votes	Votes per party		Seats	% of electorate	% of votes
1946	2,724,796	2,365,638	Catholics	1,006,293	92	36·93	42·53
			Socialists	746,738	69	27·40	31·56
			Communists	300,099	23	11·01	12·68
			Liberals	211,143	17	7·74	8·92
1949	5,635,452	5,030,886	Catholics	2,190,898	105	38·87	43·56
			Socialists	1,496,539	66	26·55	29·75
			Liberals	767,180	29	13·61	15·25
1950	5,635,452	4,942,807	Catholics	2,356,608	108	41·81	47·68
			Socialists	1,705,781	77	30·26	34·51
			Liberals	556,102	20	9·86	11·25
1954	5,863,072	5,160,486	Catholics	2,123,408	95	36·21	41·14
			Socialists	1,927,015	86	32·86	37·34
			Liberals	626,983	25	10·69	12·15
1958	5,954,858	5,302,353	Catholics	2,465,549	104	41·10	46·50
			Socialists	1,897,646	84	31·86	35·79
			Liberals	585,999	21	9·84	11·05
1961	6,036,565	5,265,025	Catholics	2,182,642	96	36·15	41·46
			Socialists	1,933,424	84	32·02	36·73
			Liberals	649,376	20	10·75	12·33
1965	6,091,534	5,181,766	Catholics	1,785,211	77	29·30	34·45
			Socialists	1,465,503	64	24·05	28·28
			Liberals	1,119,991	48	18·38	21·61
1968	6,170,167	5,177,952	Catholics	1,643,785	69	26·6	31·8
			Socialists	1,449,172	59	23·5	28·0
			Liberals	1,080,894	47	17·5	20·9
1971	6,271,240	5,281,633	Catholics	1,587,195	67	25·3	30·1
			Socialists	1,438,626	61	22·9	27·2
			Liberals	865,657	34	13·8	16·4

BULGARIA

By 1918 Bulgaria was a constitutional monarchy with an electoral system established by the 1879 *Turnovo* constitution. The legislature was the uni-cameral National Assembly, *Narodno Sŭbranie*, of deputies each representing 10,000 electors, elected by universal suffrage at 21 years for three- (later four-) year terms. To pass any constitutional amendment a Grand National Assembly, *Veliko Narodno Sŭbranie*, was elected of twice the usual number of deputies. Elections were on the proportional representation system.

ELECTIONS

	Votes per party		Seats
1923 (23 Apr)	Agrarians	569,000	212
	Communists	204,000	16
	Social Democrats	28,000	2
	Middle class and		
	traditionalist parties	275,000	15
1923 (18 Nov)	Democratic *entente*		
	in a bloc with		202
	Social Democrats	638,675	29
	Left-wing Agrarians		
	in a bloc with		31
	Communists	217,607	8
	Right-wing Agrarians	42,737	19
	National Liberals	36,507	7.

By an electoral law of 1927 proportional representation (abolished in 1923) was restored in a system favourable to the government party, Democratic *entente*, enabling it to win 168 of the 273 seats with 39% of the votes in the election of 29 May 27:

Votes per party		Seats
Democratic *entente*	504,703	168
'Iron bloc' of Agrarians,		42
Social Democrats and		10
Artisans	285,758	4
Workers (*i.e.* Communists)	29,210	4
National Liberals		14
Democrats		12
Macedonians		11
Radicals		2

A new proportional representation system was introduced for the elections of 21 June 31, the results of which were:

Votes per party		Seats
Agrarians		69
'Popular bloc' of Democrats,		43
Kyorchev Liberals and		32
Radicals	590,000	8
Democratic *entente*		
in a bloc with		63
Smilov Liberals	417,000	15
Workers (*i.e.* Communists)	166,000	33
Macedonians		8
Social Democrats		5

The government was taken over on 19 May 34 in a *coup d'état* by a group of army officers in alliance with a group of intellectuals associated with the journal *Zveno*. Tsar Boris overthrew this government in turn on 22 Jan 35 and set up a royal dictatorship.

By an electoral law of 1937 the number of deputies was reduced to 160, political parties were banned and unmarried women disfranchised.

At the election of Mar 38 Agrarians and Social Democrats stood in opposition to the government in the Bulgarian version of the Popular Front called the 'Constitutional bloc', and won 63 seats. At the elections of 30 Jan 40 opposition candidates (including 9 Communists) won 20 seats.

On 9 Sep 44 at the beginning of the Soviet occupation a 'Fatherland Front' government of Communists and anti-fascists was set up.

18 Nov 45 (Opposition boycotted election	Fatherland Front, 88·2% (85·6% of electorate voted)

A referendum was held on 8 Sep 46 at which 92·7% of the electorate voted, 3,801,160 for a Republic, and 197,176 to retain the monarchy. 119,168 votes were invalid. A People's Republic was proclaimed on 15 Sep 46.

The elections of 27 Oct 46 were for a 'Grand' National Assembly as was necessary to carry a constitutional change. The Communists and their allies stood in a Fatherland Front bloc; the opposition parties campaigned as the 'United opposition'.

	Votes per party		Seats
1946	Fatherland Front	2,980,000	366
	Communists	2,260,000	277
	Obbov Agrarians		67
	Neikov Social Democrats		9
	Zveno group		8
	Radicals		4
	United opposition	1,300,000	99
	Agrarians		89
	Social Democrats		9
	independent		1

On 4 Dec 47 the 'Dimitrov' constitution was promulgated. The National Assembly was elected for four-year terms by all citizens of 18 and over. Each deputy represented 20,000 electors. The President was to be elected by the National Assembly.

Before the elections of 1949 the Social Democrats merged with the Communists and the *Zveno* group dissolved. 97·66% of votes cast were for the single Fatherland Front list of Communist or Agrarian candidates.

	Electorate	Votes per Party	% per votes
1953	5,017,667 (99·48% voted)	Fatherland Front (465 deputies elected)	99·8
1957	5,218,602 (99·77% voted) (Votes = 5,206,428)	Fatherland Front 5,204,027 (number of deputies reduced to 253)	99·95
1962	5,485,607 (99·71% voted) (Votes = 5,466,517)	Fatherland Front (321 deputies elected)	99·9

112

	Electorate	Votes per Party	% per votes
1966	5,774,251		
	(99·63% voted)	Fatherland Front 5,744,072	99·85
	(Votes = 5,752,817)	(number of candidates = 416)	
1971	(99·85% voted)	Fatherland Front	99·9

A new constitution was promulgated on 18 May 71 by which the number of deputies was fixed at 400 and their term of service altered to five years.

CZECHOSLOVAKIA

A National Assembly was set up on 14 Nov 18 of 260 delegates of the following party composition:

Agrarians	54
Social Democrats	50
Slovaks	50
National Democrats	44
National Socialists	28
Catholics	28
Progressive Liberals	6

Representatives of the German minority refused to take part.

A constitution was promulgated on 29 Feb 20 providing for a bicameral National Assembly, *Národní Shromáždění*, to be elected by direct universal suffrage on the proportional representation method. The Chamber of Deputies of 300 members was to be elected for six years by citizens over 21; the Senate for eight years by voters over 26, and to have 150 senators.

The head of state was to be a President elected by both chambers for seven years.

Elections to the Chamber of Deputies were held on 18 Apr 20 and to the Senate on 25 Apr 20. The electorate was 6,917,956 (for the Chamber of Deputies; the Senate electorate was a proportion of this which remained more or less constant throughout later elections. At this election it was 5,804,134). Turn-out was 89·9%. Valid votes cast for the Chamber of Deputies: 6,130,318.

Pre-war Czechoslovak politics were dominated by the problem of national minorities, and the official classification of the voting figures in this election reflects this preoccupation: Czechoslovak parties polled 4,255,623 votes (68·64% of votes cast) and gained 199 seats in the Chamber of Deputies, and gained 102 seats in the Senate with 70·07% of votes cast. German parties: 72; 1,586,060 (25·58%) and 37; 26·09%. Hungarian-German parties: 9; 247,901 (4%) and 2; 1·93%. Hungarian parties: 1; 30,734 (0·50%) and 1; 0·77%.

113

Seats gained and proportion of votes polled by individual, successful, parties were:

Chamber of Deputies:		*Seats*	*%*
	Social Democrats	74	25·65
	Populist Catholics	33	11·29
	Agrarians	28	9·74
Czechoslovak	National Socialists	24	8·08
parties	National Democrats	19	6·25
	Slovak National Agrarians	12	3·9
	Professional Middle Class	6	1·98
	Working People (Progressive Socialists)	3	0·95
	German Social Democrats	31	11·12
	German Electoral Union	15	5·3
German parties	Union of German Peasants	11	3·9
	German Christian Social Party	10	3·44
	German Democratic Liberals	5	1·78
Hungarian-German	Hungarian-German Christian Socialists	5	2·25
parties	Hungarian-German Social Democrats	4	1·75
Hungarian parties	Hungarian Agrarians	1	0·43

Senate:		*Seats*	*%*
	Social Democrats	41	28·07
	Populist Catholics	18	11·91
	Agrarians	14	10·15
Czechoslovak	National Socialists	10	7·15
parties	National Democrats	10	6·78
	Slovak National Agrarians	6	3·47
	Professional Middle Class	3	2·06
	German Social Democrats	16	11·35
	German Electoral Union	8	5·75
German parties	Union of German Peasants	6	4·03
	German Christian Social Party	4	2·7
	German Democratic Liberals	3	2·26
Hungarian-German	Hungarian-German Christian Socialists	2	1·93
Hungarian	Hungarian Agrarians	1	0·77

At the elections of 15 Nov 25 all 300 seats in the chamber of Deputies and all 150 in the Senate were filled by election. The electorate was 7,855,822, the turn-out was 91·4% and 7,105,276 votes were cast.

	Chamber of Deputies			Senate		
	Votes	*% of votes*	*Seats*	*Votes*	*% of votes*	*Seats*
(Czechoslovak parties):						
Agrarians	970,489	13·66	45	841,647	13·81	23
Populist Catholics	691,238	9·73	31	618,033	10·14	16
Social Democrats	630,894	8·88	29	537,470	8·82	14
National Socialists	609,195	8·57	28	516,250	8·47	14
Professional Middle Class	285,928	4·02	13	257,171	4·22	6
National Democrats	284,628	4·01	13	256,360	4·2	7

	Chamber of Deputies			Senate		
	Votes	% of votes	Seats	Votes	% of votes	Seats
German Social Democrats	411,040	5·79	17	363,310	6·84	12
German Christian Social Party	314,440	4·43	13	289,055	4·74	7
German Nationalists	240,879	3·39	10	214,589	3·52	5
Nazis	168,278	2·37	7	139,945	2.3	3
Union of German Peasants	571,198	8·04	24	505,597	8·29	12
Hlinka's Populist Slovak Catholics	489,027	6·88	23	417,206	6·84	12
Sub-Carpathian Russian Agrarians	35,674	0·5	1			
Polish People's and Workers' Union	29,884	0·42	1			
Hungarian Christian Social Party	98,383	1·39	4	85,777	1·41	2
Communists	933,711	13·14	41	774,454	12·7	20

At the elections of 27 Oct 29 the electorate was 8,183,462, the turn-out 91·6% and 7,385,084 votes were cast.

	Chamber of Deputies			Senate		
	Votes	% of votes	Seats	Votes	% of votes	Seats
(Czechoslovak parties):						
Agrarians	1,105,429	14·97	46	978,291	15·17	24
Social Democrats	963,312	13·05	39	841,331	13·04	20
National Socialists	767,571	10·39	32	666,607	10·33	16
Populist Catholics	623,522	8·44	25	559,700	8·68	13
National Democrats	359,533	4·87	15	325,023	5·04	8
Professional Middle Class	291,238	3·94	12	274,085	4·25	6
Anti-Electoral Scrutiny	70,857	0·96	3	51,617	0.8	1
German Social Democrats	506,750	5·76	19	446,940	6·93	11
German Electoral Coalition	396,383	5·37	16	359,002	5·57	9
German Christian Social Party	348,097	4·71	14	313,544	4·86	8
Nazis	204,096	2·77	8	171,181	2·65	4
German Nationalist and Sudeten German Union	189,071	2·56	7			
Hlinka's Populist Slovak Catholics	425,052	5·76	19	377,498	5·85	9
Hungarian Christian Socialists	257,231	3·48	9	233,772	3·62	6
Polish and Jewish Union	104,539	1·42	4			
Communists	753,444	10.2	30	644,896	10·00	15

At the elections of 19 May 35 the electorate was 8,957,572, turn-out was 92·8% and 8,231,412 votes were cast.

	Chamber of Deputies			Senate		
	Votes	% of votes	Seats	Votes	% of votes	Seats
(Czechoslovak parties):						
Agrarians	1,176,593	14·29	45	1,042,924	14·33	23
Social Democrats	1.034,774	12·57	38	910,252	12·51	20
National Socialists	755,880	9·18	28	672,126	9·24	14
Populist Catholics	615,877	7·48	22	557,684	7·66	11
Artisans and Tradesmen	448,047	5·44	17	393,732	5·41	8
Fascists	167,433	2·04	6			
National Union	456,353	5·55	17	410,095	5·64	9
Sudeten Germans	1,249,531	15·18	44	1,092,255	15·01	23
German Social Democrats	299,942	3·64	11	271,097	3·73	6
German Christian Social Party	162,781	1·98	6	155,234	2·13	3
Union of German Peasants	142,399	1·73	5			

	Chamber of Deputies			Senate		
	Votes	% of votes	Seats	Votes	% of votes	Seats
Autonomous bloc (Hlinka's Slovaks, Poles and Hungarians	564,273	6·86	22	495,166	6·8	11
Hungarian-German Christian Social bloc	291,831	3·55	9	259,832	3·57	6
Communists	849,509	10·32	30	740,696	10·18	16

With the dismemberment and annexation of Czechoslovakia by Germany in 1938 all political parties were proscribed and two puppet organizations set up: The Party of National Unity and the Party of Labour.

On 3 Apr 45 Beneš established a provisional government at Košice with a cabinet of seven Communists, three Slovak Democrats, three Populist Catholics, three National Socialists and two Social Democrats. This organized an indirect election in Sep and Oct 45 of a provisional National Assembly which met on 28 Oct 45. Four parties were recognized in the Czech lands (Communists, Agrarians, National Socialists, Social Democrats) and allotted 40 deputies each, 2 in Slovakia (Populist Catholics and Slovak Democrats) 50 each, 32 seats went to the Trade Union organization and 8 to outstanding individuals in the cultural sphere, making 300 in all.

At the elections of 26 May 46 to a Constituent Assembly eight official parties were allowed to stand: no independents, no fascist parties and (at Soviet insistence) no Agrarians. The electorate was 7,583,784 (all citizens over 18) of whom 7,138,694 voted.

Party	Votes	Seats
Communists	2,695,915	114
National Socialists	1,298,917	55
Populist Catholics	1,110,920	47
Slovak Democrats	988,275	43
Social Democrats	905,654	36
Slovak Freedom	67,575	3
Slovak Labour	49,983	2

Elections were held on 30 May 45 in which the electorate of 7,998,035 were invited to vote for a single list of National Front candidates. 7,419,253 votes were cast, 6,424,734 for the National Front.

President Beneš resigned and was succeeded by K. Gottwald.

A new constitution of 9 June 48 provided for a single-chamber National Assembly, Národni Shromáždĕni, of 368 deputies elected by universal suffrage of citizens over 18 for a six-year period. The President was to be elected by the National Assembly for seven years.

An electoral law of May 54 permitted only one candidate to stand per constituency; all candidates had to be nominated by the National Front.

At the elections of 28 Nov 54 the electorate was 8,783,816, votes cast numbered 8,711,718 (99·18%), of which 8,494,102 (97·89%) were for the National Front. At the elections of 12 June 60 9,085,432 votes were cast

(99·68% of the electorate), of which 9,059,838 (99·86% of votes cast) went to the National Front.

On 11 July 60 a new constitution made Czechoslovakia a 'Socialist' instead of a 'People's' Republic, and fixed the number of National Assembly deputies at 300. The President was henceforth to be elected for a five-year term, the National Assembly for four.

At the elections of 14 June 64 9,418,349 votes were cast (99·98% of the electorate), 9,412,309 for the National Front (99·99% of votes cast).

Czechoslovakia became a Federal Republic of the Czech lands and Slovakia as of 1 Jan 69. Each federative republic elects a National Council. The Federal Assembly consists of two chambers: the Chamber of the People of 200 deputies, and the Chamber of the Nations composed of 75 Czech and 75 Slovak deputies. Elections are held every five years, to coincide with Communist Party congresses.

The elections due in 1968 were postponed until 26–27 Nov 71. In 1968 a new electoral law had permitted more than one candidate to stand for each seat, but this was annulled in the 1971 elections in which the number of candidates was once again equivalent to the number of seats. The electorate was 10,253,796 of whom 99·45% voted. Votes for candidates: Federal Assembly Chamber of the People, 99·81%; Federal Assembly Chamber of the Nations, 99·77%; Czech National Council, 99·78%; Slovak National Council, 99·94%.

DENMARK

In 1918, the capital had direct proportional elections, the provinces had direct elections in single-member constituencies with some additional seats allotted in proportion to the vote. From 1920, direct proportional elections in multi-member seats. Suffrage of men and women over 29, except those working as servants and farm helpers without their own household. Age reduced to 25 at the third election of 1920, to 23 in 1953 and to 21 in 1961. From 1918–53 there was a second chamber, the Landsting. For this there was indirect election, electors being selected by city or parish, voters having one vote per elector allocated. Voters were all men and women over 35. Electors in turn elected 53 (first two elections of the period) of the 66 Landsting members, and 55 of them in the last ten elections.

	Electorate	Valid votes	Votes per party		Seats	% of electorate	% of vote
1918	1,226,598	915,745	Liberals	269,005	44	21·9	29·4
			Soc. Dem.	262,796	39	21·4	29·4
			Rad. Lib.	192,478	33	15·7	21·0
			Con.	167,865	22	13·7	18·3

	Electorate	Valid votes	Votes per party		Seats	% of electorate	% of vote
1920(1)	1,274,377	1,024,206	Liberals	350,563	48	27·5	34·2
			Soc. Dem.	300,345	42	23·6	29·3
			Con.	201,499	28	15·8	19·7
			Rad. Lib.	122,160	17	9·6	11·9
1920(2)	1,276,302	953,561	Liberals	343,351	51	26·9	36·1
			Soc. Dem.	285,166	42	23·3	29·9
			Con.	180,293	26	14·1	18·9
			Rad. Lib.	110,931	16	8·7	11·6
1920(3)	1,576,716	1,211,695	Liberals	411,661	51	26·1	34·0
			Soc. Dem.	389,653	48	24·7	32·2
			Con.	216,733	27	13·7	17·9
			Rad. Lib.	147,120	18	9·3	12·1
1924	1,637,564	1,282,937	Soc. Dem.	469,949	55	28·7	36·6
			Liberals	362,682	44	22·1	28·3
			Con.	242,955	28	14·8	18·9
			Rad. Lib.	166,476	20	10·2	13·0
1926	1,742,604	1,337,647	Soc. Dem.	497,106	53	28·5	37·2
			Liberals	378,137	46	21·7	28·3
			Con.	275,793	30	15·8	20·6
			Rad. Lib.	150,931	16	8·7	11·3
1929	1,786,092	1,420,246	Soc. Dem.	593,191	61	33·2	41·8
			Liberals	402,121	43	22·5	28·3
			Con.	233,935	24	13·0	16·5
			Rad. Lib.	151,746	16	8·5	10·7
1932	1,902,835	1,547,082	Soc. Dem.	660,839	62	34·7	42·7
			Liberals	381,862	38	20·0	24·7
			Con.	289,531	27	15·2	18·7
			Rad. Lib.	145,221	14	7·6	9·4
1935	2,044,997	1,646,438	Soc. Dem.	759,102	68	37·1	46·1
			Liberals	292,247	28	14·3	17·8
			Con.	293,393	26	14·3	17·8
			Rad. Lib.	151,507	14	7·4	9·2
1939	2,159,356	1,699,889	Soc. Dem.	729,619	64	33·8	42·9
			Liberals	309,355	30	14·3	18·2
			Con.	301,625	26	14·0	17·8
			Rad. Lib.	161,834	14	7·5	9·5
1943	2,280,716	2,010,783	Soc. Dem.	894,632	66	39·2	44·5
			Con.	421,523	31	18·5	21·0
			Liberals	376,850	28	16·5	18·7
1945	2,381,983	2,049,148	Soc. Dem.	671,755	48	28·2	32·8
			Liberals	479,158	38	20·1	23·4
			Con.	373,688	26	15·7	18·2
1947	2,435,306	2,084,141	Soc. Dem.	834,089	57	34·2	40·0
			Liberals	574,895	49	23·6	27·6
			Con.	259,324	17	10·6	12·4
1950	2,516,118	2,054,330	Soc. Dem.	813,224	59	32·3	39·6
			Liberals	438,188	32	17·4	21·3
			Con.	365,236	27	14·5	17·8

	Electorate	Valid votes	Votes per party		Seats	% of electorate	% of vote
1953(1)	2,571,311	2,070,930	Soc. Dem.	836,507	61	32·5	40·4
			Liberals	456,896	33	17·8	22·1
			Con.	358,509	26	13·9	17·3
1953(2)	2,695,554	2,166,391	Soc. Dem.	894,913	74	33.2	41·3
			Liberals	499,656	42	18·5	23·1
			Con.	364,960	30	13·5	16·8
1957	2,772,159	2,310,175	Soc. Dem.	910,170	70	32·8	39·4
			Liberals	578,932	45	20·9	25·1
			Con.	383,843	30	13·8	16·6
1960	2,842,336	2,431,947	Soc. Dem.	1,023,794	76	36·0	42·1
			Liberals	512,041	38	18·0	21·1
			Con.	435,764	32	15·3	17·9
1964	3,088,269	2,631,384	Soc. Dem.	1,103,667	76	35·7	41·9
			Liberals	547,770	38	17·7	20·8
			Con.	527,798	36	17·0	20·1
1966	3,162,880	2,794,007	Soc. Dem.	1,068,911	69	33·8	38·2
			Liberals	539,028	35	17·0	19·3
			Con.	522,027	34	16·5	18·7
1968	3,208,646	2,854,647	Soc. Dem.	974,833	62	30·4	34·1
			Liberals	530,167	34	16·5	18·6
			Cons.	581,051	37	18·1	20·4
1971	3,332,044	2,883,900	Soc. Dem.	1,074,777	70	32·3	37·3
			Liberals	450,904	30	13·5	15·6
			Cons.	481,335	31	14·4	16·7

ESTONIA

Elections for a Constituent Assembly were held 7 and 8 Apr 19, and a coalition government formed headed by the Social Democratic Party. A constitution was adopted on 15 June 20 which provided for a single-chamber parliament (*Riigikogu*) of 100 deputies elected every 3 years by proportional representation. Elections were held in 1920, 1923, 1926, 1929 and 1932. The system favoured the proliferation of political parties. There were also national minority parties: Swedish, German and Russian. The Communist Party was outlawed in Feb 25 after an abortive *coup*. The fascist ex-servicemen's organization Vaps began to gain influence at a time of increasing dissatisfaction with government instability (between 1919 and 1933 there were 20 coalition governments) and instigated a referendum to amend the constitution in Oct 33. The amendment was approved by 416,879 votes (56·3% of the electorate), but the President (K Päts) on 12 Mar 34 assumed direct control under emergency powers and presented a third constitution to the people in Feb 36. This was approved by a majority of

76·1% and came into force on 1 Jan 38. It provided for a new two-chamber parliament: a 40-strong National Council of appointed specialists, and an 80-strong Chamber of Deputies elected every five years on the single-member constituency system. The President was to be directly elected every six years.

At the elections of 24 Apr 38 the poll was a record 90%. Päts was elected President. 55 members of the pro-Päts Patriotic League were elected. Social Democrats and extreme left-wing groups were in opposition.

FINLAND

Voting procedures. Direct proportional elections from multi-member constituencies. Suffrage for all adults over 24 until 1945, and then over 21. In 1919, part of the population disenfranchised by the civil war.

	Electorate	Valid votes	Votes per party		Seats	% of electorate	% of votes
1919	1,438,709	961,101	SSP	365,046	80	25·3	38·0
			MI	189,297	42	13·2	19·7
			KK	151,018	28	10·5	15·7
			KE	123,090	26	8·6	12·8
			RK	116,582	22	8·1	12·1
1922	1,489,022	865,421	SSP	216,861	53	14·5	25·1
			MI	175,401	45	11·7	20·3
			KK	157,116	35	10·6	18·1
			RK	107,414	25	7·2	12·4
			KE	79,676	15	5·4	9·2
1924	1,539,393	878,941	SSP	255,068	60	16·5	29·0
			MI	177,982	44	11·6	20·3
			KK	166,880	38	10·8	19·0
			RK	105,733	23	6·9	12·0
			KE	79,937	17	10·8	19·0
1927	1,638,864	910,191	SSP	257,572	60	15·7	28·3
			MI	205,313	52	12·5	22·5
			KK	161,450	34	9·9	17·7
			RK	111,005	24	6·8	12·2
			KE	61,613	10	3·8	6·8
1929	1,719,567	951,270	SSP	260,254	59	15·1	27·4
			MI	248,762	60	14·5	26·1
			KK	138,008	28	8·0	14·5
			RK	108.886	23	6·3	11·4
			KE	53,301	7	3·1	5·6
1930	1.722,588	1,130,028	SSP	386,026	66	22·4	34·2
			MI	308,280	59	17·9	27·3
			KK	203,958	42	11·8	18·1
			RK	113,318	20	6·6	10·0
			KE	65,830	11	3·8	5·8
1933	1,789,331	1,107,823	SSP	413,551	78	23·0	37·3
			MI	249,758	53	14·0	22·6

Year	Electorate	Valid votes	Party	Votes per party	Seats	% of electorate	% of votes
			RK	131,440	21	7·0	11·2
			KK	121,619	20	6·5	10·4
			IK	97,891	14	5·2	8·3
1939	1,956,807	1,297,319	SSP	515,980	85	26·3	39·8
			MI	296,529	56	15·2	22·9
			KK	176,215	25	9·0	13·6
			RK	124,720	18	6·4	9·6
1945	2,284,249	1,698,376	SSP	425,948	50	18·6	25·1
			SKDI	398,618	49	17·4	23·5
			MI	362,662	49	15·9	21·3
			KK	255,394	28	11·2	15·0
1948	2,420,287	1,879,968	MI	455,635	56	18·8	24·2
			SSP	494,719	54	20 5	26·3
			SKDI	375,820	38	15·6	20·0
			KK	320,366	33	13·2	17·1
1951	2,448,239	1,812,817	SSP	480,754	53	19·6	26·5
			MI	421,613	51	17·2	23·2
			SKDI	391,362	43	16·0	21·6
			KK	264,044	28	10·8	14·6
1954	2,526,969	2,008,257	SSP	527,094	54	20·8	26·2
			MI	483,958	53	19·1	24·1
			SKDI	433,528	43	17·2	21·6
			KK	257,025	24	10·2	12·8
1958	2,606,258	1,944,235	SKDI	450,506	50	17·3	23·2
			SSP	450,212	48	17·3	23·2
			MI	448,364	48	17·2	23·1
			KK	297,094	29	11·4	15·3
1962	2,714,838	2,301,998	MI	528,409	53	19·5	23·0
			SKDI	507,124	47	18·7	22·0
			SSP	448,930	38	16·5	19·5
			KK	346,638	32	12·8	15·0
1966	2,800,461	2,370,046	MI	503,047	49	18·0	21·2
			SKDI	502,635	41	17·9	21·2
			SSP	645,339	55	23·0	27·2
			KK	326,928	26	11·7	13·8
1970	3,094,359	2,535,782	MI	434,150	37	14·0	17·1
			SKDI	420,556	36	13·6	16·6
			SSP	594,185	51	19·2	23·4
			KK	457,582	37	14·8	18·0
1972	3,178,169	2,577,949	MI	423,039	35	13·3	16·4
			SKDI	438,757	37	13·8	17·0
			SSP	664,724	55	20·9	25·8
			KK	453,434	34	14·3	17·6

FRANCE

Voting procedures. From 1919–27, mixed proportional and majority representation. From 1927–45 the system was as in 1852. In 1945 proportional representation was restored as the sole system; this lasted until 1951 when mixed representation returned. Universal male suffrage until 1945, when women received the vote.

	Electorate	Valid votes	Votes per party		Seats	% of electorate	% of votes
1919	11,446,000	8,034,000	Rep. U.	1,820,000	201	15·9	22·3
			Rad. Soc.	1,420,000	106	12·4	17·4
			Rep. (left)	889,000	79	7·7	10·9
			Soc.	1,615,000	67	14·1	20·1
1924	11,070,000	9,000,000	Rep. U.	3,191,000	204	28·8	35·5
			Rad. Soc.	1,613,000	162	14·5	17·9
			Soc.	1,814,000	104	16·3	20·2
1928	11,396,000	9,470,000	Rep. U.	2,082,000	182	18·2	22·0
			Rad. Ind. } Rep. (left)	2,196,000	126	19·2	23·2
			Soc.	1,709,000	99	14·9	18·0
1932	11,562,000	9,579,000	Rad. Soc.	1,837,000	157	15·8	19·2
			Soc.	1,964,000	129	16·9	20·5
			Rep. U.	1,233,000	76	10·6	12·9
			Rep. (left)	1,300,000	72	11·2	13·6
			Rad. Ind.	956,000	62	8·2	10·0
1936	11,768,000	9,847,000	Centre party	2,536,000 }	222	21·5	25·8
			Right-wing	1,666,000 }		14·1	16·9
			Soc.	1,955,000	149	16·6	19·9
			Rad. Soc.	1,423,000	109	12·0	14·5
			Communist	1,502,000	72	12·7	15·3
1945	24,623,000	19,190,000	Communist } Progressive	5,005,000	148	20·3	26·1
			Soc.	4,561,000	134	18·5	23·8
			Chr. Dem.	4,780,000	141	19·4	24·9
1946(1)	24,697,000	19,881,000	Chr. Dem.	5,589,000	160	22·6	28·1
			Communist } Progressive	5,119,000	146	20·7	25·7
			Soc.	4,188,000	115	16·9	21·1
1946(2)	25,052,000	19,203,000	Communist Progressive	5,489,000	166	21·9	28·6
			Chr. Dem.	5,058,000	158	20·1	26·3
			Soc.	3,432,000	90	13·6	17·9
			Moderates	2,566,000	70	10·2	13·4
1951	24,531,000	19,129,000	Gaulliste	4,125,000	107	16·8	21·6
			Com. and Prog.	5,057,000	97	20·6	26·4
			Soc.	2,745,000	94	11·1	14·3
			Moderates	2,657,000	87	10·8	13·9
			Chr. Dem.	2,370,000	82	9·6	12·4

	Electorate	Valid votes	Votes per party		Seats	% of electorate	% of votes
1956	26,772,225	21,299,000	Com. and Prog.	5,514,000	147	20·5	25·8
			Moderates	3,258,000	95	12·1	15·2
			Soc.	3,247,000	88	12·1	15·2
			Rep. Front Radicals	1,996,000		7·4	9·3
			Right Centre		73		
			Radicals	838,000		3·1	3·9
			Chr. Dem.	2,366,000	71	8·8	11·1
1958	27,236,491	20,490,000	Gaulliste	4,165,000	198	15·2	20·4
			Moderates	4,502,000	133	16·5	22·1
			Chr. Dem.	2,273,000	57	8·3	11·1
			Soc.	3,194,000	44	11·7	15·7
			Com. and Prog.	3,908,000	10	14·3	19·2
1962	27,535,019	18,330,000	Gaulliste	5,847,000	234	21·2	31·9
			Soc.	2,320,000	64	8·4	12·6
			Com. and Prog.	3,992,000	41	14·4	21·7
			Moderates	1,743,000	37	6·3	9·6
			Chr. Dem.	1,635,000	37	5·9	8·9
1967	28,300,936	22,392,000	Gaulliste	8,454,000	232	29·8	37·7
			Dem. Soc. Fed.	4,207,000	116	14·8	18·8
			Com. and Prog.	5,030,000	72	17·7	22·4
1968	28,172,635	22,138,657	Gaulliste	10,201,024	349	36·2	46·1
			Communist	4,435,357	33	15·7	20·0
			F.G.D.S.	3,654,003	57	13·0	16·5
			Moderates	2,700,864	31	9·6	12·2

GERMANY

From 1918–33, direct proportional elections by list system with a uniform quota of 60,000 votes for one representative. Suffrage for all men and women over 20. From 1933 to 1945 there were three elections, but these are not recognized as free elections and no figures are given.

	Electorate	Valid votes	Votes per party		Seats	% of electorate	% of votes
1919	36,766,500	30,400,300	SPD	11,509,100	163	31·3	37·9
			BVP	5,980,200	91	16·3	19·7
			DDP	5,641,800	75	15·3	18·6
			DNVP	3,121,500	44	8·5	10·3
1920	35,949,800	28,196,300	SPD	6,104,400	102	17·0	21·6
			BVP	5,083,600	85	14·1	17·8
			USPD	5,046.800	84	14·0	18·0
			DVP	3,929,400	65	10·9	14·0
1924	38,375,000	29,281,800	SPD	6,008,900	100	15·7	20·5
			DNVP	5,696,500	95	14·8	19·5
			BVP	4,861,100	81	12·7	16·6
			KPD	3,693,300	62	9·6	12·6

	Electorate	Valid votes	Votes per party		Seats	% of electorate	% of votes
1924	38,987,300	30,290,100	SPD	7,881,000	131	20·2	26·0
			DNVP	6,205,800	103	15·9	20·5
			BVP	5,252,900	88	13·5	17·3
			DVP	3,049,100	51	7·8	10·7
1928	41,224,700	30,753,300	SPD	9,153,000	153	22·2	29·8
			BVP	4,657,800	78	11·3	15·2
			DNVP	4,381,600	73	10·6	14·2
			KPD	3,264,800	54	7·9	10·6
1930	42,957,700	34,970,900	SPD	8,577,700	143	20·0	24·5
			NSDAP	6,409,600	107	14·9	18·3
			BVP	5,187,000	87	12·1	14·8
			KPD	4,592,100	77	10·7	13·1
1932	44,226,800	36,882,400	NSDAP	13,745,800	230	31·1	37·4
			SPD	7,959,700	133	18·0	21·6
			BVP	5,782,000	97	13·1	15·7
			KPD	5,282,600	89	11·9	14·6
1932	44,373,700	35,471,800	NSDAP	11,737,000	196	26·4	33·1
			SPD	7,248,000	121	16·3	20·4
			KPD	5,980,200	100	13·5	16·9
			BVP	5,325,200	90	12·0	15·0
			DNVP	2,959,000	52	6·7	8·8
1933	44,685,800	39,343,300	NSDAP	17,277,200	288	38·7	43·9
			SPD	7,181,600	120	16·1	18·3
			BVP	5,498,500	92	12·3	13·9
			KPD	4,848,100	81	10·8	12·3
			DNVP	3,136,800	52	7·0	8·0

EAST GERMANY

Electors vote at 18 and may be candidates at 21. Elections to the People's Chamber (*Volkskammer*) are 'universal, equal, direct and secret' and are held every four years. East Berlin has its own Assembly (*Ostberliner Abgeordenetenhaus*) of 200 and does not elect to the *Volkskammer*. However, it nominates 66 representatives thereto without voting rights.

There are 434 seats in the *Volkskammer* (500 in all when the East Berlin nominees are added). The parties are represented in pre-arranged proportions. Since 1967 more candidates have been allowed to stand than there are seats. All candidates who receive more than 50% of the votes are considered elected; those in excess of the number of seats are placed on a reserve list in order of votes gained. As well as to parties, seats are allotted to social and cultural organizations, *e.g.* to trade unions.

The *Volkskammer* evolved through a series of People's Congresses dominated by the USSR and East German Communists which claimed to speak for all Germany. At the *Länder* elections of Oct 46 the SED failed to gain 50% of the vote and elections thereafter were conducted on the Soviet single-list model.

	Electorate	Valid votes	Seats	
1949	13,533,071	12,887,234	SED	90
			CDU	45
			LDPD	45
			NDPD	15
			DBP	15
			others	130

These elections resulted in the 3rd People's Congress of 1,525 delegates, which elected from among its members a German People's Council of 330 on 3 May 49.

On 7 Oct 49 the formation of a go-it-alone German Democratic Republic was announced and the People's Council became the Provisional *Volkskammer* of 400 representatives.

West Germany declared the GDR illegal in that it was not founded upon free elections. (West Germany and the Western Allies still do not recognize East Germany *de jure*.)

An upper chamber of representatives of provinces (*Länderkammer*) was formed in 1949 but abolished in 1958. The term 'Provisonal' was dropped from the title of the *Volkskammer* after that Chamber had been confirmed by the 1950 elections.

	Electorate	Valid votes	Seats	
1950	12,331,905	12,139,932	SED	100
			CDU	60
			LDPD	60
			NDPD	30
			others	150
1954	12,085,380	11,892,849	SED	102
			CDU	47
			LDPD	46
			NDPD	45
			DBD	45
			others	115
1958	11,839,217	11,707,715	SED	102
			CDU	47
			LDPD	46
			NDPD	45
			DBD	45
			others	115

At the 1963 elections the electorate was 11,621,158 (valid votes, 11,533,859); 1967, 11,341,729 (11,208,816); 1971, 11,401,090 (11,227,535). The distribution of seats in all 3 elections was the same: SED, 128; CDU, 52; LDPD, 52; NDPD, 52; DBP, 52; others 164.

WEST GERMANY

From 1949, direct elections for 60% of the seats in the Bundestag, the others filled by election from lists. From 1953, each voter votes (1) for a candidate in his constituency and (2) for a party list. Seats are distributed proportionally to the second vote. Suffrage since 1949 is for men and women over 21.

	Electorate	Valid votes	Votes per party		Seats	% of electorate	% of votes
1949	31,207,600	23,732,400	CDU/CSU	7,359,100	139	23·6	31·0
			SPD	6,935,000	131	22·2	29·2
			FDP	2,829,900	52	9·1	11·9
1953	33,120,900	27,551,300	CDU/CSU	12,444,000	244	37·6	45·2
			SPD	7,994,900	151	24·0	28·8
			FDP	2,629,200	48	7·9	9·5
1957	35,400,900	29,905,400	CDU/CSU	15,008,400	270	42·4	50·2
			SPD	9,495,600	169	26·4	31·8
			FDP	2,307,100	41	6·2	7·7
1961	37,440,700	31,551,100	CDU/CSU	14,298,400	242	38·2	45·4
			SPD	11,427,400	190	30·5	36·2
			FDP	4,028,800	67	10·8	12·8
1965	38,510,400	32,620,400	CDU/CSU	15,524,100	245	40·3	47·6
			SPD	12,813,200	202	33·3	39·3
			FDP	3,096,800	49	8·0	9·5
1969	38,677,325	32,966,024	CDU/CSU	15,195,187	242	39·3	46·1
			SPD	14,065,716	224	36·4	42·7
			FDP	1,903,422	30	4·9	5·8
1972	41,446,302	37,459,750	CDU/CSU	16,806,020	225	40·5	44·9
			SPD	17,175,169	230	41·4	45·8
			FDP	3,129,982	41	7·6	8·4

GREECE

Voting procedures. Party list system in electoral departments. Direct election, majority vote. Universal male suffrage. From 1926, proportional representation until 1928, and then again for the election of Sep 32 and the elections of Jan 36, Mar 46, Mar 50, Sep 51 and May 58 onwards. Vote extended to women in 1955.

	Electorate	Valid votes	Votes per party		Seats	% of electorate	% of votes
1926	1,567,378	958,392	Liberals	303,140	102	19·3	31·6
			Populists	194,243	60	12·4	20·3
			Freedom Party	151,044	51	9·6	15·8
1928	1,021,434	1.017,281	Liberals	477,502	178		46·9
			Pro-Liberals	74,976	25		2·5
			Workers and Agrarian	68,278	20		6·7
			Populists	243,543	19		23·9
1932	1,175,983	1,171,637	Liberals	391,521	98		33·4
			Populists	395,974	95		33·8
			Progressive	97,836	15		8·4
1933	1,146,943	1,141,331	Populists	434,550	118		38·1
			Liberals	379,968	80		33·3
1935	1,090,362	1.029,196	Populists } Nat. Radical	669,434	287		65·0
			Royalists	152,285	7		14·8
1936	1,278,085	1,274,002	Liberals	474,651	126		37·3
			Populists	281,597	72		22·1
			Populists and Rad. Union	253,384	60		19·9
1946	1,121,696	1,108,473	Nationalist (union of Populists, Nat. Lib., Reformist and others)	610,995	206		55·1
			Nat. Pol. Union (Venizelos Liberals, Soc. Dem., Nat. United Party and others)	213,721	68		19·3
			Liberals	159,525	48		14·4
1950	1,696,146	1,688,923	Populists	317,512	62		18·8
			Liberals	291,083	56		17·2
			Nat. Prog. Union	277,739	45		16·4
			Papandreou Party (ex-Soc. Dem.)	180,185	35		10·7
1951	2,224,246	1,708,904	Hellene Party	624,316	114	28·1	36·5
			Nat. Prog. Union	401,379	74	18·0	23·5
			Liberals	325,390	57	14·6	19·0
1952	2,123,150	1,600,172	Hellenes	783,541	247	36·9	49·2
			Nat. Prog. Union } Liberals	544,834	51	25·7	34·2
1956	4,507,907	3,364,361	Nat. Rad. Union	1,594,112	165	35·4	47·4
			Dem. Union (Populists, Liberals, Nat. Prog. Union, Agrarians and Centre)	1,620,007	132	35·9	48·2

	Electorate	Valid votes	Votes per party		Seats	% of electorate	% of votes
1958	5,119,148	3,847,785	Nat. Rad. Union	1,583,885	171	30·9	41·2
			United Democratic Left	939,902	79	18·4	24·4
			Liberals	795,445	36	15·5	20·7
1961		4,620,751	Nat. Rad. Union	2,347,824	176		50·8
			Centre Union } Progressives }	1,555,442	100		33·7
			Un. Dem. Left (under title Pan-democratic Agrarian Front)	675,867	24		14·6
1963	5,662,965	4,667,159	Centre Union	1,962,079	138	34·6	42·0
			Nat. Rad. Union	1,837,377	132	32·4	39·4
			Un. Dem. Left	669,267	28	11·8	14·3
1964	5,662,965	4,598,839	Centre Union	2,424,477	171	42·0	52·7
			Nat. Rad. Union } Progressives }	1,621,546	108	28·6	35·3
			Un. Dem. Left	542,865	21	9·5	11·8

HUNGARY

Before its extensive territorial reduction in 1918 the kingdom of Hungary formed part of the Austro-Hungarian empire. It had no codified written constitution. There was a bicameral parliament (*Országgyűles*), but only 6% of the population possessed the vote.

Towards the close of the war M. Károlyi's Party of Independence emerged on the political scene, standing for independence from Austria and unilateral withdrawal from hostilities. At a time of popular unrest Karolyi was appointed prime minister on 31 Oct 18, leading a coalition government of Party of Independence, Radicals and Social Democrats. On 13 Nov 18 King Charles IV renounced participation in affairs of state, and on 16 Nov 18 Hungary was proclaimed a Republic with Károlyi as provisional President (he became President on 11 Jan 19). Parliament was dissolved and replaced by a provisional unicameral National Assembly.

This government resigned on 22 Mar 19 in protest at Allied territorial demands, and was succeeded by a Soviet republic of Communists and Social Democrats led by Béla Kun. Elections to the Soviets were held on 17 Apr 19. The Communist régime was short-lived and harassed by hostilities with foreign invaders and native anti-Communist forces. Kun resigned on 1 Aug 19, and Romania occupied Budapest until M. Horthy entered on 16 Nov 19 at the head of an anti-Communist army.

At Allied insistence an election with universal secret suffrage was held on 25 Jan 20. The Christian Nationalists (government party) gained 77 seats, the Smallholders 49. The Social Democrats refused to take part in the election.

This government annulled all Károlyi's and Kun's legislation and re-established the former constitution. The link with Austria was dissolved. On 23 Mar 20 Hungary was proclaimed a kingdom again; Horthy had been chosen as regent on 1 Mar 20.

This government decreed a new electoral system. The upper house (House of Magnates) was re-established. Secret ballot was abolished except in towns (20% of constituencies were urban). Some 1·5m. lost the vote. Educational, property and residence qualifications were introduced. Men voted at 24, women at 30. Candidates had to be nominated by 10,000 electors. The National Assembly was to consist of 245 deputies.

On 7 Mar and 29 Oct 21 Charles IV made unsuccessful attempts to regain the throne.

At the elections of 28 May and 2 June 22 Smallholders and Christian Nationalists combined to form the Party of National Unity, which gained 143 seats. The opposition parties gained 78 (including 25 Social Democrats).

An electoral law of 11 Nov 26 gave definitive form to the House of Magnates, which was to consist of nominated members of the nobility and upper middle class, and other dignitaries. A small proportion of members were elected for ten-year terms.

1926   Party of National Unity, 171; Christian Social Union, 35; Social Democrats, 14; others, 25.

1931   Party of National Unity, 155; Christian Social Union, 32; Social Democrats, 14; Independent Smallholders, 11; independents, 21; others, 12.

1935   Party of National Unity, 170; Independent Smallholders, 23; Christian Social Union, 14; Social Democrats, 11.

By an electoral law of Dec 38 residential and educational qualifications were made stricter, and male voting age raised from 24 to 26. In order to vote women over 30 had to be self-supporting or the wives of electors. The number of deputies was raised to 260. 135 single-member constituencies were formed, election requirement being a simple majority over 40%. Multi-member constituencies elected the remainder on a proportional representation scheme.

Secret ballot was introduced in May 39, and many Jews were disfranchised.

1939   Party of Hungarian Life (formerly Party of National Unity) in alliance, 186; Christian Union, 3; Arrow Cross (fascists), 29; Independent Smallholders, 14; National Social Front Union, 5; Citizens' Freedom Party, 5; Social Democrats, 5; Racialists, 4; National Front, 3; Christian National Social Front, 3; People's Will, 1; Independents, 2.

During the war an Independence Front began to take shape of Social Democrats, crypto-Communists, Smallholders, National Peasants and Legitimists.

With the Soviet invasion a provisional government was set up at Debrecen on 21 Dec 44, which ultimately consisted of 127 Communists, 123 Smallholders, 94 Social Democrats, 63 Trade Unionists, 39 National Peasants, 22 Democrats and 30 independents.

By an electoral law of 19 Sep 45 universal secret suffrage at 20 was introduced.

		Votes	Seats
1945	Smallholders	2,688,161	245
	Social Democrats	821,566	69
	Communists	800,257	70
	National Peasants	322,988	23
	Democrats	78,522	2
			409

1947   Electorate: 5,407,893.   Voted: 4,996,100 (93%).   Seats 411.

Government bloc	Votes	Seats
Communists	1,082,597	100
Smallholders	757,821	68
Social Democrats	732,178	67
National Peasants	435,170	36
	3,007,027	271

Opposition	Votes	Seats
Popular Democrats	805,450	60
Hungarian Independence Party	718,193	49
Independent Democrats	256,396	18
Radicals	93,270	6
Christian Women's union	67,792	4
Citizen Democrats	48,055	3
	1,989,156	140

During the next two years the opposition parties were eliminated or amalgamated into the People's Front. The Social Democrats merged into the Communists in June 48. At the election of 15 May 49 candidates were presented on a single list, the People's Front. Electorate: 6,053,972. Voted: 5,730,519 (94·6%). For the People's Front: 5,478,515 (95·6%).

A new constitution of Soviet type was promulgated on 18 Aug 49. Hungary was proclaimed a 'People's Republic'. Voting age was lowered to 18. The National Assembly was to be elected every four years by universal secret suffrage.

At the election of 17 May 53 there was a single list of People's Front. Electorate: 6,501,869. Voted: 6,370,519 (98%). Votes for People's Front: 6,256,653 (98·2%).

On 27 Oct 56 there was a major reorganization of the government in response to armed insurrection: independent Smallholders and National Peasants were co-opted in. Revolutionary councils sprang up demanding a free general election. On 30 Oct 56 I. Nagy proclaimed the restoration of multi-party government. On 3 Nov 56 the government was reorganized as a coalition of Communists, Smallholders, National Peasants and Social Democrats.

This government was overthrown by armed Soviet intervention and a 'Revolutionary Worker-Peasant government' set up under J. Kádár.

At the election of 16 Nov 58, 6,493,680 voted (98·4% of electorate). For People's Patriotic Front: 6,431,832 (99·6%). There were 338 candidates for 338 seats.

At the election of 24 Feb 63 the electorate was 7,114,855. Voted: 6,915,644 (97·2%). Voted for the single list of People's Patriotic Front 6,813,058 (98·9%). 340 deputies elected.

On 11 Nov 66 an electoral law brought an end to the strict rigidity of the one seat – one candidate system by replacing the 20 multi-seat mega-constituencies by 349 single-member constituencies. All candidates remained nominees of the People's Patriotic Front, but it became possible for more than one candidate to contest a single seat.

In the election of 19 Mar 67 this happened in nine constituencies. None of the nine challengers were elected. 7,131,151 votes were cast (99·7% of the electorate), and 98·8% of these were for the People's Patriotic Front candidates.

In Oct 70 another electoral law liberalized the position further by introducing the participation of the ordinary citizenry in the nomination of candidates. In the election of 25 Apr 70 49 seats were contested by more than one candidate. Electorate: 7,432,420. Voted: 7,334,918 (98·7%). Voted for the People's Patriotic Front: 7,258,121 (98·9%). 352 deputies were elected.

ICELAND

Voting procedures. From 1915–20, the Althing had 40 members directly elected, 6 proportionally and 34 by majority. Majority elections were in 25 constituencies, 9 of them two-member, the rest single. Suffrage for the election of 34 members, all men and women property-holders over 25; for the 6, all those over 35. From 1920 onwards the Althing had additional members, including some elected by direct proportional election in Reykjavic. From 1934, suffrage extended to all men and women over 21 'in charge of their own finances and properties'.

	Electorate	Valid votes	Votes per party		Seats	% of electorate	% of votes
1923	43,932	30,362	Citizens Party	16,272	21	37·0	53·6
			Progressives	8,062	13	18·4	26·6
			Soc. Dems.	4,912	1	11·2	16·2
1927	46,047	32,007	Progressives	9,532	17	20·7	29·8
			Liberals ⎫	15,474	13	4·0	5·8
			Conservatives ⎭			29·6	42·0
			Soc. Dem.	6,097	4	13·2	19·1
1931	50,617	38,543	Progressives	13,844	21	27·3	35·9
			Independence	16,891	12	33·4	43·8
1933	52,465	35,678	Independence	17,131	17	32·7	48·0
			Progressives	8,530	14	16·3	23·9
1934	64,338	51,928	Independence	21,974	20	34·1	42·3
			Progressives	11,377	15	17·7	21·9
			Soc. Dem.	11,269	10	17·5	21·7
1937	67,195	58,413	Progressives	14,556	19	21·7	24·9
			Independence	24,132	17	35·9	41·3
			Soc. Dem.	11.084	8	16·5	19·0
1942(1)	73,440	58,131	Progressives	16,033	20	21·8	27·6
			Independence	22,975	17	31·3	39·5
			United Soc.	11,059	10	15·0	18·5
1942(2)	73,560	59,668	Independence	23,001	20	31·3	38·5
			Progressives	15,869	15	21·6	26·6
			United Soc.	11,059	10	15·0	18·5
1946	77,670	66,913	Independence	26,428	20	34·0	39·4
			Progressives	15,429	13	19·9	23·1
			United Soc.	13,049	10	16·8	19·5
			Soc. Dem.	11,914	9	15·3	17·8
1949	82,481	72,219	Independence	28,546	19	34·5	39·5
			Progressives	17,659	17	21·4	24·5
			United Soc.	14,077	9	17·0	19·5
1953	87,601	77,410	Independence	28,738	21	32·8	37·1
			Progressives	16,959	16	19·3	21·9
			United Soc.	12,422	7	14·2	16·1
1956	91,618	82,670	Independence	35,027	19	38·2	42·4
			Progressives	12,925	17	14·1	15·6
			People's Un.	15,859	8	17·3	19·2
			Soc. Dem.	15,153	8	16·5	18·3
1959(1)	95,050	84,788	Independence	36,029	20	37·9	42·5
			Progressives	23,061	19	24·2	27·2
			People's Un.	12,929	7	13·6	15·3
1959(2)	95,637	85,095	Independence	33,800	24	35·2	39·7
			Progressives	21,882	17	22·8	25·7
			People's Un.	13,621	10	14·2	16·0
			Soc. Dem.	12,909	9	13·4	15·2

	Electorate	Valid votes	Votes per party		Seats	% of electorate	% of votes
1963	99,798	89,352	Independence	37,021	24	37·0	41·4
			Progressives	25,217	19	25·2	28·2
			People's Un.	14,274	9	14·3	16·0
1967	107,101	96,090	Independence	36,036	23	33·6	37·5
			Progressives	27,029	18	25·2	28·1
			People's Un.	13,403	9	12·5	13·9
			Soc. Dem.	15,059	9	14·1	15·7
1971	118,289	105,395	Independence	38,170	22	32·3	36·2
			Progressives	26,645	17	22·5	25·3
			People's Un.	18,055	10	15·3	17·1
			Soc. Dem.	11,020	6	9·3	10·5

IRISH REPUBLIC

Voting procedures. From 1918–21, single-member constituencies, spot voting and plurality counting. From 1921, multi-member constituencies with preferential voting and quota counting. Suffrage for men of 21 and over, and women of 30 and over, until 1923 when the age limit for both was 21. From 1918–23, University graduates and owners of businesses had extra votes.

	Electorate	Valid votes	Votes per party		Seats	% of electorate	% of votes
1918	1,936,673	1,046,541	Sinn Fein	496,961	73	—	47·5
			Unionists	298,726	26	—	28·5
			Nationalists	233,690	6		22·3
1921	—	—	Sinn Fein	—	124	—	—
			Unionists	—	4		

(Note: This was not a normal election; no poll took place; all borough and county seats were taken by Sinn Fein and the Unionists were returned for Dublin University.)

1922	1.026,289	627,623	Pro-Treaty	245,336	58	—	39·1
	(first preference)		Anti-Treaty	134,801	36	—	21·5
			Labour	132,511	17		21·1

(Note: Pro- and Anti-Treaty parties were the result of the division of Sinn Fein.)

1923	1,785,436	1,052,495	Fine Gael	409,184	63	22·9	38·9
			Fianna Fail	291,191	44	16·3	27·7
			Labour	130,659	16	7·3	12·4
1927(1)	1,730,426	1,146,460	Fine Gael	314,711	46	18·2	27·5
			Fianna Fail	299,476	44	17·3	26·1
			Labour	159,046	23	9·2	13·9
1927(2)	1,728,340	1,170,856	Fine Gael	453,013	61	26·2	38·7
			Fianna Fail	411,833	57	23·8	35·2
			Labour	111,287	13	6·4	9·5
1932	1,601,933	1,274,026	Fianna Fail	566,498	72	33·5	44·5
			Fine Gael	449,506	56	26·6	35·3
			Independents	106,466	12	6·3	8·4
			Labour	114,163	9	6·7	9·0
1933	1,724,420	1,386,558	Fianna Fail	689,054	76	40·0	49·7
			Fine Gael	422,495	48	24·5	30·5
			Labour	88,347	9	5·1	6·4

	Electorate	Valid votes	Votes per party		Seats	% of electorate	% of votes
1937	1,775,055	1,324,449	Fianna Fail	599,040	68	33·7	45·2
			Fine Gael	461,171	48	26·0	34·8
			Labour	147,728	15	8·3	11·2
1938	1,697,323	1,286,259	Fianna Fail	667,996	76	39·4	51·9
			Fine Gael	428,633	45	25·3	33·3
			Labour	140,099	9	8·3	10·9
1943	1,816,142	1,331,709	Fianna Fail	557,525	66	30·7	41·9
			Fine Gael	307,499	32	16·9	23·1
			Labour	214,743	17	11·8	16·1
1944	1,776,850	1,217,349	Fianna Fail	595,259	75	33·5	48·9
			Fine Gael	249,329	30	14·0	20·5
			Labour	140,245	12	7·9	11·5
1948	1,800,210	1,323,443	Fianna Fail	553,914	67	30·8	41·9
			Fine Gael	262,393	31	14·6	19·8
			Labour	150,229	19	8·3	11·4
1951	1,785,144	1,331,573	Fianna Fail	161,212	68	34·5	46·3
			Fine Gael	342,922	40	19·2	25·8
			Labour	151,828	16	8·5	11·4
1954	1,763,209	1,335,202	Fianna Fail	578,960	65	32·8	43·4
			Fine Gael	427,031	50	24·2	32·0
			Labour	163,982	18	9·3	12·3
1957	1,738,278	1,227,019	Fianna Fail	592,994	78	34·1	48·3
			Fine Gael	326,699	40	18·8	26·6
			Labour	111,747	11	6·4	9·1
1961	1,670,860	1,168,404	Fianna Fail	512,073	70	30·6	43·8
			Fine Gael	374,099	47	22·4	32·0
			Labour	139,822	16	8·4	12·0
1965	1,683,019	1,253,122	Fianna Fail	597,414	72	35·4	47·7
			Fine Gael	427,081	47	25·4	34·1
			Labour	192,740	22	11·5	15·4
1969	1,735,388	1,318,953	Fianna Fail	602,234	75	34·7	45·7
			Fine Gael	449,749	50	25·9	34·1
			Labour	224,498	18	12·9	17·0

ITALY

The elections of 1919 and 1921 were fought on adult male suffrage and the
d'Hondt system of proportional representation. The election of 1924 was not
a free election because of Fascist intimidation. After 1945, the new Constitution provided for a bicameral Parliament, with a minimum voting age of 21.
Deputies are chosen by proportional representation using the *Imperiali* system.

	Electorate	Valid votes	Votes per party		Seats	% of electorate	% of votes
1919	10,239,326	5,684,833	Socialist	1,834,792	156	17·9	32·3
			Popular	1,167,354	100	11·4	20·5
			Centre coalition	904,195	96	8·9	15·9
			Democrats	622,310	60	6·1	10·9
1921	11,447,210	6,608,141	Socialist	1,631,435	123	14·2	24·7
			Popular	1,377,008	108	12·0	20·4
			Nat. Bloc.	1,260,007	105	11·0	19·1
			Lib. Dem.	684,855	68	5·6	10·4
1924	11,939,452	7,165,502	Fascist	4,671,550	375	39·1	65·3
			Popular	645,789	39	5·4	9·0
1946	28,005,449	23,010,479	Chris. Dem.	8,101,004	207	28·9	35·2
			Socialist	4,758,129	115	16·9	20·7
			Communist	4,356,686	104	15·5	18·9
1948	29,117,554	26,268,912	Chris. Dem.	12,741,299	305	43·8	48·5
			Communist }[1] Socialist }	8,137,047	183	27·9	31·0
1953	30,280,342	27,092,743	Chris. Dem.	10,864,282	263	35·9	40·1
			Communist	6,121,922	143	20·2	22·6
			Socialist	3,441,305	75	11·4	12·7
			Monarchist	1,855,843	30	6·1	6·9
1958	32,446,892	29,560,386	Chris. Dem.	12,520,556	273	38·6	42·4
			Communist	6,704,763	140	20·7	22·7
			Socialist	4,206,777	84	13·0	14·2
1963	34,200,589	30,752,871	Chris. Dem.	11,763,418	260	34·4	38·3
			Communist	7,763,854	166	22·7	25·3
			Socialist	4,251,966	87	12·4	13·8
1968	35,566,681	31,803,253	Chris. Dem.	12,441,553	266	34·0	39·1
			Communist	8,557,404	177	24·1	26·9
			Socialist	4,605,832	91	12·9	14·5
1972	37,039,769	33,384,492	Chris. Dem.	12,943,675	267	34·9	38·8
			Communist	9,085,927	179	24·5	27·2
			Socialist	4,925,700	89	13·3	14·7

[1] Under the name Democratic Popular Front

LATVIA

A Constituent Assembly in May 1920 established a parliament (*Saeima*) of
100 deputies to be elected every three years. Elections were held in 1922,
1925, 1928 and 1931. The system favoured a proliferation of Parties: 22 in
1922; 27 in 1925; 25 in 1928 and 24 in 1931. The more numerous parties
were, from right to left: Farmers' Union; Catholics; Democratic Centre; New
Settlers; Right-wing Socialists; Social Democrats. The Communist Party was
illegal, but ran as the Workers' Bloc in 1931, gaining seven seats. The Social
Democrats had 30 deputies in each government, except that of 1931, when

they had 22. There were Jewish, Polish, Russian and German national minority parties, and a fascist party, Thunder Cross (*Perkonkrusts*).

On 15 May 32 Ulmanis assumed dictatorial powers by dismissing the Saeima and prohibiting all party political activity.

The country was occupied by Soviet troops on 16 June 40 and an election was held on 14 and 15 July 40. The resultant People's *Saeima* voted unanimously for incorporation into the USSR.

LITHUANIA

On 22 Sep 17 a congress of 214 Lithuanian delegates elected a 20-strong council (*Taryba*) which proclaimed independence and organized elections for a Constituent Assembly. These were held by universal suffrage on the proportional representation system on 15 May 20. One representative stood for 15,000 inhabitants. There were 112 seats in the Constituent Assembly, distributed as follows: Christian Democrats, 59; Social Populist Democrats, 29; Social Democrats, 13; Jews, 6; Poles, 3; Independents, 2.

This enacted that a parliament (*Semias*) of 80 was to be elected every three years by universal suffrage on the proportional representation system, one deputy representing 25,000 electors.

At the elections of 10 Oct 22 the results were: Christian Democrats (including the Farmers' Union and the Workers' Federation), 38; Social Populist Democrats, 19; Social Democrats, 11; Workers' Party, 5; Jews, 3; Poles, 2. A. Stulginskis was elected President.

A further election was held on 5 June 23: Christian Democrats, 40; Social Populist Democrats, 16; Social Democrats, 8; Jews, 5; Poles, 5; Germans, 2; Russians, 2.

Elections 8 and 10 May 26: Christian Democrats, 30; Socialist Populist Democrats, 22; Social Democrats, 15; Poles, 4; Jews, 3; Germans, 1; and from Memel (Klaipeda) Agrarians, 3; People's Party, 2.

By a *coup d'état* of 17 Dec 26 A. Smetona assumed dictatorial powers as President, and parliamentary government lapsed.

THE NETHERLANDS

Voting procedures. Direct proportional elections on the party list system. Elections to 100 seats, the rest allocated according to the greatest remainder vote. Suffrage for men over 25, until 1922 when it was extended to women the same age. In 1946, extended to all citizens 23 and over and in 1967 all citizens over 21.

	Electorate	Valid votes	Votes per party		Seats	% of electorate	% of votes
1918	1,517,380	1,344,209	RKS	402,908	30	26·6	30·0
			S-DA-P	296,145	22	19·5	22·0
			PvV	202,972	15	13·4	15·1
			ARP	179,523	13	11·8	13·4

	Electorate	Valid votes	Votes per party		Seats	% of electorate	% of votes
1922	3,299,672	2,929,569	RKS	874,745	32	26·5	29·9
			S-DA-P	567,769	20	17·2	19·4
			ARP	402,277	16	12·2	13·7
1925	3,543,058	3,085,862	RKS	883,333	30	24·9	28·6
			S-DA-P	706,689	24	20·0	22·9
			ARP	377,426	13	10·6	12·2
1929	3,821,612	3,379,503	RKS	1,001,589	30	26·2	29·6
			S-DA-P	804,714	24	21·0	23·9
			ARP	391,832	12	10·3	11·6
			CHU	354,548	11	9·3	10·5
1933	4,126,490	3,721,828	RKS	1,037,364	28	25·1	27·9
			S-DA-P	798,632	22	19·4	21·5
			ARP	499,892	14	12·1	13·4
1937	4,462,859	4,058,077	RKS	1,170,431	31	26·2	28·8
			S-DA-P	890,661	23	20·0	22·0
			ARP	665,501	17	14·9	16·4
1946	5,275,888	4,760,711	KV	1,466,582	32	27·8	30·8
			PvA	1,347,940	29	25·5	28·3
			ARP	614,201	13	11·6	12·9
1948	5,433,663	4,932,959	KV	1,531,154	32	28·2	31·0
			PvA	1,263,058	27	23·2	25·6
			ARP	651,612	13	12·0	13·2
1952	5,792,679	5,335,745	KV	1,529,508	30	26·4	28·7
			PvA	1,545,867	30	26·7	29·0
			ARP	603,329	12	10·4	11·3
1956	6,125,210	5,727,742	PvA	1,872,209	50	30·6	32·7
			KV	1,529,508	49	29·6	31·7
			ARP	567,535	15	9·3	9·9
1959	6,427,865	6,258,521	KV	1,895,914	49	29·5	31·6
			PvA	1,821,825	48	28·3	30·3
			VVD	732,658	19	11·4	12·2
			ARP	563,091	14	8·8	9·4
1963	6,748,611	6,258,521	KV	1,993,352	50	29·6	31·9
			PvA	1,753,084	43	26·0	28·0
			VVD	643,839	16	9·5	10·3
			ARP	545,836	13	8·0	8·7
			CHU	536,801	13	8·0	8·6
1967	7,452,776	6,878,030	KV	1,822,904	42	24·4	26·5
			PvA	1,620,112	37	21·4	23·5
			VVD	738,202	17	9·9	10·7
			ARP	681,060	15	9·1	9·9
1971	8,048,726	6,318,152	KV	1,379,672	35	17·1	21·8
			PvA	1,554,280	39	19·3	24·6
			VVD	653,370	16	8·1	10·3
			ARP	542,742	13	6·7	8·6
1972	8,915,359	7,394,045	KV	1,305,401	27	14·6	17·7
			PvA	2,021,454	43	22·7	27·3
			VVD	1,068,375	22	12·0	14·4
			ARP	653,609	14	7·3	8·8

NORWAY

Voting procedures. Direct proportional elections in multi-member constituencies. Suffrage for men and women over 23 until 1949, when it was extended to men and women over 21.

	Electorate	Valid votes	Votes per party		Seats	% of electorate	% of votes
1918	1,186,602	662,521	Left	187,657	51	15·8	28·3
			Right	101,325	50	17·0	30·4
			Labour	209,560	18	17·7	31·6
1921	1,351,183	904,699	Right	301,372	57	22·3	33·3
			Left	181,989	37	13·5	20·1
			Labour	192,616	29	14·3	21·3
			Agrarian	18,657	17	8·8	13·1
1924	1,412,441	973,941	Right	316,846	54	22·4	32·5
			Left	180,979	34	12·8	18·6
			Labour	179,567	24	12·7	18·4
			Agrarian	131,706	22	9·3	13·5
1927	1,484,409	999,297	Labour	388,106	59	24·8	36·8
			Conservative	240,091	30	16·2	24·0
			Liberal	172,568	30	11·6	17·3
			Agrarian	149,026	26	10·0	14·9
1930	1,550,077	1,194,755	Labour	374,854	47	24·2	31·4
			Conservative	327,731	41	21·1	21·1
			Liberal	241,355	33	15·6	20·2
			Agrarian	190,220	25	12·3	15·9
1933	1,643,498	1,248,686	Labour	500,526	69	30·5	40·1
			Conservative	252,506	30	15·4	20·2
			Liberal	213,153	24	13·0	17·1
			Agrarian	173,634	23	10·6	13·9
1936	1,741,905	1,455,238	Labour	618,616	70	35·5	42·5
			Conservative	310,324	36	17·8	21·3
			Liberal	232,784	23	13·4	16·0
			Agrarian	168,038	18	9·6	11·6
1945	1,961,977	1,485,225	Labour	609,348	76	31·1	41·0
			Conservative	252,608	25	12·9	17·0
			Liberal	204,852	20	10·4	13·8
1949	2,159,065	1,758,366	Labour	803,471	85	37·2	45·7
			Conservative	311,819	23	14·4	17·7
			Liberal	235,876	21	10·9	13·4
1953	2,256,799	1,779,831	Labour	830,448	77	36·8	46·7
			Conservative	344,067	27	14·8	18·8
			Liberal	177,662	15	7·9	10·0
			Chr. People's	186,627	14	8·3	10·5
			Agrarian	160,583	14	7·1	9·0
1957	2,298,376	1,791,128	Labour	865,675	78	37·7	48·3
			Conservative	338,651	29	14·7	18·9
			Liberal	173,525	15	7·5	9·7
			Agrarian	166,757	15	7·3	9·3

	Electorate	Valid votes	Votes per party		Seats	% of electorate	% of votes
1961	2,340,495	1,840,206	Labour	860,526	74	36·8	46·8
			Conservative	368,340	29	14·7	20·0
			Agrarian	170,645	16	7·3	9·3
			Chr. People's	176,896	15	7·6	9·6
1965	2,406,866	2,047,394	Labour	883,320	68	36·7	43·1
			Conservative	432,025	31	18·0	21·1
			Liberal	211,853	18	8·9	10·4
			Agrarian	202,396	18	8·5	9·9
1969	2,579,566	2,158,712	Labour	1,000,348	74	38·9	46·5
			Conservative	406,209	13	15·7	18·8
			Liberal	202,553	13	7·9	9·4
			Agrarian	194,128	20	7·5	9·0

POLAND

J. Piłsudski proclaimed independence on 10 Nov 18 and appointed governments on 18 Nov 18 and 16 Jan 19.

Elections to the Sejm (parliament) were held in non-occupied Poland on 26 Jan 19 and supplemented by by-elections in Nov. There were 394 deputies from 14 parties including:

National Democrats and allies (dubbed 'Endecja' from the initials)	140 (of these 116 were National Democrats, i.e. 37% of all deputies)
Polish Peasant Party 'Liberation' (i.e. left-wing)	71
Polish Peasant Party 'Piast' (i.e. right-wing)	46
Polish Socialist Party	35
National Workers' Party	32
National minority parties	13

A constitution was promulgated on 17 Mar 21 by which a bicameral parliament was set up, to be elected by universal suffrage every five years by proportional representation, consisting of a Senate of 111 senators and the Sejm of 444 deputies.

At the elections of 5 and 12 Nov 22 the electorate was 13,109,793 of whom 8,760,195 (67%) voted. Representatives of 15 parties were elected to the Sejm, including:

	Votes	(%)	Seats
Christian League of National Union	2,551,000	29·1	169
Polish Peasant Party 'Piast'	1,150,000	13·1	70
Polish Peasant Party 'Liberation'	963,000	11	49

	Votes	(%)	Seats
Polish Socialist Party	906,000	10·3	41
National Workers' Party	474,000	5·4	18
Polish Centre	260,000	3	6
Communist Party	121,000	1·4	2
National minority parties	1,963,000	22·4	86

On 14 May 26 Piłsudski staged a *coup d'état* and issued a constitution in June which restricted the powers of the Sejm.

At the elections of 4 Mar 28 the electorate was 15m. and 11,408,218 voted.

	Votes	Seats
Non-party pro-Piłsudski Bloc (BBWR)	2,399,032	130
Polish Peasant Party 'Liberation'		66
Polish Socialist Party	1,148,279	63
People's Party (SN; formerly National Democrats)	925,744	37
Polish Peasant Party 'Piast'		21
Christian Democratic Party		19
National Workers' Party		14
Communist Party (illegal, but running under the name 'Union of Town and Country Proletariat')	940,000	8
National minority parties		86

This Sejm was dissolved on 30 Aug 30.

During the campaign before the elections of 16 and 23 Nov 30 opposition politicians were imprisoned.

The electorate was 15,520,342, of whom 13,078,682 voted. 372 deputies were elected to the *Sejm*, and the number was made up to 444 by allotments according to proportional representation:

	Votes	Seats
Non-party pro-Piłsudski Bloc (BBWR)	5,292,725	247
People's Party (SN)	1,455,399	62
6-Party Centre-Left coalition	1,907,380	
Polish Peasant Party 'Liberation'		33
Polish Socialist Party		24
Christian Democrats		15
Polish Peasant Party 'Piast'		15
National Workers' Party		10
Communist Party		5
National minority parties		33

A new constitution was promulgated on 23 Apr 35. The Sejm was reduced to 208 deputies, elected by universal suffrage at 24 years. The Senate was reduced to 96, of whom one-third were appointed by the President and the remainder elected by a college of 300,000. Methods of election were not changed but district electoral assemblies acquired a decisive role in the designation of candidates.

All political parties boycotted the elections of 8 and 15 Sep 35. The electorate was 16,332,100, of whom according to the government's own figures only 45·9% voted. (7,512,102). 153 BBWR members were returned to the Sejm and 22 members of national minority groups.

President Móscicki dissolved Sejm and Senate on 22 Sep 35.

All political parties abstained from the elections of 6 and 13 Nov 38. The turn-out was 67·4%. 161 members of the non-party Camp of National Unity (OZN) were returned to the Sejm.

The liberation of part of Poland from German occupation by Soviet forces enabled the Polish Committee of National Liberation (PKWN) to be set up on 21 July 44, proclaiming itself the sole legal Polish executive power. It was composed of Communists, left-wing socialists, left-wing peasants and Democratic party representatives. It became the provisional government on 31 Dec 44. At the Yalta conference (Feb 45), it was agreed that a Provisional Government of National Unity should be formed based on this government, and this was done on 28 June 45. It contained Communists (PPR,, i.e. Polish Workers' Party) and representatives of the Polish Socialist Party (PPS), and the Polish Peasant (PSL), Democratic (SD) and Christian Democratic Labour (SP) parties.

A referendum was held on 30 June 46, at which the electorate were asked to approve (1) the abolition of the Senate, (2) basic nationalization and land reform, (3) the fixing of Poland's borders on the Baltic and the Oder-Neisse line. The turn-out was 80·8% (11,530,551), and affirmative answers were recorded as follows: (1) 68%, (2) 77·2%, (3) 91·4%.

An electoral law of Sep 46 disfranchised collaborators: approximately 1m. people lost their vote in this way.

During the elections of 19 Jan 47 some 12·7m. votes were cast, of which 11,244,873 were valid (89·19% of electorate voted). The Communists together with the Polish Socialist, Peasant and Democratic parties stood as the Democratic Bloc, polling 9m. votes (80·1% of the vote) and gaining 392 seats in the Sejm. Other parties:

	Votes %	Seats
Polish Peasant Party	10·3	27
Christian Labour Party (SP)	4·7	15
Peasant Party 'Liberation'		7
Catholic independents		3

On 19 Feb 47 the Sejm passed an interim constitution, which became known as the 'Little Constitution'. A permanent constitution was passed on 22

July 52. This gives the ground plan of the electoral provisions now extant, although these have been liberalized by later amendments. The Sejm is elected every four years by all citizens over 18. Citizens may stand as candidates at 21. There is one deputy per 60,000 inhabitants. Only political and social organizations (trade unions, youth and cultural organizations) may nominate candidates, who must be on the single list of the National Unity Front (FJN), which groups three parties: Communist (PZPR), United Peasant (ZSL) and Democratic (SD).

The office of President was abolished. The Chairman of the Council of State would henceforth be head of state.

At the elections of 26 Oct 52 the number of candidates was the same as the number of seats. The electorate was 16,305,891: votes cast, 15,495,815. The single list of National Front candidates gained 99·8% of valid votes, and took up seats in the Sejm:

	Seats
Communist Party (PZPR)	273
United Peasant Party (ZSL)	90
Democratic Party (SD)	25
Independents	37
	425

By an electoral law of 24 Oct 56 the single list of candidates was allowed to include up to two-thirds more candidates than seats. All electors were to make their vote behind curtains. Negative votes were to be recorded by crossing out the candidates' names.

At the elections of 20 Jan 57 there were 717 candidates (51% of whom were Communists) for 459 seats. Turn-out was 94·14% (16, 892,213 votes were cast from an electorate of 17,944,081). 280,002 votes (1·6% of votes) were made against National Front candidates. Seats:

	Seats
Communists (PZPR)	239
United Peasant Party (ZSL)	118
Democratic Party (SD)	39
Independents (including 12 Catholics,	63
9 of whom from the Znak group)	459

An electoral law of 22 Dec 60 reduced the ratio of candidates to seats.

At the elections of 16 Apr 61 there were 616 candidates for 460 seats. The turn-out was 94·83%. There were 292,009 votes against the National Front list (1·57% of votes).

	Seats
Communists (PZPR)	256
United Peasant Party (ZSL)	117
Democratic Party (SD)	39
Independents (including 5 Catholics of the Znak group)	48

After the elections of 30 May 65, 1 June 69 and 19 Mar 72 the parties' positions were the same.

	Seats
Communists (PZPR)	255
United Peasant Party (ZSL)	117
Democratic Party (SD)	39
Independents (including 14 Catholics)	49
	460

	1965	1969	1972
Electorate	19,645,893	21,148,879	21,854,481
Turn-out	96·62%	97·61%	97·94%
Votes against	226,324	161,569	. .
National Front List	(1·15% of votes)	(0·78% of votes)	. .

DANZIG

Danzig was created a Free City by the Versailles treaty on 28 June 19, under a League of Nations High Commissioner and in customs union with Poland. It was incorporated into Germany during World War II, and into Poland (as Gdańsk) after it.

The constitution provided for a Senate of 20 plus a President and Vice-President elected by the People's Assembly for four years. The President was head of state: 1918, H. Sahm; 1931, E. Ziehm; 1933, H. Rauschning; 1934, A. Greiser. The Assembly (*Volkstag*) of 120 (reduced to 72 in 1930) was elected by universal secret suffrage at 20 for four-year terms on a proportional representation system.

Election 16 May 20. Social Democrats, 37 seats; German Nationalists, 34; Centre (Catholics), 17; German Democrats, 10; Poles, 7; Populists, 6; National Liberals, 3; German Liberals, 3; Communists, 3.

Election 9 Nov 23. Social Democrats, 30; German Nationalists, 26; Centre (Catholics), 15; Communists, 11; German Social Party, 7 (10,301 votes; the first appearance of a racialist party); Populists, 6; German Democrats, 5; German Liberals, 5; Poles, 5; National Liberals, 4; Middle-class Federation, 2; Independents, 4.

Election 13 Nov 27. Social Democrats, 42; German Nationalists, 25; Centre (Catholics), 18; Communists, 8; Populists, 5; National Liberals, 5;

German Liberals, 4; Middle-class Federation, 3; Poles, 3; German Social Party, 1 (2,130 votes); Nazis, 1 (1,483 votes).

Elections

	16 Nov 30		28 May 33		7 Apr 35	
	Votes	*Seats*	*Votes*	*Seats*	*Votes*	*Seats*
Social Democrats	49,965	19	38,703	13	37,804	14
Nazis	32,457	12	107,335	38	128,619	40
Centre (Catholics)	30,232	11	31,339	10	31,576	11
German Nationalists	25,938	10	13,595	4	9,822	3
Communists	20,194	7	44,766	5	7,935	2
Poles	6,377	2	6,738	2	8,311	2
People's Union		3				
Populists		2				
National Liberals		2				
Middle-class Federation		2				
German Liberals		1				
Independent		1				

The 1935 election was fought for a two-thirds majority to enable the Nazis to ask the League of Nations to revise the constitution. The Polish government and the opposition parties alleged terror and unlawful practices by the Nazis. The Danzig Court found for some illegality, and reduced the Nazi vote and number of seats as first officially proclaimed. The final figures are given above.

By dissolutions and amalgamations the Nazis became supreme in the Assembly by 1939, except for the two Polish deputies. On 22 Mar 39 it was declared that the elections then due were 'unnecessary' and would not be held.

PORTUGAL

On 19 Mar 33, the *Estado Novo* constitution (providing for an authoritarian Republic on a corporative basis) was voted upon and adopted. This constitution provides for a President, to be elected for seven years by direct suffrage by male Portuguese citizens, of age or emancipated, able to read or write, and those unable to read or write, being taxpayers to the state or administrative corporations for direct taxes, and Portuguese citizens, females, of age or emancipated, with a special, secondary school, or university diploma; and for a National Assembly (one chamber) of 90 deputies elected for four years by direct suffrage. In the two elections for the National Assembly (1934 and 1938) the only lists presented were those organized by the National Union, an association legally recognized, but without the character of a party, whose aim is to defend the principles contained in the constitution. The electoral law permits, however, the presentation of more than one list of the deputies to be elected.

At the elections of 8 Nov 53 the União Nacional (National Union) obtained all 120 seats; the 28 opposition candidates were defeated. At subsequent elections only government candidates stood for re-election.

ROMANIA

1919	Chamber of Deputies: 568 of which:	
	National Party of Transylvania	199
	Peasants	130
	National Liberals	120
	Nationalists and Democrats	27
	Conservative Democrats	16

In 1920 the number of deputies was reduced to 369 and conducted under a proportional representation.

1920	People's Party	224
	Peasants	40
	National Party of Transylvania	30
	Socialists	19
	National Liberals	17
	Germans	8
1922	National Liberals	227
	Peasants and National Party of Transylvania	62
	People's Party	11
	Conservative Democrats	8
	Germans	8
	Social Democrats	1
	Jews	1

Opposition parties challenged validity of this election and withdrew.

A new constitution of 23 Mar 23 reorganized the Senate to consist of 249 seats elected on a more restricted suffrage (over 40-year-olds and members of the ruling élite). The Chamber of Deputies was to be elected by universal secret suffrage at 21 years of age on a constituency basis.

By an electoral law of 1926 that party which obtained 40% of the vote was awarded 50% of the seats plus a proportionate share of the seats remaining.

Party	Number of votes	% of votes	Seats gained
1926 Electorate: 3,496,814, of which 75% voted.			
National Liberals	192,309	7	16
National Peasants	727,202	28	69
People's Party	1,306,100	52	292
Christian League of National Defence	124,778	5	10

Party	Number of votes	% of votes	Seats gained
1927 The electorate was 3,586,086, of which 77% voted.			
National Liberals } Peasants }	1,704,435	62	{ 298 { 22
National Peasants	610,149	22	54
Hungarians	173,517	6	15
1928 The electorate was 3,671,352, of which 77·4% voted.			
National Peasants	2,228,922	78	348
National Liberals	185,939	7	13
People's Party	70,490	2	5
Peasants	70,506	2	5
Hungarians	172,699	6	16
1931 The electorate was 4,038,464, of which 72·5% voted.			
National Union	1,389,901	48	289
National Peasants	438,747	15	30
National Liberals (G. Brătianu)	173,586	6	12
People's Party	141,141	5	10
Hungarians	139,003	5	10
Christian League of National Defence	113,863	4	8
Peasant Party	100,682	3	7
Social Democrats	94,957	3	6
Peasant Democrats Union in alliance with League against Usury	80,570	3	6
Labour and Peasant Group	73,716	3	5
Jews	64,193	2	4
1932 The electorate was 4,220,731, of which 70·8% voted.			
National Peasants	1,203,700	41	274
National Liberals (Duca)	407,023	14	28
National Liberals (Brătianu)	195,048	7	14
Peasants	170,860	6	12
Christian League of National Defence	159,071	5	11
Hungarians	141,894	5	14
National Agrarians	108,857	4	8
Social Democrats	101,068	3	7
Iron Guard	70,674	2	5
National Union	68,116	2	5
Jews	67,582	2	5
People's Party	64,525	2	4

Party	Number of votes	% of votes	Seats gained
1933 The electorate was 4,380,354, of which 68% voted.			
National Liberals	1,518,864	51	300
National Peasants	414,685	14	29
Peasants	152,167	5	11
National Liberals (Brătianu)	147,665	5	10
Christian League of National Defence	133,205	5	9
National Agrarians	121,748	4	9
Hungarians	119,562	4	8
Radical Peasants	82,930	3	6
Agrarian Union	73,208	2	5
1937 66% of the electorate voted.			
Government Party (National Liberals, etc.)	1,103,323	36	152
National Peasants	626,642	20	86
'All-for-Country' (i.e. Iron Guard)	478,378	16	66
Christian League of National Defence	281,167	9	39
Hungarians	136,139	4	19
National Liberals (Brătianu)	119,361	4	16
Radical Peasants	69,208	2	9

The government failed to get its necessary 40% of the votes. King Carol II picked on the Christian League of National Defence to form a government. He dismissed this government on 10 Feb 38 and instituted a royal dictatorship, called the Government of National Concentration.

A new constitution of 20 Feb 38 reduced the electorate to some 2m. (voting was universal and secret at age 30) and established a Senate. Political parties were banned except for the royalist monolithic National Renaissance Front. A plebiscite of 24 Feb 38, conducted by open voting, confirmed the new constitution by 4,283,395 to 5413 votes. Turn-out (compulsory): 92%. A corporatist parliament was returned at the election of 2 June 39: 86 representatives of agrarian and labour interests, 86 of commerce and industry, 86 intelligentsia and 88 senators. Turn-out was 85%. There were twice as many candidates as seats.

An electoral law of 14 July 46 abolished the Senate, enfranchised all at 21 and provided for a unicameral Assembly elected for four-year terms.

At the election of 19 Nov 46 the government bloc (National Democratic Front) obtained 71% of the votes cast and 347 seats. The National Peasants gained 33, the National Liberals 3. The validity of the results has been challenged.

1947   Electorate: 7,859,212. Voted: 6,934,563 (88.9%).

National Democratic Front	(348)	(4,766,630)
National Liberals	75	
Social Democrats	75	
Communists	73	
Ploughmen's Front	70	
National People's Party	26	
Dissident National Peasants	20	
Jews	2	
Independents	7	
Opposition parties		(1,361,536)
National Peasants	32	879,927
National Liberals	3	259,306
Democratic Peasants	2	156,775
Hungarian People's Union	29	569,651

The opposition parties protested at the falsification and terror used in these elections.

In Dec 47 King Michael abdicated, and a People's Republic was proclaimed on the 30th. On the 28 Mar 48, an election was held for a new National Assembly to pass a new constitution.

The remnants of the Social Democrats were merged with the Communists to form the Workers' Party, which ran for election in the single-list monolithic National Democratic Front comprising also the Ploughmen's Front, the National Peasants and the Hungarian People's Union. Electorate 8,417,467. Voted: 7,663,675 (91% turn-out). Voted for National Democratic Front: 6,958,531 (90·8%). The Front gained 405 of the 414 Assembly seats, the Liberals 7, the Democratic Peasants 1 with 1 Independent.

On 13 Apr 48 a new constitution, of the Soviet type, was promulgated: vote at 18, stand at 23, universal secret suffrage.

A further constitution was instituted on 24 Sep 49, in general outline the same as that of 1948. Deputies to the Grand National Assembly (*Marea Adunare Nationala* were to represent 40,000 electors for four-year terms.

1952   Electorate: 10·5m. Voted: 97%. For National Democratic Front: 98%.

1957   Electorate: 11·7m. Voted: 99·15%. For National Democratic Front: 99·88%.

At the elections of 5 Mar 61, 7 Mar 65 and 2 Mar 69 a single list of candidates was presented, the number of candidates equalling the number of seats. At least 99% of the voters turned out, at least 99% of these voted for the National Democratic Front (Socialist Unity Front since 19 Nov 68).

SPAIN

Elections held in Feb 18 were followed by a long period of political stability.

On 12 Sep 23 Primo de Rivera took over the country in a *coup d'état*. In Sep 27 the National Assembly met, members having been nominated by Primo de Rivera.

In Feb 31 elections were announced but postponed because of a government crisis and elections under a provisional government were held for the constituent *Cortes*. Franchise minimum voting age reduced from 25 to 23 years. Eligibility for *Cortes* membership extended to women and priests. Electoral divisions revised to give one deputy for every 50,000 inhabitants to a *Cortes* which was a single chamber elected by direct popular vote.

			Seats
Feb 31		Socialists	116
		Radical Socialists	60
		Azañaś Republican Action Party	30
		Radicals (following Lerroux)	90
		Progressives (following Zamona)	22
		Catalan Esquerra	43
		Casares Quirozaś Gallegan Nationalists	16
		Parties of the Right of which only 19 were members of the Monarchist Party	60
Nov 33	*Parties*	Acción Republicana	8
	of the	Socialists	58
	left	Remainder of pro-government parties	33
	centre	Radicals (following Lerroux)	167
		Parties to the right	207
Feb 36		Parties of the left	278
		Centre parties	55
		Parties of the right	134

Traditionally designated as the *Cortes* (courts), the Spanish parliament was revived by General Franco in 1942 as a unicameral body with strictly limited powers under the official name of Spanish Legislative Assembly (*Las Cortes Españolas*). Until 1967 it had no directly elected members but was made up of appointed and *ex officio* dignitaries, representatives of syndical (trade-union) and professional and business associations, and 108 indirectly elected representatives from the 53 Spanish and African provinces and the two North African *presidios*. Under the Organic Law of 1967, its membership was expanded by the addition of 108 'family representatives' to be directly elected for a four-year term by heads of families, married women and widows. The first elections of family representatives were held 10 Oct 67.

In 1969, the membership of the *Cortes* was made up of the categories and approximate numbers listed below; however, since some members sat in more than one capacity, the total membership was somewhat less than the indicated 563. The succession law of 22 July 69 was adopted by a vote of 491 in favour, 19 opposed, 9 abstaining, and 15 absent, making a total of 534.

High Officials	23
Appointed	25
Members of the National Council of the Movement	102
Representatives of cultural bodies	18
Representatives of professional associations	22
Syndical representatives	150
Municipal and provincial representatives	115
Family representatives	108
	563

SWEDEN

Voting procedures. Election to the First Chamber indirect through electoral colleges. Direct election to the Second Chamber. Proportional representation. Suffrage – for the First Chamber, universal suffrage at age 27; for the Second, suffrage for men at 24. In 1927, the First Chamber suffrage extended to age 23, and to age 21 in 1941. In 1945 suffrage for the Second Chamber altered to universal suffrage at 21.

	Electorate	Valid votes	Votes per party		Seats	% of electorate	% of votes
1917	1,123,969	739,053	Högern (Con.)	181,333	59	24·7	16·1
			Agrarians/Centre	62,658	12	8·5	5·6
			Liberaler (Lib.)	202,936	62	27·6	18·0
			Social Dem.	288,020	97	39·1	25·6
			Others	1,037	0	0·1	0·1
1920	1,192,922	660,193	Högern (Con.)	183,019	70	27·8	15·3
			Agrarians/Centre	92,941	30	14·1	7·8
			Liberaler (Lib.)	144,946	48	22·0	12·2
			Social Dem.	237,177	82	36·1	19·9
			Others	100	0	0·0	0·0
1921	3,222,917	1,747,553	Högern (Con.)	449,302	62	25·8	13·9
			Agrarians/Centre	192,269	21	11·1	6·0
			Liberaler (Lib.)	332,765	41	19·1	10·3
			Social Dem.	687,096	99	39·4	21·3
			Soc. and Comm.	80,355	7	4·6	2·5
			Others	165	0	0·0	0·0
1924	3,338,892	1,770,607	Högern (Con.)	461,257	65	26·1	13·8
			Agrarians/Centre	190,396	23	10·8	5·7
			Liberaler (Lib.)	69,627	5	3·9	2·0
			Frisinnade (Lib.)	228,913	28	13·0	6·9
			Social Dem.	725,407	104	41·1	21·7
			Soc. and Comm.	89,902	5	5·1	2·7
			Others	84	0	0·0	0·0

	Electorate	Valid votes	Votes per party		Seats	% of electorate	% of votes
1928	3,505,672	2,363,168	Högern (Con.)	692,434	73	28·9	19·8
			Agrarian/Centre	263,501	27	11·2	7·5
			Liberaler (Lib.)	70,820	4	3·0	2·1
			Frisinnade (Lib.)	303,995	28	13·4	8·7
			Social Dem.	873,931	90	37·0	25·0
			Soc. and Comm.	151,567	8	6·4	4·4
			Others	2,563	0	0·1	0·1
1932	3,698,935	2,500,769	Högern (Con.)	585,248	58	23·1	15·8
			Agrarians/Centre	351,215	36	14·1	9·5
			Liberaler (Lib.)	48,722	4	2·0	1·3
			Frisinnade (Lib.)	244,577	20	10·1	6·6
			Social Dem.	1.040,689	104	41·7	28·0
			Socialist	132,564	6	5·3	3·6
			Sommunist	74,245	2	3·0	2·0
			Others	17,846	0	0·7	0·5
1936	3,924,598	2,925,255	Högern (Con.)	512,781	44	17·6	13·0
			Agrarians/Centre	418,840	36	14·3	10·7
			Folkpartiet (Lib.)	376,161	27	12·9	9·6
			Social Dem.	1,338,120	112	45·9	34·0
			Socialist	127,832	6	4·4	3·3
			Communist	96,519	5	3·3	2·5
			Others	47,500	0	1·6	1·2
1940	4,110,720	2,889,137	Högern (Con.)	518,346	42	18·0	12·6
			Agrarians/Centre	344,345	28	12·0	8·4
			Folkpartiet (Lib.)	344,113	23	12·0	8·4
			Social Dem.	1,546,804	134	53·8	37·6
			Socialist	18,430	0	0·7	0·4
			Communist	101,424	3	3·5	2·5
			Others	955	0	0·0	0·0
1944	4,310,241	3,099,103	Högern (Con.)	488,921	39	15.9	11·3
			Agrarians/Centre	421,094	35	13·6	9·8
			Folkpartiet (Lib.)	398,293	26	12·9	9·2
			Social Dem.	1,436,571	115	46·6	33·3
			Socialist	5,279	0	0·2	0·1
			Communist	318,466	15	10·3	7·6
			Others	17,680	0	0·6	0·4
1948	4,707,783	3,895,161	Högern (Con.)	478,786	23	12·3	10·2
			Agrarians/Centre	480,421	30	12·4	10·2
			Folkpartiet (Lib.)	882,437	57	22·8	18·7
			Social Dem.	1,789,459	112	46·1	38·0
			Communist	244,826	8	6·3	5·2
			Others	3,062	0	0·1	0·0
1952	4,805,216	3,801,284	Högern (Con.)	543,825	31	14·4	11·3
			Agrarians/Centre	406,183	26	10·7	8·5
			Folkpartiet (Lib.)	924,819	58	24·4	19·2
			Social Dem.	1,742,284	110	46·1	36·3
			Communist	164,194	5	4·3	3·4
			Others	2,402	0	0·1	0·0
1956	4,887,325	3,902,114	Högern (Con.)	663,693	42	17·1	13·6
			Agrarians/Centre	366,612	19	9·4	7·5
			Folkpartiet (Lib.)	923,564	58	23·8	18·9

	Electorate	Valid votes	Votes per party		Seats	% of electorate	% of votes
			Social Dem.	1,729,463	106	44·6	35·4
			Communist	194,016	6	5·0	4·0
			Others	1,982	0	0·1	0·0
1958	4,992,421	3,864,963	Högern (Con.)	750,332	45	19·5	15·0
			Agrarians/Centre	486,760	32	12·7	9·7
			Folkpartiet (Lib.)	700,019	38	18·2	14·0
			Social Dem.	1,776,667	111	46·2	35·6
			Communist	129,319	5	3·4	2·6
			Others	1,155	0	0·0	0·0
1960	4,972,177	4,271,610	Högern (Con.)	704,365	39	16·5	14·2
			Agrarians/Centre	579,007	34	13·6	11·6
			Folkpartiet (Lib.)	744,142	40	17·5	15·0
			Social Dem.	2,033,016	114	47·8	40·9
			Communist	190,560	5	4·5	3·8
			Others	3,024	0	0·1	0·0
1964	5,095,850	4,273,595	Högern (Con.)	582,609	33	13·7	11·4
			Agrarians/Centre	559,632	36	13·2	11·0
			Folkpartiet (Lib.)	720,733	43	17·0	14·1
			Social Dem.	2,006,923	113	47·3	39·4
			Communist	221,746	8	5·2	4·4
			Others	154,137	0	3·6	3·0
1968	5,445,333	4,829,379	Högern (Con.)	621,031	29	11·4	12·9
			Agrarians/Centre	757,215	37	13·9	15·7
			Folkpartiet (Lib.)	688,456	32	12·6	14·3
			Social Dem.	2,420,277	125	44·4	50·1
			Communist	145,172	3	2·7	3·0
			Others	197,228	7	3·6	4·1
1970	5,645,804	4,976,196	Högern (Con.)	573,812	41	10·2	11·5
			Agrarians/Centre	991,208	71	17·6	19·9
			Folkpartiet (Lib.)	806,667	58	14·3	16·2
			Social Dem.	2,256,369	163	40·0	45·3
			Communist	236,659	17	4·2	4·8
			Others	111,481	0	2·0	2·3

SWITZERLAND

A general election takes place by ballot every four years. Every citizen of the Republic who has entered on his 20th year is entitled to vote, and any voter, not a clergyman, may be elected as a deputy. Laws passed by both chambers may be submitted to direct popular vote, when 30,000 citizens or eight cantons demand it; the vote can be only 'Yes' or 'No'. This principle, called the *referendum*, is frequently acted on.

Women's suffrage, although advocated by the Federal Council and the Federal Assembly, was repeatedly rejected but at a *referendum* held on 7 Feb 71 women's suffrage was carried.

	Electorate	Valid votes	Votes per party		Seats	% of electorate	% of votes
1919	946,271	749,954	Liberal Democratic	28,497	9	3·0	3·8
			Peasant and Middle Class	114,537	31	12·1	15·3
			Catholic Conservative	156,702	41	16·5	21·0
			Radical	215,566	58	22·8	28·8
			Socialist	175,292	41	18·5	23·5
			Others	59,360	9	6·3	7·6
1922	983,238	737,423	Liberal Democratic	29,041	10	2·9	4·0
			Peasant and Middle Class	118,382	35	12·0	16·1
			Catholic Conservative	153,836	44	15·6	20·9
			Radical	208,144	58	21·1	28·3
			Socialist	170,974	43	17·7	23·3
			Communist	13,441	2	1·3	1·8
			Others	43,605	6	4·4	5·6
1925	995,551	747,138	Liberal Democratic	30,523	7	3·0	4·1
			Peasant and Middle Class	113,512	31	11·4	15·3
			Catholic Conservative	155,467	42	15·8	20·9
			Radical	206,485	59	20·7	27·8
			Socialist	192,208	49	19·3	25·8
			Communist	14,837	3	1·5	2·0
			Others	34,106	7	3·4	4·1
1928	1,043,823	807,472	Liberal Democratic	23,752	6	2·3	2·9
			Peasant and Middle Class	126,961	31	12·1	15·8
			Catholic Conservative	172,516	46	16·5	21·4
			Radical	220,135	58	21·1	27·4
			Socialist	220,141	50	21·1	27·4
			Communist	14,818	2	1·4	1·8
			Others	29,149	5	2·8	3·3
1931	1,118,841	866,575	Liberal Democratic	24,573	6	2·2	2·8
			Peasant and Middle Class	131,809	30	11·8	15·3
			Catholic Conservative	184,602	44	16·5	21·4
			Radical	232,562	52	20·8	26·9
			Socialist	247,946	49	22·1	28·7
			Communist	12,778	2	1·1	1·5
			Others	32,305	4	2·9	3·4
1935	1.194,910	917,575	Independent	37,861	7	3·2	4·2
			Liberal Democratic	30,476	7	2·5	3·3
			Peasant and Middle Class	100,300	21	8·4	11·0
			Catholic Conservative	185,052	42	15·5	20·3
			Radical	216,664	48	18·1	23·7
			Socialist	255,843	50	21·4	28·0
			Communist	12,569	2	1·0	1·4
			Others	78,810	10	6·8	8·1
1939	861,266	623,740	Independent	43,735	9	5·1	7·1
			Liberal Democratic	10,241	6	1·2	1·6
			Peasant and Middle Class	91,182	22	10·6	14·7
			Catholic Conservative	105,018	43	12·2	17·0
			Radical	128,163	51	14·9	20·8
			Socialist	160,377	45	18·6	25·9
			Communist	15,962	4	1·8	2·6
			Others	69,062	7	8·0	10·3

153

	Electorate	Valid votes	Votes per party		Seats	% of electorate	% of votes
1943	1,300,784	887,676	Independent	48,557	7	3·8	5·5
			Liberal Democratic	28,434	8	2·2	3·2
			Peasant and Middle Class	101,998	22	7·8	11·6
			Catholic Conservative	182,916	43	14·1	20·8
			Radical	197,746	43	15·2	22·5
			Socialist	251,576	56	19·3	28·6
			Others	76,449	11	5·8	7·8
1947	1,360,453	966,680	Independent	42,428	9	3·1	4·4
			Liberal Democratic	30,492	7	2·3	3·2
			Peasant and Middle Class	115,976	21	8·5	12·1
			Catholic Conservative	203,202	44	14·9	21·2
			Radical	220,486	52	16·2	23·0
			Socialist	251,625	48	18·5	26·2
			Communist	49,353	7	3·6	5·1
			Others	53,118	6	3·9	4·8
1951	1,386,146	967,989	Independent	49,100	10	3·5	5·1
			Liberal Democratic	24,813	5	1·8	2·6
			Peasant and Middle Class	120,819	23	8·7	12·6
			Catholic Conservative	216,616	48	15·6	22·5
			Radical	230,687	51	16·6	24·0
			Socialist	249,857	49	18·1	26·0
			Communist	25,659	5	1·9	2·7
			Others	50,438	5	3·6	4·5
1955	1,425,421	982,020	Independent	53,450	10	3·8	5·5
			Liberal Democratic	21,688	5	1·5	2·2
			Peasant and Middle Class	117,847	22	8·3	12·1
			Catholic Conservative	226,122	47	15·8	23·2
			Radical	227,370	50	15·9	23·3
			Socialist	263,664	53	18·5	27·0
			Communist	25,060	4	1·8	2·6
			Others	46,819	5	3·2	3·4
1959	1,473,155	989,005	Independent	54,049	10	3·7	5·5
			Liberal Democratic	22,934	5	1·5	2·3
			Peasant and Middle Class	113,611	23	7·7	11·6
			Catholic Conservative	229,088	47	15·5	23·3
			Radical	232,557	51	15·8	23·7
			Socialist	259,139	51	17·6	26·3
			Communist	26,346	3	1·8	2·7
			Others	51,281	6	3·5	4·1
1963	1,531,164	969,037	Independent	48,224	10	3·5	5·0
			Liberal Democratic	21,501	6	1·4	2·2
			Peasant and Middle Class	109,202	22	7·1	11·4
			Catholic Conservative	225,160	48	14·7	23·4
			Radical	230,200	51	15·1	24·0
			Socialist	256,063	53	16·7	26·6
			Communist	21,088	4	1·4	2·2
			Others	49,693	6	3·3	4·2
1967	1,599,479	1,001,863	Independent	89,950	16	5·6	9·1
			Liberal Democratic	23,208	6	1·4	2·3
			Peasant and Middle Class	109,621	21	6·8	11·0
			Catholic Conservative	219,184	45	13·7	22·1

Electorate	Valid votes	Votes per party		Seats	% of electorate	% of votes
		Radical	230,095	49	14·4	23·2
		Socialist	233,873	51	14·6	23·5
		Communist	28,723	5	1·8	2·9
		Others	59,194	7	3·5	3·6
1971 3,551,008	1,992,422	Independent	150,684	13	4·2	7·6
		Liberal Democratic	43,338	6	1·2	2·2
		Peasant and Middle Class	217,909	23	6·1	11·0
		Catholic Conservative	402,528	44	11·3	20·4
		Radical	431,364	49	12·1	21·8
		Socialist	452,194	46	12·7	22·9
		Communist	50,834	5	1·4	2·6
		Republican Movement	88,327	7	2·5	4·5
		Others	138,417	7	3·9	5·3

TURKEY

The first Turkish Grand National Assembly met in Ankara on 23 Apr 20. In these circumstances, only indirect elections proved possible, every province putting forward five delegates. The Assembly consisted of 337 members, 232 of whom had been newly elected. Under the constitution of 20 Jan 21, which the Assembly adopted and which legalized the organization it had set up, the deputies' term of office was set at two years.

The first Assembly was prorogued on 1 Apr 23 after deciding that new elections should be held. On 19 Oct 23, the Republic was proclaimed and the 1924 constitution extended the franchise to all men aged 18 or over. Candidates had to be at least 30 years old, and the deputies' term of office was lengthened to four years. A constitutional amendment adopted on 5 Jan 34 extended the franchise to women, but raised the minimum voting age to 22. Elections continued to be indirect: voters chose an electoral college which then elected the Assembly. This practice was continued until 1946. The membership of the Assembly increased constantly until the adoption of the 1961 constitution, since it had been laid down that there should be one deputy per 40,000 citizens.

The first effective political party in the history of the Turkish Republic, the People's Party, was formed in Oct 23; in Nov 24 its name was changed to Republican People's Party. This party remained in power until 1950. The Free Republican Party, formed in 1930, had a brief existence. Then between 1930 and 1945 Turkey had a single-party regime. On 5 June 45 the authorities allowed the formation of political parties without a preliminary permit, and as a consequence the elections held on 21 July 46 were for the first time contested by more than one party. Voting was direct and public, electors were allowed to divide their votes between party lists of candidates (producing 'mixed' lists), but votes were counted in secret. To win, candidates needed to obtain the simple majority of the votes cast. Two changes were introduced in the elections held on 14 May 50: voting became secret, and the counting of votes open. In 1957 mixed lists were banned, but electors were allowed to delete the names of individual candidates from the party lists of their choice. After 27 May 60, the National Unity Committee first assumed all the powers vested in the Grand National Assembly under the 1924 constitution. This transfer of power, legalized by the provisional constitution of 12 June 60, was followed on 13 Dec of the same year by a law setting up a Constituent Assembly, which was opened on 6 Jan 61. The constitution which this Assembly drew up governed the elections held on 15 Oct 61 which produced a new Turkish Grand National Assembly. Article 55 of the constitution requires voting to be free, direct, universal and secret, and the counting of votes to be open. However, the constitution does not define the system of representation which is to be used, and this is regulated by electoral laws. Proportional representation was introduced for the first time in the elections of 15 Oct 61 and has been retained since, although the basic d'Hondt formula has been varied: first candidates had to obtain a minimum number of votes (known as the 'barrage') to qualify for consideration: then the country-wide pooling and redistribution of wasted votes ('the national residue') was introduced in time for the elections of 12 Oct 65, but dropped together with the 'barrage' requirement before the 1969 elections.

In the 1920 elections Kemalists held 197 seats; Opposition, 118; Non-aligned, 122. In 1923, Grand National Assembly Party, ..; Progressive Republican Party, ..; Republican People's Party, 304. In 1946, Democratic Party, 64; Republican People's Party, 64; Independents, 6.

		Votes per party	Seats
1950	Democratic Party	4,242,831	396
	Republican People's Party	3,165,096	68
	Nation Party	240,209	1
	Independents	258,698	7
1954	Republican People's Party	3,161,696	31
	Republican Nation Party	434,085	5
	Democratic Party	5,151,550	505
	Peasant Party	57,011	–
	Independents	137,318	1
1957	Republican People's Party	3,753,136	178
	Republican Nation Party	652,064	4
	Democratic Party	4,372,621	424
	Freedom Party	350,497	4
	Independents	4,994	–
1961	Justice Party	3,527,435	158
	Republican People's Party	3,724,752	173
	Republican Peasants and Nation Party, renamed Nationalist Action Party	1,415,390	54

		Votes per party	Seats
	New Turkey Party	1,391,934	65
	Independents	81,732	–
1965	Justice Party	4,921,235	240
	Republican People's Party	2,675,785	134
	Republican Peasants and Nation Party, renamed Nationalist Action Party	208,696	11
	Nation Party	582,704	31
	Turkish Workers' Party	276,101	14
	New Turkey Party	346,514	19
	Independents	296,528	1
1969	Justice Party	4,219,712	256
	Republican People's Party	2,487,006	143
	Republican Peasants and Nation Party, renamed Nationalist Action Party	275,091	1
	Nation Party	292,961	6
	Turkish Workers' Party	243,631	2
	New Turkey Party	197,929	6
	Independents	511,023	13
	Unity Party	254,695	8
	Reliance Party, renamed National Reliance Party in 1971	597,818	15

Senators are elected for six years, but one-third of the membership is re-elected every other year. Voting is free, equal, universal, direct and secret, and counting open. The Senate was first set up in 1961. That year and in 1964, a simple majority sufficed for the election of a senator; in 1966 and 1968, proportional representation (with 'national residue') was introduced.

		Votes per party	Seats
1961	Justice Party	3,560,675	71
	Republican People's Party	3,734,285	76
	Republican Peasants and Nation Party	1,350,892	16
	New Turkey Party	1,401,636	27
	Independents	39,558	–
1964	Justice Party	1,385,655	31
	Republican People's Party	1,125,783	19
	Republican Peasants and Nation Party	88,400	–
	New Turkey Party	96,427	–
	Independents	64,498	1
1966	Justice Party	1,688,316	35
	Republican People's Party	877,066	13
	Republican Peasants and Nation Party	57,367	1
	Nation Party	157,115	1

		Votes per party	Seats
	Turkish Workers' Party	116,375	1
	New Turkey Party	70,043	1
	Independents	980	–
1968	Justice Party	1,656,802	38
	Republican People's Party	899,444	13
	Republican Peasants and Nation Party	66,232	–
	Reliance Party, renamed	284,234	1
	National Reliance Party		
	Nation Party	200,737	1
	Turkish Workers' Party	157,062	–
	Independents	58,317	–

USSR

In 1917 the Provisional Government had been organizing elections to establish a Constituent Assembly, and these the Bolsheviks allowed to take place on 25 Nov 17. Suffrage was universal, and the electorate numbered 41·7m. Figures are uncertain and contradictory (some reputable variant figures are given in brackets).

	Votes cast	Delegates returned
	17·1m. (17·4m.)	419 (of whom 380 of the right-wing faction)
Bolsheviks	9·6m. (9·8m.)	168 (175)
Mensheviks	1·4m.	18
Kadets	2m.	17
Monarchists	300,000	..
Various national minority parties	1·7m.	..

The Kadets were proscribed at the end of 1917. The Constituent Assembly met on 18 Jan 18, just over half the delegates being present. It was dissolved by the Bolsheviks the following day after rejecting by 237 votes to 136 a Bolshevik motion which would have recognized the Congress of Soviets to be the supreme government authority.

The Congress of Soviets was therefore the supreme organ of state power until it was replaced by the Supreme Soviet in 1937. There were altogether ten All-Russian Congresses until the formation of the USSR (30 Dec 22) and eight All-Union Congresses thereafter.

Elections were indirect, from amongst the deputies in the hierarchy of soviets throughout the country. The latter were elected on a franchise restricted to workers, peasants and the armed forces. Deputies to town soviets were elected on a basis of 1 per 25,000 electors; to rural soviets on a basis of 1 per 125,000.

By 1922 all public opposition to the Communist Party had been brought to an end. Party allegiance in the early Congresses of Soviets (for the first two see above):

3rd (Jan 18)   Bolsheviks 61%
4th Extraordinary (Mar 18)   Bolsheviks 66%
5th (July 18)   Bolsheviks (now called Communists) 66%
6th (Nov 18)   Communists 90%
7th (Dec 19)   Communists 95%
8th (Dec 20)   Communists 95%

The 'Stalin' Constitution of 1936 replaced the Congresses of Soviets with the Supreme Soviet (*Verkhovnyi Sovet*). This has two chambers: the Soviet of the Union (*Sovet Soyuza*) and the Soviet of Nationalities (*Sovet Natsional-nostei*). Elections are held every four years. Suffrage universal at 18 years; candidates may stand at 23. The Soviet of the Union is elected on a basis of 1 deputy per 300,000 electors. Deputies to the Soviet of Nationalities are elected in the following proportions: 32 from each federative republic, 11 from each Autonomous Republic, 5 from each Autonomous Oblast (Province) and 1 from each National District.

Although it is constitutionally the supreme legislative body, the Supreme Soviet has no significance in the realm of policy-making: *de facto* supreme power is in the hands of the Communist Party. Candidates for election may be nominated only by recognized organizations: the Communist Party, trade unions, industrial co-operatives, agricultural collectives, youth organizations and cultural organizations. Candidates need not belong to the party, but they must support its programme. On the average, some 75% of deputies are party members.

More than one candidate may be nominated, and there is no constitutional bar to more than one standing for election, but the practice is that one only of the nominees is selected to stand by local party officials, and the elector's choice is thus limited to voting for or against him.

The ballot is secret but so arranged that only a contrary vote actually requires entry into the polling booth.

Elections were held in Dec 37, Feb 46, Mar 50, Mar 54, Mar 58, Mar 62, June 66 and June 70. In 1937 91,113,153 votes were cast out of an electorate of 93,139,478, and subsequently the turn-out has always exceeded 99%. Less than 1% of votes cast have been against candidates, and no candidate has ever failed to be elected.

INDEPENDENT TERRITORIES (1918–21)

ARMENIA, AZERBAIJAN and GEORGIA proclaimed independence jointly as the Transcaucasian Federative Republic on 22 Apr 18; reconquered respectively 29 Nov 20, 27 Apr 20 and 18 Mar 21.

The Transcaucasian Federative Republic was governed by a *Seim* of delegates based upon the elections to the Russian Constituent Assembly (dissolved on 18 Jan 18): Mensheviks, 33; Musavat (Moslem Nationalists), 30; Dashnaktsutiun, (Armenian Nationalists), 27, Moslem Socialists, 7; Socialist revolutionaries, 5; others, 10.

The Federation collapsed upon the secession of Georgia on 26 May 18, and each republic became separately independent.

ARMENIA set up a National Council (*Khorhurd*) on 1 Aug 18, the party composition of which was: Dashnaktsutiun, 18; Populists, 6; Moslems, 6; Mensheviks, 5; independents, 2; Bolsheviks, 1; Yezidis, 1; Russians, 1.

AZERBAIJAN set up a National Council composed as follows: Musavat (Moslem Nationalists) and Neutral Democratic Group (Sunni Moslems), 30; Socialists, 11; Moslem Union, 3. In June 18 the Council was reformed under the insistence of the Turkish military commander to exclude socialists and give predominance to the conservative Moslem Union. In turn the British military commander after the surrender of the Turks objected to the council as unrepresentative. A new Council was created in Dec 18: Musavat, 38; Neutral Democratic Group, 7; Unity Party, 13; Socialists, 11; Dashnaktsutiun (Armenian Nationalists), 7; other Armenian parties, 4; Bolsheviks, 1; others, 15.

GEORGIA In Feb 19 the National Council held elections for a Constituent Assembly. Suffrage was universal and by proportional representation. 15 parties presented candidates for election. 505,477 votes were cast (some 60% of the electorate). The Assembly had 130 deputies, distributed as follows:

	Votes cast	Deputies in the Assembly
Mensheviks	409,766	109
National Democrats	30,154	8
Social-Federalists	33,721	8
Social-Revolutionaries	21,453	5

UNITED KINGDOM

In 1911 the maximum duration of a parliament, which since 1715 had been seven years, was reduced to five years.

By 1918 virtually all men were enfranchised together with all women over thirty years of age who were householders or the wives of householders. Voting in more than two constituencies was prohibited. General elections which had hitherto been spread over two weeks and more were concentrated on a single day. Candidates were required to provide a deposit of £150 to be forfeit if they failed to secure one-eighth of the votes cast in their constituency. Seats were redistributed, for the first time on the basis of approximately equal electorates, and the House of Commons was increased to 707 members (this fell to 615 in 1922, with the independence of Southern Ireland).

The age of women voting was lowered to 21 in 1928 and they were given the vote on exactly the same basis as men.

In 1948 university seats and all plural voting were abolished. Machinery was set up for Permanent Boundary Commissions to redraw constituencies once in the life of every normal five-year parliament, but because the first routine distribution of seats in 1954–5 (which increased the House to 630 members) had caused so much annoyance and difficulty, an Act was passed in 1958 to reduce the frequency of redistribution to between 10 and 15 years.

		Votes	% share of total vote	Members	Candi-dates	Unopposed returns
1918	Electors:	21,392,322	Turnout: 58·9%			
	Total votes cast	10,766,583	100·0	707	1,625	107
	Coalition Unionist	3,504,198	32·6	335	374	42
	Coalition Liberal	1,455,640	13·5	133	158	27
	Coalition Labour	161,521	1·5	10	18	–
	(Coalition)	(5,121,259)	(47·6)	(478)	(550)	(69)
	Conservative	370,375	3·4	23	37	–
	Irish Unionist	292,722	2·7	25	38	–
	Liberal	1,298,808	12·1	28	253	–
	Labour	2,385,472	22·2	63	388	12
	Irish Nationalist	238,477	2·2	7	60	1
	Sinn Fein	486,867	4·5	73	102	25
	Other	572,503	5·3	10	197	–
1922	Electors:	21,127,663	Turnout: 71·3%			
	Total votes cast	14,393,632	100·0	615	1.443	57
	Conservative	5,500,382	38·2	345	483	42
	National Liberal	1,673,240	11·6	62	162	5
	Liberal	2,516,287	17·5	54	328	5
	Labour	4,241,383	29·5	142	411	4
	Other	462,340	3·2	12	59	1
1923	Electors:	21,281,232	Turnout: 70·8%			
	Total votes cast	14,548,521	100·0	615	1,446	
	Conservative	5,538,824	38·1	258	540	35
	Liberal	4,311,147	29·6	159	453	11
	Labour	4,438,508	30·5	191	422	3
	Other	260,042	1·8	7	31	1
1924	Electors:	21,731,320	Turnout: 76·6%			
	Total votes cast	16,640,279	100·0	615	1,428	32
	Conservative	8,039,598	48·3	419	552	16
	Liberal	2,928,747	17·6	40	340	6
	Labour	5,489,077	33·0	151	512	9
	Communist	55,346	0·3	1	8	–
	Other	126,511	0·8	4	16	1
1929	Electors:	28,850,870	Turnout: 76·1%			
	Total votes cast	22,648,375	100.0	615	1,730	7
	Conservative	8,656,473	38.2	260	590	4
	Liberal	5,308,510	23.4	59	513	–
	Labour	8,389,512	37.1	288	571	–
	Communist	50,614	0.3	–	25	–
	Other	243,266	1.0	8	31	3

		Votes	% share of total vote	Members	Candidates	Unopposed returns
1931	Electors:	29,960,071	Turnout: 76·3%			
	Total votes cast	21,656,373	100·0	615	1,292	67
	Conservative	11,978,745	55·2	473	523	56
	National Liberal	341,370	1·6	13	20	–
	Liberal National	809,302	3·7	35	41	–
	Liberal	1,403,102	6·5	33	112	5
	(National government)	(14,532,519)	(67·0)	(554)	(696)	(61)
	Independent Liberal	106,106	0·5	4	7	–
	Labour	6,649,630	30·6	52	515	6
	Communist	74,824	0·3	–	26	–
	New Party	36,377	0·2	–	24	–
	Other	256,917	1·2	5	24	–
1935	Electors:	31,379,050	Turnout: 71·2%			
	Total votes cast	21,997,054	100·0	615	1,348	40
	Conservative	11,810,158	53·7	432	585	26
	Liberal	1,422,116	6·4	20	161	–
	Labour	8,325,491	37·9	154	552	13
	Independent Labour Party	139,577	0·7	4	17	–
	Communist	27,117	0·1	1	2	–
	Other	272,595	1·2	4	31	1
1945	Electors:	33,240,391	Turnout: 72·7%			
	Total votes cast	25,085,978	100·0	640	1,682	3
	Conservative	9,988,306	39·8	213	624	2
	Liberal	2,248,226	9·0	12	306	–
	Labour	11,995,152	47·8	393	604	1
	Communist	102,780	0·4	2	21	–
	Common Wealth	110,634	0·4	1	23	–
	Other	640,880	2·0	19	104	–
1950	Electors:	33,269,770	Turnout: 84·0%			
	Total votes cast	28,772,671	100·0	625	1,868	2
	Conservative	12,502,567	43·5	298	620	2
	Liberal	2,621,548	9·1	9	475	–
	Labour	13,266,592	46·1	315	617	–
	Communist	91,746	0·3	–	100	–
	Other	290,218	1·0	3	56	–
1951	Electors:	34,645,573	Turnout: 82·5%			
	Total votes cast	28,595,668	100·0	625	1,376	4
	Conservative	13,717,538	48·0	321	617	4
	Liberal	730,556	2·5	6	109	–
	Labour	13,948,605	48·8	295	617	–
	Communist	21,640	0·1	–	10	–
	Other	177,329	0·6	3	23	–
1955	Electors:	34,858,263	Turnout: 76·7%			
	Total votes cast	26,760,493	100·0	630	1,409	–
	Conservative	13,286,569	49·7	344	623	–
	Liberal	722,405	2·7	6	110	–
	Labour	12,404,970	46·4	277	620	–
	Communist	33,144	0·1	–	17	–
	Other	313,410	1·1	3	39	–

		% share of		Candi-	Unopposed
	Votes	*total vote*	*Members*	*dates*	*returns*
1959 Electors:	35,397,080	Turnout: 78·8%		1,536	–
Total votes cast	27,859,241	100·0	630	1,536	–
Conservative	13,749,830	49·4	365	625	–
Liberal	1,638,571	5·9	6	216	–
Labour	12,215,538	43·8	258	621	–
Communist	30,897	0·1	–	18	–
Other	224,405	0·8	1	56	–
1964 Electors:	35,892,572	Turnout: 77·1%			–
Total votes	27,655,374	100·0	630	1,757	–
Conservative	12,001,396	43·4	304	630	–
Liberal	3,092,878	11·2	9	365	–
Labour	12,205,814	44·1	317	628	–
Communist	45,932	0·2	–	36	–
Other	302,982	1·1	–	98	–
1966 Electors:	35,964,684	Turnout: 75·8%			–
Total votes cast	27,263,606	100·0	630	1,707	–
Conservative	11,418,433	41·9	253	629	–
Liberal	2,327,533	8·6	12	311	–
Labour	13,064,951	47·9	363	621	–
Communist	62,040	0·2	–	57	–
Other	390,649	1·4	2	89	–
1970 Electors:	39,384,364	Turnout: 72%			–
Total votes cast	28,344,807	100·0	630	1,837	–
Conservative	13,144,692	46·4	330	628	–
Liberal	2,117,638	7·5	6	332	–
Labour	12,179,166	42·9	287	624	–
Communist	38,431	0·1	–	58	–
Other	864,880	3·1	7	195	–

YUGOSLAVIA

The 1920 elections were held on proportional principles by universal male suffrage. 65% of electorate voted.

	Party	*Seats*	*% of votes*
1920	Democrats (a combination of S. Pribičević's Hapsburg Serbs and the Independent Radicals)	92	19·9
	Radicals	91	17
	Communists (became illegal 1921)	58	12·4
	Croat Peasants	50	14·3
	Serbian Agrarians	39	
	Moslems	32	
	Slovene Catholic People's Party	27	
	Social Democrats	10	
	Others	19	

The proportional system was modified in the 1923 election. 73% of the electorate voted.

	Party	Seats	% of votes
1923	Radicals	108	25·8
	Croat Peasants	70	21·8
	Democrats	51	
	Slovene Catholic People's Party	22	
	Moslems of Bosnia	18	
	Moslems of Macedonia	14	
	Serbian Agrarians	10	
	Germans	8	
	Social Democrats	2	
	Others	9	

At the 1925 elections 76·9% of the electorate voted.

	Party	Seats
1925	Radicals in a bloc with ⎱	142
	Independent Democrats ⎰	22
	Croat Peasants	67
	Slovene Catholic People's Party	20
	Moslems	15
	Serbian Agrarians	5
	Germans	5
	Montenegrans	3
	Others	34

At the 1927 elections 68% of the electorate voted.

	Party	Seats
1927	Radicals	112
	Croat Peasants	61
	Democrats	59
	Independent Democrats	22
	Slovene Catholic People's Party	21
	Moslems	18
	Serbian Agrarians	9
	Germans	6
	Social Democrats	1
	Others	6

The *Vidovdan* constitution and the *Skupština* were abolished on 6 Jan 29 by King Alexander, who set up a royal dictatorship which found permanent expression in the constitution of 3 June 31. This instituted a bicameral legislature: a National Assembly elected every four years publicly by all males over 21, each deputy representing 50,000 inhabitants; and a Senate half appointed and half elected by regional colleges of electors. The powers of the *Skupština* were reduced. In an attempt to eliminate regionalism all parties centred about ethnic or religious particularities were declared illegal. The name of the kingdom was changed to Yugoslavia in a similar gesture against separatism. Proportional representation was abolished: any party which won a majority of votes would henceforth be allotted two-thirds of the seats in the *Skupština*.

At the elections of 8 Nov 31 only the government list was presented. 65% of the electorate voted.

In 1933 this electoral law was relaxed. The winning party was to receive three-fifths of the seats; and conditions for establishing countrywide lists of candidates were made easier.

On 9 Oct 34 King Alexander was assassinated, and Prince Paul became Regent.

The elections of 25 May 35 were public. The opposition parties (Croat Peasants, Independent Democrats, Democrats, Serbian Agrarians and Moslems) formed a united bloc. 73·7% of the electorate voted.

	Votes	*Seats*
The Government	1,746,982	303
The Opposition	1,076,345	67

At the elections of 11 Dec 38 74·5% of the electorate voted.

The Government	1,643,783	306
(Yugoslav Radical Union)		
The Opposition	1,364,524	67

All opposition parties abstained from the elections to the Constituent Assembly of 11 Nov 45 leaving only a single Popular Front list. 88% of the electorate voted, 90% for the Popular Front.

In 1950 an electoral law abolished the single list system, and candidates were nominated individually. In the election of 26 Mar 50 the number of candidates was still the same as the number of seats: there was no contest. Popular Front candidates polled 93·25% of the votes cast.

At the elections of 22 Nov 53 the electorate for the Federal Council was 10,580,648. 527 candidates stood for 484 seats (Federal Council, 282; Council of Producers, 202, of whom 135 were industrial and 67 were agricultural). 89·4% of the electorate voted.

At the elections of 23–26 Mar 58 307 candidates stood for the 301 seats of the Federal Council. The electorate was 11,331,727: 94% of the electorate voted. 216 representatives were elected to the Council of Producers: 168 industrial, 48 agricultural.

By the constitution of 7 Apr 63 Yugoslavia became a 'Socialist' instead of a

'People's' Republic. This constitution did away almost entirely with direct elections, replacing these by an electoral filtering system. The electoral emphasis moved from the formal act of voting to the nominating process in which citizens participate through their local government wards and workers through their workplace. The Council of Producers was abolished and replaced by four specialised councils (Administration; Culture; Economy; Welfare). The Federal Assembly of 670 was to be elected for four-year terms. Every second year one-half of each council was renewed.

Elections were held on 25 May and 16 June 63. The number of candidates was the same as the number of seats. 95·5% of the electorate voted. Half the seats came up for renewal on 19 Mar and 18 Apr 65, when a few constituencies had more than one candidate. 93·6% of the electorate voted.

At the elections of 9 and 23 Apr 67 there were 81 candidates for 60 seats. Campaigning was vigorous. 89% of the electorate voted.

By a constitutional amendment in 1968 the Federal Council was abolished and divided into its two political components: (1) Social and Political Council, elected by citizens in local government wards; (2) Council of Nations, representing the republican legislatures.

At the elections of 12 Apr and 10 May 69 for the Social and Political Council there were 179 candidates for the 120 seats. 87% of the electorate voted. There were 624 candidates for the 360 seats of the four specialized councils.

BIBLIOGRAPHY

Adam, G., *Atlas des élections sociales en France*. Paris, 1964
Bergasse, H., *Histoire de l'assemblée: des élections de 1789 aux élections de 1967*. Paris, 1967
Butler, D., *The Electoral System in Britain since 1918*. Oxford, rev. ed. 1963
Carson, G. B., *Electoral Practices in the U.S.S.R.* New York, 1955
Cook, C., and Ramsden, J., *By-Elections in British Politics*. London, 1973
Delruelle, N., *Le comportement politique des électeurs belges*. Brussels, 1970
Drashkovich, M., *Tito's Elections*. Chicago 1953
Galli, G., *Il comportamento elettorale in Italia*. Bologna, 1968
Goguel, F., *Géographie des élections françaises de 1870 à 1951*. Paris, 1951
Kitzinger, U., *German Electoral Politics: A Study of the 1957 Campaign*. Oxford, 1960
Mackie, T. T., and Rose, R., *The International Almanac of Electoral History*. London, 1974
Rokkan, S., and Meyriat, J. (ed.) *International Guide to Electoral Statistics*. Paris, 1967
Rusinow, D. I., *Yugoslav Elections, 1969*. Hanover, U.S.A., 1969
Stiefold, R., *Wahlen und Parteien in Österreich*. Vienna, 1966
Törnudd, K., *The Electoral System of Finland*. London, 1968

6 POLITICAL PARTIES

ALBANIA

ALBANIAN PARTY OF LABOUR

Founded 1941, present name adopted in 1948. Communist; the only recognized party in the state.
Membership in 1971, 63,000. First Secretary 1971, Enver Hoxha.

AUSTRIA

SOCIAL DEMOCRATIC PARTY 1889
Socialist social and economic aims, supported political union with Germany. After World War II, changed its name to the *Austrian Socialist Party* (*SPO*), no longer pan-German.
Membership in 1971, 700,000. Chairman 1971, B. Kreisky.

CHRISTIAN SOCIALIST PARTY 1892

Conservative with strong clerical Roman Catholic influence. Politically divided with one section monarchist and the other pan-German. In 1945 it was reformed as the *Austrian People's Party* (*OVP*) with a conservative Christian-Democrat programme.
Chairman 1971, H. Withalm.

ALL-GERMANY PARTY 1917

Developed out of the German National Club and some sections of the old National Democratic Party. Politically centre, committed to union with Germany. Dissolved by World War II.

COMMUNIST PARTY (KPO) 1918

Communist programme includes committal to strict neutrality.
Chairman 1971, F. Muhri.

AUSTRIAN LIBERAL PARTY (FPO) 1955

Partially succeeds the previous Independent League dissolved in 1956. Programme of moderate social reform and inter-Europe co-operation.
Chairman 1971, F. Peter.

DEMOCRATIC PROGRESSIVE PARTY (DPF) 1965

Centre party, formed as a balance between the OVP and SPO. Chairman 1971, F. Olah.

BELGIUM

CATHOLIC PARTY

This, with the Liberal Party, was one of the main parties of the nineteenth century. It was divided on the French-Flemish language question, and had clearly defined left and right wings but was mainly conservative and clerical. It survived until 1945, when it was reformed as the *Christian Socialist Party* (*PSC*) which is now undenominational and has a Christian-Democrat moderate reform programme.
Membership 1971, 300,000. Chairman 1971, R. Houben.

LIBERAL PARTY

The other main party of the nineteenth century, less influential since. It had a moderate social and religious policy. In 1961 it was succeeded by the *Party for Liberty and Progress* (*PLP*). This is anti-federalist and concerned specially with farmers and industrial workers.
Membership 1971, 100,000. President 1971, M. Drumaux.

BELGIAN SOCIALIST PARTY (PSB) 1885

Founded as Parti Ouvrier Belge. Orthodox socialist programme. Chairman 1971, L. Collard.

FRONT PARTY 1918

Founded to divide Belgium by setting up a separate Flemish state. Modern counterpart is the *People's Union*, Flemish nationalist party founded in 1953.

FRONT DEMOCRATIQUE DES FRANCOPHONES

Front composed of several small Walloon parties.

BULGARIA

COMMUNIST PARTY 1918

Dominant party of the Fatherland Front organization which claims 4m. members. Founded from a splinter group of the moderate left *Social Democratic Party* (1893).

AGRARIANS' UNION 1899

Founded to protect farming and related industries. Main body continued as Stamboulinsky's party when Draghyeff's party broke away in 1919 as a more moderate group, defending parliamentary methods in politics.

DEMOCRATIC PARTY 1895

Founded as a group to reconcile differing parties with a centre policy. In 1906 the *Radical Party* split off, in support of co-operatives, radical tax reforms and a federation of Balkan states.

NATIONAL LIBERAL PARTY 1920

United three small parties to rebuild post-war Bulgaria and gain a revision of the peace treaty. *Stambouloff's National Liberal Party* broke away in 1925.

PARTY OF THE DEMOCRATIC ENTENTE 1923

Moderate reform party committed to peace and strengthening of the law and the economy.

CYPRUS

AKEL—PROGRESSIVE PARTY OF THE WORKING PEOPLE 1941

Communist.
Membership 1971, 14,000. Secretary-General 1971, E. Papaioannou.

CYPRUS TURKISH NATIONAL UNION 1959

Formed from *Cyprus-is-Turkish* party. Anti-Communist, concerned for the welfare of the Turkish minority.
Chairman 1971, Dr Kucuk.

UNIFIED PARTY 1960

Greek, pro-Makarios.
Chairman 1971, G. Clerides.

DEMOCRATIC NATIONAL PARTY 1968

Opposition to Makarios, left-wing.
Chairman 1971, T. Evdokas.

PROGRESSIVE FRONT 1970

Right-wing pro-government farmers' party.

CZECHOSLOVAKIA

COMMUNIST PARTY OF CZECHOSLOVAKIA 1921

Incorporated extreme left elements of the former Czech. Social Democratic Labour Party, a working-class and mainly anti-communist socialist party, and the Slovak Labour Party.

Membership 1971, 1,700,000. First Secretary 1971, G. Husak.

CZECH CATHOLIC PEOPLE'S PARTY 1918

Founded from three smaller Catholic parties, with mainly peasant support. The *Slovak Catholic People's Party* seceded from it in 1921.

CZECH NATIONAL DEMOCRATIC PARTY 1917

Developed from the Young Czech Party (liberals), the Radical Party (right-wing), the Moravian Progressive Party and the Realist Party. The bulk of membership of the last two seceded in 1925 to form the National Party of Labour. The party represented big industrial and banking interests and the anti-Socialist bourgeoisie.

NATIONAL PARTY OF LABOUR 1925

Liberal intellectual support. Programme of moderate social reform, its socialist tendencies evolutionary and not revolutionary.

CZECH PEOPLE'S PARTY 1919

Christian party supporting the National Front government.
Secretary 1971, J. Pauly.

SLOVAK RECONSTRUCTION PARTY 1948

Developed from the former Slovak Democratic Party. Supports the National Front government.
Chairman 1971, J. Mijartan.

DENMARK

LIBERAL-DEMOCRATIC PARTY 1870

Support mainly from farmers, and its main aim the dominance of the Folkesting (second chamber) over Landsting (first chamber). Name changed to *Venstre*, a moderate liberal party with support no longer confined to farmers. Programme of free trade and a minimum of state interference.
President 1971, P. Hartling.

SOCIAL DEMOCRATIC PARTY 1871

Non-communist socialist party supported mainly by industrial and farm workers.
Membership 1971, 200,000. Chairman 1971, J. O. Krag.

CONSERVATIVE PEOPLE'S PARTY 1916

Originally supported by propertied class and concerned to support the authority of the Landsting over the Folkesting. Developed as a party of free initiative, maintaining private property, restricting state action to necessary economic and social intervention.
Chairman 1971, K. Thestrup.

RADICAL LIBERAL PARTY 1905

Smallholders' party, committed to reduction of armaments, international co-operation through UN, state control of large trusts and monopolies, but encouragement for small private enterprise.
Chairman 1971, S. Haugaard.

ESTONIA

CHRISTIAN PEOPLE'S PARTY 1918

Formed mainly to introduce religious teaching into the elementary and secondary schools. A centre party, slightly to the right.

REFORMIST LABOUR PARTY 1917

Left of centre, formed from the old Radical Socialist Party.

PEOPLE'S PARTY

Right of centre, developed from the old Democratic and Radical-Democratic parties.

FINLAND

SOCIAL DEMOCRATIC PARTY 1899

Constitutional socialist.
Membership 1971, 100,000. Chairman 1971, R. Paasio.

CENTRE PARTY 1906

Formed as the Agrarian Union, name changed in 1965. Centre with tendencies to the left, aims to support the interests of smallholders and small farmers.
Membership 1971, 290,000. Chairman 1971, J. Virolainen.

FINNISH PEOPLE'S DEMOCRATIC LEAGUE 1944

Union of Communists and left-wing socialist, including the old Socialist Union Party.
Membership 1971, 158,000. Chairman 1971, E. Alenius.

COMMUNIST PARTY 1918

Established in Moscow in 1917 before becoming active in Finland. It did not become legal in Finland until 1944.
General Secretary 1971, A. Aalto.

NATIONAL COALITION PARTY 1918

Conservative, supporting private enterprise.
Membership 1971, 72,000. Secretary 1971, H. Holkeri.

SWEDISH PEOPLE'S PARTY 1906

To protect the interests of the Swedish minority; divided politically, but mainly liberal.
Chairman 1971, J. M. Jansson.

FRANCE

ACTION FRANÇAISE 1898

Right-wing, nationalist, monarchist, anti-democratic and originally anti-semitic. Supported considerable autonomy for the provinces and a government of ministers responsible only to a king.

ACTION NATIONALE 1918

A combination of the former Action Liberale Populaire (Catholic), the Federation of Democratic Republicans and the Republican Federation. A centre party supporting indirect taxation, the free play of economic laws, decentralized administration and free enterprise.

DEMOCRATIC AND SOCIAL REPUBLICAN PARTY 1901

Founded as Republican Democratic Alliance. Favoured direct taxation, diplomatic relations with the Vatican, but a careful balance between clerical and anti-clerical influences and the separation of church and state.

GAUCHE RADICALE

Moderate socialist party, most active following 1918. Conciliatory in foreign policy.

FEDERATION OF RADICALS AND RADICAL SOCIALISTS POST—1918

Socialist reform party supporting state monopolies, supporting the League of nations and the full implementation of the Treaty of Versailles.

SOCIALIST PARTY 1905

Amalgamation of the Socialist Party of France (revolutionary) and the French Socialist Party (moderate evolutionary). The union split in 1920 and the resulting party was anti-communist, collectivist in theory but moderate in practice. Moved towards the eventual abolition of private property.
First Secretary 1971, A. Savary.

UNION OF DEMOCRATS FOR THE REPUBLIC

Development through several former parties with successive titles;
Democratic Labour Union
Union for the New Republic
Democratic Union for the Fifth Republic
Union for the Defence of the Republic
The Gaulliste party, now actively supporting continuation of Gaullist policy and a more independent role for France in the Western Alliance.

NATIONAL FEDERATION OF INDEPENDENT REPUBLICANS 1962

Liberal policy.
President 1971, V. Giscard d'Estaing.

REPUBLICAN RADICAL AND RADICAL-SOCIALIST PARTY

Traditional centre party of the third Republic. Extreme left-wing dissidents broke away in 1956, the remaining body continued with a liberal economic policy, support for NATO and European unity.
President 1971, M. Faure.

FRENCH COMMUNIST PARTY 1920

Marxist. Aims for a positive and independent French role in the UN.
Secretary-General 1971, W. Rochet.

UNITED SOCIALIST PARTY 1960

Developed from the Independent Socialist Party, the Union of the Left Socialist Party and the Tribune of Communism dissident section.
Membership 1971, 20,000. National Secretary 1971, M. Rocard.

DEMOCRATIC CENTRE

Formed from former sections of the Independent and Republican Movement parties. Centre left policy, supporting a united Europe and NATO.
President 1971, J. Lecanuet.

FEDERAL REPUBLIC OF GERMANY

CHRISTIAN-DEMOCRATIC UNION (CDU)

CHRISTIAN SOCIAL UNION (CSU) – EQUIVALENT BAVARIAN PARTY
1945

United Catholic-Protestant action on Christian principles, supporting maintenance of private property and individual freedom. Moderate conservative.
Membership 1971, 445,000. Chairman 1971, K. G. Kiesinger.

SOCIAL DEMOCRATIC PARTY OF GERMANY (SPD) 1945

Orthodox social-democrat policies, supporting a competitive economy,
moderate social policy.
Membership 1971, 710,500. Chairman 1971, W. Brandt.

FREE DEMOCRATIC PARTY (FDP)

Liberal social policies, policy of appeasement in Central Europe.
Membership 1971, 100,000. Chairman 1971, W. Scheel.

ZENTRUM PARTY

Catholic party, to the left of the CDU.
Chairman 1971, J. Brockman.

NATIONAL DEMOCRATIC PARTY OF GERMANY (NPD) 1964

Right-wing, nationalist.
Membership 1971, 35,000. Chairman 1971, A. von Thadden.

DEMOCRATIC GERMAN REPUBLIC

SOCIALIST UNITY PARTY OF GERMANY 1946

Founded as a union of the Social Democratic Party and the Communist
Party. Communist policy.
Membership 1971, 1·7m. First Secretary 1971, W. Ulbricht.

CHRISTIAN DEMOCRAT UNION OF GERMANY 1945

Chairman 1971, G. Gotting.

*These and six others belong to a National Front and issue a joint manifesto
before elections.*

GERMANY 1918–45

GERMAN NATIONAL PEOPLE'S PARTY (DNVP) 1918

Conservative, formed from a union of the Free Conservative Party, the Economic Union, the Conservative Party and the Christian Socialists. Aimed at a restoration of German sovereignty and a revision of the Treaty of Versailles. Protection for home industries, anti-Communist, pro-Christian.

NATIONAL PARTY OF GERMAN MODERATES (RDM) 1920

Supported by and concerned for the industrial and commercial middle classes. Anti-Socialist and against state controls.

SOCIAL DEMOCRATIC PARTY OF GERMANY 1875

Republican, democratic. Unqualified support for peace and reconciliation after 1918. Repudiated nationalism, aimed at socialization of large-scale production.

GERMAN DEMOCRATIC PARTY 1918

Formed from the former Progressive People's Party of 1910 and the left-wing of the National Liberal Party. Republican and moderate reformist.

GERMAN COMMUNIST PARTY 1919

Revolutionary communist.

GERMAN CENTRE PARTY 1870

Catholic centre party committed to fulfilling Versailles treaty obligations with a view to reconciliation. Supported the Weimar constitution.

GERMAN PEOPLE'S PARTY 1918

Formed from the right-wing of the former National Liberal Party. Protectionist in trade, nationalist and monarchist in politics.

NATIONAL SOCIALIST GERMAN WORKERS' PARTY 1925

Seceded from the German People's Party. Nationalist, supporting rearmament. Anti-Semitic. Protectionist in trade policy. Committed to social and educational reform, expansion of German sovereignty in Europe.

GIBRALTAR

GIBRALTAR LABOUR PARTY AND ASSOCIATION FOR THE ADVANCEMENT OF CIVIL RIGHTS

Leader 1971, Sir J. Hassan.

175

INTEGRATION WITH BRITAIN PARTY

Leader 1971, Major R. J. Peliza.

GREECE

POPULAR PARTY 1920

Parliamentary methods, moderate socialist policies.

LIBERAL-CONSERVATIVE PARTY 1920s

Republican. Aimed at government through a state council.

REPUBLICAN UNION 1920s

Formerly the extreme left of the Liberal Party. Committed to increased industrial production and the welfare of industrial workers. Supported proportional representation.

COMMUNIST PARTY

Supported proportional representation, women's suffrage, confiscation of large properties. Anti-armament.

NATIONAL RADICAL UNION 1956

Concerned with stimulating production and economic stability. Moderate. Chairman, K. Karamanlis.

> This and other parties were suspended in 1967 when all political parties ceased to function. Other parties recently formed and now suspended:
>> Union of Democratic Left – extreme left-wing.
>> Progressive Agrarian Democratic Union – moderate.
>> Union of Populist Parties – right-wing, monarchist.
>> Centre Union – liberal and progressive coalition.
>> Liberal Democratic Centre Party – breakaway group from the CU.

HUNGARY

PARTY OF NATIONAL UNITY 1921

Developed from the Party of Christian Small Landowners and Citizens. Conservative.

CHRISTIAN ECONOMY PARTY 1923

Formed from the former People's Party, Unionist Party, and Christian Socialists. Conservative and legitimist.

SOCIAL DEMOCRATIC PARTY 1894

Extreme left.

HUNGARIAN SOCIAL WORKERS' PARTY 1956

The Communist Party and the Social Democratic Party merged to create the Working People's Party. The name was later changed. Moscow-oriented Communist.
Membership 1971, 662,397. First Secretary 1971, J. Kadar.

PATRIOTIC PEOPLE'S FRONT 1954

Replaced the former Hungarian Independent People's Front. Represents the mass organizations such as Trade Unions. Independent Communist.
Chairman 1971, G. Kallai.

ICELAND

INDEPENDENCE PARTY 1929

Amalgamation of Conservative (1924) and Liberal (1925) parties. Aimed at social reform within a capitalist framework and furtherance of national independence through renunciation of the Act of Union with Denmark.

PROGRESSIVE PARTY 1916

Supports co-operatives, aims at educational and social reform.
Chairman 1971, O. Johannesson.

LABOUR PARTY 1916

Moderate evolutionary socialist.
President 1971, E. Jonsson.

PEOPLE'S UNION 1956

Formed from sections of the Social Democrats and the Socialist Unity Party. Marxist.
Chairman 1971, H. Valdimarsson.

IRISH REPUBLIC

CUMAN-NA-GAEDHEAL

Moderate party accepting partition and the Act of Settlement in 1921. Aimed for economic and social stability within the Empire.
Leader, W. Cosgrave.

FIANNA FAIL 1926

Republican. Successor to those bodies not accepting the Act of Settlement. Neutralist.
Leader, E. de Valera. General Secretary 1971, T. Mullins.

FINE GAEL 1933

Formed by amalgamating Cuman-na-Gaedheal, the Centre Party and the National Guard Party. Centre.
Leader 1971, L. Cosgrave.

LABOUR PARTY 1912

Formed as an organ of the Trades Unions, separated from them in 1930. Socialist.
Chairman 1971, D. Browne.

SINN FEIN 1905

Formed to end British occupation, and then to end partition and achieve a Democratic Socialist Republic of all Ireland.

ITALY

ITALIAN LIBERAL PARTY 1848

Founded by Cavour as a democratic force in the re-unification of Italy. Liberal.
Membership 1971, 180,000. President 1971, V. Badini-Confalonieri.

ITALIAN REPUBLICAN PARTY 1897

Founded on the doctrines of Mazzini.
Membership 1971, 80,000. Political Secretary 1971, U. la Malfa.

CHRISTIAN DEMOCRAT PARTY 1943

Successor to the pre-Fascist Popular Party. Anti-Communist, moderate social policy.
Political Secretary 1971, A. Forlani.

ITALIAN COMMUNIST PARTY 1921

The largest in Western Europe. Advocates nationalization and land redistribution.
General Secretary, L. Longo.

178

ITALIAN SOCIALIST PARTY (PSI) 1966

Founded by a merger of the Italian Socialist Party and the Italian Democratic Socialist Party. The latter broke away in 1969. Centre left, adhering to the second international.
Secretary General 1971, Fr. de Martino.

UNITED SOCIALIST PARTY (PSU) 1969

Democrat splinter from the Unified Socialists. Centre party.
President 1971, M. Tanassi.

ITALIAN SOCIAL MOVEMENT 1946

Extreme right.
Membership 1971, 650,000. President 1971, A. de Marsanich.

UNITED PROLETARIAN ITALIAN SOCIALIST PARTY 1964

Further left than the Italian Socialist Party, from whom it broke away.
Secretary 1971, T. Vecchietti.

NATIONAL FASCIST PARTY 1919

Formed to resist Bolshevism by force. Policies developed as conservative, nationalist, militarist and imperialist. ('Fascismo' = absolute and dictatorial government.)
Leader, B. Mussolini.

ITALIAN POPULAR PARTY 1919

Catholic independent party with social-democrat policies.
Leader, L. Sturzo.

(All non-fascist parties were dissolved in 1926)

UNITED PARTY 1922

Formed from a section of the old Socialist Party. Revolutionary socialist and reformist.

MASSIMALIST PARTY 1922

Hard-core theoretical socialists remaining after the United Party breakaway.

LATVIA

SOCIAL DEMOCRATIC PARTY

Allied with the Jewish Bund. Moderate.

DEMOCRATIC CENTRE PARTY

Middle-class support, policy left of centre.

FARMERS' UNION

Left-of-centre party to support rural interests.

INDEPENDENT NATIONALISTS

Right wing, support from the commercial and industrial class.

LITHUANIA

Christian Democrats ⎱
Farmers' Union   ⎰ Extreme right.
Labour Federation

Populist Party   ⎱
Nationalist Party   ⎰ Liberal.

Social Democrats   Left of centre.

LIECHTENSTEIN

PROGRESSIVE CITIZENS' PARTY

Secretary 1971, G. Kieber.

FATHERLAND UNION

Secretary, F. Nagele.

CHRISTIAN-SOCIALIST PARTY 1962

Chairman 1971, R. Walser.

LUXEMBOURG

LUXEMBOURG SOCIALIST WORKERS' PARTY 1902

Orthodox socialist policies.
Chairman 1971, F. Georges.

COMMUNIST PARTY 1921

Secretary 1971, D. Urbany.

CHRISTIAN SOCIALIST PARTY 1914

Dominant party in government since its foundation.
Chairman 1971, J. Dupong.

MALTA

NATIONALIST PARTY

Supports the European and Catholic tradition in Malta. Democratic conservative.
Leader 1971, Dr Borg Olivier.

MALTA LABOUR PARTY 1920

Socialist. Foreign policy of non-alignment and security through the United Nations.
Leader 1971, D. Mintoff.

CHRISTIAN WORKERS' PARTY 1961

Aims to base national progress on workers' interests.
Leader 1971, A. Pellegrini.

PROGRESSIVE CONSTITUTIONAL PARTY 1953

Supports association with EEC, close relations with Britain and NATO.
Leader 1971, Hon. M. Strickland.

THE NETHERLANDS

ROMAN CATHOLIC STATE PARTY

Influential nineteenth-century party. Policies based on encyclicals: 'Quanta cura', 'Immortale Dei', and 'Rerum Novae'. Right wing.

CATHOLIC PEOPLE'S PARTY 1925

Democratic section seceding from the above. Present-day membership open to Protestants.
Membership 1971, 200,000. President 1971, A. P. J. J. M. van der Stee.

ANTI-REVOLUTIONARY PARTY 1877

Originally neo-Calvinist, basing policies on the traditional Dutch native character as it was thought to be expressed in Calvinism. Conservative, becoming Christian-Democrat in policies.
Membership 1971, 100,000. President 1971, A. Veerman.

CHRISTIAN-HISTORICAL UNION 1908

Seceded from the Anti-Revolutionaries. Protestant, and to the left of the ARP.
Chairman 1971, A. D. W. Tilanus.

PEOPLE'S PARTY FOR FREEDOM AND DEMOCRACY 1948

Undenominational. Liberal. Free enterprise and social security within one system.
Chairman 1971, H. van Someren.

SOCIAL DEMOCRATIC WORKERS' PARTY

Developed from the previous Socialist Party which it saw as anarchical and non-parliamentary. Moderate left. In 1946 the most active section broke away and formed the Labour Party, farther left.
Labour Party Chairman 1971, A. Vorderling.

NORWAY

HØYRE 1884

Conservative. Aimed at a property-owning democracy, private enterprise.
Chairman 1971, S. Lindebrække.

CENTRE PARTY 1920

Moderate democratic party. Formed as Farmers' party, name changed in 1959.
Chairman 1971, J. Austrheim.

CHRISTIAN PEOPLE'S PARTY 1933

Christian-Democrat.
Chairman 1971, L. Korvald.

LIBERAL PARTY (VENSTRE) 1884

Moderate reform party.
Chairman 1971, H. Seip.

WORKERS' PARTY 1887

Orthodox evolutionary socialist.
Chairman 1971, T. Bratteli.

SOCIALIST PEOPLE'S PARTY 1961

Broke away from Workers' Party, being farther to the left. Opposes nuclear weapons and the Atlantic alliance. Neutralist.
Membership 1971, 7,000. Chairman 1971, T. Solheim.

POLAND

Polish People's Party National Christian Club Christian Democrats	The right wing, Catholic, alliance of Church and State, nationalist, anti-Communist and anti-Socialist.

PEASANTS' UNION 1924

Aimed for the abolition of the senate and universal franchise for men and women.

UNION OF POLISH PEASANT PARTIES 1923

Radical, concerned for small farmers and labourers. Aimed for peasant proprietorship.

RADICAL PEASANTS' PARTY 1918

Bolshevik.

NATIONAL LABOUR PARTY 1905

Workers' reform party, nationalist.

POLISH SOCIALIST PARTY 1892

Orthodox socialist, evolutionary reform party.

POLISH UNITED WORKERS' PARTY 1948

Formed by merging the former Socialist Party and Workers' Party. Communist.
Membership 1971, 2m. First Secretary 1971, E. Gierek.

UNITED PEASANTS' PARTY 1949

Formed from merging the Peasant Party and the Polish Peasant Party. Communist, concerned for small farmers and rural workers.
Membership 1971, 450,000. Chairman 1971, S. Gucwa.

DEMOCRATIC PARTY 1939

Progressive intellectual communist.
Membership 1971, 86,000. President 1971, Z. Moskwa.

PORTUGAL

MONARCHIST PARTY

Formed to support the claims of former King Manuel or Prince Duarte Nuno.

CATHOLIC PARTY

Conservative.

pre-Salazar

NATIONALIST PARTY

Conservative policy, republican.

REPUBLICAN PARTY

Democratic policy, republican.

POPULAR NATIONAL ACTION

Formerly National Union, the ruling conservative party. President 1971, M. Caetano.

ROMANIA

LIBERAL PARTY

Nineteenth-century moderate party, becoming conservative in 1916 on the introduction of universal suffrage and break-up of the great estates. (The old conservative party disappeared with this change.)

NATIONAL PEASANT PARTY

Liberal economic policies, supported co-operatives for agriculture.

ROMANIAN COMMUNIST PARTY 1921

Merged with Socialist Democratic Party in 1948 to form the Romanian Workers' Party. Name changed in 1965.
Membership 1971, 2m. General Secretary 1971, N. Ceausescu.

SPAIN

CONSTITUTIONAL LIBERAL PARTY 1875

Advocated religious toleration, a bicameral system of government, a constitutional monarchy and universal suffrage. Split into left and right factions in 1903.

REFORMISTS' PARTY 1913

Sovereignty to be vested in the people. Foreign policy for friendship with neighbouring states.

PATRIOTIC UNIONISTS 1924

'Religion, country, monarchy' – party formed and inspired by the Military Directory.

FALANGISTS

Only party currently existing. Conservative.
President 1971, Gen. F. Franco Bahamonde.

SWEDEN

SOCIAL DEMOCRATIC LABOUR PARTY 1880

Socialist party, economical reform policy, supports United Nations.
Membership 1971, 890,000. Chairman 1971, O. Palme.

PEOPLE'S PARTY 1902

Liberal.
Chairman 1971, S. Weden.

MODERATE UNION PARTY 1904

Conservative, free enterprise and private property.
Chairman 1971, G. Bohman.

COMMUNIST PARTY OF THE LEFT 1917

Formed as the Left Social Democratic Party of Sweden, renamed the Communist Party in 1921 and renamed again in 1967. Marxist.
Chairman 1971, C. H. Hermansson.

CENTRE PARTY 1922

Formed from a coalition of two smaller moderate parties. Developed more progressive social policies.
Chairman 1971, G. Hedlund.

CHRISTIAN DEMOCRATIC UNION 1964

Orthodox Christian-Democrat policies.
Membership 1971, 14,000. Chairman 1971, B. Ekstedt.

SWITZERLAND

RADICAL DEMOCRATIC PARTY

Led the movement towards the confederation of 1848. Liberal policies, supports strong central, federal power.
Chairman 1971, H. Schmitt.

CHRISTIAN DEMOCRATIC PEOPLE'S PARTY OF SWITZERLAND 1912

Formed by parties which had opposed centralization since 1848. Joined also by the Kulturkampf of the Radical Majority Party. Non-sectarian Christian; the most numerous parliamentary group in the Council of States.

SOCIAL DEMOCRATIC PARTY OF SWITZERLAND 1870

Socialist. Its influence dates mainly from the first Proportional Representation in 1919.
Chairman 1971, Fr. Crutter.

FARMERS', ARTISANS' AND CITIZENS' PARTY 1919

Seceded from the Radical Democrats. Mainly agrarian concerns, liberal social policies.
President 1971, H. Conzett.

LABOUR PARTY 1944

Communist and left-wing socialist; aims to co-ordinate all left-wing influences.
President 1971, R. Suter.

TURKEY

REPUBLICAN PEOPLE'S PARTY 1923

Founded by Kemal Atatürk. Left of centre, favoured a combination of state and private enterprise.
Leader 1971, I. Inonu.

PROGRESSIVE REPUBLICANS 1924

Liberal policies, free trade programmes. Dissolved for 'being in league with reactionary groups'.

JUSTICE PARTY 1961

Private enterprise party.
Leader 1971, S. Demirel.

RELIANCE PARTY 1967

Broke away from the Republican People's Party. Belief in political democracy. Policies left of centre.
Leader 1971, T. Feyzioglu.

NATIONAL ORDER PARTY 1969

Extreme right-wing, aims for the abolition of the Senate.
Leader, P. Erbakan.

TURKISH WORKERS' PARTY 1961

Left wing socialist.
Leader 1971, B. Boran.

USSR

COMMUNIST PARTY OF THE SOVIET UNION 1903

Began as the Bolshevik movement, named the Russian Communist Party in 1917, the All-Union Communist Party of Bolsheviks in 1925, the present name given in 1952.
General Secretary 1971, L. Brezhnev.

UNITED KINGDOM

CONSERVATIVE AND UNIONIST PARTY 1886

Formed by merger of the original Tory Party, renamed Conservative, with Liberals who did not accept Home Rule for Ireland. Policy imperialist and protectionist. Current policy free enterprise, entry into EEC, and the strengthening of the Commonwealth.
Leader 1971, E. Heath.

LABOUR PARTY 1900

Formed as a federation of trades unions and similar organizations. Socialist economic and social policies, support for UN in foreign relations, opposes entry into EEC.
Leader 1971, H. Wilson.

LIBERAL PARTY 1832

Formed from amalgamation of the old Whig Party, the Radical Party and the Reformers. Originally aimed at free trade, Home Rule for Ireland, reform of the House of Lords and moderate social reform and land reform. Supported the League of Nations and later the United Nations. Supports entry into EEC. Leader 1971, J. Thorpe.

CO-OPERATIVE PARTY 1917

Sponsors Labour and Co-operative candidates through a formal agreement of 1926, in which Co-operative parties became eligible for affiliation to Labour parties, and a further agreement of 1946 whereby Co-operative candidates were to run as Co-operative and Labour candidates.
Membership 1971, 15,000. Chairman, H. Kemp.

INDEPENDENT LABOUR PARTY 1893

Originally affiliated to the Labour Party until policy differences grew and the parties split in 1932. Its members gradually returned to the Labour Party after 1946.

WELSH NATIONALIST PARTY (PLAID CYMRU) 1925

Membership 1971, 40,000. President 1971, G. Evans.

SCOTTISH NATIONAL PARTY 1928

Formed as the National Party of Scotland. Merged with the Scottish Party in 1933.
President 1971, G. Wolfe.

COMMUNIST PARTY OF GREAT BRITAIN 1920

Membership 1971, 30,000. Chairman 1971, J. Gollan.

YUGOSLAVIA

LEAGUE OF COMMUNISTS OF YUGOSLAVIA

The only effective party.
Membership 1971, 1m. President, J. Broz Tito.

National Radical Party	– monarchist, centralist and nationalist	
Slovenian People's Party	– anti-centralist, demanding autonomy for different groups	
National Democratic Party	– split from the Radicals, centralists but ready to grant autonomy as a concession in some cases	pre-1945
Peasants' Party	– originally republican, by 1925 veering towards monarchy. Supported co-operatives and agrarian reform	

BIBLIOGRAPHY

Andrén, N., *Government and Politics in the Nordic Countries.* Stockholm, 1964
Barnes, S. H., *Party Democracy: Politics in an Italian Socialist Federation.* Yale Univ. Press, 1967
Barron, R. W., *Parties and Politics in Modern France.* Washington, D.C., 1959
Barzel, R., *Die Deutschen Parteien.* Geldern, Schaffrath, 1952
Berchtold, K. (ed.), *Österreichische Parteiprogramme 1868–1966.* Vienna, 1967
Buchheim, K., *Geschichte der christlichen Parteien in Deutschland.* Munich, 1953
Butler, D., *The Electoral System in Britain since 1918.* 2nd ed. OUP, 1963
Butler, D. E., and Freeman, J., *British Political Facts, 1900–68.* London, 1969
Buttinger, J., *In the Twilight of Socialism. A History of the Revolutionary Socialists of Austria.* New York, 1953
Capelle, R. B., *The M.R.P. and French Foreign Policy.* New York, 1963
Childs, D., *From Schumacher to Brandt.* Oxford, 1966
Chubb, B. (ed.), *A Source Book of Irish Government.* Dublin, Institute of Public Administration, 1964
Couwenberg, S. W., *Het Nederlandse Partijstelsel in Toekomstperspectief.* The Hague, 1960
Deguelle, C., and others, *Les élections législatives belges du 1er juin, 1958.* Brussels, 1959
Derry, J. W., *Political Parties.* London, 1968
De Tarr, F., *The French Radical party, from Herriot to Mendès-France.* OUP, 1964
Faucher, J. A., *Les clubs politiques en France.* Paris, 1965
Galli, G., and Facchi, P., *La sinistra democristiana: storia e ideologia.* Milan, 1962
Gruner, E., *Die Parteien in der Schweiz.* Bern, 1969
Hancock, M. D., *Sweden: a Multiparty System in Transition?* Univ. of Denver Press, 1968
Harrison, M., *Trade Unions and the Labour Party since 1945.* London, 1960
Höjer, C. H., *Le régime parlementaire belge de 1918 à 1940.* Uppsala and Stockholm, 1946
Hughes, C. J., *The Parliament of Switzerland.* London, 1962
Laponce, J., *The Government of the Fifth Republic; French Political Parties and the Constitution.* Univ of California Press, 1961
MacRau, D., *Parliament, Parties and Society in France 1946–58.* London and New York, 1967
Magri, F., *La democrazia cristiana in Italia.* 2 vols. Milan, 1954–5
McCracken, J. L., *Representative Government in Ireland.* OUP, 1959
McKenzie, R. T., *British Political Parties.* 2nd ed. London, 1964
Molin, B., 'Swedish Party Politics: A Case Study', *Scandinavian Political Studies*, No. 1. Helsinki, 1966
Neumann, S. (ed.), *Modern Political Parties.* Rev. ed. Univ. of Chicago Press, 1965
Nissen, B. A., *Political Parties in Norway: an Introduction to their History and Ideology.* Oslo, 1949
Olzog, G., *Die Politischen Parteien.* 3rd ed. Munich and Vienna, 1967
Pickles, D., *The Fifth French Republic.* 3rd ed. London, 1965
Pickles, D., *The Fourth French Republic.* 2nd ed. London, 1958
Schumann, H.-G., *Die Politischen Parteien Deutschlands nach 1945. Ein bibliographisch-systematischer Versuch.* Frankfurt am Main, 1967
Sjöblom, G., 'Analysis of Party Behavior', *Scandinavian Political Studies*, No. 2. Helsinki, 1967
Storing, J. A., *Norwegian Democracy.* Oslo, 1963
Valen, H., and Katz, D., *Political Parties in Norway.* London, 1964
Verney, D., *Parliamentary Reform in Sweden.* OUP, 1957
The Times *Guide to the House of Commons.* Rev. ed. after each General Election

7 JUSTICE

ALBANIA

Justice is administered by People's Courts. In 1952 a new penal code was introduced, modelled on Soviet law, but with severer penalties (41 offences carry the death penalty). Minors (14–18 years) are criminally responsible, but may not receive the death penalty. In Sep 66 the Ministry of Justice was incorporated into the Ministry of the Interior. In 1968 tribunals were set up in towns and villages to try minor crimes which had previously been dealt with by district courts.

AUSTRIA

The Supreme Court of Justice (*Oberster Gerichtshof*) in Vienna is the highest court in the land. Besides there are 4 higher provincial courts (*Oberlandesgerichte*), 18 provincial and district courts (*Landes- und Kreisgerichte*) and 229 local courts (*Bezirksgerichte*).

BELGIUM

Judges are appointed for life. There is a court of cassation, 3 courts of appeal, and assize courts for political and criminal cases. There are 26 judicial districts, each with a court of first instance. In each of the 236 cantons is a justice and judge of the peace. There are, besides, various special tribunals. There is trial by jury in assize courts.

BULGARIA

The constitution of 1947 provides for the election (and recall) of the judges by the people and, for the Supreme Court, by the National Assembly. The lower courts include laymen ('assessors') as well as jurists. There are a Supreme Court, 28 provincial (including Sofia) courts and 103 people's courts.

In June 61 'Comrades' Courts' were set up for the trial of minor offenders by their fellow-workers.

New family and penal codes were approved by the National Assembly in Apr 68. The maximum term of imprisonment is now 15 years except for murder which is punishable by a minimum of 20 years' imprisonment.

The Prosecutor-General, elected by the National Assembly for five years and subordinate to it alone, exercises supreme control over the correct observance of the law by all government bodies, officials and citizens. He appoints and discharges all Prosecutors of every grade. Prosecutors are independent of judges and government.

CZECHOSLOVAKIA

A new criminal code came into force on 1 Jan 62. The main emphasis in this and in the new criminal procedure law associated with it is on re-education rather than on punishment. Capital punishment is retained only as an extreme measure.

The emergency laws of 1969 have been incorporated into the criminal code.

Judges in local and district courts are elected by universal suffrage, those in regional courts by the regional local authority and the bench of the Supreme Court by the National Assembly.

DENMARK

The lowest courts of justice are organized in 105 tribunals (*underretter*), where minor cases are dealt with by a single judge. The tribunals at Copenhagen have 29 judges and Aarhus 8 and the other tribunals have 1 to 3. Cases of greater consequence are dealt with by the superior courts (*Landsretterne*); these courts are also courts of appeal for the above-named minor cases. Of superior courts there are two: *Østre Landsret* in Copenhagen with 33 judges, *Vestre Landsret* in Viborg with 20 judges. From these an appeal lies to the Supreme Court (*Højesteret*) in Copenhagen, composed of 15 judges. Judges under 70 years of age can be removed only by judicial sentence.

FINLAND

The lowest courts of justice are the municipal courts in towns and district courts in the country. Municipal courts are held by the burgomaster and at least two members of court, district court by judge and five jurors, the judge alone deciding, unless the jurors unanimously differ from him, when their decision prevails. From these courts an appeal lies to the courts of appeal (*Hovioikeus*) in Turku, Vaasa, Kuopio and Helsinki. The Supreme Court

(*Korkein oikeus*) sits in Helsinki. Judges can be removed only by judicial sentence.

Two functionaries, the *Oikeuskansleri* or Chancellor of Justice, and the *Oikeusasiamies*, or Solicitor-General, exercise control over the administration of justice. The former acts also as counsel and public prosecutor for the government; while the latter, who is appointed by the parliament, exerts a general control over all courts of law and public administration.

FRANCE

The French judicial system has been reorganized by a number of ordinances and decreees dated 22 Dec 1958.

Before this reform, the lowest courts were those of the Justices of Peace (*juges de paix*), one in each *canton*, who tried less important civil cases. The Tribunals of First Instance (*Tribunaux de Première Instance* or *Tribunaux Civils*), one in each *arrondissement*, dealt with more important civil cases and served as Tribunals of Appeal for the Justices of Peace, when their decisions were susceptible of appeal.

Since 2 Mar 59, 467 *tribunaux d'instance* (ten in overseas departments), under a single judge each and with increased material and territorial jurisdiction, have replaced the cantonal justices of the peace; and 178 *tribunaux de grande instance* (six in overseas departments) have taken the place of the 357 *tribunaux de première instance*.

The *tribunaux de grande instance* usually have a collegiate composition: however a law dated 10 July 70 has allowed them to administer justice under a single judge in some civil cases.

All petty offences (*contraventions*) are disposed of in the Police Courts (*Tribunaux de Police*) presided over by the *Juge d'Instance*. The Correctional Courts pronounce upon all graver offences (*délits*), including cases involving imprisonment up to five years. They have no jury, and consist of three judges who administer both criminal and civil justice. In all cases of a *délit* or a *crime* the preliminary inquiry is made in secrecy by an examining magistrate (*juge d'instruction*), who either dismisses the case or sends it for trial before a court where a public prosecutor (*Procureur*) endeavours to prove the charge.

The Conciliation Boards (*Conseils des Prud'hommes*) composed of an equal number of employers and employees deal with small trade and industrial disputes. Commercial litigation goes to the Commercial Courts (*Tribunaux de Commerce*) composed of tradesmen and manufacturers elected for two years.

When the decision of any of these Tribunals are susceptible of appeal, the cases go to the Courts of Appeal (*Cours d'Appel*). There are 31 Courts of Appeal (3 in overseas departments), composed each of a president and a variable number of members.

The Courts of Assizes (*Cours d'Assises*), composed each of a president, assisted by two other magistrates who are members of the Courts of Appeal, and by a jury of nine people, sit in every *département*, when called upon to try very important criminal cases. The decisions of the Courts of Appeal and the Courts of Assizes are final; however, the Court of Cassation (*Cour de Cassation*) had discretion to verify if the law had been correctly interpreted and if the rules of procedure have been followed exactly. The Court of Cassation may annul any judgment, and the cases have to be tried again by a Court of Appeal or a Court of Assizes.

A State Security Court has been established by 2 laws dated 15 Jan 63. It is usually composed of three civilian judges, including the president, and two judges of general or field officer rank, and has jurisdiction to deal with subversion in peace-time.

The French penal institutions have been reorganized by the procedural code which came into force on 2 Mar 59, and was modified by a law dated 17 July 70. They consist of: (1) *maisons d'arrêt* and *de correction*, where persons awaiting trial as well as those condemned to short periods of imprisonment are kept; (2) central prisons (*maisons centrales*) for those sentenced to long imprisonment; (3) special establishments, namely (a) schools for young adults, (b) hostels for old and disabled offenders, (c) hospitals for the sick and psychopaths, (d) institutions for recidivists. Special attention is being paid to classified treatment and the rehabilitation and vocational re-education of prisoners, including work in open-air and semi-free establishments.

Juvenile delinquents go before special judges and courts; they are sent to public or private institutions of supervision and re-education.

EAST GERMANY

The judicial system of East Germany (G.D.R.) was instituted following World War II. The principles on which the judicial system functions are embodied in the constitution. Judges are elected by the people's representative bodies or by the citizens directly. State Prosecuting Counsels are nominated by the Prosecutor-General. Jurisdiction is exercised by the Supreme Court, by the *Bezirke* Courts and by the *Kreis* Courts. All courts decide on the appointment of one presiding and two assistant magistrates. The Assistant Magistrates in the first instance are jurors (lay magistrates from all classes of society); the Labour Law Tribunal of the Supreme Court appoints two official judges and three lay magistrates.

Judges are independent and subject only to the constitution and the Legislature. A judge can be recalled only if he has committed a breach of the law, grossly neglected his duties or been convicted by a court.

Lay magistrates are elected for a period of four years after nomination by the democratic parties and organizations. Magistrates of the *Kreis* Courts are directly elected by the people; Magistrates of the *Bezirke* Courts, by the *Bezirkstag*; Magistrates of the Labour Law Tribunal of the Supreme Court, by the *Volkshammer*. All are equally authorized Judges.

Attached to the *Volkshammer* is a Constitutional and Legislature Commission in which all parties are represented according to their numbers. In addition there are on the Commission three members of the Supreme Court as well as three State Law Teachers who may not be members of the *Volkshammer*. All members of the Constitutional and Legislature Commission are appointed by the *Volkshammer*.

On 14 Jan 68 the whole judicial and penal system was reformed; the most important reform being the introduction of a new criminal code to replace the German Criminal Code of 1871.

WEST GERMANY

Justice is administered by the federal courts and by the courts of the Länder. In criminal procedures, civil cases and procedures of non-contentious jurisdiction the courts on the Land level are the local courts (*Amtsgerichte*), the regional courts (*Landgerichte*) and the courts of appeal (*Oberlandesgerichte*). On the federal level decisions regarding these matters are taken by the Federal Court (*Bundesgerichtshof*) at Karlsruhe. In labour law disputes the courts of the first and second instance are the labour courts and the Land labour courts and in the third instance, the Federal Labour Court (*Bundesarbeitsgericht*) at Kassel. Disputes about public law in matters of social security, unemployment insurance, maintenance of war victims and similar cases are dealt with in the first and second instances by the social courts and the Land social courts and in the third instance by the Federal Social Court (*Bundessozialgericht*) at Kassel. In most tax matters the finance courts of the Länder are competent and in the second instance, the Federal Finance Court (*Bundesfinanzhof*) at Munich. Other controversies of public law in non-constitutional matters are decided in the first and second instance by the administrative and the higher administrative courts (*Oberverwaltungsgerichte*) of the Länder, and in the third instance by the Federal Administrative Court (*Bundesverwaltungsgericht*) at Berlin.

For the inquiry into maritime accidents the admiralty courts (*Seeämter*) are competent on the Land level and in the second instance the Federal Admiralty Court (*Bundesoberseeamt*) at Hamburg.

The constitutional courts of the Länder decide on constitutional questions. The Federal Constitutional Court (*Bundesverfassungsgericht*) as the supreme German court decided such questions as loss of basic rights, unconstitutional character of political parties, validity of laws, charges against judges and complaints regarding violations of basic rights by the public force. The death sentence is abolished. (It is retained in East Germany for espionage or sabotage and for treason.)

HUNGARY

The administration of justice is the responsibility of the Procurator-General, who is elected by parliament for a term of six years. Civil and criminal cases fall under the jurisdiction of the district courts, county courts and the Supreme Court in Budapest. Criminal proceedings are dealt with by district courts through three-member councils and by county courts and the Supreme Court in five-member councils.

District courts act only as courts of first instance; county courts as either courts of first instance or of appeal. The Supreme Court acts normally as an appeal court, but may act as a court of first instance in cases submitted to it by the Public Prosecutor. All courts, when acting as courts of first instance, consist of one professional judge and two people's assessors, and, as courts of appeal, of three professional judges. Local government Executive Committees may try petty offences.

District or county judges and assessors are elected by the district or county councils, all members of the Supreme Court by Parliament.

There are also military courts of the first instance. Military cases of the second instance go before the Supreme Court.

Judges are appointed for life, subject to removal for disciplinary reasons.

ITALY

Italy has 1 court of cassation, in Rome, and is divided for the administration of justice into 23 appeal court districts (and 3 detached sections), subdivided into 159 tribunal districts, and these again into *mandamenti* each with its own magistracy (*Pretura*), 899 in all. There are also 85 first degree assize courts and 26 assize courts of appeal. For civil business, besides the magistracy above mentioned, *Conciliatori* have jurisdiction in petty plaints.

THE NETHERLANDS

Justice is administered by the High Court of the Netherlands (Court of Cassation), by 5 courts of justice (Courts of Appeal), by 19 district courts and by 62 cantonal courts; trial by jury is unknown. The Cantonal Court, which deals with minor offences, is formed by a single judge; the more serious cases are tried by the district courts, formed as a rule by three judges (in some cases one judge is sufficient); the courts of appeal are constituted of three and the High Court of five judges. All judges are appointed for life by the Sovereign (the judges of the High Court from a list prepared by the Second Chamber of the States-General). They can be removed only by a decision of the High Court.

Juvenile courts were set up in 1922. The juvenile court is formed by a single judge specially appointed to try children's civil cases, at the same time charged with the administration of justice for criminal actions committed by young persons who are between 12 and 18 (in special cases up to 21) years old, unless imprisonment of 6 months or more ought to be inflicted; such cases are tried by three judges.

NORWAY

The judicature in Norway is common to both civil and criminal cases. The same judges, who are state officials, preside over both kinds of cases. The participation of lay assessors and jurors, summoned for each case, varies according to the civil or criminal nature of the case.

The ordinary Court of First Instance (*Herreds- og Byrett*) is presided over by a judge who in criminal cases is, and in civil cases may be, assisted by two lay assessors, chosen by ballot from a panel elected by the district council. In criminal matters the Court of First Instance is generally competent in cases where the maximum penalty incurred is five years imprisonment. Altogether there are 104 Courts of First Instance. There is a Conciliation Council (*Forliksråd*) for each community, consisting of three men or women, elected by the district council, before which, as a general rule, civil cases must first be brought for mediation.

The Court of Second Instance (*Lagmannsrett*) is presided over by a judge, together with two other judges. In civil matters they may be assisted by lay assessors, ordinarily four but in some cases two, chosen and elected in the same way as mentioned above. In criminal cases the lay element is a jury composed of ten jurors. This court is a court of appeal in both civil and criminal cases. In addition, as a court of first instance, it takes cognizance of all criminal cases (other than those coming under the *Riksrett* – the court for impeachments) which do not come under the competence of the Court of First Instance. The kingdom is divided into five districts (*Lagdømmer*) for the purpose of the Courts of Second Instance.

The Supreme Court (*Høyesterett*) is the ultimate court of appeal. In criminal cases the competence of the court, however, is limited to the complaints against the application of laws, the measuring out of the penalty and the trial of the case of the subordinate courts. The Supreme Court consists of a president and 17 judges. In each single case the court consists of 5 judges.

All serious offences are prosecuted by the state. The public prosecution is led by a general prosecutor (*riksadvokat*) and there are 15 district prosecutors (*statsadvokater*). Counsel for the defence is, generally, paid by the state.

POLAND

The legal system was reorganized in 1950. A new penal code was adopted in 1969. Espionage and treason carry the severest penalties and severer punishment is provided for 'serious crimes'. For minor crimes there is more provision for probation sentences and fines. Previous jurisprudence was based on a penal code of 1932 supplemented by the Concise Penal Code of 1946.

There exist the following courts: The Supreme Court; voivodship, district and special courts. Judges and lay assessors are elected. The State Council elects the judges of the Supreme Court for a term of five years and appoints the Prosecutor-General. The office of the Prosecutor-General is separate from the judiciary.

Lawyers belong to 'legal collectives'; private practice has been abolished.

PORTUGAL

Portuguese law distinguishes civil (including commercial) and penal, labour, administrative and fiscal law, each branch having its lower courts, courts of appeal and the Supreme Court.

The Republic is divided for civil and penal cases into 171 *comarcas*; in every *comarca* there is a lower court. In the *comarca* of Lisbon there are 33 lower courts (16 for criminal procedure and 17 for civil or commercial cases); in the *comarca* of Oporto there are 17 lower courts (8 for criminal and 9 for civil or commercial cases); at Braga, Setúbal, Guimarães, Santarém, Leiria Aveiro, Viseu, Almada, Feira, Anadia, Cascais and Funchal there are 2 courts; at Coimbra there are 3 courts. There are 3 courts of appeal (*Tribunal de Relação*) at Lisbon, Coimbra and Oporto, and a Supreme Court in Lisbon (*Supremo Tribunal de Justiça*). There are also 33 municipal courts, which are lower courts, similar to those of the *comarcas*; their jurisdiction is, however, limited.

Capital punishment is abolished, except, in the case of war, by court martial.

ROMANIA

Justice is administered by the Supreme Court, the 39 district courts and lower courts. People's assessors (elected for four years) participate in all court trials, collaborating with the judges. The Procurator-General exercises 'supreme supervisory power to ensure the observance of the law' by all authorities, central and local, and all citizens. The Procurator's Office and its organs are independent of any organs of justice or administration, and only responsible to the Grand National Assembly (which appoints the Procurator-General for four years) and, between its sessions, to the State Council. Since 1968 the Ministry of the Interior has been responsible only for 'ordinary' police work. State security is the responsibility of a new, separate State Security Council. A new penal code came into force on 1 Jan 69. It is based on 'the rule of law' and is aimed at preventing illegal trials. The death penalty is retained for 'specially serious offences' (treason, some classes of murder, theft of state property having serious consequences).

SPAIN

Justice is administered by *Tribunales* and *Juzgados* (Tribunals and Courts), which conjointly form the *Poder Judicial* (Judicial Power). Judges and magistrates cannot be removed, suspended or transferred except as set forth by law.

The Judicature is composed of the *Tribunal Supremo* (Supreme High Court); 15 *Audiencias territoriales* (Division High Courts); 50 *Audiencias Provinciales* (Provincial High Courts); 579 *Juzgados de Primera Instancia* (Courts of First Instance), and 9,203 *Juzgados Municipales, Comarcales y de paz* (District Court, or Court of Lowest Jurisdiction held by Justices of the Peace).

The *Tribunal Supremo* consists of a president (appointed by the government) and various judges distributed among six chambers: one for trying civil matters, three for administrative purposes, one for criminal trials and one for social matters. The *Tribunal Supremo* has disciplinary faculties; is court of cassation in civil criminal trials; for administrative purposes decides in first and second instance disputes arising between private individuals and the state, and in social matters resolves in the last instance all cases involving over 100,000 pesetas.

The *Audiencias Territoriales* have power to try in second instance sentences passed by judges in civil matters.

The *Audiencias Provinciales* try and pass sentence in first instance on all cases filed for delinquency. The jury system is in operation except for military trials.

The *Juzgados Municipales* try small civil cases and petty offences. The *Juzgados Comarcales* deal with the same charges, but their jurisdiction embraces larger districts.

Military cases are tried by the *Tribunal Supremo de Justicia Militar*.

198

SWEDEN

The administration of justice is entirely independent of the government. The *Justitiekansler*, or Chancellor of Justice (a royal appointment) and the *Justitieombudsmän* (Judical Commissioners appointed by the Diet), exercise a control over the administration. In 1968 a reform was carried through which meant that the offices of the former *Justitieombudsman* (Ombudsman for civil affairs) and the *Militieombudsman* (Ombudsman for military affairs) were turned into one sole institution with three Ombudsmen, each styled *Justitieombudsman*. They exert a general supervision over all courts of law, the civil service, military laws and the military services. In 1969 they received altogether 3,128 cases; of these, 393 were instituted on their own initiative and 2,735 on complaints. They dismissed 747 cases, investigated 1,527 without taking direct action, offered criticisms in 557 cases, instituted 5 prosecutions and made 7 proposals to government.

The *Riksånlagaren* (a royal appointment) is the chief public prosecutor.

The kingdom has a Supreme Court of Judicature and is divided into 6 high-court districts and 135 district-court divisions.

These district courts (or courts of first instance) deal with both civil and criminal cases. More serious criminal cases are generally tried by a judge and a jury (*nämnd*) of seven to nine members; in minor criminal cases the jury is reduced to three; petty cases are tried by the judge alone. In larger towns civil cases are tried as a rule by three to four judges or in minor cases by one judge. In rural districts and small towns civil cases are tried in the same way as criminal cases.

In trials by jury the judge decides the case except when the whole jury – or at least seven members if the jury consists of more than seven – differs from him, when the decision of the jury prevails.

Persons of poor or moderate means may be provided with the services of lawyers in civil and criminal proceedings from special state-aided legal aid centres, and may also be granted costs for their proceedings. Moreover, the community may bear the cost of free legal advice to poor persons by private lawyers in cases not brought before a court.

SWITZERLAND

The Federal Tribunal (*Bundes-Gericht*), which sits at Lausanne consists of 26–28 members, with 11–13 supplementary judges, appointed by the Federal Assembly for six years and eligible for re-election; the president and vice-president serve for two years and cannot be re-elected. The president has a salary of 100,000 francs a year, and the other members 90,000 francs. The

Tribunal has original and final jurisdiction in suits between the Confederation and cantons; between cantons and cantons; between the Confederation or cantons and corporations or individuals, the value in dispute being not less than 8,000 francs; between parties who refer their case to it, the value in dispute being at least 20,000 francs; in such suits as the constitution or legislation of cantons places within its authority; and in many classes of railway suits. It is a court of appeal against decisions of other federal authorities, and of cantonal authorities applying federal laws. The Tribunal also tries persons accused of treason or other offences against the Confederation. For this purpose, it is divided into four chambers: Chamber of Accusation, Criminal Chamber (*Cour d'Assises*), Federal Penal Court and Court of Cassation. The jurors who serve in the Assize Courts are elected by the people, and are paid 70 francs a day when serving.

On 3 July 38 the Swiss electorate accepted a new federal penal code, to take the place of the separate cantonal penal codes. The new code, which abolished capital punishment, came into force on 1 Jan 42.

By federal law of 5 Oct 50 several articles of the penal code concerning crime against the independence of the state have been amended with a view to reinforcing the security of the state.

TURKEY

The unified legal system consists of: (1) justices of the peace (single judges with limited but summary penal and civil jurisdiction); (2) courts of first instance (single judges, dealing with cases outside the jurisdiction of (3) and (4): (3) central criminal courts (a president and two judges, dealing with cases where the crime is punishable by imprisonment over five years): (4) commercial courts (three judges).

The Court of Cassation sits at Ankara.

The Council of State is the highest administration tribunal; it consists of five chambers. Its 31 judges are nominated from among high-ranking personalities in politics, economy, law, the army, etc. The Military Court of Cassation in Ankara is the highest military tribunal.

The Constitutional Court, set up under the 1961 constitution, can review and annul legislation and try the President of the Republic, Ministers and senior judges. It consists of 15 regular and 5 alternate members.

The Civil Code and the Code of Obligations have been adapted from the corresponding Swiss codes. The Penal Code is largely based upon the Italian Penal Code, and the Code of Civil Procedure closely resembles that of the Canton of Neuchâtel. The Commercial Code is based on the German.

UNION OF SOVIET SOCIALIST REPUBLICS

The basis of the judiciary system is the same throughout the Soviet Union, but the constituent republics have the right to introduce modifications and to make their own rules for the application of the code of laws. The Supreme Court of the USSR is the chief court and supervising organ for all constituent republics and is elected by the Supreme Soviet of the USSR for five years. Supreme Courts of the Union and Autonomous Republics are elected by the Supreme Soviets of these republics, and Territorial, Regional and Area Courts by the respective Soviets, each for a term of five years.

Court proceedings are conducted in the local language with full interpreting facilities as required. All cases are heard in public, unless otherwise provided for by law, and the accused is guaranteed the right of defence.

Laws establishing common principles of criminal legislation, criminal responsibility for state and military crimes, judicial and criminal procedure and military tribunals were adopted by the Supreme Soviet on 25 Dec 58 for the courts both of the USSR and the constituent Republics.

The Law Courts are divided into People's Courts and higher courts. The People's Courts consist of the People's Judge and two Assessors, and their function is to examine, as the first instance, most of the civil and criminal cases, except the more important ones, some of which are tried at the Regional Court, and those of the highest importance at the Supreme Court. The regional Courts supervise the activities of the People's Courts and also act as Courts of Appeal from the decisions of the People's Court. Special chambers of the higher courts deal with offences committed in the Army and the public transport services.

People's Judges and rota-lists of assessors are elected directly by the citizens of each constituency: judges for five years, assessors for two: they must be over 25 years of age. Should a judge be found not to perform his duties conscientiously and in accordance with the mandate of the people, he may be recalled by his electors.

The People's Assessors are called upon for duty for two weeks in a year. The People's Assessors for the Regional Court must have had at least two years' experience in public or trade-union work. The list of Assessors for the Supreme Court is drawn up by the Supreme Soviet of the Republic.

The Labour Session of the People's Court supervises the regulations relating to the working conditions and the protection of labour and gives decisions on conflicts arising between managements and employees, or the violation of regulations.

Disputes between state institutions must be referred to an arbitration commission. Disputes between Soviet state institutions and foreign business firms may be referred by agreement to a Foreign Trade Arbitration Commission of the All-Union Chamber of Commerce.

The Procurator-General of the USSR is appointed for seven years by the Supreme Soviet. All procurators of the republics, autonomous republics and autonomous regions are appointed by the Procurator-General of the USSR for a term of five years. The procurators supervise the correct application of the law by all state organs, and have special responsibility for the observance of the law in places of detention. The procurators of the Union republics are subordinate to the Procurator-General of the USSR, whose duty it is to see that acts of all institutions of the USSR are legal, that the law is correctly interpreted and uniformly applied; he has to participate in important cases in the capacity of State Prosecutor.

Capital punishment was abolished on 26 May 47, but was restored on 12 Jan 50 for treason, espionage and sabotage, on 7 May 54 for certain categories of murder, in Dec 58 for terrorism and banditry, on 7 May 61 for embezzlement of public property, counterfeiting and attack on prison warders and, in particular circumstances, for attacks on the police and public order volunteers and for rape (15 Feb 62) and for accepting bribes (20 Feb 62).

In view of criminal abuses, extending over many years, discovered in the security system, the powers of administrative trial and exile previously vested in the security authorities (MVD) were abolished in 1953; accelerated procedures for trial on charges of high treason, espionage, wrecking, etc., by the Supreme Court were abolished in 1955; and extensive powers of protection of persons under arrest or serving prison terms were vested in the Procurator-General's Office (1955). Supervisory commissions, composed of representatives of trade unions, youth organizations and local authorities, were set up in 1956 to inspect places of detention.

Further reforms of the civil and criminal codes were decreed on 25 Dec 58. Thereby the age of criminal responsibility has been raised from 14 to 16 years; deportation, banishment and deprivation of citizenship have been abolished; a presumption of innocence is not accepted, but the burden of proof of guilt has been placed upon the prosecutor; secret trials and the charge of 'enemy of the people' have been abolished.

UNITED KINGDOM

Although the United Kingdom is a unitary state, it does not have a single body of law applicable universally within its limits. Scotland has its own distinctive legal system and law courts, and although the existence of a single Parliament for Great Britain since 1707, common opinions on broader issues, and a common final court of appeal in civil cases have resulted in substantial identity on many points, differences in legal procedure and practice remain. In Northern Ireland on the other hand, the structure of the courts and legal procedure and practice have closely resembled those of England and Wales for centuries but, as Northern Ireland has its own parliament with defined powers (as well as being represented in the parliament at Westminster), its enacted law derives in certain spheres from a different source and may differ in substance from that which operates in England and Wales. However, a large volume of modern legislation, particularly in the social field, applies throughout the United Kingdom. A feature common to all the systems of law in the United Kingdom (which differentiates them from some continental systems) is that there is no complete code, although the Law Commission is working on the codification of certain branches of law. The sources of law in all the systems include legislation and unwritten or 'common' law.

Legislation includes some 3,000 Acts of Parliament and delegated or subordinate legislation made by ministers and others under powers conferred by parliament, Acts of Parliament being absolutely binding on all courts of the United Kingdom, and taking precedence over any other source of law. The common law of England originated in the customs of the realm and was built up by decisions of the courts. A supplementary system of law, known as 'equity', came into being during the Middle Ages to provide and enforce more effective protection for existing legal rights. It was administered by a separate court and later became a separate body of legal rules. In 1875 the courts of equity were fused with the courts of common law, so that all courts now apply both systems but, where they conflict, equity prevails. In Scotland the basis of common law, which largely depends on the canon law of Rome, helped by continental commentators, is embodied in the writings of certain seventeenth-, eighteenth- and early nineteenth-century lawyers who, between them, de-scribed systematically almost the whole field of private and criminal law as existing in their times. Broadly speaking, the principles enunciated by these lawyers, together with the many judicial decisions which have followed and developed from those principles, form the body of Scots non-statutory law. Scotland has never had a separate system of equity – equitable principles having always permeated the ordinary rules of law. A feature common to the legal systems of the United Kingdom is the distinction made between the criminal law and the civil law. Criminal law is concerned with wrongs against the community as a whole; civil law is concerned with the rights, duties and obligations of individual members of the community between themselves.

YUGOSLAVIA

There are county tribunals, district courts, the Supreme Court of the Auto-nomous Province of Vojvodina, Supreme Courts of the constituent republics and the Supreme Court of the Socialist Federal Republic of Yugoslavia. In county tribunals and district courts the judicial functions are exercised by professional judges and by lay assessors constituted into collegia. There are no assessors at the supreme courts.

All judges are elected by the social-political communities in their jurisdiction. The judges exercise their functions in accordance with the legal provisions enacted since the liberation of the country.

BIBLIOGRAPHY

Bebr, G., *Judicial Control of the European Communities*. London, 1962
David, R., and Hazard, J. N., *Le Droit Soviétique*. Paris, 1954
Jackson, R. M., *The Machinery of Justice in England*. 5th ed. London, 1967
Rowat, D. C., *The Ombudsman: Citizen's Defender*. London, 1965
Schlesinger, R., *Soviet Legal Theory*. London, 1945

8 DEFENCE AND TREATIES

PRINCIPAL EUROPEAN ARMED CONFLICTS
1918–72

RUSSIAN CIVIL WAR. *June 1918–November 1920*

Civil War between Soviet Communists and White Russian forces, with intervention by outside powers on behalf of the anti-Communists. The first landing of British forces took place at Murmansk in June 18, and further French and British troops landed at Archangel in Aug 18; Japan and the United States also sent troops. The Civil War effectively ended when White Russian forces under General Wrangel evacuated the Crimea in Nov 20.

RUSSO-POLISH WAR. *April 1919–October 1920*

Invasion by Polish forces of territory occupied by the Soviet Union as the German army withdrew at the end of World War I, in the hope of establishing a Soviet-Polish frontier which would give Poland possession of all the areas it traditionally claimed. After a Soviet counter-attack had been defeated, an armistice was signed on 12 Oct 20, and a settlement was reached in the treaty of Riga (18 Mar 21).

GRECO-TURKISH WAR. *January 1921–October 1922*

Greek invasion of Asian Turkey (Anatolia). This was repelled by the Turkish republican forces, and the Armistice of Mudanya (11 Oct 22) ended the fighting. By the Treaty of Lausanne (24 July 23), Greece renounced any claim to territory in Asia Minor, whilst Turkey surrendered all claims to territories of the Ottoman empire occupied by non-Turks.

SPANISH CIVIL WAR. *July 1936–March 1939*

A revolt by military leaders in Spanish Morocco against the civilian government led to general civil war. Unofficial military assistance was given by Germany, Italy, Portugal and the USSR; in all, 40,000 foreign volunteers, including 2,000 British, fought in the International Brigade on the Republican side. The civil war ended when General Franco's Nationalist forces entered Madrid on 28 Mar 39.

WORLD WAR II (EUROPE). *September 1939–May 1945*

German forces invaded Poland on 1 Sep 39, which led Britain and France to declare war on Germany on 3 Sep. The Germans invaded the Low Countries on 10 May 40, and France was compelled to sign an armistice on 22 June, the British army being evacuated from Dunkirk. Italy declared war on Britain and France on 10 June 40. Breaking the Nazi-Soviet Pact of Aug 39, Hitler invaded Russia on 22 June 41. Allied forces drove Italian and German armies out of North Africa and invaded Italy in 1943. The invasion of Normandy was launched on 6 June 44, and Germany was forced to accept unconditional surrender on 7 May 45.

RUSSO-FINNISH WAR. *November 1939–March 1940*

Soviet forces invaded Finland following Finnish rejection of demands for territorial concessions. The war was ended by the Treaty of Moscow (12 Mar 40), in which the Finns surrendered to Russia the south-eastern part of the country.

GREEK CIVIL WAR. *1946–1949*

Civil war between Communist partisan forces and the civilian government. The likelihood of a Communist victory was reduced by the break between Yugoslavia and the Communist bloc in 1948, which led to the closing of one stretch of Greece's northern frontier to the rebels. The Greek Communist broadcasting station announced the end of open hostilities on 16 Oct 49.

EAST GERMAN UPRISING. *June 1953*

Demonstrations in East Berlin and other East German cities against Russian domination began on 17 June 53, but were suppressed by Soviet armed forces.

HUNGARIAN UPRISING. *October 1956*

Student demonstrations on 23 Oct 56 led to a general uprising against the civil government and Soviet occupying power. On 27 Oct Soviet troops were forced to evacuate Budapest, but reinforcements arrived to surround the capital, and after ten days' fighting the uprising was suppressed.

INVASION OF CZECHOSLOVAKIA. *August 1968*

During the night of 20–21 Aug, Soviet troops and Warsaw Pact forces from Poland, Hungary, East Germany and Bulgaria occupied Prague and other leading cities to reverse the liberalizing reforms of the Czechoslovakian government. Though the Czechoslovakian armed forces were ordered to offer no resistance, there were extensive civilian demonstrations against the occupying forces.

PRINCIPAL ARMED CONFLICTS (OUTSIDE EUROPE) IN WHICH EUROPEAN POWERS PARTICIPATED 1918–72

ABYSSINIAN WAR. *October 1935–July 1936*

Italy invaded Abyssinia on 3 Oct 35. Addis Ababa was captured on 5 May 36, and the Emperor Haile Selassie was forced into exile in Britian. The League of Nations imposed sanctions on Italy, but these proved ineffective; they were lifted in July 36.

WORLD WAR II (ASIA). *December 1941–August 1945*

Japan attacked the American base at Pearl Harbour on 7 Dec 41, and within six months the Japanese were masters of South-east Asia and Burma. The Allied counter-offensive culminated in the dropping of the first atomic bombs on Hiroshima and Nagasaki in Aug 45. On 15 Aug 45 the Emperor of Japan broadcast to the nation to cease fighting. The principal European powers involved in the conflict were Britain and the Netherlands; the Soviet Union also declared war on Japan on 8 Aug 45.

FIRST VIETNAM WAR. *December 1946–July 1954*

The war between the French colonial government and Communist forces led by Ho Chi Minh began with attacks on French garrisons by Vietminh troops throughout Vietnam on 19 Dec 46. The French army was defeated at Dien Bien Phu in May 54, and the war was ended by the Geneva Agreement of 21 July 54, which divided Vietnam into the area north of the 17th parallel and an independent South Vietnam.

MALAYAN EMERGENCY. *June 1948–July 1960*

Insurgency by Communist forces, eventually suppressed by British and Malayan troops. The State of Emergency was ended on 31 July 60. British troops were also involved in the 'confrontation' with Indonesia after the creation of the Malaysia Federation on 16 Sep 63. An agreement was reached ending confrontation on 1 June 66.

KOREAN WAR. *June 1950–July 1953*

The invasion of South Korea by North Korea on 25 June 50 led to intervention by United Nations forces following an emergency session of the Security Council. The advance of the United Nations forces into North Korea on 1 Oct 50 led to the entry of the Chinese into the war. An armistice was signedat Panmunjon on 27 July 53. The European powers which contributed to the United Nations force were Britain, France, Turkey, Belgium, Luxembourg, the Netherlands and Greece.

ALGERIAN REVOLUTIONARY WAR. *October 1954–March 1962*

The uprising by the FLN (Front de Libération Nationale) against the French colonial government began during the night of 31 Oct–1 Nov 54. A cease-fir? agreement was signed on 18 Mar 62, and after a referendum the independence of Algeria was recognized on 3 July 62.

SUEZ WAR. *October–November 1956*

The Israeli army attacked Egypt on 29 Oct 56. The rejection of a British and French ultimatum by Egypt resulted in a combined British and French attack on Egypt on 31 Oct. Hostilities ended at midnight on 6–7 Nov following the call for a cease-fire by the United Nations.

WORLD WAR I
EUROPEAN BELLIGERENTS

	Population (in millions)	Total mobilized (in thousands)	Soldiers killed or died of wounds (in thousands)
Austria-Hungary	47	7,800	1,200
Belgium	7	267	14
Britain	41	8,904	908
Bulgaria	4	560	87
France	39	8,410	1,363
Germany	63	11,000	1,774
Italy	33	5,615	560
Romania	7	750	336
Russia	150	12,000	1,700
Serbia	3	707	45
Turkey	26	2,850	325

Source: Quincy Wright, *A Study of War*, The University of Chicago Press, 1942: second edition, 1965.

WORLD WAR II
PRINCIPAL EUROPEAN BELLIGERENTS

	Population (in millions)	Total mobilized (in thousands)	Soldiers killed or died of wounds (in thousands)	Civilians killed (in thousands)
Belgium	8	625	8	101
Britain	48	5,896	557	61
Bulgaria	7	450	10	..
Czechoslovakia	15	150	10	490
Denmark	4	25	4	..
Finland	4	500	79	..
France	39	5,000	202	108
Germany	71	10,200	3,250	500
Greece	6	414	73	400
Hungary	9	350	147	..
Italy	44	3,100	149	783
Netherlands	9	410	7	242
Norway	3	75	2	2
Poland	35	1,000	64	2,000
Romania	14	1,136	520	—
Soviet Union	175	22,000	7,500	7,500
Yugoslavia	15	3,741	410	1,275

Source: Quincy Wright. *A Study of War.* University of Chicago Press, 1942: second edition, 1965.

EUROPEAN ARMED FORCES 1971–2

	Population	Army	Navy	Air-force	Para-Military	Defence expenditure US $ m. in 1971	Total regular Forces
Albania	2,190,000	35,000	3,000	4,000	37,000	116	42,000
Austria	7,445,000	44,000	—	4,350	12,000	170	48,350
Belgium	9,800,000	71,500	5,000	20,000	13,500	594	96,500
Britain	56,000,000	185,300	84,600	111,000	—	6,108	380,900
Bulgaria	8,555,000	117,000	9,000	22,000	15,000	279	148,000
Czechoslovakia	14,700,000	145,000	—	40,000	35,000	1,765	185,000
Denmark	4,990,000	24,000	6,500	10,000	—	410	40,500
Finland	4,600,000	34,000	2,500	3,000	3,000	154	39,500
France	51,225,000	329,000	68,500	104,000	65,000	5,202	501,500
Germany (East)	17,150,000	90,000	16,000	20,000	46,000	2,124	126,000
Germany (West)	60,000,000	327,000	36,000	104,000	18,500	5,961	467,000
Greece	8,960,000	118,000	18,000	23,000	25,000	338	159,000
Hungary	10,300,000	90,000	500	12,500	277,000	511	103,000
Italy	54,000,000	295,000	45,000	74,000	80,000	2,651	414,000
Luxembourg	342,000	550	—	—	350	8.59	550
Netherlands	13,175,000	76,000	19,000	21,500	3,200	1,161	116,500
Norway	3,915,000	18,000	8,500	9,400	—	411	35,900
Poland	33,200,000	190,000	20,000	55,000	65,000	2,220	265,000
Portugal	9,730,000	179,000	18,000	21,000	9,700	398	218,000
Romania	20,400,000	130,000	9,000	21,000	540,000	798	160,000
Soviet Union	245,700,000	2 million	475,000	550,000	300,000	39,700	3,375,000
Spain	33,600,000	220,000	47,500	33,500	65,000	681	301,000
Sweden	8,125,500	12,500	4,700	5,800	325,000	1,192	23,000
Switzerland	6,375,000	2,500	—	3,000	—	459	5,500
Turkey	36,100,000	420,000	38,500	50,000	75,000	446	508,500
Yugoslavia	20,800,000	195,000	18,000	20,000	19,000	596	233,000

Source: *Military Balance 1971–72*

PEACE TREATIES ARISING FROM WORLD WAR I
1918–23

TREATY OF BREST-LITOVSK. *3 March 1918*

The Soviet Union surrendered the Baltic Provinces and Russian Poland to the Central Powers, recognized the independence of Finland and the Ukraine, and ceded to Turkey the districts of Kars, Ardahan and Batum. The Treaty was formally invalidated by the Armistice in the West on 11 Nov 18.

TREATY OF VERSAILLES. *28 June 1919*

The peace treaty between Germany and the Allied Powers. Germany surrendered territory to Belgium, Denmark, Poland and Czechoslovakia; Alsace-Lorraine was ceded to France. Germany also surrendered all her overseas territories. The Rhineland was declared a demilitarized zone, with Allied occupation for fifteen years from when the Treaty came into effect on 10 Jan 20. Severe restrictions were placed on the German Armed Forces; the army was limited to 100,000 men. The union of Germany and Austria was forbidden. The Treaty declared Germany's responsibility for causing the war, and made Germany liable for the payment of Reparations. The treaty also contained the Covenant of the League of Nations.

TREATY OF ST. GERMAIN. *10 September 1919*

The peace treaty between the Austrian Republic and the Allied Powers. By the settlement Austria lost territory to Italy, Yugoslavia, Czechoslovakia, Poland and Romania. Hungary was recognized as an independent state, and the union of Austria and Germany was forbidden. The Austrian army was limited to 30,000 men, and the Republic was made liable for the payment of Reparations.

TREATY OF NEUILLY. *27 November 1919*

The peace treaty between Bulgaria and the Allied Powers. Bulgaria lost Western Thrace to Greece, and territory to Yugoslavia. The Bulgarian army was limited to 20,000 men, and Bulgaria was made liable for Reparations.

TREATY OF TRIANON. *4 June 1920*

The peace treaty between Hungary and the Allied Powers. Hungary surrendered territory to Romania, Czechoslovakia, Yugoslavia, Poland, Italy and the Austrian Republic, to a total of about two-thirds of its pre-war lands. The Hungarian army was limited to 35,000 and Hungary was made liable for Reparations.

TREATY OF SÈVRES. *10 August 1920*

The peace treaty made with Ottoman Turkey, but never ratified by the Turks.

TREATY OF LAUSANNE. *24 July 1923*

Treaty made necessary by Turkey's refusal to accept the treaty of Sèvres. Turkey surrendered its claims to territories of the Ottoman Empire occupied by non-Turks, whilst retaining Constantinople and Eastern Thrace in Europe. The Greeks surrendered Smyrna, but were confirmed in possession of all the Aegean Islands except Imbros and Tenedos which were returned to Turkey. Turkey recognized the annexation of Cyprus by Britain and of the Dodecanese by Italy. The Bosphorus and the Dardanelles were declared to be demilitarized. (By the Montreux Convention of 20 July 36 Turkey was permitted to re-fortify the Straits.)

TREATIES, AGREEMENTS AND ALLIANCES 1918–72

3 Mar 18	Treaty of Brest-Litovsk	Russia and the Central Powers
Aug 19	Franco-Belgian Military Convention	
28 June 19	Treaty of Versailles	Germany and the Allied Powers
10 Sep 19	Treaty of St Germain	Austrian Republic and the Allied Powers
27 Nov 19	Treaty of Neuilly	Bulgaria and the Allied Powers
4 June 20	Treaty of Trianon	Hungary and the Allied Powers
10 Aug 20	Treaty of Sèvres	Turkey and the Allied Powers (not ratified by Turkey)
19 Feb 21	Franco-Polish Treaty	
3 Mar 21	Polish-Romanian Treaty	
18 Mar 21	Treaty of Riga	Poland and the Soviet Union
16 Apr 22	Treaty of Rapallo	Russia and Germany
31 Aug 22	Little Entente	Czechoslovakia, Yugoslavia and Romania
24 July 23	Treaty of Lausanne	
1 Dec 25	Locarno Treaties	France, Belgium, Germany; guaranteed by Britain and Italy
24 Apr 26	Soviet-German Neutrality Pact	
25 July 32	Polish-Soviet Treaty	
26 Jan 34	Polish-German Pact	
2 May 35	Franco-Russian Alliance	
20 July 36	Montreux Convention	Turkey permitted to re-fortify the Straits
25 Nov 36	Anti-Comintern Pact	Germany and Japan; signed by Italy 6 Nov 37
2 Jan 37	Anglo-Italian Gentleman's Agreement	
29 Sep 38	Munich Agreement	Britain, France, Germany, Italy
22 May 39	Pact of Steel	Germany and Italy
23 Aug 39	Nazi-Soviet Pact	
25 Aug 39	Polish-British Treaty	
19 Oct 39	British-French-Turkish Agreement	
12 Mar 40	Treaty of Moscow	Ended war between Finland and Soviet Union
27 Sep 40	Tripartite Pact	Germany, Italy, Japan
26 May 42	Anglo-Soviet Treaty	
12 Dec 43	Soviet-Czech Pact	
10 Dec 44	Franco-Soviet Treaty	
21 Apr 45	Soviet-Polish Pact	
4 Mar 47	Dunkirk Treaty	Britain and France
10 Mar 47	Polish-Czech Pact	
16 Dec 47	Bulgarian-Albanian Pact	
16 Jan 48	Bulgarian-Romanian Pact	

24 Jan 48	Hungarian-Romanian Pact	
4 Feb 48	Soviet-Romanian Pact	
18 Feb 48	Soviet-Hungarian Pact	
17 Mar 48	Brussels Treaty	Britain, France, Benelux
18 Mar 48	Soviet-Bulgarian Pact	
5 Apr 48	Soviet-Finnish Pact	
23 Apr 48	Bulgarian-Czech Pact	
9 June 48	Polish-Hungarian Pact	
18 June 48	Bulgarian-Hungarian Pact	
21 July 48	Romanian-Czech Pact	
21 Jan 49	Polish-Romanian Pact	
4 Apr 49	North Atlantic Treaty	
16 Apr 49	Hungarian-Czech Pact	
9 Aug 54	Balkan Pact	Greece, Turkey, Yugoslavia
24 Feb 55	Baghdad Pact	Turkey and Iraq; Britain 5 Apr 55; Pakistan 23 Sep 55
5 May 55	London and Paris Agreements	
13 May 55	Warsaw Pact	
15 May 55	Austrian State Treaty	
22 Jan 63	Franco-West German Treaty	
27 Nov 63	Soviet-Czech Pact	
12 June 64	Soviet-East German Pact	
8 Apr 65	Soviet-Polish Pact	
1 Mar 67	Polish-Czech Treaty	
15 Mar 67	Polish-East German Treaty	
17 Mar 67	East German-Czech Treaty	
13 May 67	Soviet-Bulgarian Pact	
18 May 67	Hungarian-East German Pact	
6 Apr 67	Polish-Bulgarian Pact	
7 Sep 67	Soviet-Hungarian Pact	
7 Sep 67	Bulgarian-East German Pact	
26 Apr 68	Bulgarian-Czech Pact	
16 May 68	Polish-Hungarian Pact	
10 July 69	Bulgarian-Hungarian Pact	
20 Mar 70	Soviet-Czech Pact	
7 July 70	Soviet-Romanian Pact	
12 Aug 70	Soviet-West German Treaty	
12 Nov 70	Polish-Romanian Treaty	
7 Dec 70	Polish-West German Treaty	

OUTLINE OF PRINCIPAL EUROPEAN DEFENCE TREATIES AND AGREEMENTS 1918–72

FRANCO-BELGIAN MILITARY CONVENTION. *August 1920*

The abrogation of treaties for the neutralization of Belgium was confirmed in a treaty signed by Britain, France and Belgium on 22 May 26. Belgium announced its return to neutrality in Oct 36 after the remilitarization of the Rhineland (7 Mar 36), thereby preventing the vital co-ordination of strategic planning with France prior to World War II.

FRANCO-POLISH TREATY. *19 February 1921*

Provided for mutual defence against unprovoked aggression. Poland concluded a similar treaty with Romania on 3 Mar 21.

TREATY OF RAPALLO. *16 April 1922*

Germany and Soviet Russia re-established diplomatic relations, renounced financial claims on either side, and pledged economic co-operation. The Treaty was reaffirmed by the German-Soviet Neutrality Pact of 24 Apr 26.

THE LITTLE ENTENTE. *31 August 1922*

Bilateral agreements between Yugoslavia, Czechoslovakia and Romania were consolidated into a single treaty in Aug 22, and further strengthened in May 29. The object of the Little Entente was the maintenance of the *status quo* in Central Europe.

LOCARNO TREATIES. *1 December 1925*

The signatories, France, Germany and Belgium, recognized the inviolability of the Franco-German and Belgo-German frontiers, and the existence of the demilitarized zone of the Rhineland; this was guaranteed by Britain and Italy. Franco-Polish and Franco-Czech Treaties of Mutual Guarantee were also signed, and action under these treaties was not to be regarded as aggression against Germany. The treaty was violated on 7 Mar 36 when Hitler sent troops into the Rhineland.

POLISH-SOVIET TREATY. *25 July 1932*

A non-aggression treaty, valid for five years. It was prolonged for ten years in Dec 34 after the signing of a Polish-German Treaty.

POLISH-GERMAN TREATY. *26 January 1934*

A non-aggression treaty, valid for ten years; repudiated by Hitler on 28 Apr 39.

FRANCO-RUSSIAN ALLIANCE. *2 May 1935*

Provided for mutual aid in the event of unprovoked aggression.

ANGLO-GERMAN NAVAL AGREEMENT. *18 June 1935*

Limited the German navy to 35% of the British, with submarines at 45% or equality in the event of danger from Russia.

ANTI-COMINTERN PACT. *25 November 1936*

Signed by Germany and Japan to oppose the spread of communism. Italy joined the Pact on 6 Nov 37.

ANGLO-ITALIAN 'GENTLEMAN'S AGREEMENT'. *2 January 1937*

An agreement to maintain the *status quo* in the Mediterranean.

MUNICH AGREEMENT. *29 September 1938*

An agreement reached by Britain, France, Italy and Germany, by which territorial concessions were to be made to Germany, Poland and Hungary at the expense of Czechoslovakia. The rump of Czechoslovakia was to be guaranteed against unprovoked aggression, but German control was extended to the rest of Czechoslovakia in Mar 39.

THE PACT OF STEEL. *22 May 1939*

The formal treaty of alliance between Italy and Germany. Prior to this Mussolini had announced the existence of the 'Rome-Berlin Axis' in a speech at Milan on 1 Nov 36.

NAZI-SOVIET PACT. *23 August 1939*

The Soviet Union agreed to remain neutral if Germany was involved in a war. The Pact was broken when Hitler invaded Russia on 22 June 41.

BRITISH-POLISH TREATY. *25 August 1939*

A mutual assistance treaty, subsequent to the Franco-British guarantee against aggression given to Poland on 31 Mar 39.

BRITISH-FRENCH-TURKISH AGREEMENT. *19 October 1939*

A mutual assistance treaty. Turkey, however, remained neutral until 1 Mar 45, and signed a treaty of non-aggression with Germany in June 41.

TRIPARTITE PACT. *27 September 1940*

Germany, Italy and Japan undertook to assist each other if one of them was attacked by a power not already in the war. The Pact was signed by Hungary, Romania, Slovakia, Bulgaria and Yugoslavia 1940–41.

ANGLO-SOVIET TREATY. *26 May 1942*

A treaty of alliance and mutual assistance, valid for twenty years. The treaty was abrogated by the Soviet Union on 7 May 55 as a result of the ratification of the London and Paris Agreements by the British government.

FRANCO-SOVIET TREATY. *10 December 1944*

A treaty of alliance and mutual assistance, valid for twenty years. The Treaty was abrogated by the Soviet Union on 7 May 55 as a result of the ratification of the London and Paris Agreements by the French government.

DUNKIRK TREATY. *4 March 1947*

Treaty of alliance between Britain and France, valid for fifty years.

BRUSSELS TREATY. *17 March 1948*

An agreement signed by France, Britain and the Benelux countries for mutual aid in military, economic and social matters.

NORTH ATLANTIC TREATY. *4 April 1949*

Collective Security treaty signed by Belgium, Britain, Canada, Denmark, France, Iceland, Italy, Luxembourg, the Netherlands, Norway, Portugal, and the United States. Greece and Turkey joined NATO in Feb 52, and the Federal Republic of Germany in May 55.

BALKAN PACT. *9 August 1954*

A treaty of alliance, political co-operation and mutual assistance signed by Greece, Turkey and Yugoslavia, and valid for twenty years.

BAGHDAD PACT. *24 February 1955*

A mutual assistance treaty signed by Turkey and Iraq. Britain joined the Pact on 5 Apr 55, and Pakistan on 23 Sep 55.

LONDON AND PARIS AGREEMENTS. *5 May 1955*

The occupation régime in West Germany was ended, and the German Federal Republic attained full sovereignty and independence. The Federal Republic became a member of NATO, and of the Western European Union, the expanded Brussels Treaty Organization which came into being on 5 May.

WARSAW PACT. *13 May 1955*

A treaty of friendship, co-operation and mutual assistance signed by the Soviet Union, Poland, Czechoslovakia, East Germany, Hungary, Romania, Bulgaria and Albania. The Treaty also provided for the creation of a unified command for all the countries.

AUSTRIAN STATE TREATY. *15 May 1955*

Signed by the Soviet Union, Britain, France and the United States, the treaty re-established Austria as a sovereign, independent and neutral state.

FRANCO-WEST GERMAN TREATY. *22 January 1963*

Treaty of co-operation, providing for co-ordination of the two countries' policies in foreign affairs, defence, information and cultural affairs.

SOVIET-WEST GERMAN TREATY. *12 August 1970*

A treaty renouncing the use of force.

POLISH-WEST GERMAN TREATY. *7 December 1970*

An agreement that the existing boundary line on the Oder and the West Neisse constitutes the western frontier of Poland, and renouncing the use of force for the settlement of disputes.

BIBLIOGRAPHY

Brodie, B., *Strategy in the Missile Age*. Princeton Univ. Press, 1959

Carr, E. H., *The Bolshevik Revolution, 1917–1923*. London, 1963

Gilbert, M., and Gott, R., *The Appeasers*. London, 1963

Knapp, W., *A History of War and Peace, 1939–1965*. OUP, 1967

Liddell Hart, Sir B. H., *History of the Second World War*. London, 1970

Northedge, F. S., *British Foreign Policy: The Process of Adjustment, 1945–61*. London, 1962–

    The Foreign Policy of the Powers. London, 1968

Osgood, R. E., *NATO: The Entangling Alliance*. Univ. of Chicago Press, 1962

Taylor, A. J. P., *English History 1914–1945*. OUP, 1965–

    The Origins of the Second World War. London, 1961

Thomas, H., *The Spanish Civil War*. London, 1961

Wolfe, T. W., *Soviet Power and Europe, 1945–1970*. London, 1970

Woodward, Sir E. L., *British Foreign Policy in the Second World War*. HMSO, London, 1961

9 DEPENDENCIES

BELGIUM

Zaïre, formerly Belgian Congo and then Congo (Kinshasa). Until the middle of the nineteenth century the territory drained by the Congo River was practically unknown. When Stanley reached the mouth of the Congo in 1877, King Leopold II of the Belgians recognized the immense possibilities of the Congo Basin and took the lead in exploring and exploiting it. The Berlin Conference of 1884–85 recognized King Leopold II as the sovereign head of the Congo Free State.

The annexation of the state to Belgium was provided for by treaty of 28 Nov 07, which was approved by the chambers of the Belgian Legislature in Aug and Sep and by the King on 18 Oct 08. The law of 18 Oct 08, called the Colonial Charter (last amended in 1959), provided for the government of the Belgian Congo, until the country became independent on 30 June 60.

The departure of the Belgian administrators, teachers, doctors, etc., on the day of independence left a vacuum which speedily resulted in complete chaos. Neither Joseph Kasavubu, the leader of the Abako Party, who on 24 June 60 had been elected head of state, nor Patrice Lumumba, leader of the Congo National Movement, who was the prime minister of an all-party coalition government, could establish his authority. Personal, tribal and regional rivalries led to the breakaway of Katanga province under premier Moïse Tshombe. Lumumba found his main support in the Oriental and Kivu provinces. Early in July the *Force Publique* mutinied and removed all Belgian officers. Lumumba called for intervention by the UN as well as the USSR. The Secretary-General dispatched a military force of about 20,000, composed of contingents of African and Asian countries. Lumumba was kidnapped by Katanga tribesmen and, in early Feb 61, murdered; his place was taken by Antoine Gizenga, who set up a government in Stanleyville.

On 15 Aug 61 the UN recognized the government of Cyrille Adoula as the central government. UN forces, chiefly Irish and Ethiopians, in mid-Sep invaded Katanga.

On 15 Jan 62 the forces of Gizenga in Stanleyville surrendered to those of the central government, and on 16 Jan Adoula dismissed Gizenga. UN forces, chiefly Ethiopians and Indians, again invaded Katanga in Dec 62 and by the end of Jan 63 had occupied all key towns; Tshombe left the country. The UN troops left the Congo by 30 June 64.

The Gizenga faction started a fresh rebellion and after the capture of Albertville (19 June) and Stanleyville (5 Aug) proclaimed a People's Republic on 7 Sep 64. Government troops, Belgian paratroopers and a mercenary contingent captured Stanleyville on 24 Nov after the rebels had massacred thousands of black and white civilians. The last rebel strongholds were captured at the end of Apr 65.

DENMARK

The Faroe Islands, Faerøerne. The islands were first colonized in the ninth century and were Norwegian possessions until 1380 and subsequently belonged to Denmark. They were occupied by British troops in World War II. In Sep 46 they voted for independence from Denmark but now return two members to the *Folketing*. Home rule was granted in 1948.

Greenland, Grønland. From 1261 to 1953 Greenland was a Danish colony. On 5 June 53 Greenland became an integral part of the Danish Realm with the same rights as other counties in Denmark, returning two members to the *Folketing*, and with a democratically elected council (*landsråd*). A Danish-American agreement for the common defence of Greenland was signed on 27 Apr 51.

Iceland, Island. The first settlers came to Iceland in 874. Between 930 and 1264 Iceland was an independent republic, but by the 'Old Treaty' of 1263 the country recognized the rule of the King of Norway. In 1381 Iceland, together with Norway, came under the rule of the Danish kings, but when Norway was separated from Denmark in 1814, Iceland remained under the rule of Denmark. Since 1 Dec 18 it has been acknowledged as a sovereign state. It was united with Denmark only through the common sovereign until it was proclaimed an independent republic on 17 June 44.

FRANCE

The French Community, La Communauté. The constitution of the Fifth Republic 'offers to the oversea territories which manifest their will to adhere to it new institutions based on the common ideal of liberty, equality and fraternity and conceived with a view to their democratic evolution'. The territories were offered three solutions: they could keep their status; they could become overseas *départements*; they could become, singly or in groups, member states of the Community (Art. 76).

According to the amendment of the constitution adopted on 4 June 60, member-states of the Community could become independent and sovereign republics without ceasing to belong to the Community. The 12 African and Malagasy members availed themselves of this *loi constitutionnelle* and became independent by the transfer of 'common powers' (*compétences communes*).

The territorial structure of the Community and affiliated states was as follows:

I. FRENCH REPUBLIC

A. Metropolitan Departments

B. Oversea Departments:

(i) Martinique; (ii) Guadeloupe; (iii) Réunion; (iv) Guiana.

C. Overseas Territories:

(i) French Polynesia; (ii) New Caledonia; (iii) French Territory of the Afars and the Issas; (iv) Comoro Archipelago; (v) Saint-Pierre and Miquelon; (vi) Southern and Antarctic Territories; (vii) Wallis and Futuna Islands.

II. MEMBER STATES

1. French Republic; 2. Central African Republic; 3. Republic of Congo; 4. Republic of Gabon; 5. Madagascar; 6. Republic of Senegal; 7. Republic of Chad.

These countries concluded formal 'Community participation agreements'.

III. 'Special relations' or 'special links' were established by agreements between France and the other Franc zone countries and the following states:

1. Republic of Ivory Coast; 2. Republic of Dahomey; 3. Republic of Upper Volta; 4. Islamic Republic of Mauritania; 5. Republic of Niger; 6. Federal Republic of Cameroun.

IV. Co-operation in certain fields was established by special agreements between France and the Republic of Mali.

V. Co-operation was established between France and the Togo Republic by a convention signed on 10 July 63.

VI. The states listed under II, 2–7, III, 1–3, 5 and 6, and V are members of the *Organisation Commune Africaine et Malgache*.

VII. Other regional organizations:

1. The Customs and Economic Unon of Central Africa, comprising the Central African Republic, Congo, Gabon, Chad and Cameroun; the common external tariff, effective from 1 July 62, did not apply to the countries listed under II and III;

2. The entente of Ivory Coast, Dahomey, Upper Volta, Niger;
3. The customs union of Senegal, Mali, Ivory Coast, Dahomey, Upper Volta, Niger and Mauritania;
4. The West-African monetary union of Senegal, Mauritania, Ivory Coast, Upper Volta, Niger, Dahomey and Togo.

VIII. Relations between France and Algeria (comprising the former Algerian and Sahara Departments) are governed by the Évian agreements of 19 Mar 62 and subsequent agreements.

IX. The Anglo-French Condominium of the New Hebrides is administered according to the London Protocol of 6 Aug 14.

Algeria. Algeria was annexed by France in 1885 and became a department of France. French policy was to integrate Algeria completely into France itself but this was not acceptable to the French settlers, *colons.*

On 1 Nov 54 the National Liberation Front (FLN), founded 5 Aug 51, went over to open warfare against the French administration and armed forces. In Sep 58 a free Algerian government was formed in Cairo with Ferhat Abbas as provisional president.

A referendum was held in Metropolitan France and Algeria on 6–8 Jan 61 to decide on Algerian self-determination as proposed by President de Gaulle. His proposals were approved by 15,200,073 against 4,996,474 votes in Metropolitan France, and by 1,749,969 against 767,546 votes in Algeria. In Metropolitan France 20·2m. out of 27·2m. registered voters went to the polls; in Algeria 2·5m. out of 4·5m. registered voters.

Long delayed by the terrorism, in Metropolitan France as well as Algeria, of a secret organization (OAS) led by anti-Gaullist officers, a cease-fire agreement was concluded between the French government and the representatives of the Algerian Nationalists on 18 Mar 62; but OAS terror acts continued for some months. On 7 Apr a provisional executive of 12 members was set up, under the chairmanship of Abderrhaman Farès.

On 8 Apr 62 a referendum in Metropolitan France approved the Algerian settlement with 17,505,473 (90·7%), against 1,794,553 (9·3%) and 1,102,477 invalid votes; 6,580,772 voters abstained. On 1 July 62, 5,975,581 Algerians voted in favour of, 16,534 against the settlement.

Morocco. From 1912 to 1956 Morocco was divided into a French protectorate (established by the Treaty of Fez concluded between France and the Sultan on 30 Mar 12), a Spanish protectorate (established by the Franco-Spanish convention of 27 Nov 12) and the international zone of Tangier (set up by France, Spain and Britain on 18 Dec 23).

On 2 Mar 56 France and the Sultan terminated the Treaty of Fez; on 7 Apr 56 Spain relinquished her protectorate, and on 29 Oct 56 France, Spain,

Britain, Italy, USA, Belgium, the Netherlands, Sweden and Portugal abolished the international status of the Tangier Zone.

Indo-China, Cambodia. Attacked on either side by the Vietnamese and the Thai from the fifteenth century on, Cambodia was saved from annihilation by the establishment of a French protectorate in 1863. Thailand eventually recognized the protectorate and renounced all claims to suzerainty in exchange for Cambodia's north-western provinces of Battambang and Siem Reap, which were, however, returned under a Franco-Thai convention of 1907, confirmed in the Franco-Thai treaty of 1937. In 1904 the province of Stung Treng, formerly administered as part of Laos, was attached to Cambodia.

A nationalist movement began in the 1930s, and anti-French feeling strengthened in 1940–41, when the French submitted to Japanese demands for bases in Cambodia and allowed Thailand to annex Cambodian territory. On 9 Mar 45 the Japanese suppressed the French administration and the treaties between France and Cambodia were denounced by King Norodom Sihanouk, who proclaimed Cambodia's independence. British troops occupied Phnom Penh in Oct 45, and the re-establishment of French authority was followed by a Franco-Cambodian *modus vivendi* of 7 Jan 46, which promised a constitution embodying a constitutional monarchy. Elections for a National Consultative Assembly were held on 1 Sep 46 and a Franco-Thai agreement of 17 Nov 46 ensured the return to Cambodia of the provinces annexed by Thailand in 1941.

In 1949 Cambodia was granted independence as an Associate State of the French Union. The transfer of the French military powers to the Cambodian government on 9 Nov 53 is considered in Cambodia as the attainment of sovereign independence. In Jan 55 Cambodia became financially and economically independent, both of France and the other two former Associate States of French Indo-China, Vietnam and Laos.

Laos. In 1893 Laos became a French protectorate and in 1907 acquired its present frontiers. In 1945 French authority was suppressed by the Japanese. When the Japanese withdrew in 1945 an independence movement known as *Lao Issara* (Free Laos) set up a government under Prince Phetsarath, the Viceroy of Luang Prabang. This government collapsed with the return of the French in 1946 and the leaders of the movement fled to Thailand.

Under a new constitution of 1947 Laos became a constitutional monarchy under the Luang Prabang dynasty, and in 1949 became an independent sovereign state within the French Union.

Vietnam. French interest in Vietnam started in the late sixteenth century with the arrival of French and Portuguese missionaries. The most notable of these was Alexander of Rhodes, who, in the following century, romanized Vietnamese writing. At the end of the eighteenth century a French bishop and

222

several soldiers of fortune helped to establish the Emperor Gia-Long (with whom Louis XVI had signed a treaty in 1787) as ruler of a unified Vietnam, known then as the Empire of Annam.

An expedition sent by Napoleon III in 1858 to avenge the death of some French missionaries led in 1862 to the cession to France of part of Cochin-China, and thence, by a series of treaties between 1874 and 1884, to the establishment of French protectorates over Tonkin and Annam, and to the formation of the French colony of Cochin-China. By a Sino-French treaty of 1885 the Empire of Annam (including Tonkin) ceased to be a tributary to China. Cambodia had become a French protectorate in 1863, and in 1899, after the extension of French protection to Laos in 1893, the Indo-Chinese Union was proclaimed.

In 1940 Vietnam was occupied by the Japanese and used as a military base for the invasion of Malaya. During the occupation there was considerable underground activity among nationalist, revolutionary and Communist organizations. In 1941 a nominally nationalist coalition of such organizations, known as the Vietminh League, was founded by the Communists.

On 9 Mar 45 the Japanese interned the French authorities and proclaimed the 'independence' of Indo-China. In Aug 45 they allowed the Vietminh movement to seize power, dethrone Bao Dai, the Emperor of Annam, and establish a republic known as Vietnam, including Tonkin, Annam and Cochin-China with Hanoi as capital. In Sep 45 the French re-established themselves in Cochin-China and on 6 Mar 46, after a cease-fire in the sporadic fighting between the French forces and the Vietminh had been arranged, a preliminary convention was signed in Hanoi between the French High Commissioner and President Ho-Chi-Minh by which France recognized 'the Democratic Republic of Vietnam' as a 'Free State within the Indo-Chinese Federation'. Subsequent conferences convened in the same year at Dalat and Fontainebleau to draft a definitive agreement broke down chiefly over the question of whether or not Cochin-China should be included in the new republic. On 19 Dec 46 Vietminh forces made a surprise attack on Hanoi, the signal for hostilities which were to last for nearly eight years.

An agreement signed by the Emperor Bao Dai on behalf of Vietnam on 8 Mar 49 recognized the independence of Vietnam within the French Union, and certain sovereign powers were forthwith transferred to Vietnam. Others remained partly under French control until Sep 54. The remainder connected with services in which Cambodia, France, Laos and Vietnam had a common interest were regulated by the Pau conventions of Dec 50. These conventions were abrogated by the Paris agreements of 29 Dec 54, which completed the transfer of sovereignty to Vietnam. Supreme authority in the military field remained with the French until the departure of the last French C.-in-C. in Apr 56. Treaties of independence and association were initiated by representatives of the French and Vietnamese governments on 4 June 54.

ITALY

Ethiopia. In 1936 Ethiopia was conquered by the Italians, who were in turn defeated by the Allied forces in 1941 when the Emperor returned.

The former Italian colony of Eritrea, from 1941 under Britsh military administration, was in accordance with a resolution of the General Assembly of the United Nations, dated 2 Dec 50, handed over to Ethiopia on 15 Sep 52. Eritrea thereby became an autonomous unit within the federation of Ethiopia and Eritrea, under the Ethiopian Crown. This federation became a unitary state on 14 Nov 62 when Eritrea was fully integrated with Ethiopia.

Somalia. The Somali Republic came into being on 1 July 60 as a result of the merger of the British Somaliland Protectorate, which became independent on 26 June 60, and the Italian Trusteeship Territory of Somalia.

THE NETHERLANDS

Netherlands Antilles, De Nederlandse Antillen. Since Dec 54, the Netherlands Antilles have been fully autonomous in internal affairs, and constitutionally equal with the Netherlands and Surinam. The Sovereign of the Kingdom of the Netherlands is head of the Government of the Netherlands Antilles and is represented by a Governor.

Netherlands East Indies. From 1602 the Netherlands East India Company conquered the Netherlands East Indies, and ruled them until the dissolution of the company in 1798. Thereafter the Netherlands government ruled the colony from 1816 to 1945.

Company and unconditional sovereignty was transferred to the Republic of the United States of Indonesia on 27 Dec 49, except for the western part of New Guinea, the status of which was to be determined through negotiations between Indonesia and the Netherlands within one year after the transfer of sovereignty. A union was created to regulate the relationship between the two countries. A settlement of the New Guinea (West Irian) question was, however, delayed until 15 Aug 62, when, through the good offices of the UN, an agreement was concluded for the transfer of the territory to Indonesia on 1 May 63.

Surinam, Dutch Guiana. At the peace of Breda (1667) between Great Britain and the United Netherlands, Surinam was assigned to the Netherlands in exchange for the colony of New Netherland in North America, and this was confirmed by the Treaty of Westminster of Feb 1674. Since then Surinam has been twice in British possession, 1799–1802 (when it was restored to the

Batavian Republic at the peace of Amiens) and 1804–16, when it was returned to the Kingdom of the Netherlands according to the convention of London of 13 Aug 14, confirmed at the peace of Paris of 20 Nov 15.

NORWAY

Svalbard. The main islands of the archipelago are Spitsbergen (formerly, Vestspitsbergen), Nordaustlandet, Edgeøya, Barentsøya, Prins Karls Forland, Bjørnøya, Hopen, Kong Karls Land, Kvitøya, and many small islands.

The archipelago was probably discovered by Norsemen in 1194 and rediscovered by the Dutch navigator Barents in 1596. In the seventeenth century the very lucrative whale-hunting caused rival Dutch, British and Danish-Norwegian claims to sovereignty and quarrels about the hunting-places. But when in the eighteenth century the whale-hunting ended, the question of the sovereignty of Svalbard lost its actuality; it was again raised in the twentieth century, owing to the discovery and exploitation of coalfields. By a treaty, signed on 9 Feb 20 in Paris, Norway's sovereignty over the archipelago was recognized. On 14 Aug 25 the archipelago was officially incorporated in Norway.

Jan Mayen. The island was possibly discovered by Henry Hudson in 1608, and it was first named Hudson's Tutches (Touches). It was again and again rediscovered and renamed. Its present name derives from the Dutch whaling captain Jan Jacobsz May, who indisputably discovered the island in 1614. It was uninhabited, but occasionally visited by seal hunters and trappers, until 1921 when Norway established a radio and meteorological station. On 8 May 29 Jan Mayen was officially proclaimed as incorporated in the Kingdom of Norway. Its relation to Norway was finally settled by law of 27 Feb 30.

Bouvet Island, Bouvetøya. This uninhabited island was discovered in 1739 by a French naval officer, Jean Baptiste Lozier Bouvet, but no flag was hoisted until, in 1825, Capt. Norris raised the Union Jack. In 1928 Britain waived its claim to the island in favour of Norway, which in Dec 27 had occupied it. A law of 27 Feb 30 declared Bouvetøya a Norwegian dependency.

Peter I Island, Peter I øy. This uninhabited island was sighted in 1821 by the Russian explorer, Admiral von Bellingshausen. The first landing was made in 1929 by a Norwegian expedition which hoisted the Norwegian flag. On 1 May 31 Peter I Island was placed under Norwegian sovereignty, and on 24 Mar 33 it was incorporated in Norway as a dependency.

Queen Maud Land, Dronning Maud Land. On 14 Jan 39 the Norwegian cabinet placed that part of the Antarctic Continent from the border of Falkland Islands dependencies in the west to the border of the Australian

Antarctic Dependency in the east (between 20°W. and 45° E.) under Norwegian sovereignty. The territory had been explored only by Norwegians and hitherto been ownerless. Since 1949 expeditions from various countries have explored the area. In 1957 Dronning Maud Land was given the status of a Norwegian dependency.

PORTUGAL

On 11 June 51 the status of the Portuguese overseas possessions was changed from 'colonies' to 'overseas territories'. Each one has a Governor and enjoys financial and administrative autonomy. Their budgets are under approval of the Minister for the Overseas Territories. They are not allowed to contract public loans in foreign countries. Under the Organic Law for Overseas Territories, of May 72, the overseas provinces were given greater autonomy 'without affecting the unity of the nation'. Angola and Moçambique were designated States instead of overseas provinces.

On 6 Sep 61 all Africans were given full Portuguese citizenship, thereby achieving the same status as the inhabitants of Portuguese India and the other provinces.

All customs duties between Portugal and the overseas provinces were abolished with effect from 1 Jan 64.

Cape Verde Islands. The Cape Verde Islands were discovered in 1460 by Diogo Gomes, the first settlers arriving in 1462. In 1587 its administration was unified under a governor. The territory consists of ten islands and five islets which are administered by a Governor, whose seat is at Praia, the capital. The islands are divided into two groups, named Barlavento (windward) and Sotavento (leeward), the prevailing wind being north-east. The former is constituted by the islands of São Vicente, Santo Antão, São Nicolau, Santa Luzia, Sal and Boa Vista, and the small islands named Branco and Raso. The latter is constituted by the islands of Santiago, Maio, Fogo and Brava, and the small islands named Rei and Rombo. São Vicente is an oiling station which supplies all navigation to South America. The total area is 4,033 sq. km. (1,557 sq. miles). The population (census, 1970) was 272,071.

Portuguese Guinea. Portuguese Guinea, on the coast of Guinea, was discovered in 1446 by Nuno Tristão. It became a separate colony in 1879. It is bounded by the limits fixed by the convention of 12 May 86 with France, and is bounded by Senegal in the north and by Guinea in the east and south. It includes the adjacent archipelago of Bijagoz, with the island of Bolama. The capital is, since 1942, Bissau. Area is 36,125 sq. km. (13,948 sq. miles); population (census, 1970), 487,448.

São Tomé e Principe. The Islands of S. Tomé and Principe, which are about 125 miles off the coast of Africa, in the Gulf of Guinea, were discovered in 1471 by Pedro Escobar and João Gomes, and since 1522 constitute a province under a Governor. The province also includes the islands of Pedras Tinhosas and Rolas; the fort of St Jean Baptiste d'Ajudã on the coast was annexed by the Dahomey Republic on 1 Aug 61. Area of the islands 964 sq. km. (372 sq. miles). According to the census of 1970 the population of the islands was 73,811.

Angola. Angola, with a coastline of over 1,000 miles, is separated from the Congo by the boundaries assigned by the convention of 12 May 86; from Zaïre by those fixed by the convention of 22 July 27; from Rhodesia in accordance with the convention of 11 June 91, and from South-West Africa in accordance with that of 30 Dec 86. The Congo region was discovered by the Portuguese in 1482, and the first settlers arrived there in 1491. Luanda was founded in 1575. It was taken by the Dutch in 1641 and occupied by them until 1648. The area is 1,246,700 sq. km. (481,351 sq. miles). By a decree of 20 Oct 54 it is divided into 13 districts. The important towns are S. Paulo de Luanda (capital), Benguela, Moçâmedes, Lobito, Sá da Bandeira, Malange and Huambo (Novo Lisboa) the future capital. The population at census, 1970, was 5,673,046, of whom 300,000 are white.

Moçambique. Moçambique was discovered by Vasco da Gama's fleet on 1 Mar 1498, and was first colonized in 1505. The frontier with British Central and South Africa was fixed between Great Britain and Portugal in June 1891. The border with Tanganyika, according to agreements of 1886 and 1890, ran from Cape Delgado at 10° 40′ S. Lat. until it meets the courses of the Rovuma, which it follows to the point of its confluence with the 'Msinje, the boundary thence to Lake Nyasa being the parallel of latitude of this point. The Treaty of Versailles, 1919, allotted to Portugal the original Portuguese territory south of the Rovuma, known as the 'Kionga Triangle' (formerly part of German East Africa).

Moçambique, with an area of 784,961 sq. km. (303,070 sq. miles) is administered by the state, since 19 July 42, when the state took over the territory of Manica and Sofala, which was incorporated as a fourth district of the province, with Beira as its capital. Lourenço Marques is the capital of the province. As established by decree of 20 Oct 54, the province is divided into nine districts: Lourenço Marques, Gaza, Inhambane, Manica and Sofala, Tete, Zambézia, Moçambique, Cabo Delgado, Niassa.

There is a government council composed of officials and elected representatives of the commercial, industrial and agricultural classes, and also an executive council. The population, according to the census of 1970, was 8,233,034.

Macao. Macao, in China, situated on a peninsula of the same name at the mouth of the Canton River, which came into possession of the Portuguese in 1557, forms with the two small adjacent islands of Taipa and Colôane a province, divided into two wards, each having its own administrator. The boundaries have not yet been definitely agreed upon; at present Portugal holds the territory in virtue of the treaty with China of 1 Dec 1887. The area of the province is 16 sq. km (6 sq. miles). The population, according to the census of 1970, is 248,316; the steady influx of Chinese refugees is creating serious social and economic difficulties while Chinese communists cause sporadic political unrest.

Timor. Portuguese Timor has been under Portuguese administration since 1586. It consists of the eastern portion of the island of that name in the Malay Archipelago, with the territory of Ambeno and the neighbouring islands of Pulo Cambing and Pulo Jako, a total area of 14,925 sq. km. By a treaty of Apr 1859, ratified 18 Aug 1860, the island was divided between Portugal and Holland; by convention of 1 Oct 04, ratified in 1908, the boundaries were straightened and settled. The territory, formerly administratively joined to Macao, was in 1896 (confirmed in 1926) made an independent province. Population in 1970, 610,541.

Portuguese India, Estado da India, was under Portuguese rule 1505–1961. It consisted of Goa, containing the capital, Goa, together with the islands of Angediva, São Jorge and Morcegos, on the Malabar coast; Damão, with the territories of Dadrá and Nagar-Haveli, on the Gulf of Cambis; and Diu, with the continental territories of Gogola and Simbor, on the coast of Gujerat.

Indian troops invaded Goa, Damão and Diu without declaration of war on 18–19 Dec 61 and forcibly incorporated the Portuguese territory in the Indian Union.

SPAIN

In Jan 58 the territory of 'Spanish West Africa' was divided into the provinces of Ifni and Spanish Sahara; both were under the jurisdiction of the commanding officer of the Canary Islands. The former colony of Equatorial Guinea became the independent Republic of Equatorial Guinea on 12 Oct 68 and the province of Ifni was returned to Morocco on 30 June 69.

The Province of Spanish Sahara consists of two districts: Sekia El Hamra (82,000 sq. km.) and Rio de Oro (184,000 sq. km.). Area 266,000 sq. km. (102,680 sq. miles). The population consists of some 10,000 Spanish civilians, about 15,000 Spanish soldiers and perhaps 30,000–50,000 nomadic Saharans.

The capital is El Aaiún (population, 4,000–5,000). The strip between 27° 40′ N. and Wad Draa was ceded by Spain to Morocco on 10 Apr 58. Strong pressure was brought, in 1970, by Morocco, Mauritania and Algeria for a referendum to be conducted by Spain in the province. A Saharan nationalist party claims the independence of the country from Spain.

UNITED KINGDOM

The Commonwealth is a free association of the United Kingdom, Canada, Australia, New Zealand, India, Sri Lanka, Ghana, Nigeria, Cyprus, Sierra Leone, Jamaica, Trinidad and Tobago, Uganda, Kenya, Malaysia, Tanzania, Malawi, Malta, Zambia, The Gambia, Singapore, Guyana, Botswana, Lesotho, Barbados, Mauritius, Swaziland, Tonga, Fiji, Western Samoa, Nauru, Bangladesh, Bahamas and their dependent territories.

Up to July 25 the affairs of all the British Empire, apart from the United Kingdom and India, were dealt with by the Colonial Office. From that date a new secretaryship of state, for Dominion Affairs, became responsible for the relations between the United Kingdom and all the independent members of the Commonwealth.

In July 47 the designations of the Secretary of State for Dominion Affairs and the Dominions Office were altered to 'Secretary of State for Commonwealth Relations' and 'Commonwealth Relations Office'. The following month, on the independence of India and Pakistan, the India Office ceased to exist and the staff were transferred to the Commonwealth Relations Office, which then became responsible for relations with India and Pakistan.

The Colonial Office was merged with the Commonwealth Relations Office on 1 Aug 66 to form the Commonwealth Office, and the post of Secretary of State for Commonwealth Relations became Secretary of State for Commonwealth Affairs. The post of Secretary of State for the Colonies was retained until 6 Jan 67. The Commonwealth Office was merged with the Foreign Office on 17 Oct 68.

The Secretary of State for Foreign and Commonwealth Affairs is now responsible for relations with the independent members of the Commonwealth, with the Associated States, with the protected state of Brunei and for the administration of the UK dependent territories, in addition to his responsibilities for relations with foreign countries.

On 18 Apr 49, when the Republic of Ireland Act 1948 came into force, Southern Ireland ceased to be a member of the Commonwealth.

The Imperial Conference of 1926 defined Great Britain and the Dominions, as they were then called, as 'autonomous communities within the British Empire, equal in status, in no way subordinate one to another in any aspect of their domestic or foreign affairs, though united by a common allegiance to the

Crown, and freely associated as members of the British Commonwealth of Nations'. On 11 Dec 31 the Statute of Westminster, which by legal enactment recognized the status of the Dominions as defined in 1926, became law. Each of the Dominions, which then included Canada, Australia, New Zealand, South Africa and Newfoundland (which in 1949 became a Canadian Province) had signified approval of the provisions of the Statute.

India and Pakistan became independent on 15 Aug 47; Ceylon, now Sri Lanka, on 4 Feb 48; Ghana (formerly the Gold Coast) on 6 Mar 57; the Federation of Malaya on 31 Aug 57 (renamed the Federation of Malaysia on 16 Sep 63, including from that date North Borneo, Sarawak and Singapore until 9 Aug 65 when Singapore became a separate independent state); Nigeria on 1 Oct 60; Cyprus on 16 Aug 60; Sierra Leone on 27 Apr 61; Tanganyika on 9 Dec 61 (renamed United Republic of Tanzania on 26 Apr 64 when she joined with Zanzibar, which had become independent on 10 Dec 63); Jamaica on 6 Aug 62; Trinidad and Tobago on 31 Aug 62; Uganda on 9 Oct 62; Western Samoa on 1 Jan 62; Kenya on 12 Dec 63; Malawi (formerly Nyasaland) on 6 July 64; Malta on 21 Sep 64; Zambia (formerly Northern Rhodesia) on 24 Oct 64; The Gambia on 18 Feb 65; Guyana (formerly British Guiana) on 26 May 66; Botswana (formerly Bechuanaland) on 30 Sep 66; Lesotho (formerly Basutoland) on 4 Oct 66; Barbados on 30 Nov 66; Mauritius on 12 Mar 68; Swaziland on 6 Sep 68; Nauru on 31 Jan 68; Tonga on 4 June 70; Fiji on 10 Oct 70; Bangladesh on 4 Feb 72; Bahamas on 10 July 73. All became members of the Commonwealth on independence, except Cyprus, Western Samoa and Bangladesh which joined on 13 Mar 61, 28 Aug 70 and 18 Apr 72 respectively.

India became a republic on 26 Jan 50, Ghana on 29 June 60, Cyprus on 16 Aug 60, Tanganyika on 9 Dec 62, Nigeria on 1 Oct 63, Kenya on 12 Dec 63, Tanzania (on the unification of Tanganyika and Zanzibar) on 26 Apr 64, Zambia on 24 Oct 64, Singapore on 9 Aug 65, Malawi on 6 July 66, Botswana on 30 Sep 66, Uganda on 8 Sep 67, Nauru on 31 Jan 68, Guyana on 23 Feb 70, The Gambia on 24 Apr 70, Sierra Leone on 19 Apr 71 and Ceylon as the Republic of Sri Lanka on 22 May 72. They accept the Queen as the symbol of the free association of its independent member nations and as such Head of the Commonwealth.

On 4 Jan 48 Burma became an independent republic outside the Commonwealth.

South Africa withdrew from the Commonwealth on becoming a republic on 31 May 61.

To cater for the special circumstances of Nauru, a 'special membership' of the Commonwealth has been devised in close consultation with the independent government of Nauru.

Nauru has the right to participate in all functional activities of the Commonwealth and to receive appropriate documentation in relation to them as well as the right to participate in non-Governmental Commonwealth organizations. Nauru is not represented at meetings of Commonwealth Heads of Government, but may attend Commonwealth meetings at ministerial or official level in such fields as education, medical co-operation, finance and other functional and technical areas as the Nauruan Government desires. It is eligible for Commonwealth technical assistance.

Pakistan withdrew from the Commonwealth on 30 Jan 72.

The Caribbean islands of Antigua, St Christopher-Nevis-Anguilla, Dominica, Grenada and St Lucia entered into a new form of association with Britain in Feb 67. St Vincent became an associated state on 27 Oct 69. Each has control of its internal affairs, with the right to amend its own constitution (including the power to end the associated status and declare itself independent). Britain continues to be responsible for external affairs and defence. Grenada became independent on 7 Feb 74 and has applied for Commonwealth membership.

Territories dependent on the United Kingdom comprise dependent territories (properly so-called), a protectorate, a protected state and a Condominium. A dependent territory is a territory belonging by settlement, conquest or annexation to the British Crown. A protectorate is a territory not formally annexed but in which, by treaty, grant and other lawful means the Crown has power and jurisdiction. A protected state is a territory under a ruler which enjoys Her Majesty's protection, over whose foreign affairs she exercises control, but in respect of whose internal affairs she does not exercise jurisdiction.

United Kingdom dependencies administered through the Foreign and Commonwealth Office comprise in the Far East: Hong Kong (dependent territory); in the Indian Ocean: British Indian Ocean territory, Seychelles (dependent territories); in the Mediterranean: Gibraltar (dependent territory); in the Atlantic Ocean: Falkland Islands and St Helena (both dependent territories with dependencies); in the Caribbean: Bermuda, British Honduras, now Belize, British Virgin Islands, Cayman Islands, Turks and Caicos Islands (dependent territories); in the Western Pacific: British Solomon Islands Protectorate (protectorate), Gilbert and Ellice Islands Colony, Pitcairn (dependent territories), New Hebrides (Anglo-French Condominium).

The Island of Anguilla, although technically still a part of the State of Saint Christopher-Nevis-Anguilla, has now, through the Anguilla Act of 1971 and the Anguilla (Administration) Order 1971, come under the direct administration of the United Kingdom. Provision is thereby made for Her Majesty's Commissioner to administer the Island in consultation with the Anguilla council.

While constitutional responsibility to parliament for the government of the dependent territories rests with the Secretary of State for Foreign and Commonwealth affairs, the administration of the territories is carried out by the governments of the territories themselves.

A protected state is a territory under a ruler which enjoys Her Majesty's protection, over whose foreign affairs she exercises control but in respect of whose internal affairs she does not exercise jurisdiction. Brunei is a protected state. Under the 1959 Agreement, as amended Nov 71 the UK remains responsible for the external affairs of Brunei, while Brunei has full responsibility for all internal matters. The two governments would consult together about measures to be taken separately and jointly in the event of any external threat to the State of Brunei.

Commonwealth Secretariat. In the communiqué issued at the end of the Commonwealth Prime Ministers' Conference in July 64, instructions were given for the preparation of proposals for the establishment of a Commonwealth Secretariat. These proposals were approved at the Commonwealth Prime Ministers' Conference in June 65, and the first Secretary-General, Arnold Smith (Canada), took up his duties on 17 Aug 65.

BIBLIOGRAPHY

Blet, H., *Histoire de la colonisation français.* 3 vols. Paris, 1946–50

Bradley, K. (ed.), *The Living Commonwealth.* London, 1961

Brunschwig, H., *Mythes et réalités de l'impérialisme colonial français.* Paris, 1960

Burns, Sir Alan, *In Defence of Colonies.* London, 1957

Caetano, M., *Tradições, princípios e métodos da colonização portuguêsa* (in Portuguese, French and English). Lisbon, 1951

Casey, Lord, *The Future of the Commonwealth.* London, 1963

Crick, W. F. (ed.), *Commonwealth Banking Systems.* OUP, 1965

Duffy, J., *Portuguese Africa.* Harvard Univ. Press, 1959
    Portugal in Africa. Harmondsworth, 1962

Hailey, Lord, *An African Survey.* Rev. ed. Oxford, 1957
    Native Administration in the British African Territories. 5 vols. HMSO, 1951 ff.

Jeffries, Sir C., *Colonial Office.* London, 1956

Keeton, G. W. (ed.), *The British Commonwealth: its laws and constitutions.* 9 vols. London, 1951 ff.

Kuczynski, R. R., *Demographic Survey of the British Colonial Empire.* 3 vols. London, New York, Toronto, 1948–53

Ligot, M., *Les accords de coopération entre la France et les États africains et Malgache d'expression française.* Paris, 1964

Mansergh, N., *The Commonwealth Experience.* London, 1969

Maxwell, W. H. and L. F., *A Legal Bibliography of the British Commonwealth of Nations.* 2nd ed. London, 1956

Nera, G., *La Communauté.* Paris, 1960

Pattee, R., *Portugal na Africa contemporânea.* Coimbra, 1959

Patterson, A. D., *Handbook of Commonwealth Organizations.* London, 1965

Wade, E. C. S., and Phillips, G. G., *Constitutional Law: an outline of the law and practice of the constitution, including central and local government and the constitutional relations of the British Commonwealth and Empire.* 7th ed. London, 1965

Walker, P. Gordon, *The Commonwealth.* London, 1962

Wheare, K. C., *The Statute of Westminster and Dominion Status.* 5th ed. Oxford, 1953
    Constitutional Structure of the Commonwealth. Oxford, 1960

Wiseman, V. H., *The Cabinet in the Commonwealth.* London, 1958

10 POPULATION[1]

ALBANIA

	Population	Area	Density
1924	831,877	27,529	30·2
1930	1,003,124	27,529	36·4
1947	1,150,000	28,748	40·0
1960	1,626,315	28,748	56·6
1967	1,964,730	28,748	68·3
1970	2,135,600	28,748	74·2

AUSTRIA

	Population	Area	Density
1910	7,529,935	101,010	74·5
1920	6,428,336	83,792	76·7
1923	6,534,481	83,835	77·9
1934	6,760,233	83,835	80·6
1951	6,933,905	83,850	82·7
1961	7,073,807	83,850	84·4
1971	7,456,403	83,850	88·9

BELGIUM

	Population	Area	Density
1910	7,423,784	29,456	252·0
1920	7,465,782	30,437	245·3
1930	8,092,004	30,437	265·9
1940	8,294,674	30,497	272·0
1947	8,512,195	30,497	279·1
1961	9,189,741	30,513	301·2
1970	9,690,991	30,513	317·6

[1] area in sq. km.

BULGARIA

	Population	Area	Density
1910	4,337,516	87,146	49·8
1921	4,909,700	103,188	47·6
1926	5,478,741	103,188	53·1
1934	6,077,939	103,146	58·9
1946	7,022,206	110,841	63·3
1956	7,629,254	110,911	68·8
1965	8,227,866	110,911	74·2
1970	8,467,300	110,911	76·3

CYPRUS

	Population	Area	Density
1931	347,959	9,251	37·6
1946	450,114	9,251	48·7
1956	528,879	9,251	57·2
1960	573,566	9,251	62·0
1970	633,000	9,251	68·4

CZECHOSLOVAKIA

	Population	Area	Density
1921	13,613,172	140,490	96·9
1930	14,729,536	140,490	104·8
1947	12,164,661	127,827	95·2
1961	13,745,577	127,870	107·5
1970	14,445,301	127,870	112·9

DENMARK

	Population	Area	Density
1911	2,775,076	40,357	68·8
1921	3,289,195	44,403	74·1
1930	3,550,656	42,931	82·7
1935	3,706,349	42,931	86·3
1950	4,281,275	42,931	99·7
1960	4,585,256	43,069	106·5
1971	4,950,048	43,069	115·0

ESTONIA

	Population	Area	Density
1922	1,110,538	47,549	23·4
1934	1,126,413	47,549	23·7
1939	1,134,000	47,549	23·8

FINLAND

	Population	Area	Density
1910	3,115,197	343,209	9·1
1920	3,364,807	343,209	9·8
1930	3,667,067	343,405	10·7
1942 (est.)	3,887,217	343,405	11·3
1950	4,029,803	305,475	13·2
1960	4,446,222	305,475	14·6
1970	4,707,000	305,475	15·4

FRANCE

	Population	Area	Density
1911 (excluding Alsace-Lorraine)	39,601,509	536,464	73·8
1921 (including Alsace-Lorraine)	39,209,518	550,986	71·1
1931	41,834,923	550,986	76·0
1946	40,506,639	550,986	73·5
1954	42,777,174	551,601	77·6
1962	46,519,997	551,601	84·3
1968	49,778,540	551,601	90·2
1972	51,500,000	551,601	93·3

GERMANY (to 1940)

	Population	Area	Density
1910 (including Alsace-Lorraine)	64,925,993	540,740	120·1
1925 (after reduction at Versailles)	62,410,619	468,728	133·1
1933 (including Waldeck and Saarland)	66,030,491	470,600	140·3
1939 (including Austria and Sudetenland)	79,576,758	583,265	136·4

WEST GERMANY

	Population	Area	Density
1950	47,695,672	245,317	194·4
1971	61,502,500	248,593	247·4

EAST GERMANY

	Population	Area	Density
1947	19,102,000	108,173	176·6
1950	17,313,734	108,173	160·1
1964	17,003,655	108,173	157·2
1971	17,042,363	108,178	157·5

GIBRALTAR

	Population	Area	Density
1911	19,586	6.5	301·3
1921	17,160	6.5	264·0
1931	17,613	6.5	270·9
1951	23,232	6.5	357·4
1961	24,075	6.5	370·4
1968	26.007	6.5	400·1
1970	26,833	6.5	412·7

GREECE

	Population	Area	Density
1913	4,821,300	108,606	44·4
1920	5,536,375	108,606	51·0
1928	6,204,684	130,199	47·7
1940	7,347,002	132,561	55·4
1951	7,403,599	132,727	55·8
1961	8,388,553	131,944	63·6
1971	8,745,084	131,944	66·3

HUNGARY

	Population	Area	Density
1910 (including Croatia and Slavonia)	20,886,787	324,773	64·3
1920	7,980,143	92,916	85·9
1931	8,688,349	92,916	93·5
1941	14,670,000	92,916	157·9
1960	9,961,044	93,030	107·0
1970	10,314,152	93,030	110·9

ICELAND

	Population	Area	Density
1910	85,183	102,968	0·83
1920	94,679	102,846	0·92
1930	108,870	102,846	1·05
1940	121,618	102,846	1·18
1950	144,263	102,846	1·40
1960	177,292	102,819	1·72
1971	207,174	102,819	2·01

IRISH REPUBLIC

	Population	Area	Density
1921	3,096,000	68,893	44·9
1936	2,968,420	68,893	43·1
1946	2,955,107	68,893	42·9
1956	2,898,264	68,893	42·1
1961	2,818,341	68,893	40·9
1971	2,971,230	68,893	43·1

ITALY

	Population	Area	Density
1911	35,441,918	286,324	123·8
1921	37,143,102	305,573	121·5
1931	40,309,621	310,057	130·0
1936	42,024,584	310,189	135·4
1951	46,737,629	301,023	155·3
1961	50,463,762	301,225	167·5
1970	54,418,831	301,225	180·7

LATVIA

	Population	Area	Density
1920	1,503,193	51,945	28·9
1935	1,950,502	51,945	37·5
1939	1,994,506	51,945	38·4

LIECHTENSTEIN

	Population	Area	Density
1930	10,213	160	63·8
1960	16,628	160	103·9
1970	21,350	160	133·4

LITHUANIA

	Population	Area	Density
1923	2,168,971	59,463	36·5
1940	2,879,070	66,119	43·5

237

LUXEMBOURG

	Population	Area	Density
1916	263,824	2,586	102·0
1950	298,578	2,586	115·4
1970	339,848	2,586	131·4

MALTA

	Population	Area	Density
1911	211,864	305.6	693·3
1921	213,024	305.6	697·1
1931	244,002	316.0	772·2
1948	306,996	316.0	971·5
1957	319,620	316.0	1011·4
1967	314,216	316.0	994·4
1971	322,072	316·0	1019·2

THE NETHERLANDS

	Population	Area	Density
1911	6,022,452	32,758	183·8
1920	6,865,314	32,587	210·7
1930	7,935,565	32,580	243·6
1938	8,728,569	32,924	265·1
1947	9,625,499	33,328	288·8
1960	11,556,008	33,612	343·8
1970	13,119,430	33,686	389·4

NORWAY

	Population	Area	Density
1910	2,391,782	321,496	7·4
1920	2,649,775	323,658	8·2
1930	2,814,194	322,683	8·7
1946	3,156,950	323,917	9·7
1950	3,278,546	323,917	10·1
1960	3,591,234	323,917	11·1
1970	3,866,468	323,878	12·6

POLAND

	Population	Area	Density
1921	27,092,025	380,266	71·2
1931	31,948,027	388,396	82·3
1950	24,976,926	311,732	80·1
1960	29,776,000	312,700	95·2
1970	32,670,000	312,700	104·5

PORTUGAL

	Population	Area	Density
	Population	*Area*	*Density*
1920	6,032,991	89,329	67·5
1930	6,360,347	89,329	71·2
1940	7,722,152	89,329	86·4
1950	8,441,312	91,709	92·0
1960	8,889,392	91,641	97·0
1970	8,668,267	91,641	94·5

ROMANIA

	Population	*Area*	*Density*
1920	17,393,149	316,710	54·9
1930	18,025,037	316,710	56·9
1941	13,551,756	195,198	69·4
1948	15,872,624	237,428	66·9
1956	17,489,794	237,428	73·7
1966	19,103,163	237,428	80·5
1970	20,140,000	237,428	84·8

SPAIN

	Population	*Area*	*Density*
1910	19,588,688	504,488	38·8
1920	21,303,162	504,488	42·2
1930	23,563,867	509,212	46·3
1940	25,877,971	492,229	52·5
1950	27,976,755	503,061	55·6
1960	30,430,698	503,545	60·4
1970	33,823,918	503,545	67·1

SWEDEN

	Population	*Area*	*Density*
1910	5,522,403	447,749	12·3
1920	5,904,489	448,161	13·2
1930	6,141,571	448,992	13·7
1940	6,370,538	449,101	14·2
1950	7,041,829	449,206	15·7
1960	7,495,129	449,793	16·7
1965	7,766,424	449,793	17·3
1970	9,076,903	449,793	20·1

SWITZERLAND

	Population	Area	Density
1910	3,741,971	41,378	90·4
1920	3,880,320	41,378	93·8
1930	4,066,400	41,288	98·5
1941	4,265,703	41,288	103·3
1950	4,714,992	41,288	114·2
1960	5,429,061	41,288	131·5
1970	6,269,783	41,288	151·8

TURKEY

	Population	Area	Density
1927	13,648,270	762,537	17·9
1935	16,158,018	762,537	21·2
1940	17,820,950	762,537	23·4
1950	20,936,524	767,119	27·3
1960	27,754,820	767,119	36·2
1965	31,391,421	767,119	40·9
1970	35,666,549	767,119	46·5

USSR

	Population	Area	Density
1920	135,710,423	24,900,000	5·4
1926	147,013,609	21,300,000	6·9
1939	170,467,186	21,200,000	8·0
1959	208,826,000	22,400,000	9·3
1970	241,748,000	22,400,000	10·8

UNITED KINGDOM

	Population	Area	Density
1911	41,126,040	230,609	178·3
1921	43,176,521	230,609	187·2
1931	44,937,444	230,609	194·9
1951	49,012,362	230,609	212·5
1961	51,435,567	230,609	223·0
1971	55,347,000	230,609	240·0

YUGOSLAVIA

	Population	Area	Density
1921	12,017,323	248,987	48·3
1931	13,934,039	247,495	56·3
1953	16,927,275	256,393	66·0
1961	18,549,291	255,804	72·5
1970	20,529,000	255,804	80·3

BIBLIOGRAPHY

Pressat, R., *Démographie sociale*. Paris, 1971
Robinson, T., *The Population of Britain*. London, 1968
Savvy, A., *General Theory of Population*. London, 1969
Solomon, M. E., *Population Dynamics*. London, 1970
Bibliography on Population. Population Reference Bureau, Washington D.C., 1966
Growth of the World's Urban and Rural Population 1920–2000. UN, New York, 1969
International Assistance for Population Programmes. OECD Paris, 1970
Proceedings of the World Population Conference Belgrade, 1965. UN, New York, 1966–67

11 ECONOMICS, PLANNING AND NATIONALIZATION

ALBANIA

Confirmed in its independence at Versailles, Albania at that time was a backward isolated country, 80% of the population peasants working dwarf holdings or landless labourers on the vast estates.

Albania has always been a client state: of Fascist Italy before the war, then of Yugoslavia till the latter's expulsion from the Cominform in 1948, then of USSR, and finally (with the Sino-Soviet rift) of China since 1961.

Under Yugoslav tutelage Albania instituted a thoroughgoing nationalization policy as soon as the war ended and retains a Stalinist model of economic administration.

Oil was extracted before the war and there were a few consumer industries. Industry remains small: agricultural tools, oil products, cement, non-ferrous metallurgy. Chemical and electricity supply and engineering industries are being developed. Government policy is to transform Albania from an 'agricultural-industrial' into an 'industrial-agricultural' state. The leaders are aware of the dangers of top-heavy industrialization and agriculture expanded faster than industry in the 4th five-year plan.[1]

Soil resources are meagre. Some 11% of land is arable[2] (of which almost a half is under olives or vines) but only about 5% could be called good agricultural land. There is little land along the narrow valley bottoms. The alluvial soil of the lowland plains is sterile and poorly drained. The elevated land between the mountains and coastal plains is excellent arable. One-half of the unproductive area (22% of all area)[3] has a potential for development. The introduction of scientific agricultural techniques is improving crop yields. Pasture covers 635,300 hectares, forest (nearly half oaks; beech and conifers also important) 1,238,400 hectares.

[1] 1st five-year plan, 1951–5; 2nd, 1956–60; 3rd, 1961–5; 4th, 1966–70; 5th, 1971–5.
[2] According to Western estimates in 1969, Albania claims 20% of land arable but much of this is likely to be marginally so.
[3] 2,874,800 ha.

Exploitation of minerals generates the largest share of the gross industrial product and uses the largest section of the labour force. However, the country is not especially rich in minerals. There are large reserves of oil and natural gas. Oilfields are at Qytet Stalin and there is a pipeline to the port of Vlorë. The oil has a high sulphur content and is expensive to refine. Albania is the largest chrome source in Eastern Europe and can supply 2% of world total output. Considerable copper ore is available. There is no hard coal but ample lignite. Asphalt has been worked for centuries. Iron is plentiful, but in low-grade ores. Salt is abundant. Limestone is available everywhere. There are deposits of bauxite, nickel, gold, silver.

The economy is administered through a small number of economic bodies.[1] Economic policy is governed by annual and five-year plans prepared by the State Planning Commission in accordance with party directives.

Agriculture is organized into state and collective farms dependent upon machine and tractor stations for the performance of mechanized operations. Industry is badly balanced with regard to domestic needs and is export-oriented. The economy is dependent on foreign assistance. The loss of Soviet aid in 1961 had serious repercussions on the economy and has only partly been made good by Chinese aid.

Labour productivity is low owing to lack of mechanization and workers' inexperience: a campaign of educating and training labour has been under way since 1969. Two-thirds of the labour force is peasantry. Of the rest (369,106 in 1969) 128,897 were employed in industry, 72,732 were employed as agricultural labourers[2] and mechanics (as opposed to the two-thirds of peasantry mentioned above) and 47,989 in building. Shock groups of people 'volunteering' from all walks of life are used in specific projects.

Government policy in agriculture is to mechanize and modernize to attain self-sufficiency. There has been a history of dependence on grain imports and there is special emphasis therefore in raising grain and potato output. Emphasis is also placed on the expansion of industrial crops: cotton, beets, sunflowers, tobacco, for export and as an industrial resource. Farm output remains inadequate to the population's needs. Large-scale land reclamation and irrigation projects are in hand.

The 5th five-year plan (1971–5) provides for a marked increase in industrial development and modernization: an average annual increase in capital goods production of 12·5% and one of 7·5% in consumer goods production is forseen, made possible by increased investments of 70–75%. Output of crops is scheduled to rise by 60–65% and meat by 35%. Copper ore and crude oil targets for 1975 are 600,000 tons and 2·7m. tons respectively.

[1] Finance, State Control; State Planning Commission; Committee for Labour and Prices; Directorate of Statistics. Also involved State Bank and Ministries of Agriculture, Trade, Industry and Mining, Building.
[2] *i.e.* workers on state farms.

From 1961 to 1965 national income increased at an annual average rate of 5·7%. From 1966–9 the rate was 6·9%.

GDP *per capita* (1970 estimate) £198.

AUSTRIA

In 1968 the total area sown amounted to 1,549,512 hectares. In 1970 the chief products (area in hectares, yield in metric tons) were as follows:

	Area	*Yield*
Wheat	275,229	810,424
Rye	136,498	362,521
Barley	290,229	913,301
Oats	101,567	272,280
Potatoes	109,924	2,703,894

Mineral production (in metric tons) was as follows:

Lignite	3,669,558
Iron ore	3,996,700
Lead and zinc ore[1]	219,407
Copper ore[1]	176,391
Raw magnesite[1]	1,609,340
Pig-iron	2,967,231
Raw steel	4,078,757
Rolled steel	2,859,932

[1] Including recovery from slag.

On 26 July 46 the Austrian Parliament passed a government bill, nationalizing some 70 industrial concerns. As from 17 Sep 46 ownership of the three largest commercial banks, most oil-producing and refining companies and the principal firms in the following industries devolved upon the Austrian state: River navigation; coal extraction; non-ferrous mining and refining; iron-ore mining; pig-iron and steel production; manufacture of iron and steel products, including structural material, machinery, railroad equipment and repairs, and shipbuilding; electrical machinery and appliances. Six companies supplying electric power were nationalized in accordance with a law of 26 Mar 47.

In 1968 the percentage of the production of nationalized industries in relation to total production was as follows: Copper ore, lead-zinc ore, chemical fertilizers, 100%; pig-iron, 99·9%; iron ore, 100%; raw steel, 95·3%; coal, 90·4%; rolled steel, 95·5%; electrical energy, 82·8%; aluminium, 66%.

GDP *per capita* (1970) £897.

BELGIUM

By the convention concluded in Brussels on 25 July 21 between Belgium and Luxembourg and ratified on 5 Mar 22 an economic union was formed by the two countries, and the customs frontier between them was abolished on 1 May 22. Dissolved in Aug 40, the union was re-established on 1 May 45.

On 14 Mar 47, in execution of an agreement signed in London on 5 Sep 44, there was concluded a customs union between Belgium and Luxembourg, on the one hand, and the Netherlands, on the other. The union came into force on 1 Jan 48, and is now known as the Benelux Customs Union. A joint tariff has been adopted and import duties are no longer levied at the Netherlands frontier, but import licences may still be required. A full economic union of the three countries came into operation on 1 Nov 60.

Mining output (in metric tons):

	1966	1967	1968	1969	1970
Coal	17,499,000	16,435,000	14,806,000	13,200,000	11,362,293
Briquettes	972,000	869,000	823,000	793,000	745,174
Coke	6,961,000	6,857,000	7,243,000	7,249,000	7,119,210
Cast iron	8,229,663	8,902,000	10,370,505	11,211,074	10,844,707
Wrought steel	8,916,677	9,716,000	11,572,670	12,836,978	12,611,440
Finished steel	6,867,635	7,511,000	8,669,743	9,829,314	9,298,154

In 1970 there were 21 sugar factories, output 170,125 metric tons of raw sugar; 6 sugar refineries, output 229,792 metric tons; 13 distilleries, output 406,212 hectolitres of potable and industrial alcohol; 232 breweries, output 13,014,777 hectolitres of beer; margarine factories, output 135,750 metric tons; match factories, output 55,303m. matches.

Six trusts control the greater part of Belgian industry: the Société Générale (founded in 1822) owns about 40% of coal, 50% of steel, 65% of non-ferrous metals and 35% of electricity; Brufina-Confinindus operates in steel, coal, electricity and heavy engineering; the Groupe Solvay rules the chemical industry; the Groupe Copée has interests in steel and coal; Empain controls tramways and electrical equipment; the Banque Lambert owns petroleum firms and their accessories.

Of the total area of 3,051,338 hectares, there were, in 1969, 1,609,901 hectares under cultivation, of which 477,253 were under cereals, 23,463 (1968: 19,959) vegetables, 108,801 industrial plants, 85,591 root crops, 803,629 pastures and meadows.

Chief crops	Area in hectares			Produce in metric tons		
	1968	1969	1970	1968	1969	1970
Wheat	202,544	198,647	181,206	839,334	753,816	707,526
Barley	152,948	155,214	169,701	574,441	555,249	525,455
Oats	87,208	87,360	71,962	314,821	280,752	194,297
Rye	27,182	22,448	19,890	86,982	69,739	61,261
Potatoes	54,874	50,292	46,473	1,566,180	1,252,604	1,373,365
Beet (sugar)	89,568	89,994	89,688	4,107,588	4,216,531	3,868,243
Beet (fodder)	33,587	34,784	32,743	3,303,446	3,141,531	2,965,860
Tobacco	569	611	570	1,837	1,785	1,853

On 1 Dec 70 there were 67,399 horses, 2,714,746 cattle (including 1,042,453 milch cows), 65,700 sheep, 2,612 goats and 3,835,260 pigs.

In 1961 the forest area covered 21·8% of the land surface. In 1969, 2,565,000 cu. metres of timber were felled.

The total quantity of fish landed amounted to 46,392 tons valued at 925·7m. francs in 1970. The fishing fleet had a total tonnage of 31,185 gross tons at 31 Dec 70.

GDP *per capita* (1970) £1,196.

BULGARIA

Industry during the period 1918–39 was one of light, small-scale and semi-handicraft industry for domestic consumption. The industrial labour force was around 8–9% of the whole work force throughout this period. Between the two wars industrial output rose only 2·8 times. Percentage of industrial production in 1939: Food industry, 60; textiles, 16; engineering, chemicals, metals, energy, 8·4.

Bulgaria escaped serious war damage and this facilitated the rapid introduction of a Soviet-type economy.

A start was made on collectivization of agriculture (started 1944 and completed 1958, in both cases before any other East European country). This was preceded by a land reform, but this was of no great significance because of the absence of great estates. The idea of agricultural co-operation was not new. The peasant commune (*zadruga*) had survived under Turkish hegemony into the twentieth century, and more modern forms of co-operative had been set up inter-war to make possible modern equipment acquisition: in 1944 there were, *e.g.*, some 1,000 agricultural credit co-operatives with 1m. members. It is arguable whether this predisposed the peasantry to Soviet-type collectivization. It was not until 1950 that large numbers of collectives were formed.

Nationalization also was not new. In 1947 the nationalized sector was expanded to include all industry, banks and financial institutions. By 1948 this sector was responsible for 85% of gross industrial output.

A two-year plan for 1947–8 was claimed fulfilled 106%. Resources were generated by nationalization and technical assistance and subventions from the USSR (who lent $237m. at 2–3% in 1947–51 and $213m. in 1955–8. There were further massive loans in 1961 and 1966).

The 1st five-year plan (1949–53) was declared fulfilled a year ahead of time. No real assessment can be made but it is likely that only overall targets were fulfilled. The 2nd five-year plan covered 1953–7. By the end Bulgaria was declared 'industrial-agrarian'.

The 3rd five-year plan (1958–60) was wound up early after a 'Great Leap Forward' type spurt. Plans since: 4th (1961–6); 5th (1966–70); 6th (1971–5).

There has been a rapid expansion in industry since the Communist takeover: industrial output in 1963 was 17 times 1939. Average annual increase in industrial output between 1949 and 1963 was 15·2%. The scale of production unit also increased, and productivity went up 2·7 times in this period.

Crude oil output expanded from 4,700 tons in 1954 to 499,000 tons in 1967 to 1m. tons in 1971. Engineering has grown until it accounts for 30% of industrial growth. Great iron and steel works have been built at Pernik and Kremikovtsi. Machine-building developed rapidly in order to supply the Soviet market. Bulgaria is a deeply-involved member of COMECON.

One-third of Bulgaria's exports are agricultural. Under the first five-year plan 17·4% of all investment was earmarked for agriculture and 13·4% actually allotted.

GDP *per capita* (1970 estimate) £394.

CZECHOSLOVAKIA

The country is not rich in minerals generally. Coal is ample, and there is iron ore, uranium, glass sand, kaolin and salt. 87% of extracted materials is coal, 4% metal ores, 1% oil and natural gas.

Inter-war Czechoslovakia classified itself as an agricultural/industrial country. 52% of the industry of Austria-Hungary found itself on Czecho-slovak territory as delineated by the peace treaty. Industry was concentrated in the west – Slovakia was less developed.

Mining is ancient: silver mining at Joachimsthaler for 'thalers' (whence 'dollar') originated in the Middle Ages. Extraction of iron ore began in the eighteenth century, of coal in the nineteenth. Coal production in 1913 was 14m. tons; in 1929, 16·5m.; in 1933, 10·5m.; in 1937, 17m. Iron and other ore mines supplied about half the raw material needs of domestic industry in the inter-war period. The textile industry was most important, and the most important branch of this was cotton. The glass industry was founded early and had a world-wide reputation. About half the pig iron production of

Austria-Hungary found itself in Czechoslovakia, and about 83% of this went into domestic steel production.

The value of milk and milk products was equal to heavy industrial production in 1937.

STRUCTURE OF INDUSTRY IN 1930

Employees in thousands

Metal	391
Textiles	360
Building	297
Clothes and shoes	284
Timber	174
Stone and clay	165
Mining	121
Glass	64
Chemicals	41

In 1930 89% of factories had 5 or fewer employees, and 3% had 20 or more. Consumer goods production accounted for 76% of plant and 55% of employees. The number of large-scale concerns was not negligible, however. There was a large number of independent craftsmen, and the nature of certain branches of production (artistic china and glass, for example) made mass assembly-line methods unsuitable. There were also huge industrial establishments with thousands of workers, producing machinery, engineering goods, armaments, shoes (Škoda, Bren guns, Bat'a).

Industry was largely in private hands though there was a nationalized sector: railways, an airline, posts, some mines and metal works, tobacco.

A land reform was carried out in 1919 to break up the great Austro-Hungarian estates and dislodge the ruling gentry. Vast estates had co-existed with dwarf holdings and (in Slovakia under Hungarian tutelage) a landless peasantry. By the reform no proprietor might own more than 250 hectares, including no more than 150 hectares of arable. About a quarter of agricultural land fell to the state in this way, and about half of this again had been distributed by the mid 1930s. Smallholdings thus produced were fragmented into strips, averaging some 30 to each farm. The break-up of the large estates may have retarded modernization (the land reform was primarily a political move) but the standards of agriculture were very high, especially in the west, and compared favourably in productivity with Western Europe. There was no rural over-population problem and little poverty except in Slovakia and Ruthenia.

Co-operatives (agricultural and other) were an important feature. Amongst the latter the Communists ran a very powerful one. There were 11,454 agricultural co-operatives in 1935. In this way farmers had access to modern equipment. The co-operatives also handled distribution of produce.

Livestock was the mainstay of the small and medium farmers. In 1936 there were 4·3m. breeding cattle, including 2·4m. milch cows, and 2·7m. pigs.

Until 1927 Czechoslovakia had been the world's second producer of sugar ('white gold' from sugar beet). The world sugar crisis brought about a dramatic fall in production. The area set free tended to be sown to wheat (60% of all arable by mid 1930s) and small exportable surpluses were obtained, although wheat had previously been imported. The increase in wheat production was felt to have an undesirable effect on industry: in 1934 a grain monopoly was granted to the Czechoslovak Grain Company, which was not state-controlled, but subject to state requirements on occasion to take economic measures regardless of business interests.

Although by 1945 industry stood at about half its pre-war capacity, and machinery, capital and stocks were run down, Czechoslovakia, relatively speaking, did not suffer serious damage during World War II. The official estimate of costs and damage is 347,512m. Kc.

Before the Communist take-over in 1948 the foundations of planning and nationalization were laid. It was not only Communists (a legal and mass party) and Social Democrats but a prevalent weight of opinion which felt that the previous free enterprise system could not undertake reconstruction and avoid recurrent crises. Furthermore, the Nazis had expropriated and reorganized industry so that it would have been difficult to restore it to former owners or their heirs.

The Communists presented themselves as agrarian reformers before their takeover and explicitly denied any intention to collectivize agriculture. In the 1945 government they secured the Ministries of the Interior and of Agriculture, which played a key part in the land reform which confiscated land from Germans and native collaborators and produced some 1·2m. cultivable hectares for distribution.

In 1947 the Communists carried through by a s.nall majority a third reform which put a ceiling on smallholdings of 50 hectares, and this was embodied in the first Communist constitution.

In 1945 nationalization was applied to different branches in different degrees. Mining, power, iron and steel, armaments, pharmaceuticals, cellulose and gramophone records, and some types of chemicals and glass were completely nationalized. In other fields only firms over a certain size were nationalized. Banking and insurance were entirely nationalized. Building ? ¹ printing were left alone, although even here the government took into possession a number of units. By 1946 17·4% of plants had been nationalized, involving 57·7% of employees.

The Czechoslovak Economic Plan came into force in 1946. Its aims were to raise overall industrial production by 10% over the 1937 level, with special emphasis on heavy and basic industries which were to rise 50% over 1937.

After the Communist take-over enterprises with more than 50 employees were nationalized. New nationalization laws banned private enterprise from many additional industries. The private sector was reduced to 5·1%. All wholesale and foreign trade was nationalized.

The application of the Soviet-type model to industry destroyed the balance of Czechoslovakia's matured industrial pattern by developing heavy and capital goods industry at the expense of all other branches in the 1st five-year plan (1949–53). The initial targets were even revised upwards in 1950–1. The plan provided for an average expansion of industrial production by 57%. The base was 1948s output, which was roughly that of 1937. This was revised up to 80%.

The 2nd five-year plan ran from 1954–8.

The increase in industrial growth was impressive. By 1958 overall output was 200% above 1948, of which engineering grew 477% and chemicals 384%.

42% of gross fixed investments went into industry in the period 1948–57. National income originating in industry rose 101% (at 1955 constant prices).

There was a pause in the pace of heavy industrial production after the death of Stalin, and later output was spread more evenly over heavy and light industry.

The failure of agriculture has had an unbalancing effect upon trade which already has to sustain the strain of Soviet internationalist policies developed without regard for conditions within Czechoslovakia.

In the period 1948–57 not only did imports rise 90% and exports 80% but the pattern of trade changed from the pre-war one. Export of machinery and capital equipment rose from 7% of exports in 1937 to 20% in 1948 and 40% in 1957. This new emphasis deprived domestic industry of the machines it needed itself, and increased the need to import raw materials and foodstuffs, (after 1959). By 1964 19·7% of all imports were foodstuffs. The inefficiency of Czechoslovak industry means that production costs are high and thus the exports of machinery are at little profit to Czechoslovakia. Similarly the cost of importing food is higher than that of producing it domestically.

Trade with the USSR was only 1% in 1937 and has grown to a third.

In 1963 the formerly advanced and efficient Czechoslovakia became the only country in the world to register a decline in industrial growth:

ANNUAL INDUSTRIAL GROWTH RATE (in %)

1949	1950	1951–5	1956–9	1960	1961	1962	1963
19	16	11·2	10	10·7	8·9	6·1	−2

Planners felt that fundamental reform was necessary and politically possible since the 12th Party Congress resolved that ways and means should be sought to adapt the economy to 'the conditions of the advanced stage of socialist development'. A blueprint for such a reform was worked out for the 13th Party Congress in 1966. As approved the 'New Economic Model' bore the marks of compromise between the ideas of conservative leaders and the new planners. It was introduced on 1 Jan 67.

The New Economic Model interposed a market between state-owned enterprises. It recognized supply and demand, and the drive for profit and higher income as natural motives, permissible and efficient in Communist economies. It devolved the rigid, clumsy, centralized decision-making to industrial units[1] except for the setting up of basic targets. Prices were to be gradually freed except for raw materials, power and imported capital goods. Price ceilings were to be imposed on basic commodities. The NEM brought only a modicum of improvement in 1967.

The Dubček administration published its 'Action Programme' in Apr 68, a vital part of which was the economic section. The NEM was to be followed in its unrestricted original form: decentralization in production and planning, profits and premiums to be used as signals, technical experts to replace party trusties. Special attention was given to foreign trade. The adverse balance of payments with freely-convertible currency countries and the vast surpluses in inconvertible currencies were to be remedied. Trade with the West was to be considerably enlarged.[2] The Soviet intervention in Aug 68 led to the abandonment of the NEM.

The 4th five-year plan (1971–5) contains fewer detailed targets than previous plans, and confines itself largely to minima and maxima. This will permit greater flexibility in implementation.

National income is to rise by 28% through a series of yearly 5% increases. The share of industry in national income is to rise from 60·6% in 1970 to 62·2% in 1975. Investment priority is given to the export-producing industries: machinery, plant, foodstuffs.

GDP *per capita* (1970 estimate) £672.

DENMARK

Although only very few industrial raw materials are produced within the country, considerable industries have been developed.

According to the census of manufacturing, 2 June 58, there were 65,700

---

[1] 'Trusts' or groups of individual enterprises.
[2] It was hoped to make the crown convertible eventually.

establishments employing altogether 616,100 persons. The following are some data for the most important industries in 1968. The table covers establishments with more than five employees.

Branch of industry	Number of wage-earners	Value of production (1,000 kroner)	Value added (1,000 kroner)
Mining and quarrying	1,003	132,726	107,924
Food industry	36,789	11,255,196	2,706,407
Beverage industry	8,812	1,180,578	772,740
Tobacco factories	5,294	679,972	330,160
Textile industry	16,760	1,843,321	837,965
Footwear and clothing industry	19,430	1,630,385	770,935
Wood industry (except furniture)	9,103	914,407	455,570
Manufacturing of furniture	9,773	965,775	515,592
Paper industry	8,245	1,203,520	528,868
Graphic industry	16,869	2,168,170	1,429,985
Leather products (except footwear)	1,750	211,689	88,878
Rubber industry	2,740	277,900	147,130
Chemical industry	11,315	3,662,046	1,734,570
Oil and coal products	1,332	1,608,516	339,600
Stone, clay and glass industry	18,023	2,019,956	1,301,743
Metal Works	5,669	1,105,094	357,597
Manufacture of metal products	22,344	2,429,037	1,248,811
Engine works, including iron foundries	31,736	3,831,434	2,063,607
Manufacture of electrical machines, etc.	20,334	2,427,165	1,268,037
Transportation equipment	26,171	2,695,818	1,282,842
Other manufacturing industries	11,705	1,458,258	823,724
Total	285,197	43,700,913	19,112,685

The soil of Denmark is greatly subdivided. In 1970 the total number of farms was 140,197. There were 44,038 small holdings (0·55–10 hectares), 90,686 medium-size holdings (10–60 hectares) and 5,473 holdings with more than 60 hectares.

The number of agricultural workers has declined from 128,319 in July 60 to 34,126 in June 70, while the index of production increased from 100 in 1960 to 101 in 1968 (1963–64 = 100).

In July 70 the cultivated area was utilized as follows (in 1,000 hectares): grain, 1,739; peas and beans, 27; root crops, 289; other crops, 84; green fodder and grass, 800; fallow, 2; total cultivated area, 2,941.

Livestock, 3 July 70: horses, 45,413; cattle, 2,842,271; pigs, 8,360,575; sheep, 69,610; poultry, 17,846,768.

Production (in 1,000 metric tons) in 1970: milk, 4,637; butter, 132; cheese, 111; beef, 237; pork and bacon, 771; eggs, 86.

In June 70 farm tractors numbered 175,000 and harvester-threshers 42,253.

Few countries in Western Europe have such a small state-owned sector. The railways, apart from some small local lines, are state owned, and of Denmark's 30% share in Scandinavian Airlines Systems, the state owns 50%.

The postal service is state-run. The telephone service and electrical power supply are in the hands of private concession companies, but the state owns 51% of shares in the former.

GDP *per capita* (1970) £1,393.

FINLAND

Agriculture is one of the chief occupations of the people, although the cultivated area covers only 9% of the land. The arable area was divided in 1969 into 297,257 farms, and the distribution of this area by the size of the farms was: Less than 5 hectares cultivated, 108,796 farms; 5–20 hectares, 165,924 farms; 20–50 hectares, 20,625 farms; 50–100 hectares, 1,620 farms; over 100 hectares, 292 farms.

The principal crops (area in 1,000 hectares, yield in metric tons) were in 1970:

Crop	Area	Yield
Rye	65·9	131,400
Barley	403·5	933,400
Wheat	175·5	409,300
Oats	527·3	1,329,700
Potatoes	60·1	1,135,900
Hay	873·3	3,120,200

The total are under cultivation in 1970 was 2,663,100 hectares. Creamery butter production in 1970 was 86,500 metric tons, and production of cheese was 40,600 metric tons.

Livestock (1971): horses, 72,900; milch cows, 849,300; other cattle, 1,016,100; sheep, 175,200; pigs, 1,182,700; poultry, 8·7m.; reindeer, 145,100.

The total forest land amounts to 21·87m. hectares. The productive forest land covers 16,909,000 hectares. The growing stock was valued at 1,410m. cu. metres in 1960–63 and the annual growth at 43m. cu. metres.

In 1970 there were exported: round timber, 1,078,000 cu. metres; sawn wood, 1,008,134 standards; plywood and veneers, 604,922 cu. metres.

The most important mines are Outokumpu (copper, discovered in 1910) and Otanmäki (iron, discovered in 1953). In 1970 the metal content (in metric tons) of the output of copper concentrates was 33,665, of zinc concentrates 68,875, of nickel concentrates 6,682 and of iron concentrates and pellets 575,000.

The following data cover establishments with a total personnel of five or more in 1970:

Industry	Value of production Gross value (1m. marks)	Value added (1m. marks)
Metal mining	371	307
Other mining and quarrying	95	59
Food	6,592	1,232
Beverages	483	208
Tobacco	121	59
Textiles	1,362	484
Clothing, etc.	1,056	499
Wood	2,037	725
Furniture and fixtures	486	227
Pulp and paper	6,044	1,958
Printing and publishing	1,149	643
Leather	121	48
Rubber	239	136
Chemical products	1,723	652
Petroleum and coal products	885	258
Non-metallic mineral products	890	479
Basic metal industries	2,542	526
Metal products	1,249	603
Non-electrical machinery	2,106	1,017
Electrical machinery, etc.	1,250	524
Transport equipment	1,882	892
Other manufacturing	553	270
Electricity	1,630	875
Gas and steam	229	62
Water	111	94
Total	35,205	12,837

GDP *per capita* (1970) £917.

FRANCE

Following World War II reconstruction and expansion of the French economy began under the guidance of the first 'Monnet plan' (1947–50), named after the then director of the planning office, Jean Monnet. This was followed by the second and third plans (1954–7, 1958–61), an intermediate plan for 1960 and

1961, and the fourth plan, 1962–5, and fifth plan, 1966–70. The preparation of the sixth plan (1971–5) has been completed.

Of the total area of France (54·9m. hectares in 1970) 17m. are under cultivation, 13·9m. are pasture, 1·3m. are under vines, 13·8m. are forests and 7·7m. are uncultivated land.

The following table shows the area under the leading crops and the production for two years:

| | Area (1,000 hectares) | | Produce (1,000 quintals) | |
Crop	1969	1970	1969	1970
Wheat	4,034	3,746	144,587	129,219
Rye	154	135	3,090	2,871
Barley	2,859	2,953	94,521	81,264
Oats	851	805	23,091	21,025
Potatoes	391	401	85,370	86,942
Industrial beet	401	403	179,002	175,215
Maize	1,184	1,483	57,227	75,809

Other crops in 1969 (figures for 1970 in brackets) include (in 1,000 quintals); rice, 954 (907); tobacco, 445 (465); hops, 17 (17).

The annual production of wine and cider (in 1,000 hectolitres) appears as follows:

	Vineyards (1,000 hectares)	Wine produced	Wine import	Wine export	Cider produced
1938	1,513	60,332	16,257	1,032	34,601
1948	1,433	47,437	9,894	620	13,092
1958	1,315	47,735	19,862	1,266	27,440
1970	1,200	75,531	10,560	3,769	11,200

The production of fruits (other than for cider making) and nuts for 1970 (figures for 1969 in brackets) is given in 1,000 quintals, as follows: apples, 18,753 (18,316); pears, 5,362 (4,407); plums, 910 (923); peaches, 5,175 (5,199); apricots, 759 (580); cherries, 1,198 (1,186); nuts, 292 (354); grapes, 3,409 (2,617); chestnuts, 504 (659).

On 31 Dec 70 the numbers of farm animals (in 1,000) were (figures for 1969 in brackets); horses, 629 (697); mules, 32 (33); asses, 33 (34); cattle, 21,738 (21,719); sheep, 10,239 (10,037); goats, 924 (925); pigs, 11,572 (10,463).

There were in 1970 35,799 fishermen, and 13,430 sailing-boats, steamers and motor-boats. Catch (in 1,000 tons): fresh fish, 434; salted cod, 31·4; crustaceans, 25; shell fish, 54·7; oysters, 59·3.

Principal minerals produced, in 1,000 metric tons:

	1969	1970
Coal	40,583	37,254
Lignite	2,950	2,785
Iron ore	55,425	56,805
Bauxite	2,773	2,992
Potash salts	1,938	1,904
Pig-iron	18,212	19,221
Crude steel	22,511	23,773
Aluminium	372	381

Output of petroleum in 1969, 2·5m. and 1970, 2·31m. metric tons. The greater part came from the Parentis oilfield in the Landes. France has an important oil-refining industry, utilizing imported crude oil. Total yearly capacity at the end of 1970 was about 116·5m. metric tons. The principal plants are situated in Nord (production, in metric tons, 1970), 9m.; Basse Seine, 37·3m.; Atlantic, 15·4m; Mediterranean, 29·1m.; and Alsace, 12·1m.

There has been considerable development of the production of natural gas and sulphur in the region of Lacq in the foothills of the Pyrenees. Production of natural gas was 9,779m. cu. metres in 1969; 10,284m. in 1970.

Engineering Industry (1970): 2·5m. vehicles (excluding small vehicles); 1,511,000 television sets; 2,922,000 radio sets; 68,800 agricultural tractors; 39·4m. tyres.

Chemical Industry (1970, in 1,000 metric tons): sulphuric acid, 3,682; caustic soda, 1,094; sulphur, 1,733; polystyrene, 132; polyvinyl, 412; polyethylene, 409; ammonia, 1,545; nitric acid, 604.

Textiles (1970, in 1,000 metric tons): woollen, 63·5; cotton, 186·5; linen, 15·1; silk, 41·2; man-made fibres, yarns, 133·8; jute, 42.

Food (1970, in 1,000 metric tons): cheese, 769; chocolate, 86·2; biscuits, 253; sugar, 2,478; fish preparations, 98; jams and jellies, 84.

Construction (1970): houses, 455,000; cement, 28·9m. tons.

GDP *per capita* (1970) £1,314.

EAST GERMANY

In 1970 the arable land was 4,678,075 hectares; meadows and pastures 1,469,172 hectares; forests 2,947,988 hectares. Since 1945, the estates of Junkers, war criminals and leading Nazis have been sequestrated: 3·1m. hectares have been distributed among farmers. In 1970 there were 9,009 collective farms of 5·39m. hectares, 511 state farms of 442,638 hectares.

The yield of the main crops in 1970 was as follows (in 1,000 metric tons):

wheat, 2,132; rye, 1,483; barley, 1,926; oats, 558; potatoes, 13,054; sugar-beet, 6,135.

Livestock (in 1,000) on 31 Dec 70: cattle, 5,190·2 (including 2,162·9 milch cows); pigs, 9,683·6; sheep, 1,597·5; goats, 135·2; horses, 126·5; poultry, 43,033·7.

The Ministry of Agriculture was abolished on 8 Feb 63 and replaced by an Agricultural Council.

Total catch of fish (1970) 319,296 metric tons. Inland catch was 13,156 metric tons, of which 8,693 tons was carp.

In the production of lignite, the German Democratic Republic takes first place in world output. Rare metals, such as uranium, cobalt, bismuth, arsenic and antimony, are being exploited in the western Erzgebirge and eastern Thuringia.

The principal minerals raised are as follows (in 1,000 metric tons):

	1970
Coal	1,049
Lignite	260,582
Iron ore	422
Potash	2,419

Industry produced about 60% of the national income in 1970; the nationally owned and co-operative undertakings were responsible for 82·9% of the gross national product and the semi-state enterprises for 11·4%. The percentage of privately owned enterprises was 31·2 in 1950 and 5·7 in 1970.

There were, at 31 Dec 70, 11,564 industrial establishments employing 2,817,767 employees, including 3,184 private firms with 73,195 employees.

Production of iron and steel (in 1,000 metric tons):

	1970
Crude steel	5,052·7
Pig-iron	1,994·0
Rolled steel	3,406·5

Leading chemical products in 1970 were (in 1,000 metric tons): nitrogen fertilizers, 378; synthetic rubber, 118; sulphuric acid, 1,099; calcined soda, 676; caustic soda, 413; ammonia, 585; other industrial products: cement, 7,987; cotton fabrics, 248m. sq. metres; leather shoes, 36·4m. pairs.

The 340-km. pipeline from Schwedt on the Oder to Leuna near Halle was completed in Jan 67; it carries Soviet oil direct to the industrial centre of the GDR. Total pipeline length within GDR (1970) 681 km.

GDP *per capita* (1970 estimate) £667.

WEST GERMANY

The agricultural area of Germany within the boundaries of 1937 comprised 28·5m. hectares, of which 14·7m. are now situated in the Federal Republic. In 1969 the arable land within the Federal Republic was 7,570,600 hectares: meadows and pastures, 5,661,000 hectares; gardens, vineyards, orchards, nurseries, 616,800.

The total number of agricultural holdings (with an agricultural area of 0·5 hectare or more) in the Federal Republic, and their classification by size, according to the agricultural area, were as follows (spring 1969):

	Total	0·5–5 hectares	5–20 hectares	20–100 hectares	Over 100 hectares
Schleswig-Holstein	51,032	14,431	13,908	22,077	616
Hamburg	2,942	2,089	559	270	6
Lower Saxony	212,558	89,617	75,039	46,973	929
Bremen	1,165	631	236	295	3
North Rhine-Westphalia	166,308	77,721	61,318	26,858	411
Hessen	119,619	68,884	42,335	8,215	185
Rhineland-Palatinate	130,378	77,812	45,186	7,323	57
Baden-Württemberg	264,632	157,441	94,528	12,498	165
Bavaria	375,008	139,322	196,638	38,585	463
Saarland	18,139	13,899	3,094	1,132	14
Berlin (West)	370	269	68	33	–
Federal Republic	1,342,133	642,116	532,909	164,259	2,849

There were a further 5·5m. households with a total area of less than 0·5 hectare used for horticultural, agricultural or forestry purposes (census, 6 June 61).

Area (in 1,000 hectares) and yield (in 1,000 metric tons) of the main crops in the Federal Republic, were as follows:

	Area 1969	Yield 1969
Wheat	1,494	6,000
Rye	873	2,889
Barley	1,387	5,130
Oats	860	2,976
Potatoes	589	15,985
Sugar-beet	295	12,941

Wine must production (in 1m. hectolitres): 7·4 in 1960; 3·6 in 1961; 3·9 in 1962; 6 in 1963; 7·2 in 1964; 5 in 1965; 4·8 in 1966; 6·1 in 1967; 6 in 1968; 5·9 in 1969.

Livestock on 3 Dec 69 were as follows: cattle, 14,285,900 (including 5,848,300 milch cows); horses, 254,000; sheep, 840,700; pigs, 19,323,000; goats, 60,300; poultry, 98,954,100.

Forestry is an industry of great importance, conducted under the care of the state on scientific methods. The forest area of Germany within the boundaries of 1937 was 12·9m. hectares, of which 7m. are now in the Federal Republic. In 1968–9 cuttings amounted to 27m. cu. metres in the Federal Republic.

In 1969 the yield of sea and coastal fishing in the Federal Republic was 641,700 metric tons, live weight, valued at DM.340·5m.

At the end of 1969 the number of vessels of the fishing fleet was 118 trawlers (124,449 gross tons), 34 luggers and 1,005 cutters.

The great bulk of the minerals in Germany is produced in North Rhine-Westphalia (for coal, iron and metal smelting-works), Central Germany (for brown coal), Lower Saxony (Salzgitter for iron ore; the Harz for metal ore). The chief oilfields are in Lower Saxony (Emsland).

The quantities of the principal minerals raised in the Federal Republic (until 1963 excluding Berlin) were as follows (in 1,000 metric tons):

Minerals	1969
Coal	111,630
Lignite	107,424
Iron ore	7,451
Metal ore	1,453
Potash	20,310
Crude oil	7,876

The production of iron and steel in the Federal Republic was (in 1,000 metric tons):

	1969
Pig-iron	33,764
Steel ingots and castings	45,316
Rolled products finished	32,247

In June 70, 56,303 establishments (with ten and more employees) in the Federal Republic employed 8,573,242 persons; of these 1,113,578 were employed in machine construction; 500,858 in textile industry; 1,092,206 in electrical engineering; 310,001 in mining; 592,992 in chemical industry.

The production of important industrial products in the Federal Republic was as follows:

Products	1969
Electricity (1m. kwh.)	226,049
Aluminium (1,000 tons)	263
Petrol (1,000 tons)	13,148
Diesel oil (1,000 tons)	9,012
Potassium fertilizers, K_2O (1,000 tons)	2,283

Products	1969
Sulphuric acid, SO_3 (1,000 tons)[1]	3,658
Soda, Na_2CO_3 (1,000 tons)[1]	1,324
Cement (1,000 tons)[1]	35,079
Rayon:	
Staple fibre (1,000 tons)	185
Continuous rayon filament (1,000 tons)[1]	77
Cotton yarn (1,000 tons)[1]	252
Woollen yarn (1,000 tons)[1]	87
Passenger cars (1,000)[2]	3,313
Commercial cars and buses (1,000)	281
Bicycles (1,000)	1,614

[1] Including the quantities processed in the same factories.
[2] Including dual-purpose vehicles.

GDP *per capita* (1970) £1,467.

GREECE

The Greek economy was completely ruined as the result of the occupation of the country by the Italians, Germans and Bulgarians from 1941 to 1944.

Of the economically active population in 1967, 50% were engaged in agriculture, 21% in industry and 29% provided services.

Of the total area only 32% is cultivable, but it supports 50% of the whole population. The total area under cultivation in 1970 was 3,527,961 hectares, forest area (1965) was 2,512,418 hectares (445,715 of which were privately owned).

Among products cultivated in Greece are wheat (about 1m. hectares), which covers the needs of the Greek people, fodder and export crops, such as cotton and tobacco, also citrus fruits, grapes, olives, vegetables, apples, peaches, apricots, etc. Cattle breeding does not cover the requirements, and Greece imports meat and dairy products.

There were about 52,300 two-axle tractors, 34,361 single-axle tractors, 7,020 harvesters in 1968.

The further development of the Greek agriculture requires a continuous increase of the area under irrigation. The irrigated areas reached 730,000 hectares in 1970 (600,000 in 1967).

Yield (1,000 metric tons) of the chief crops:

Crop	1964	1966	1968	1969
Wheat	2,088	2,020	1,515	1,752
Maize	249	275	375	428
Barley	242	563	487	529
Oats	139	167	105	119

Crop	1964	1966	1968	1969
Rice (paddy)	107	80	108	103
Potatoes	544	531	648	718
Vegetables	1,111	1,242	..	..
Cotton	225	260	210	300
Tobacco	134	104	78	70
Must	359	..	478	504
Sultanas	73	90	96	78
Currants	90	93	91	92
Grapes	153	157	184	182
Citrus	556	642	426	580
Olive oil	135	180	154	150
Olives	36	73	45	47

Tobacco normally furnishes, by value, 17% of Greece's total exports (US $102m. in 1970). The harvested area was 99,000 hectares in 1970.

Olives are abundant, about 496,260 hectares being under cultivation.

Rice is cultivated in Macedonia, the Peloponnese, Epirus and Central Greece. Successful experiments have been made in growing rice on alkaline land previously regarded as unfit for cultivation. The main kinds of cheese produced are sliced cheese in brine (commercially known as Fetta) and hard cheese, such as Kefalotyri.

Greece produces a variety of ores and minerals, including iron (average content 44–52%; annual production about 300,000 tons); iron-pyrites (104,000 metric tons in 1965); emery (7,600 metric tons in 1967); bauxite (1·5m. metric tons in 1967); zinc, lead (14,800 short tons in 1965); silver (238,000 troy oz. in 1967); manganese (73,600 metric tons in 1965); chromite (42,400 metric tons in 1965); antimony, nickel, magnesite ore, baryte (131,361 metric tons in 1965); gold (4,823 troy oz. in 1960); sulphur (225,000 metric tons in 1964); ochre, bitumen, marble (white and coloured) and various other earths, chiefly from the Laurium district, Thessaly, Euboea and the Aegean islands. There is no coal, only lignite of indifferent quality (5m. metric tons in 1967). Oil was struck in 1963 by British Petroleum at Kleisoura in west central Greece.

The main products are canned vegetables and fruit, fruit juice, beer, wine, alcoholic beverages, cigarettes, textiles, yarn, leather, shoes, synthetic timber, paper, plastics, rubber products, chemical acids, pigments, pharmaceutical products, cosmetics, soap, disinfectants, fertilizers, glassware, porcelain sanitary items, wire and power coils and household instruments.

Production in 1967 (in 1,000 metric tons): cement, 3,450; fertilizers, 700; steel and steel products, 600; aluminium, 75.

GDP *per capita* (1970) £405.

HUNGARY

Hungary is generally poor in minerals except for bauxite. There is brown coal and lignite, oil and natural gas (with further prospecting taking place) and uranium ore. There are rich mineral waters.

The soil cover is very fertile, and the number of soils diverse: forest soils in the hill regions, meadow, steppe and alkali soils on the plains. Some 15% of the country is forested.

In 1918 industry was comparatively undeveloped. Early industry was concerned mainly with the processing of agricultural produce and the manufacture of agricultural machinery, although some attempts to stimulate industry had been made at the opening of the century, mainly in mining and metallurgy. Considerable foreign capital flowed into these branches, and a further impetus was given by the development of railways. Finally industrial production had been boosted by the needs of World War I.

43% of landed properties were great estates of more than 200 hold. (1 hold = 0·57 ha). There were few medium holdings, but many dwarf holdings: 1 in 3 of the rural labour force were landless or dependent upon dwarf holdings.

In the land reform of 1920, of 1·2m. hold, only 495,000 were distributed, 298,000 beneficiaries receiving an average of 1·6 hold each. Landlords tended to part only with their inferior and inaccessible land, the reform was not fully implemented until 1936, and the government deliberately discouraged the introduction of labour-saving machinery in order to maintain employment for seasonal labour.

Immigration into the USA was curtailed, resettlement programmes and the labour market of an expanding industry changed the position only slightly. There were still 746,000 landless peasants in 1941.

The occupational distribution of the population in 1930 was as follows:

		%
Agriculture, forestry, fisheries	4,499,393	51·8
Mines and blast furnaces	115,041	1·3
Industry	1,883,257	21·7
Commerce and finance	469,059	5·4
Communications	338,875	3·9
Public services and professions	434,782	5·0
Defence	72,541	0·8
Casual labourers	122,338	1·4
Pensioners, rentiers, etc.	360,901	4·2
Other occupations	114,251	1·3
Domestic servants	197,179	2·3
No occupation or occupation unknown	80,702	0·9
	8,688,319	100·0

262

39% of the agricultural population were landless labourers.

A moderate degree of recovery had been attained by the end of the 1920s. National income increased from 4,631m. pengo in 1924–5 to 5,728m. in 1928–9. This was terminated by the world Depression.

In a land reform of 1945 all estates over 115 hectares were confiscated and distributed. 3·2m. hectares changed hands (*i.e.* 34·8% of Hungary's total area). 1·9m. hectares were distributed to 642,000 smallholders and landless peasants; 1·3m. hectares were retained by the state. Because not all areas contained great estates about one-third of the peasantry remained landless and left agriculture or were later employed in state farms.

Nationalization began in 1946. There had been some state ownership before the war: railways, Danube shipping, the post office, tobacco, salt. In 1946 the state took over coal mines, electricity, and iron and steel. Banks and their industrial companies followed in 1947, and all firms employing more than 100 in 1948.

PERCENTAGE OF WORKERS EMPLOYED BY NATIONALIZED INDUSTRY

1945	10·5
1946	43·2
1947	58·0
1948	83·5
1949	100·0

A three-year plan was brought in to raise production above 1938 levels. It was scheduled for 1947–50 but completed in 1949. This plan consisted of overall directives and did not contemplate major structural changes in the economy. During this plan, however, the People's Republic came into being and the tempo of nationalization increased. Increase in national income[1] and industrial production[2] during the plan was very impressive. Agricultural output was 84% of 1938.

The 1st five-year plan (1950–55) was a Soviet-type classic of over-emphasis on heavy industry accompanied by collectivization of agriculture (*see below*). Targets were stepped up in 1951, and this is now officially acknowledged to have been 'unrealistic'. Investment was to reach 30% of national income. Heavy industry received 86% of all industrial investments. Potentially more productive sectors were starved of investments: *e.g.* agriculture only received 15%. The typical drive to autarchy was ill-suited to Hungary since 90% of coking coal and 80% of iron ore had to be imported. Real incomes (not including agricultural) dropped 18% in 1949–52.

[1] 24% over 1938, official figures.
[2] 53% over 1938, official figures.

The over-emphasis on heavy industry was moderated in the 2nd five-year plan (1961–5). Technical experts replaced party officials: 5% charges were made on capital. The switch to economic signals and levers was reflected in the planning offices by the elaboration of the 'New Economic Mechanism', conceived in 1965, implemented in 1968. National income grew by 25% in this planning period (36% had been the target). Industrial production rose by 47%.

The 3rd five-year plan was distinguished by more realistic projections. It emphasized productivity and proposed some decentralization of responsibility.

GDP *per capita* (1970 estimate) £562.

IRISH REPUBLIC

General distribution of surface (in acres) in 1969: Crops and pasture, 11,902,200; other land, including grazed mountain, 5,121,500; total, 17,023,700.

Estimated area (statute acres) under principal crops, and estimated yield (in tons), calculated from sample returns:

Crops	Area 1969	Produce 1969
Wheat	203,600	357,100
Oats	189,500	247,500
Barley	490,200	775,600
Rye	800	700
Potatoes	136,300	1,429,700
Turnips	99,200	1,975,700
Mangels	27,200	661,200
Sugar-beet	61,500	902,400
Hay	2,192,000	5,218,300

Agricultural output for the year 1969 was valued at £312,512,000.

Livestock at 1 June 69: cattle, 5·69m.; sheep, 4,006,200; pigs, 1,115,500; horses, 124,900; poultry, 10,334,600.

The total area of state forests was 530,902 acres in 1970.

The number of vessels and men engaged in fishing in 1970 were 932 motor, 1,075 boats propelled by outboard engines, sails and oars; men, 5,861. The quantitites and values of fish landed during 1970 were: Demersal fish, 301,974 cwt., value £1,428,363; pelagic fish, 993,005 cwt., value £1,381,030; shell-fish, value £1,111,369. Total value, £3,920,762.

The census of industrial production for 1968 gives the following details of the values (in £) of gross and net output for the principal manufacturing industries. The figures for net output are those of gross output minus cost of materials, including fuel, light and power.

	Gross output	Net output
Tobacco	62,587,754	6,565,158
Creamery butter, cheese, condensed milk, chocolate crumb, ice-cream and other edible milk products	78,852,654	13,102,976
Grain milling and animal feeding stuffs	49,444,827	9,737,952
Bacon factories	45,563,544	7,547,893
Assembly, construction and repair of mechanically propelled road and land vehicles	44,976,758	12,900,231
Manufacture and refining of sugar and manufacture of cocoa, chocolate and sugar confectionery	31,452,333	9,511,951
Bread, biscuit and flour confectionery	30,164,301	12,787,669
Slaughtering, preparation and preserving of meat other than by bacon factories	54,854,162	5,593,860
Brewing[1]	23,160,171	17,017,036
Metal trades (excluding machinery and transport equipment)	39,566,410	17,166,952
Woollen and worsted (excluding clothing)	23,621,418	10,322,931
Printing, publishing and allied trades	24,607,018	16,010,672
Manufacture of paper and paper products	21,190,824	8,866,012
Manufacture of electrical machinery, apparatus and appliances	36,653,068	16,385,396
Hosiery	22,045,145	10,928,957
Structural clay products, asbestos goods, plaster, gypsum and concrete products, slate, dressed stone and cement	22,807,454	12,313,189

[1] Excluding excise duty £21,499,270.

GDP *per capita* (1970) £539.

ITALY

The area of Italy on 30 June 70 comprised 301,253 sq. km. of which 273,569 sq. km. was agricultural and forest land and 27,684 sq. km. was unproductive; the former was mainly distributed as follows (in 1,000 hectares): cereals, 5,864; leguminous plants, 761; garden produce, 575; olive trees, 974; woods, 6,162; forage and pasture, 10,411; olive trees grown among other crops, 1,280.

At the first general census of agriculture (15 Apr 61) agricultural holdings numbered 4,310,134 and covered 26,016,195 hectares. 3,529,556 owners (81·9%) farmed directly 14,250,860 hectares (54·8%); 295,157 owners (6·9%)

worked with hired labour on 7,380,751 hectares (28·4%); 336,876 share-croppers (7·8%) tilled 3,199,103 hectares (12·3%); the remaining 148,545 holdings (3·4%) of 1,185,481 hectares (4·5%) were operated in other ways.

Under the land reform laws of 1950, about 800,000 hectares have been acquired for allocation to peasants; by 30 June 62 more than 634,000 hectares had been allocated to 113,901 families.

According to the labour force survey in Apr 70 persons engaged in agriculture numbered 3·75m. (2,618,000 males and 1,137,000 females).

In 1970, 630,677 farm tractors were being used.

The production of the principal crops (in 1,000 metric quintals) in 1970: wheat, 96,886; barley, 3,146; oats, 4,858; rye, 685; maize, 47,543; sugar-beet, 95,180; potatoes, 36,677; tomatoes, 36,179; rice, 8,185; olive oil, 4,244; hemp, 10; oranges, 13,623; tangerines, 2,786; lemons, 7,696; other citrus fruit, 516.

The Italian mining industry is most developed in Sicily (Caltanissetta), in Tuscany (Arezzo, Florence and Grosseto), in Sardinia (Cagliari, Sassari and Iglesias), in Lombardy (particularly near Bergamo and Brescia) and in Piedmont.

Italy's fuel and mineral resources are wholly inadequate. Only sulphur and mercury outputs yield a substantial surplus for exports. In 1969 outputs, in metric tons, of coal and similar fuels was 2,235,895; cast-iron ingots, 7,780,521; raw steel, 16,428,135; rolled iron, 13,353,547.

Production of metals and minerals (in metric tons) was as follows:

	1965	1970
Iron pyrites	1,401,395	1,518,432
Iron ore	784,694	756,729
Manganese	47,810	50,091
Lead	54,481	55,268
Zinc	225,075	244,090
Crude sulphur	649,073	354,218
Bauxite	244,393	224,701
Mercury	1,976	1,530
Lead	45,420	54,288
Aluminium	128,505	146,476

The Sicilian district of Ragusa, Gela and Fontanarossa is rapidly developing into one of the largest European oilfields. Production in 1969 amounted to 1,519,914 metric tons, of which 1,387,077 came from Sicily.

The textile industry is the largest and most important. In the cotton industry, 891 factories had, in Dec 70, 4·3m. spindles. Silk culture, while flourishing most extensively in Lombardy, Piedmont and Venezia, is carried on all over Italy. The silk industry, Dec 70, had 810,229 spindles and 20,639 looms; output of raw silk in 1970, 560 metric tons. The production of artificial and synthetic fibre (including staple fibre and waste) in 1970 was 400,609 metric tons in 33 factories with 784,806 spindles. The woollen industry had, in 1970, 815 combing and spinning factories with 2,735 combers, 641,890 carding spindles and 1,148,289 combing spindles; woollen weaving was done in 245 factories with 11,047 looms. Output, 1970 (in metric tons): pure cotton yarns, 188,531; pure cotton fabrics, 104,730; jute yarns, 26,447; pure wool yarns, 53,991.

The chemical industry produced, in 1970 (in metric tons): sulphuric acid (at 50 Be), 5,328,797; mineral superphosphate, 1,394,394; sugar, 1,102,329.

Production of motor cars was 1,854,252 in 1970.

A considerable proportion of industrial activity is government-controlled. The *Istituto per la Ricostruzione* (IRI) group of companies accounts for 90% of total output of pig iron; 50% of steel and almost all shipyards. IRI also controls four of the main national banks, the national airline, *Alitalia*, a large proportion of cement output, the RAI-TV broadcasting corporation and main toll motorway company and other enterprises from electronics to textiles.

Ente Nazionale Idrocarburi (ENI) is mainly concerned with oil and has about 25% of the market for petroleum products, nearly all of the natural gas output is also controlled by ENI and it has large interests in petrochemicals and petroleum engineering.

GDP *per capita* (1970) £758.

THE NETHERLANDS

The Netherlands, Belgium and Luxembourg are part of a customs union, *Benelux* (see p. 245).

INDUSTRY

Numbers employed (in 1,000) and turnover (in 1m. guilders) in manufacturing enterprises with ten workers and more, excluding building and public utilities (figures for 1970 are not comparable exactly with 1969):

| | Numbers employed | | Turnover | |
	1969	1970	1969	1970
Earthenware, glass, lime and stoneware	48·4	47·1	2,239	2,626
Graphic industry	50·6	50·8	1,982	2,174
Chemical industry	99·2	99·8	11,669	13,842
Manufacture of goods of wood and straw	47·5	43·2	1,882	2,097
Clothing	61·6	58·6	2,042	2,144
Cleaning	12·5	12·0	232	244
Leather and rubber industry	32·9	31·8	1,382	1,441
Mining and quarrying	32·9	20·1	1,760	2,222

	Numbers employed		Turnover	
	1969	1970	1969	1970
Metal industry, including diamond industry	444·9	444·0	21,413	25,464
Paper industry	32·5	32·7	2,143	2.361
Textile industry	87·8	82·9	4,430	4,409
Manufacture of foodstuffs	159·2	158·3	20,817	23,421
Total	1,094·9	1,081·2	71,992	82,446

On 1 Jan 71 only three coalmines were still being operated. The daily average of workers was 12,200 in 1970 (of whom 7,200 worked underground).

Production of coal in 1,000 metric tons: 1938, 13,488; 1948, 11,032; 1958, 11,800; 1967, 8,065; 1968, 6,663; 1969, 5,564; 1970, 4,334.

The production of crude petroleum (in 1,000 metric tons) amounted in 1943 (first year) to 0·2; 1953, 820; 1968, 2,147; 1969, 2,020; 1970, 1,919.

There are saltmines at Hengelo and Delfzijl; production (in 1,000 metric tons), 1950, 412·6; 1960, 1,096; 1968, 2,414; 1969, 2,668; 1970, 2,871.

The net area of all holdings[1] was divided as follows (in hectares):

	1968	1969	1970
Field crops	742,506	720,498	692,776
Grass	1,359,698	1,364,378	1,374,534
Market gardening	103,163	102,319	100,893
Land for flower bulbs	11,694	12,214	12,365
Flower cultivation	2,400	2,476	2,556
Nurseries	3,617	3,748	3,824
Fallow land	8,385	9,335	9,621
Total	2,231,463	2,214,968	2,196,569
Plantations with undercropping	5,157	4,314	3,358
Total agricultural area	2,226,306	2,210,654	2,193,211

[1] Excluding non-agrarian holdings of less than 1 hectare.

The net areas[1] under special crops were as follows (in hectares):

Products	1970
Autumn wheat	105,042
Spring wheat	37,177
Rye	56,639
Autumn barley	8,690
Spring barley	96,547
Oats	55,531
Peas	12,745
Colza	7,493

Products	1970
Flax	5,221
Agricultural seeds	10,981
Potatoes, edible[2]	91,903
Potatoes, industrial[3]	66,521
Sugar-beets	104,493
Fodder-beets	9,599

[1] Excluding non-agrarian holdings of less than 1 hectare.
[2] Including early and seed potatoes.
[3] Including seed potatoes.

The yield of the more important products, in metric tons, was as follows:

Crop	Average 1940–49	Average 1950–58	1969[1]	1970[1]
Wheat	322,003	348,464	677,181	643,219
Rye	439,055	454,992	206,532	172,347
Barley	145,892	258,049	389,393	334,330
Oats	315,642	464,041	321,655	200,566
Field beans	15,799	5,693	269	..
Peas	65,460	93,664	40,095	38,770
Colza	24,763	18,358	12,192	21,819
Flax, fibre	82,906	138,165	50,152	24,034
Potatoes, edible[2]	2,861,793	2,745,505	2,727,001	3,273,158
Potatoes, industrial	1,242,326	1,003,994	1,976,911	2,374,525
Sugar-beet	1,667,711	2,935,881	5,001,966	4,739,402
Fodder-beet	..	..	853,967	742,013

[1] Excluding non-agrarian holdings of less than 1 hectare.
[2] Including early potatoes.

Livestock, May 70: 4,366,485 cattle, 5,650,485 pigs, 47,718 horses (3 years old and over, for agricultural purposes), 610,272 sheep, 57m. poultry.

In 1970 the production of butter, under state control, amounted to 118,561 metric tons; that of cheese, under state control, to 270,881 metric tons. Export value of arable crops amounted to 3,807m. guilders; animal produce, 5,156m. guilders, and horticultural produce, 2,390 guilders.

The total produce of fish landed from the sea and inshore fisheries in 1970 was valued at 270,179,000 guilders; the total weight amounted to 249,667 tons. In 1970 the herring fishery had a value of 47,312,000 guilders and a weight of 45,441 tons. The quantity of oysters produced in 1970 amounted to 824 tons (6,336,000 guilders).

GDP *per capita* (1970) £1,080.

NORWAY

Norway is a barren and mountainous country. The arable soil is found in comparatively narrow strips, gathered in deep and narrow valleys and around fiords and lakes. Large, continuous tracts fit for cultivation do not exist. Of the total area, 75·9% is unproductive, 21% productive forest and 3·1% under cultivation.

Principal crops	Area (hectares) 1970	Produce (metric tons) 1970
Wheat	3,858	11,601
Rye	1,510	4,800
Barley	184,036	580,475
Oats	67,691	227,687
Mixed corn	475	1,433
Potatoes	33,503	856,835
Hay	426,364	2,637,112

Livestock, 20 June 70: 35,177 horses, 943,002 cattle (424,257 milch cows), 1,752,910 sheep, 84,314 goats, 641,746 pigs, 3,745,900 poultry.

Fur production in 1970–71 was as follows (1969–70 in brackets): silver fox, 1,000 (1,300); blue fox, 136,000 (155,000); mink, 2·27m. (2·24m.).

The forests are one of the chief natural sources of wealth. The total area covered with forests is estimated at 83,300 sq. km., of which 64,800 sq. km. is productive forest. 81% of the productive forest area consisted of conifers and 19% of broadleaves. Forests in public ownership cover 8,970 sq. km. of productive forests and 5,820 sq. km. of unproductive forests. Besides the home consumption of timber and fuel wood, the essential part of the cut is consumed as raw material in the paper industry. The annual natural increase is about 13·2m. cu. metres. In 1969–70, 7·5m. cu. metres were cut for production of pulp and other industrial wood products. In 1970 the export of timber products was 15% of the total exports.

The number of persons in 1969 engaged in cod fisheries was 20,071; in winter herring fisheries, 1,973; the total number of persons engaged in the fisheries was 44,972, of whom 11,699 had another chief occupation. The number of fishing vessels with motor was 36,402 in 1969; of these, 27,521 were open boats.

The value of sea fisheries in kroner in 1970 was: Cod, 404m.; mackerel, 152m.; coal-fish (saithe), 88m.; haddock, 44m.; herring, 162m.; dogfish, 17m.; deep-water prawn, 42m. The catch totalled in 1970, 2·7m. metric tons, valued at 1,403m. kroner.

Whale oil and sperm oil (in 1,000 bbls): 109 in 1967, 36 in 1968, 6 in 1969,

5 in 1970. Total value of oil and by-products was, in 1967, 55m.; 1968, 22m.; 1969, 3m.; 1970, 3m. kroner.

The Norwegian fishery limit is 12 miles from 1 Sep 61, for the coast east of Lindesnes from 1 July 67.

Industry is chiefly based on raw materials produced within the country (wood, fish, etc.) and on water power, of which the country possesses a large amount. The pulp and paper industry, the canning industry and the chemical and basic metal industries are the most important export manufactures. In the following table are given figures for industrial establishments in 1969, excluding one-man shops. Electrical plants, construction and building industry are not included. The values are given in 1,000 kroner.

Industries	Establish-ments	Gross value of production	Value added by manufacture
Coal mining	1	32,908	29,938
Metal mining	19	463,303	371,788
Stone-quarrying	363	207,934	184,964
Other non-metallic mining and quarrying	75	116,288	107,121
Food industries	3,373	8,410,522	1,727,894
Beverages	117	823,332	649,595
Tobacco	8	535,970	457,639
Textiles	329	1,171,146	606,358
Clothing, etc.	1,100	1,423,750	721,898
Wood	1,631	1,879,447	837,832
Furniture and fixtures	1,548	1,410,510	705,283
Pulp and paper	249	3,732,905	1,288,776
Printing and publishing	1,195	2,233,764	1,337,457
Leather	91	128,511	59,658
Rubber	111	322,877	196,877
Chemical	425	3,588,981	1,619,428
Manufacture of products of petroleum and coal	54	1,023,855	252,113
Non-metallic mineral products	721	1,322,303	796,510
Basic metal industries	148	5,260,662	2,011,209
Metal products	1,254	2,560,371	1,398,293
Machinery	971	1,770,935	870,980
Electrical machinery, etc.	414	2,008,454	1,065,845
Transport equipment	2,640	5,465,007	2,536,653
Total (all included)	17,413	46,722,327	20,285,773

Production and value of the chief concentrates, metals and alloys were:

Concentrates and minerals	*1969* Metric tons
Copper concentrates	54,931
Pyrites	766,607
Iron ore and titaniferrous concentrates	4,344,591
Zinc and lead concentrates	28,547
Molybdenum concentrates	480

Metals and alloys	
Copper	27,890
Nickel	35,601
Aluminium	507,943
Ferro-alloys	759,079
Semi-finished steel	644,625
Pig-iron	681,873
Zinc	58,775
Lead and tin	641

GDP *per capita* (1970) £1,317.

POLAND

After World War II Poland lost eastern territory to USSR (45% of inter-war area) and gained territory in the west to bring present total area to 80% of pre-war. Poland gained on balance in resources by these changes: the eastern lands were poor in minerals except petroleum and not industrialized, whereas the lands in the west were heavily industrialized (especially Silesia and Szczecin). It added 7,000m. tons of coal reserves and doubled lead and zinc ore deposits.

About a quarter of Poland is forested, mainly by conifers, but with some beech and oak.

19·5m. hectares of the land is farmed (out of 31·27m. hectares) and 15m. of this is arable. Poland is the world's second producer of rye and potatoes after the USSR.[1]

Poland is the sixth largest producer of bituminous coal in the world and has the highest *per capita* output after Britain.

The Upper Silesian coalfield has accessible reserves of 85,000m. tons. There is some brown coal but little petroleum or natural gas. Hydro-electric potential is small; most electricity is generated by thermal means.

Iron ores are not sufficient to needs and are imported.

[1] Grain output is insufficient to needs. During 1971–2 3m. tons of cereals were imported (50% from USSR).

Poland is Europe's biggest zinc producer apart from the USSR. Lead ores also are substantial and there is some copper.

State control and intervention was a very marked feature of pre-war Poland. During the war with Russia (1919–21) the government took control of many economic activities, and not all of these were relinquished. State monopolies (alcohol, salt, tobacco and matches) were retained from some of the partitioning powers. Private capital on a scale necessary to develop industry was lacking. In 1927 state ownership amounted to about one-eighth of national wealth. Armaments, air lines and the potash industry were entirely owned by the state, and in addition 95% of shipping, 90% of railways, 70% of iron production, 50% of other metals, 37% of forests and 30% of coal. State intervention in agriculture was much smaller though there were model farms staffed by specialists.

Industrial production declined from a peak in 1929 but was beginning to recover by World War II: industrial production was 119·3% of 1928 in 1938.

INDICES OF REAL INVESTMENT AND INDUSTRIAL PRODUCTION IN POLAND, 1928–38

	Investment			Industrial production			
	Investment in Machinery						
Year	Sale of rolled products, pipe, bricks, cement, and lime	Industry and communications	Agri-culture	General index	Producer goods	Consumer goods	Other (electric energy and export goods)
1928	100·0	100·0	100·0	100·0	100·0	100·0	100·0
1929	92·1	99·0	72·8	101·9	99·5	100·8	107·9
1930	65·4	69·0	42·5	89·7	86·9	90·0	93·5
1931	49·2	48·1	25·6	78·2	73·2	78·0	86·8
1932	34·9	33·7	11·8	63·7	56·6	67·1	69·6
1933	41·4	34·8	14·3	70·0	67·7	71·4	71·4
1934	52·5	40·1	16·1	78·8	79·7	78·6	77·7
1935	58·4	48·4	22·0	84·9	88·0	86·1	77·8
1936	73·8	61·9	30·5	94·3	103·1	93·0	82·2
1937	94·5	82·3	46·0	110·7	127·3	102·7	97·1
1938	105·0	··	··	119·3	139·8	109·2	103·2

Source: Edward Lipinski (ed.), *Koniunktura Gospodarcza Polski, Miesieczne Tablice Statystyczne* (Economic Conditions in Poland, Monthly Statistical Tables), Special Issue, December 1938, p. 24.

In 1936 for military reasons and to provide an industrial base for overall planned development the government began to develop the Central Industrial District 'industrial triangle' (south Poland, the upper plain of the Vistula). Plans going through to 1954 were envisaged, and transport, energy and agriculture were to be developed in harmony. This enjoyed some modest success but was cut short by World War II.

Poland was not over-dependent on foreign capital, and was not tied to the Nazi war economy like many other Eastern European states. German capital dropped from 25% of all foreign investment in 1931 to 13·8% in 1937.

Foreign capital (in 1m. zloty):

1929	1930	1931	1932	1933	1934	1935
5,654	5,211	4,871	4,508	4,297	3,964	3,791

Main areas of foreign investment: iron and steel, mining, utilities, chemicals, communications. Of all foreign capital, in 1937 France had 27·1%, USA 19·2, Germany 13·8, Belgium 12·5, Switzerland 7·2, UK 5·5.

The damage caused by World War II was vast and incalculable, both for lack of statistics[1] and the shifting of Poland's boundaries westwards.

Area in 1,000 sq. km.:

Poland in 1938	Ceded to USSR	Gained from Germany	1946
388·6	178·6	102·6	312·6

From 1945–7 Poland received $481m. relief from UNRRA: otherwise the economy was rebuilt without foreign aid.

A land reform law was published in Sep 44 which gave the government a reserve of 9m. hectares. Between 1945–9 some 814,000 new farms were created and 254,000 enlarged. About one-third of the land was retained for state farms and a National Land Fund.

In 1945 the state assumed the power to direct labour.

The government in its early policies favoured a balance of state, co-operative and private sectors, but gradually underwent a process of Sovietization until by 1948 its aim was complete 'socialization', squeezing out the private sector by controls and unfavourable quotas and regarding the co-operative as an intermediate step to state-ownership. The nationalization law was passed in Jan 46: German assets were confiscated; all heavy industry, most light industry, transport, utilities, communications were nationalized, and also all enterprises employing more than 50. By the end of 1946 less than 10% of gross industrial output came from the private sectors (by 1950, 5%; by 1953, 1%). The state controlled wholesale supply, and gradually took over retailing.

A three-year plan of national reconstruction was implemented in 1947–9.[2] By 1950 the economic administrative machinery of a Soviet-type economy had been established which survives (though with much modification) to this day. At the apex was the Economic Committee of the Council of Ministers,

---

[1] A government estimate of loss of fixed assets reckoned in pre-war zloty was 38·1%. A private estimate (J. Kobylinski, *Granica pokojn*, Poznan, 1948) puts losses at 84% of industrial buildings and plant, 40% of urban dwellings and 28% of farm buildings.

[2] Claimed fulfilled but this was on account of the new industrial resources in the West. If 'old Poland' alone is considered it did not regain pre-war levels in all respects.

which passed its own and party directives to the Central Planning Administration (later State Commission for Economic Planning). The next link is a number of economic ministries.

The next plan was called the 1st six-year plan and covered 1949–55.[1] Some 45% of investment went into industry. Industrial employment expanded from 1·8m. in 1950 to 2·7m. in 1955 (slightly short of the planned target of 2·8m.). Apart from bias to heavy industry this plan brought about the Soviet-type planning troubles and deteriorated social conditions gave rise to the riots of 1956.

The 2nd five-year plan took cognizance of discontent and also benefitted from cessation of enforced free deliveries to USSR with de-Stalinization. Less investment was made to producer and more to consumer goods and agriculture.

The rate of economic growth slowed (average annual growth in national income 6·7%). Restrictions on private handicrafts were relaxed and employment rose in this sector (1955: 129,600, 1960: 223,300, 1970: 431,000).

These trends were continued in the 3rd five-year plan (1960–5).[2]

Labour discontent broke out in strikes in the early 1960s and may have persuaded conservative planners to the limited reforms adopted in 1965.

Spontaneous popular and industrial action has been a feature in bringing about economic reforms and such an outbreak in Gdansk, Gdynia and Szczecin in Dec 70 actually brought down Gomulka and ushered in Gierek's government. This has led to a modification of the current five-year plan (1971–5).

GDP *per capita* (1970 estimate) £427.

PORTUGAL

During the 1st six-year plan (1953–8), 16·5m. contos were invested (11·6m. in metropolitan Portugal, 4·9m. in the overseas provinces). The 2nd six-year plan (1959–64) envisaged investments of 31m. contos (22m. in metropolitan Portugal, 9m. overseas). The interim plan 1965–7 envisaged expenditures of 34·78m. contos in metropolitan Portugal and 14·4m. contos overseas. The third six-year plan (1968–73) envisages investments of 122m. contos in metropolitan Portugal and 46·5m. in the overseas provinces. The main items in metropolitan Portugal are industry (30·85m.), transport and

---

[1] Detailed targets were never published and therefore the official claim of fulfilment was received sceptically.

[2] Subsequent five-year plans: 1966–70, 1971–5.

communications (27·1m.), energy (17·9m.), agriculture and forestry (14·6m.) and tourism (11·85m.).

The following figures show the area (in hectares) and yield (in metric tons) of the chief crops:

| | 1969 | | 1970 | |
Crop	Area	Yield	Area	Yield
Wheat	567,734	451,932	601,685	539,811
Maize	426,878	552,592	417,476	581,448
Oats	217,858	79,354	191,869	72,348
Barley	119,011	54,382	104,961	53,972
Rye	235,769	167,279	233,004	156,954
Rice	37,559	175,807	41,721	194,876
French beans	381,819	50,616	382,808	54,283
Potatoes	106,842	1,126,382	111,838	1,220,015

Wine production, 1970, 11,327,605 hectolitres, and olive oil, 1970, 687,476 hectolitres. In 1955, 228,996 hectolitres of port wine were exported; 1960, 211,560; 1967, 303,324; 1968, 337,986; 1969, 327,207; 1970, 352,090.

In 1968 Portugal (continental only) possessed 26,654 horses, 92,986 mules, 156,869 asses, 950,264 cattle, 4·36m. sheep, 530,680 goats and 1,514,652 pigs.

The forest area covers 3·2m. hectares, of which 1·41m. are pine, 758,000 cork oak, 704,000 other oak, 75,000 chestnut, 155,000 eucalyptus and 135,000 other species.

Portugal surpasses the rest of the world in the production of cork (1968, 197,152; 1969, 163,490; 1970, 132,308 metric tons). Most of it is exported crude; exports of cork and cork products totalled 139,208 metric tons in 1968; 152,070 in 1969; 147,002 in 1970. Production of resin (in metric tons) was 91,369 in 1967; 91,954 in 1968; 93,562 in 1969; 106,625 in 1970, more than two-thirds are exported. Exports of turpentine (in metric tons) were 14,014 in 1968; 5,692 in 1969; 6,908 in 1970.

The fishing industry is of importance. At 31 July 70 there were 35,304 men and boys employed, with 9,964 boats. The sardine catch, 1970, was 69,214 metric tons valued at 346,702 contos; 1969, 64,133 metric tons valued at 362,989 contos; 1968, 79,645 metric tons valued at 326,989 contos; 1967, 114,817 metric tons valued at 381,313 contos. Exports of tinned sardines (in metric tons) amounted to 52,016 in 1967; 45,999 in 1968; 30,898 in 1969; 23,328 in 1970. The most important centres of the sardine industry are at Matosinhos, Setúbal, Portimão and Olhão.

Portugal possesses considerable mineral wealth. Production in metric tons:

	1969	1970
Coal	424,425	270,890
Cupriferous pyrites	531,125	457,824
Copper (precipitated)	107	81
Tin ores	710	621
Kaolin	44,830	53,023
Gold (refined)	0.508	0.373
Beryl	29	14
Cement	2,034,761	2,346,935
Wolframite	2,289	2,531
Hematite	39,837	4,434
Magnetite	67,428	10,524
Manganese	6,928	5,526
Lead concentrates	51	..

GDP *per capita* (1970) £285.

ROMANIA

The most important natural resources are crude oil, natural gas, methane gas, oilwell gas, coal, iron ore, nonferrous ores (gold, silver, mercury, bauxite) and salt. Fuel resources: natural gas, 44%; crude oil, 38%; coal, 10% (73% bituminous, 24% lignite).

There is a national electricity grid. The Iron Gates hydroelectric power station is the largest in Europe outside the USSR, with a capacity of 2,000 MW and an output of 5,000m. KWH. It is shared with Yugoslavia.

Soils are varied: 56% forest soils (brownsoils, podzols); 31% steppe and forest-steppe soils (black-earths and grey forest soils); 9% flood plain soils; and 4% saline or marshy soils. 63% of all land is agricultural, and 41% of this is arable. Forests cover 25% of the land.

Between 1921 and 1925 the average annual production of wheat was 24·4m. quintals, and of maize, 35·6m. By 1938 87% of the arable area was sown to cereals (41·2% to maize, which was the peasants' mainstay). Wheat production was 49·1m. quintals in this year, and maize 52·2m. Yields per hectare: wheat, 8·8 q.; maize, 9·9 q.

AGRICULTURAL PROPERTIES BY
SIZE OF EXPLOITATION, 1930

Size of holdings (in hectares)	Holdings		Total Area		Tilled Area	
	Number	Per cent of total	Hectares	Per cent of total	Hectares	Per cent of total
0–1	610,000	18·6	320,000	1·6	275,000	2·1
1–3	1,100,000	33·5	2,200,000	11·1	1,850,000	14·4
3–5	750,000	22·8	3,015,000	15·3	2,475,000	19·3
Total, 0–5	2,460,000	74·9	5,535,000	28·0	4,600,000	35·8
5–10	560,000	17·1	3,955,000	20·0	3,110,000	24·2
10–20	180,000	5·5	2,360,000	12·0	1,715,000	13·3
20–50	55,000	1·7	1,535,000	7·8	1,015,000	7·9
Total, 0–50	3,255,000	99·2	13,385,000	67·8	10,440,000	81·2
50–100	12,800	0·4	895,000	4·5	540,000	4·2
100–500	9,500	0·3	2,095,000	10·6	920,000	7·2
500 and over	2,700	0·1	3,375,000	17·1	950,000	7·4
Total, 50 and over	25,000	0·8	6,365,000	32·2	2,410,000	18·8
Total	3,280,000	100·0	19,750,000	100·0	12,850,000	100·0

Romania had developed an industrial nucleus by 1938 and should be classified as 'agricultural-industrial'. It is certainly true that such industrialization as there was increased in tempo in the 1930s. Before the depression industrial capacity increased (1922–9) at an annual average of 4%. During and after the depression the government intensified the protection of industry, limiting the importation of industrial consumer goods and encouraging the import of the means of production. Between 1931 and 1936 industrial production increased by 26%. Both production and capacity were boosted by World War II, but this of course was in turn subjected to destruction and damage. By 1939 industrial production was 385% of 1921. There were state inducements to invest in industry, and government-sponsored cartels were official instruments of industrialization. Another factor in Romania's economic growth in the late 1930s was the economic and political penetration of Nazi Germany into this area.

Oil was known from the fifteenth century and first exploited industrially in 1857. Modernization after World War II led to a dramatic increase in output. The extraction was carried out by international oil companies which had no interest in establishing processing plant. Crude oil, not petroleum products, was exported, and high octane fuels actually had to be imported. By 1936 the extraction methods used led to a premature exhaustion of the primary energy and the wells were considered virtually exhausted.

Crude oil production (in m. tons):
1921, 1·2;   1936, 8·7;   1939, 6·2

In 1946 the Central Bank was nationalized. In 1948 all factories and mines, except the smallest, banks, credit, insurance and transport concerns were nationalized. Foreign trade became a state monopoly. By 1950 four-fifths of the industrial labour force worked in nationalized industries, and thereafter the private sector virtually disappeared.

A currency reform of 1947 crippled the bourgeois and *Kulak* elements by imposing an unequal revaluation according to relative wealth.

The State Planning Commission was founded in 1948. Annual plans were implemented for 1949 and 1950.

By 1950 the work of reconstruction could be considered finished. National income was 99% that of 1938 (for comparable territory). Industrial output: (1938 equals 100) 164; building, 238; agriculture, 70.

The planning era began with the 1st five-year plan (1951–5), a typical Soviet model with over-emphasis on heavy industry. Industrialization results were impressive, but the consumer and housing needs of the increasingly urbanized population were not met.

The process of collectivizing agriculture was begun in 1949 (finally completed 1962). The very rich agricultural resources made it possible to exploit this sector savagely to generate funds for industrialization while under-investing in it.

The first period of collectivization was marked by peasant resistance and government coercion. In a post-Stalin phase until 1958 the pressures to collectivize were eased, living standards were improved, and reliance was placed on transitional semi-collective 'agricultural associations' (TOZ) to accustom the peasantry gradually.

The targets of the 1st five-year plan were raised in 1953 which led to a noticeable unsatisfactory standard of living.

In the post-Stalin period there was a second monetary reform and conditions were eased by some change in the balance of investments.

The 2nd five-year plan (1956–60) was revised in 1956 and replaced by the 1st six-year plan (1960–5) in its final year.

GDP *per capita* (1970 estimate) £418.

SPAIN

A four-year development plan, 1963–7, envisaged a total investment of 355,000m. pesetas. The second development plan, 1968–71, provided 552,700m. pesetas, of which 466,900m. represented real investment and 85,800m. loans.

The economically active population numbered 12,520,100 at the end of 1968 (38·5% of the total population). Of these, 3.9m. were occupied in agriculture and fishing, 3·25m. in manufactures, 1·29m. in trade, 2·15m. in public and personal services.

Spain is mainly an agricultural country. In 1967 the total value of agricultural produce was 222m. pesetas; of livestock, 152·6m.; of forestry, 17·3m. Land under cultivation in 1967 (in 1,000 hectares) included: Cereals, 7,286; vegetables, 875; potatoes, 754. In 1969, 240,000 tractors and 30,000 harvesters were in use.

Principal crops	Area (in 1,000 hectares)		Yield (in 1,000 metric tons)	
	1968	1969	1968	1969
Wheat	3,977	3,744	5,312	4,691
Barley	1,940	2,164	3,441	3,855
Oats	515	498	539	533
Rye	371	333	355	348
Rice	61	66	362	404
Maize	528	525	1,473	1,577
Potatoes	383	386	4,546	4,717
Sugar beet	180	194	4,620	5,079
Tomatoes	52	55	1,310	1,407

In 1967, 1,584,000 hectares were under vines; in 1967 production of wine was 2·47m. hectolitres. The area of onions in 1967 was 33,000 hectares, yielding 843,000 tons. Production of oranges and mandarines in 1969 was 2,111,000 tons. Other products are esparto (41,477 tons in 1964), flax, hemp and pulse. Spain has important industries connected with the preparation of wine and fruits. Silk culture is carried on in Murcia, Alicante and other provinces; 27 tons were produced in 1969. Spain produced in 1968, 8,951 tons of honey and 500 tons of beeswax. Beer factories produced 10·8m. hectolitres in 1969.

Tobacco crop in 1969 was 25,000 tons; sugar-cane (1968), 407,000 tons.

The most important catches are those of sardines, tunny fish and cod. The total catch amounted in 1968 to 1,184,500 tons, representing a value of 21,611·3m. pesetas.

Spain is rich in minerals. The production of the more important minerals in 1969 were as follows (in 1,000 metric tons):

Anthracite	2,767	Potash	4,065
Coal	8,817	Sulphur	38·5
Lignite	2,736	Tin ore (1968)	2
Copper blister	37·6	Zinc ore	149
Copper refined	76·02	Wolfram ore (1968)	1·4
Iron ore	5,200	Silver	55
Lead ore	104	Gold (1965)	276 kg
Manganese ore	23		

In June 64 oil was struck about 40 miles north of the city of Burgos.

In 1964, 332,200 workers were employed in the mining and metallurgical industries. In 1965 the total value of the mining production was 21,998m. pesetas; of metallurgical production, in 1966, 108,732m. pesetas. In 1967 Spain produced 2·69m. tons of pig-iron and 4·33m. tons of steel ingots and castings. A uranium plant to supply the material for nuclear energy was inaugurated at Andujar in Andalusia in Feb 60.

The manufacture of cotton and woollen goods is important, principally in Catalonia. In 1966 there were 4,732 textile factories in operation, with 53,669 looms and 2,378,000 spindles, employing 209,850 workmen. Production, in 1,000 metric tons (1967): Silk yarn, 42; wool yarn, 33; cotton (yarn, 103·7; fabrics, 101·8), rayon fabrics, 20·91. 280 paper-mills produced in 1969, 581,234 tons of writing, printing, packing and cigarette paper. The production of cork in 1966 was 58,400 tons. The production of cement reached 13,117,000 tons in 1967.

Spanish shipyards launched 343,117 BRT in 1966. In 1967, 531,227 motor vehicles were built, including 275,017 passenger cars.

The economic policy is centred on vertical syndicates (trade unions) created under the Charter of Labour on 8 Aug 39, replacing the former local and provincial syndicates. The law of 23 June 41 classified these syndicates into 26 branches of production, each working within its own respective economic sphere, without interrupting their unity or formation. The individual is replaced by the producing concern as a whole, made up of the capitalists, managers, experts and all those rendering some sort of labour, whether intellectual or manual. The vertical syndicate is invested with authority and hierarchy. The appointments are made from top to bottom. At the top stands the National Delegate of Syndicates, who is responsible for his conduct to the Minister who appoints him. Production, wages, prices and the distribution of domestic and foreign merchandise are controlled, and legislation has been adopted requiring government permission for the establishment of new industries.

The daily minimum wage of workers is 156 pesetas (from 1 Apr 72).

The biggest industrial complex in Spain is run by the government-owned *Instituto Nacional de Industria*. INI owns all the share capital of 10 companies, more than three-quarters of 37 companies and has a minority interest in others. INI has invested about £720m. in industry since it was formed in 1941. The government intends that INI should withdraw from ventures that are incompatible with the present policy of complementing rather than supplementing private industry, and concentrate on coal mining, oil refining, steel and power plants.

GDP *per capita* (1970) £432.

SWEDEN

In 1970 the number of farms in cultivation, of more than 2 hectares of arable land, was 155,364; of these there were 111,848 of 2–20 hectares; 40,940 of 20–100 hectares; 2,576 of above 100 hectares. Of the total land area of Sweden (41,140,600 hectares), 3,032,393 hectares (except kitchen gardens and fruit gardens) were arable land, 141,769 hectares cultivated pastures and 22,794,000 hectares forests.

Chief crop	Area (1,000 hectares)[1] 1970	Produce (1,000 metric tons) 1970
Wheat	266·4	962
Rye	80·0	225
Barley	656·8	1,904
Oats	546·3	1,686
Mixed grain	82·3	209
Peas and vetches	2·3	..
Potatoes	65·0	1,490
Sugar-beet	40·0	1,560
Tame hay	801·7	2,763
Oil seed	96·2	194

[1] Figures refer to holdings of over 2 hectares of arable land.

Area of rotation meadows for pasture was (in 1,000 hectares): 1968, 237; 1969, 222; 1970, 237.

Total dairy production of milk (in 1,000 metric tons): 1968, 3,308; 1969, 3,139; 1970, 2,955. Butter production in the same years was (in 1,000 metric tons): 66, 63, 42; and cheese, 59, 58, 60.

Livestock, 1970: cattle, 1,925,628; sheep, 334,616; pigs, 2,073,559.

Number of farm tractors in 1970, 181,517.

The number of pelts produced in 1970 was as follows: Fox, 13,000; mink, 1·7m.

Nearly 23·5m. hectares or 55% of the total land area are covered with forests. The total amount of standing timber is estimated at 2,300m. cu. metres with bark; 85% of this volume consists of coniferous wood (pine and spruce). Half of the forest area is privately owned, the other half is equally divided between public authorities (Crown, Church, communities, etc.) and joint-stock companies. The total cut in 1970 was 60m. cu. metres solid volume (without bark); of these 23m. were coniferous timber, 33m. pulpwood, 3m. fuel wood. In 1968 and in 1969 the total cut was 49 and 53m. cu. metres respectively.

In 1970 there were over 900 saw-mills with 5 or more workers, the total production of which – representing some 90% of the country's total production – amounted to 12m. cu. metres sawn and planed wood. The production of the 100 pulp-mills in Sweden in 1970 amounted to 8·1m. metric tons pulp (dry weight). There was an export of approximately 4·2m. cu. metres of roundwood; exports of sawn coniferous wood amounted to 6·9m. cu. metres, of plywood (including blockboards) to 4,900 metric tons and of pulp 3·8m. metric tons.

In 1970 the total value of the catches of the sea fisheries was estimated at 211m. kr.; of this sum, 154m. kr. came from Göteborg, Bohus and Halland.

Sweden is one of the leading exporters of iron ore. The largest deposits are found north of the polar circle in the area of Kiruna and Gällivare-Malmberget. The ore is exported *via* the Norwegian port of Narvik and the Swedish port of Luleå. There are also important resources of iron ore in southern Sweden (Bergslagen). The most important fields are Grängesberg and Stråssa and the ores are shipped *via* the port of Oxelösund. Some of the southern deposits have, in contrast to the fields in North Sweden, a low phosphorus content.

There are also some deposits of copper, lead and zinc ores, especially in the Boliden area in the north of Sweden. These ores are often found together with pyrites. Non-ferrous ores, except zinc ores, are used in the Swedish metal industry and barely satisfy domestic needs.

The total production of iron ores amounted to 31·5m. tons in 1970 and exports to 28m. tons. The production of copper ore was 114,100 tons, of lead ore 108,200 tons, of zinc ore 167,500 tons.

There are also deposits of raw materials for aluminium not worked at present. In southern Sweden there are big resources of alum shale, containing oil and uranium.

The most important sector of Swedish manufacturing is the production of metals, metal products, machinery and transport equipment, covering almost half of the total value added by manufacturing. Production of high-quality steel is an old Swedish speciality. A large part of this production is exported. The production of ordinary steel is also steadily increasing but is still short of domestic demand. The total production of steel amounted to 5m. tons in 1969, 28% of which was high-quality steel. There is also a corresponding production of other metals (aluminium, lead and copper) and rolled semi-manufactured goods of these metals.

These basic metal industries are an important basis for the production of more developed metal products, machinery and equipment, which are to a large extent sold on the world market, *i,e,* hand tools, mining drills, ball-bearings, turbines, pneumatic machinery, refrigerating equipment, machinery for pulp and paper industries, etc., sewing machines, machine tools, office machinery, high-voltage electric machinery, telephone equipment, cars and trucks, ships and aeroplanes.

Another important manufacturing sector is based on Sweden's forest resources. This sector includes saw-mills, plywood factories, joinery industries, pulp- and paper-mills, wallboard and particle board factories, accounting for about 15% of the total value of manufacturing.

The state-owned sector includes public utilities such as the Post Office and the telephone system, the Postal Bank and the Export Credit Bank, as well as the Arctic iron ore mining company, LKAB, a monopoly for the sales of all wines, spirits and strong beer, forest industries, shipyards, lotteries and transport.

GDP *per capita* (1970) £1,812.

SWITZERLAND

Of the total area of the country of 4,128,790 hectares, about 1,007,710 hectares (24·4%) are unproductive. Of the productive area of 3,121,090 hectares, 980,650 hectares are wooded. The agricultural area, in 1969, consisted of 260,400 hectares arable land (including vineyards), 106,751 hectares artificial meadows, 693,371 hectares permanent meadow and 1,079,630 hectares pasture land. In 1969 there were 149,306 farms with a total area of 1,079,599 hectares. The gross value of agricultural products was estimated at 3,953m. in 1966, 4,224m. in 1967, 4,195m. in 1968, 4,187m. in 1969.

In 1969, 175,315 hectares were planted with cereals, of which 98,841 hectares were wheat; rye, 11,328; barley, 31,256; potatoes, 31,528; sugar-beet, 8,520; vegetables, 6,993; tobacco, 728. Production, 1969 (in 1,000 metric tons): wheat, 350; rye, 43; barley, 132; potatoes, 979; sugar-beet, 392; tobacco, 2·4. Milk production (in 1m. quintals): 1955, 28·3; 1960, 31·1; 1965, 31·2; 1968, 33·2; 1969, 32·1; 1970, 32.

The fruit production (in 1,000 metric tons) in 1969 was: apples, 530; pears, 180; cherries, 44; plums, 44; apricots, 15; nuts, 7.

Wine is produced in 18 of the cantons. In 1970 Swiss vineyards (11,900 hectares) yielded 1,267,000 hectolitres of wine, valued at 278,669,000 francs.

Livestock, 1970: 49,660 horses; 292,400 sheep; 74,707 goats (1966); 1,822,700 cattle (including 869,000 cows): 1,871,000 pigs; 6·3m. poultry.

Of the forest area of 962,677 hectares, 50,841 were owned by the Federation or the cantons, 630,447 by communes and 281,389 by private persons or companies in 1970. The utilization of timber, in 1970, was 3,401,852 cu. metres, of which 274,500 is in state-owned, 2,354,000 in communal and 772,900 in private forests.

There are two salt-mining districts; that in Bex (Vaud) belongs to the canton, but is worked by a private company, and those at Schweizerhalle, Rheinfelden and Ryburg are worked by a joint-stock company formed by the cantons interested. The output of salt of all kinds in 1970 was 333,492 metric tons. At Sargans (St. Gallen) and Herznach (Aargau) iron ore and manganese ore were mined; output (in 1,000 metric tons) 1960, 125; 1965, 113. Since 1966 the mine of Gonzen (at Sargans) and since 1967 Herznach are closed.

The chief food-producing industries, based on Swiss agriculture, are the manufacture of cheese, butter, sugar and meat. The production in 1970 was (in tons): cheese, 86,100; butter, 29,300; sugar, 53,300; meat, 330,100. There are 61 breweries, producing in 1970, 4·73m. hectolitres of beer. Tobacco products in 1970: cigars, 757m.; cigarettes, 29,230m.

Among the other industries, the manufacture of textiles, wearing apparel and footwear, chemicals and pharmaceutical products, bricks, glass and cement, the manufacture of basic iron and steel and of other metal products, the production of machinery (including electrical machinery and scientific and optical instruments) and watch and clock making are the most important. In 1970 there were 11,954 factories with 879,889 workers. Of these 59,990 were working in textile industries, 62,809 in the manufacture of textile goods and footwear, 64,701 in chemical works, 28,324 in the manufacture of clay products, glass and glass products, cement and cement products, 120,873 in manufacture of metal products, 267,445 in the manufacture of machinery and 76,809 in watch and clock making and in the manufacture of jewellery.

Production in 1969 was: cotton yarn pure and mixed, 40,702 metric tons; woven cotton fabrics pure and mixed, 160·9m. metres, rayon and acetate filament yarn, 11,892 metric tons; rayon and acetate staple, 200 metric tons; footwear, 13m. pairs; cement, 4,797,250 metric tons; raw aluminium, 91,490 metric tons; chocolate, 60,698 metric tons. 52,607,700 watches and clocks were exported.

The state has a large interest in railways and owns the communications system. Utilities, and road passenger transport services are generally owned by the cantons or communes.

GDP *per capita* (1970) £1,477.

TURKEY

In the 1920s and 1930s agriculture was extremely primitive and industries relatively unimportant although in 1934 a five-year plan was inaugurated with the aim of improving and increasing industrialization.

Effective planned development in Turkey dates back to 1962, when the State Planning Organization (SPO) was set up and given the task of drawing up three five-year development plans. The first extended from 1963 to 1967, and implementation of the second started in 1968. The first plan aimed at a growth rate of 7% per annum. The rate achieved was in fact 6·7% per annum.

Agriculture remains the main source of national income. As a result, weather conditions continue to cause fluctuations in national income figures.

Turkey's gross national product has grown as follows:

	1948	1954	1958	1962	1966	1969	1970[1]
Million TL	10,000	17,000	36,000	62,000	79,500	90,000	94,000

[1] Provisional

The distribution of the national product by sectors is as follows:

	1948	1958	1969
	%	%	%
Agriculture	47	39	26·7
Trade	9·6	7	7·3
Building	3	5·5	6
Industry	9·7	15·2	18
Other	30	33	42

The 2nd five-year plan provides for a total growth of 40·3% in the national income. Traditional agricultural methods of production are to be supplemented by the use of technology, and the contribution of industry to the national income is to increase from 16·3% in 1967 to 20·5% in 1972. During the transition from an agricultural to an industrial economy, dependence on weather conditions is to decrease, excess manpower is to be drawn away from agriculture, and attempts are to be made to deal with problems caused by urbanization, itself the result of industrialization.

Employment and Labour Supply. With the population increasing at the rate of about 3% per annum, the provision of new jobs is very important. Approximately 1,300,000 persons were unemployed in 1967. The increase in labour supply leads also to an increase in social investment at the expense of productive investment. 65% of the population live in localities having fewer than 10,000 inhabitants, *i.e.* in agricultural settlements suffering from excess manpower. The 2nd five-year plan aims at an improved use of the country's labour resources.

An important labour problem concerns the employment of Turkish workers abroad. By mid-1970 their number approached 450,000, some 90% of whom were employed in Western Germany. Efforts have been made to put to productive use the savings made by these workers, and limited companies formed for this purpose have proved successful.

Workers' remittances from foreign countries constitute an important source of foreign exchange for the Turkish Treasury. In 1969 these remittances exceeded $140m. and in 1970 $273m.

Agriculture. The agricultural sector continues to occupy first place in the composition of the national income, consumption and exports. The consumption of farm produce is, of course, increasing in line with the increase in population. However, technological development has not yet spread to the mass of the peasantry, traditional farming methods still prevail, and marketing leaves much to be desired.

LAND USE IN TURKEY
(Thousands of hectares)

	1963	1967	1968	1969
Agricultural area	23,823	23,896	24,092	24,731
Fields and pastures	28,347	26,135		
Orchards and gardens	2,207	2,414	2,976	3,012
Forests	10,584	12,578	18,273	18,273
Unsuitable for use	13,097	13,095		
Total area	78,058	78,058		

Some 90% of the sown area is used for cereals, largely wheat. Even so, wheat production does not meet domestic needs. Agricultural products which are exported include fresh and dry fruit, hazelnuts, tobacco and cotton.

AGRICULTURAL PRODUCTION IN 1969
(Thousands of tons)

Cereals	17,090
Pulses	591
Fresh fruit	5,147
Tea	160
Tobacco	127
Olives	308
Sugar beet	3,356
Cotton	400
Potatoes	1,936
Sunflower seed	310
Hazelnuts	170

In 1968, of the total cultivated area of 23,836,000 hectares, 6,411,000 hectares were ploughed by tractor. The number of tractors increased from 16,585 in 1950 to 85,475 in 1968. Nevertheless there were still 1,983,000 wooden ploughs in use in 1968.

INDUSTRY: *Mining.* Turkey has rich underground resources, of which only limited use is being made at present. However, the rational development of the production of raw materials goes hand in hand with the growth of home industry. 75% of the mines belong to the state. The 2nd five-year plan proposes a number of measures to deal with the main problems of private mining companies – the inadequacy and dispersion of resources. 29 different minerals are produced in Turkey. The production of the most important of these was as follows in 1969:

MINING PRODUCTION
(Tons)

Metals

Iron	2,505,364
Copper	19,274
Lead	3,538
Zinc	27,740
Mercury	226
Chrome	665,122
Manganese	25,258
Bauxite	1,900

Non-metallic

Sulphur	25,700
Boracite	432,475
Meerschaum (Case)	825
Amianthus	5,533

Fuels

Coal	7,743,277
Lignite	8,551,561

Oil. Turkey's oil reserves are at present estimated at 45,000m. tons. Oil production has been growing, as the following table shows.

OIL PRODUCTION AND IMPORTS
(Tons)

	1963	*1967*	*1969*
State-owned	613,650	991,287	1,184,346
Privately owned	132,385	1,760,453	2,438,846
Total production	746,035	2,751,720	3,623,192
Imports	2,893,515	3,036,580	3,413,000

The increase in imports in spite of growing home production is the result of a steep increase in consumption.

Three oil refineries are in operation in Turkey (at Batman, Izmit and Mersin) and a fourth (near Izmir) is under construction.

GDP *per capita* (1970 estimate) £169.

USSR

Natural conditions for industrial and agricultural development are not particularly favourable. There are rich natural resources for industrial development but these are in the main poorly placed in terms of climate, terrain and the historically-established centres of population.[1] (There has, however, been substantial development in the east, the impetus to which came from World War II.) Agricultural conditions are also relatively unfavourable. There is a shortage of good arable land, and conditions of temperature and humidity are often adverse.

Economic policy has been to develop industry at the expense of agriculture (industry is now second in size to the United States), and to develop heavy industry at the expense of light and food industries. Priority in industrial development has always been accorded to the power industries and capital goods industries, particularly machine-building and the steel industry. In the 1960s the growth of the crude oil, natural gas, electronic and chemical industries was stressed, plus the introduction of new technology in wide areas. The share of capital goods in the total industrial output is 75%. The production of consumer goods has had a low priority, although the position has improved since the 1960s. Heavy industry plays an important part in consumer goods production (bicycles, TV sets, washing machines and other household equipment).

The economy is organized as a hierarchy vertically divided into sectors. Supreme control is exercised by the Central Committee of the Communist Party, and by the Council of Ministers (cabinet). These issue instructions to the various economic ministries responsible for the sectors. Each ministry administers its sector through a series of 'main administrations' (*glavk*) responsible for groups of enterprises. At the bottom of the hierarchy enterprises are managed by officially-appointed directors. In some sectors associations of enterprises are found midway between individual enterprises and administrations. A similar organization exists in the constituent republics (Ukraine etc.). Usually, large enterprises are under central government control, and small ones under local party and local government control. State and collective farms are subject to ministerial and local party control.

Economic performance is organized through time in a series of 'perspective' plans (usually five-year) which set targets for fulfilment. Annual, quarterly and monthly plans guide current operations.

The Communist Party Central Committee's and Supreme Soviet's requirements are made known to the Central Planning Committee (*Gosplan*) in the form of directives from the Council of Ministers. Gosplan develops a draft plan in the form of 'control figures' which are passed down the chain of command to individual enterprise level for elaboration and comment. The draft is then sent

[1] 90% of coal deposits, 80% of hydroelectric potential, 60% of natural gas deposits and 60% of forest reserves are located in Siberia and the Far East.

back to the summit for review and integration. Gosplan then balances requirements against anticipated resources and formulates the national plan.

Gosplan is also charged with the responsibility of supervising the fulfilment of the plan, distributing the national product amongst the various groups of consumers, ensuring a correct balance amongst the different branches of the economy, speeding-up the growth of national income and raising productivity. A parallel organization exists in each constituent republic. There are also planning authorities for major economic regions.

Other agencies participate in the planning process: the State Committee for Material-Technical Supply, which shares with Gosplan over the allocation of materials and administers the wholesale trading network; the SC for Construction (industrial investment planning and construction); the SC for Science and Technology (introduction of new technology); the SC for Labour and Wages; and the Academy of Sciences, which develops the theory for a unified system of optimal planning.

Planning is carried out in physical units (quantities, man-hours). Total volumes of output only are given in money terms, and corollary financial plans are developed in terms of government-fixed prices and applied to the physical plans to control enterprise performance through the banking system.

Economic directives have the force of law. In addition, directors are rewarded for exceeding planned targets and penalized for falling short. An incentives system based on government-established production norms is used to raise worker productivity. Incentives are both material and 'moral' (honours, publicity).

The progress of the plan is also checked by various control bodies which are charged also with detecting planning defects and suggesting remedies.

Enterprises are run on the basis of 'self-accounting' (*khozraschet*), *i.e.*, are accounting units responsible for their own financial survival.

Since 1965 a reform associated with the economist E. Liberman has been progressively instituted. Charges for interest and rent have been imposed to promote a more economical use of capital and natural resources. The standard for measuring enterprise performance has been changed from volume of output to sales and profits. Managers have also received slightly more autonomy in decision-making.

Enterprises sell their products at wholesale prices determined by the State Committee for Prices and various planning authorities and included in the enterprise's annual plan. Prices are not fully correlated with production costs.

The economy before the revolution was backward and unevenly developed, but making rapid progress since industrialization began in the 1890s. Because industrialization started late it was dominated by foreign investments,[1] tended

[1] Percentage of foreign capital of total capital invested in 1916 in certain industries: mining, 91; metallurgy, 42; textiles, 28; chemicals, 50. Percentage of total foreign capital: French, 32·6; British, 22·6; German, 19·7; Belgian, 14·3; US, 5·2; others 5·6; total 100.

to be organized in large-scale units and under a great deal of government control and development.

SOURCES OF NATIONAL INCOME IN 1913

	%
Agriculture	51·4
Industry	28
Trade	8·6
Transport	7·9
Building	8·6
	100

OCCUPATIONS IN 1897

	%
Agriculture	74·6
Industry	9·3
Private service	4·6
Trade	3·8
Transport	1·6
Military services	1
Clergy	0·6
Others	4·5
	100

Serfdom had been abolished in 1861 and in 1905 Stolypin had attempted to put agriculture on to a capitalist footing by ending peasant indemnity and the village commune system. In 1913 there were 367m. hectares of agricultural land. 41% was owned by large landowners, 22% by prosperous farmers (*kulaks*) and 37% by peasants in communal plots. 11m. peasants were landless.

After the February revolution of 1917 peasants and small farmers seized the holdings of the large landowners. This was given legal sanction by the Bolsheviks on their seizure of power by a decree nationalizing land (Nov 17). Food requisitioning and the forcible establishment of state and co-operative farms aroused peasant hostility, and this together with the adverse circumstances of the civil war affected production as the peasants turned to subsistence farming and the hoarding of surpluses. By 1920 production had fallen to 50% of 1913.

Industrial production was also adversely affected by losses of raw materials, territory and manpower (both in military action and back to the rural areas). The finance and transport systems broke down, and there was almost no foreign trade. By 1921 industrial production had fallen to one-fifth of 1913.

In these circumstances there were some attempts to apply thorough-going communist principles (abolition of money, workers' control at factory level) but these were abandoned in the name of practicality.

The New Economic Policy (NEP) announced in 1921 was an ideological compromise with capitalism designed to alleviate peasant hostility and correct the imbalance between agricultural and industrial production. Peasants were no longer subject to compulsory requisitions of produce but had their dues fixed in relation to property and income. Ownership of the land remained with the state, but the peasant could farm as he wished and hire labour.

The 'controlling heights' of the economy remained under close government control, but managers (many former owners) were given more autonomy. All industrial enterprises employing five men and mechanical power or ten men without mechanical power had been nationalized in Nov 20, but NEP allowed entrepreneurs to own small enterprises and conduct most of the retail trade.

Production picked up and surpassed the 1913 level, but this led to a feeling amongst Bolshevik theoreticians that the economy was running away with them into unplanned courses. The 1923–4 'scissors crisis' (so-called from its representation on a graph) reflected the continuing imbalance of agriculture and industry now threatened by the recalcitrance of the peasants in withdrawing from the market as a response to low prices. In the party, and the planning and economic bodies (State Planning Commission founded 1923, Supreme Economic Council, 1918) debate crystallized around a 'left-wing' position (Trotsky) which argued for a forcible transfer of peasant resources into industrial investment, and a 'right-wing' position (Bukharin) which supported a policy of incentives to create an agricultural surplus which would permit the voluntary transfer of funds into industry. Stalin, who had by now begun his political take-off, took a centrist line, suppressed both factions, and in 1928 set the country on its modern footing by introducing enforced agricultural collectivization and the 1st five-year plan.

Annual economic plans ('control figures') were issued from 1925. The early 'geneticist' school of planning, which took cognizance of the dependence of underdeveloped economies on natural forces was gradually supplanted in the late 1920s by the 'technological' school associated with Strumilin which started out from final aims rather than initial possibilities.

Despite the well-known inefficiencies of small-scale farming, enforced collectivization was not *primarily* a move to increase agricultural efficiency but a political move to establish control in the countryside to ensure a supply source to the towns and the transfer of surplus agricultural resources into industrialization regardless of peasant attitudes and of natural calamities which henceforth would be absorbed by the peasantry.

Limited collectivization began in 1928. The hope that peasants could be persuaded to form collectives was defeated by stubborn peasant resistance. In the summer of 1929 the government announced a policy 'to eliminate the *kulaks* as a class'. In Dec, because collectivization was still moving slowly, Stalin demanded their 'liquidation'. By 1930 a species of civil war had spread over the countryside. All peasants who resisted collectivization were dubbed *kulaks*, deprived of rights and property, killed on the spot or sent into exile, their families scattered. During this struggle and the famine which ensued, Stalin told Churchill at Teheran, 10m. perished. By Mar resistance was at an end and some 55m. persons had been driven into collective farms.

At the end of this phase the collectives could not be operated for lack of agricultural machinery and properly formulated plans, and peasants were permitted to leave them. These recalcitrants were driven back gradually by unremitting tax discrimination against the private sector until by 1938 93% of peasant households were collectivized.

The effect of enforced collectivization on planning policy was to enable it to move from a position of economic choice between competing given resources to a quasi-military command system in which the ends were fixed and only the means remained open to logistic choice. Agriculture provided the resources for industry. Industry returned nothing, concentrating on producer goods for its own development. Consumers were satisfied only to the extent of keeping them functioning as workers.

The 1st five-year plan[1] ran from 1928 until it was declared fulfilled in 1932. It was successful in achieving sustained industrial growth, heavily weighted to producer goods (especially coal and steel) and concentrated in very large production units.

In the social sphere the socialist tenets of the old Bolsheviks were sacrificed in the course of this industrial revolution. Working-class living standards fell, the powers of working-class organs were obliterated, earning and hierarchical inequalities were instituted, the Stakhanovite system based on norms or maxima.

After the devastation of World War II reconstruction was brought about by the same traditional system of priorities.

Until after the death of Stalin in 1953 the tasks set industry were still fulfillable by the yardstick of targets met in terms of gross physical output. With the sophistication of the economy, however, calling for a highly skilled labour force in industry and in the country, the exhaustion of pools of surplus labour and the need to introduce new technology, the defects always present in the Stalinist model began to emerge as real impediments and a low standard of living became a hindrance. The desire to excel in physical output was seen to be detrimental to all other aspects of economic performance. It became increasingly difficult to co-ordinate the complex of contradictory targets.

[1] 2nd, 1933–7; 3rd, 1938 – interrupted by war; 4th, 1946–50; 5th, 1951–5; 6th, 1956 – superseded by seven-year plan 1958–65; 8th, 1966–70; 9th, 1971–5.

Output was sought for its own sake, leading to inventories cluttered with unwanted goods biassed in terms of targets.

The reform of 1965[1] attempted to deal with these problems, notably by redefining targets in terms of sales and profits.[2] True to its centralizing outlook, however, the government has not relinquished its direct control right down to enterprise level in favour of a system of natural stimuli (market prices, interest levels, profits at enterprise disposition).

GDP *per capita* (1970 estimate) £596.

UNITED KINGDOM

General distribution of the surface, in acres (1970):

Divisions	Total land surface	Rough grazing land	Permanent pasture	Arable land
England	32,030,000	3,116,000	8,059,000	13,167,000
Wales and Monmouth	5,100,000	1,554,000	1,826,000	738,000
Scotland	19,071,000	11,328,000	1,018,000	3,140,000
Isle of Man	141,000	45,000	24,000	54,000

Distribution of the cultivated area in Great Britain (in acres):

	England and Wales 1970	Scotland 1970
Corn crops[1]	7,855,692	1,128,999[5]
Green crops[2]	2,076,386	320,938
Hops	17,493	–
Small fruit	33,145[3]	10,842
Orchards	153,725	..
Bare fallow	232,310	9,006
Clover and rotation grasses	3,537,803[4]	1,670,658
Permanent pasture	9,885,465	1,018,435
Total	23,790,479	4,158,878

[1] Includes wheat, barley, oats, mixed corn and rye, for threshing.
[2] Green crops include beans, potatoes, turnips and swedes, mangolds, sugar-beet, cabbage, etc., for fodder, vegetables, and all other crops.
[3] Includes acreage of small fruit in orchards.
[4] Including lucerne.
[5] Excludes rye for threshing.

[1] Associated with the economist E. Liberman.
[2] Collective farmers received better pay conditions at this time and were admitted to the social security benefits system. The machine and tractor stations (MTS) which also served as units of political surveillance were disbanded in 1958. In 1967 state farms were made responsible in some cases for their own profits and losses.

The number of workers employed in agriculture in Great Britain was, in June 70, 400,000 (300,300 males, 99,700 females).

In 1970, in the UK, land under the plough amounted to 17·8m. acres (crops and fallow, 12·1m. acres; temporary grassland (including lucerne), 5·7m. acres). Permanent grassland amounted to 12·2m. acres.

Principal crops in the UK as at June 70:

Wheat	Barley	Oats	Beans	Potatoes	Fodder crops[2]	Mangold[1]	Sugar-beet
			Acreage (1,000 acres)				
2,495	5,542	929	189	669	248	24	463
			Total produce (1,000 tons)[3]				
4,108	7,378	1,214	157	7,364	5,561	571	6,311

[1] Fodder crops.
[2] Turnips and swedes for stock-feeding, including fodder beet.
[3] Provisional.

Livestock in the UK as at June 71 (in 1,000):

Cattle	12,836
Sheep	26,061
Pigs	8,789
Poultry	143,430[1]

[1] 1970.

Quantity (in tons) and value (in £) of fish of British taking landed in Great Britain (excluding salmon and sea-trout):

Quantity	1970[1]
England and Wales	505,331
Scotland	390,599
GB (excluding shell-fish)	895,930
Value	
England and Wales	45,918,821
Scotland	23,287,428
GB (excluding shell-fish)	69,206,249
Value of shell-fish	6,278,987

[1] Provisional figures.

The number of National Coal Board mines producing coal on 27 Mar 71 was 292, and there were also (Sep 71) 210 licensed mines. Statistics of the coal mining industry (including licensed mines) for recent years are as follows:

	1967–8[1]	1968–9[1]	1969–70[1]	1970–1[1]
Saleable output of coal:				
Total deep-mined (1,000 tons)	163,800[2]	154,000	140,800	134,100
Opencast (1,000 tons)	7,100	6,600	6,600	8,300
Average weekly number of wage-earners on colliery books:				
All workers (NCB only)	391,900	336,300	305,100	287,200
Underground workers (NCB only)	309,100	226,000	240,000	224,800
Coal exports:				
Total (1,000 tons)	1,961	3,066	3,500	2,982

[1] 12-month period ending March.
[2] Includes licensed mines – 1·02 m. tons.

Total stocks of coal on 27 Mar 71 amounted to 19·8m. tons (13·63 tons distributed, 6·17m. tons undistributed). Operating profits made by the NCB for the year ended 28 Mar 71 amounted to £34·1m. (collieries, £5·5m. profit; opencast, £16·4m. profit). Interest payable to the Secretary of State for Trade and Industry, £35·3m.

Production of coke (including coke breeze) amounted in 1970–1 to 4·46m. tons.

There were no imports of coal or coke by the NCB in 1970–1; exports, 1970–1, amounted to 2,982,679 tons coal, 16,796 tons manufactured fuel and 436,961 tons coke (including coke breeze), valued at £20m. (4m. tons valued at £20m. in 1969–70).

In 1970–1 inland consumption (1,000 tons) of coal at home is estimated to have been 148,286, some of the principal users being: power stations, 73,511; domestic, 18,407; coke ovens, 24,666; other conversion industries, 4,183; gas works, 3,472; chemicals and allied trades, 3,667; collieries, 1,763; paper industry, 2,499; cement industry, 3,818; engineering and other metal trades, 1,525; food, drink and tobacco industry, 1,412; other industrial users (including iron and steel, railways, textiles, bricks, pottery and glass), 5,531.

Production of petroleum 1970, 1,000 tons (1971 in brackets): Through-put of crude process and shale oil, 100,298 (100,301); output of refinery fuel, 5,928 (5,913); aviation and motor spirits, 22,151 (11,448); kerosene, 5,747 (5,760); diesel oil, 22,151 (22,159); fuel oil, 42,170 (42,180); lubricating oils, 1,298 (1,303); bitumen, 1,881 (1,886).

The UK is the fifth largest steel-producing country in the world.

Output in recent years was as follows (in 1,000 tons):

	Iron ore	Pig-iron	Crude steel	Home consumption[1]
1970	11,828	17,393	27,883	24,150
1971	10,067	15,173	23,793	..

[1] Finished steel (ingot equivalent).

In 1971 imports of iron ore amounted to $17 \cdot 47$m. tons valued at £108m. (compared with $19 \cdot 8$m. tons in 1970 valued at £106m.). Exports of finished steel products were $4 \cdot 7$m. tons in 1971 and were valued at £365m. (compared with $3 \cdot 8$m. tons in 1970 valued at £306m.).

Iron Castings. Production of iron castings was $3 \cdot 29$m. tons in 1971 ($3 \cdot 77$m. tons in 1970). At the end of 1971 the number of persons employed in the production of iron castings was some 188,000.

Capital Expenditure. Capital expenditure in 1971 in the iron and steel industry (including iron foundries) is estimated to have been about £230m. (compared with £153m. in 1970).

The industry is divided between the 'public sector' and the 'private sector'. The former consists of the British Steel Corporation which was established on 22 Mar 67 under the Iron and Steel Act 1967. This Act brought into public ownership the 14 major steel producers who together accounted for over 90% of the UK output of crude steel. These companies, including nearly 200 subsidiaries, of which some 50 were overseas subsidiaries, vested in the Corporation on 28 July 67. Following the transfer to the Corporation under the Iron and Steel Act 1969, of the assets and undertakings, as distinct from the shares, of the publicly owned companies and the subsequent dissolution of many of the companies, the Corporation is operated as a single business entity with six product divisions. The creation of the Corporation represented a massive merger, resulting in the second largest steel business in the free world and one of the world's largest industrial undertakings. It produces and sells steel and other products with an annual value of over £1,500m. and employs some 230,000 people. The Act left a substantial part of the British iron and steel industry in private ownership accounting for a turnover of approximately a third of the total for the whole industry at that time with particular strengths in finished steels and in the high-value special steels such as alloy, stainless, high speed and tool steels.

The private sector of the steel industry has formed the British Independent Steel Producers Association (BISPA), 109 members, to protect and represent its interest to the Corporation and the government, and to ensure that liaison continues between the public and private sectors in areas of mutual interest, such as research, standards and statistics.

Production of non-ferrous metals in 1969 (in 1,000 tons): refined copper, $195 \cdot 1$ ($194 \cdot 6$ in 1968); refined lead, $139 \cdot 4$ ($141 \cdot 4$ in 1968); tin metal, $28 \cdot 3$

(27·7 in 1968); virgin aluminium, 33·3 (37·6 in 1968); slab zinc, 151 (130·7 in 1968).

Statistics of a cross-section of industrial production are as follows:

	1970
Sulphuric acid (1,000 tons)	3,200
Synthetic resins (1,000 tons)	1,329
Commercial motor vehicles (no. 1,000)	457
Cotton single yarn (1m. lb)	268
Wool tops (1m. lb.)	175
Woollen yarn (1m. lb.)	286
Man-made fibres (rayon, nylon, etc.) (1m. lb.)	1,320
Newsprint (1,000 tons)	744

Engineering. In 1970 the number (in 1,000) of passenger cars produced amounted to 1,641; aircraft production was 35.

Electrical Goods. Production (in 1,000) for 1970: Radio sets and radiograms, 1,303; gramophone records, 112,941; television sets, 2,214; domestic washing machines, 956.

Textile Manufacture. Production for 1970: woven cloth, cotton (1m. yd), 689; man-made fibres (1m. yd), 1,436; woven woollen and mixture fabrics (1m. sq. yd), deliveries, 257.

Construction. Total value (in £1m.) of constructional work by all agencies in 1970 was 4,971, including new housing, 1,135. Value of industrial buildings for private developers completed in 1970 was £554m. New work (other than housing) for public authorities was valued at £1,170m.

NATIONALIZATION

1926 The Central Electricity Board was set up by the Electricity (Supply) Act, 1926, to regulate central distribution of electricity.

1926 The British Broadcasting Corporation was granted its first charter as a public corporation.

1933 The London Passenger Transport Board was established.

1946 The Bank of England was nationalized, and received a charter.

1946 The Coal Industry was nationalized by the Coal Industry Nationalization Act, 1946, which set up the National Coal Board.

1946 Civil Aviation was formally nationalized by the Civil Aviation Act, 1946. This covered the British Overseas Airways Corporation (set up in 1939), and two new corporations, British European Airways and British South American Airways.

1947 Public Transport (and some private transport) was nationalized by the Transport Act, 1947. The British Transport Commission was established, and the Docks and Inland Waterways, Hotels, Railways,

London Transport, Road Haulage, and Road Passenger Transport were administered by six executive boards. The Transport Act, 1953, denationalized Road Haulage. The Transport Act, 1962, reorganized nationalized transport undertakings and provided for the establishment of separate Boards for Railways, London Transport, Docks and Waterways, and for a Transport Holding Company, as successors to the British Transport Commission.

1948 Gas was nationalized by the Gas Act, 1948, which established the Gas Council and twelve Area Gas Boards.

1949 Iron and Steel were nationalized by the Iron and Steel Act, 1949, and the Iron and Steel Corporation of Great Britain was established. The vesting date of the Act was 1 Jan 51. The Iron and Steel Act, 1953, denationalized the industry, and set up the Iron and Steel Board. In 1967 the Iron and Steel Act renationalized the industry, as from 28 July 67.

1954 The UK Atomic Energy Authority was established by the UK Atomic Energy Authority Act, 1954.

1957 Electricity was nationalized by the Electricity Act, 1947, which set up the British Electricity Authority in place of the Central Electricity Board. The Electricity Act, 1957, set up the Electricity Council and the Central Electricity Generating Board. The twelve area boards became financially autonomous.

1968 The Post Office was to become a Public Corporation under legislation before Parliament during 1968–9.

PLANNING

The National Economic Development Council (NEDC), which first met in 1962, is the national forum for economic consultation between government, management and unions. The 19-member council, with the Chancellor of the Exchequer in the chair, includes leading representatives of the government, CBI and TUC besides chairmen of nationalized industries and independent members. Discussions at the monthly council meetings are normally based on papers, presented by the participating parties, which deal primarily with questions of long-term national economic performance and prospects for both government and industry, besides seeking to agree on ways of improving industrial efficiency through consultation. Council meetings are held in private to encourage the frank exchange of views between members, and the discussions are summarized at a press conference taken by the Director-General of NEDC following each meeting. The Economic Development Committees, like the NEDC, bring together representatives of management and unions, and officials from government, who use this neutral meeting place to study the efficiency and prospects of individual industries. The National

Economic Development Office (NEDO) provides the professional staff for the NEDC and the EDCs.

An attempt by the Department of Economic Affairs in 1964 to frame and supervise a national plan aiming at 25% increase in national product between 1964 and 1970 was published in 1965.

GDP *per capita* (1970) £887.

YUGOSLAVIA

In Yugoslavia there is extensive mineral wealth. Prospecting still continues. There are some 21,300m. tons of coal reserves, two-thirds accessible. Only 1·5% is good bituminous. There is some oil and natural gas. There are estimated to be 167m. tons of iron. Yugoslavia is Europe's leading producer of antimony, chrome, copper, lead and molybdenum, and a major producer of mercury, bauxite and zinc.

The damage of the 1914–18 war was vast, and in the inter-war period Yugoslavia was one of the poorest countries of Europe. This was a period of economic stagnation.

Agriculture was the main occupation. The total number of people dependent on it was 9m. in 1921, 12·5m. in 1941. 81% of the population (6·2m.) were employed in agriculture in 1941. An agrarian reform of 1919 had divided up the big commercial holdings (particularly prevalent in the north) into small holdings and thus diminished capital accumulation opportunities and efficiency. During the inter-war period the population increased 34%. There was grave over-population especially in rural districts which further fragmented holdings and put grave pressure on land. The safety valve of emigration to America was largely shut down in this period. Between 1931 and 1941 agricultural land increased by 4% and population by 20%. At the census of 1931 67·8% of farms were smaller than 5 hectares and comprised only 28% of total land. 0·4% were larger than 50 hectares and comprised 62·3% of the land. In 1938 46·5% of national income was derived from agriculture.

SHARE OF NATIONAL INCOME

	1923–5	*1936–9*
Agriculture	58·1%	52·9%
Industry	20·5%	28·7%
Other	21·4%	19·0%

In the absence of private capital the state took over coal mining, railways and much of heavy industry and attempted to stimulate engineering, steel and paper works. High protective tariffs were introduced in 1925 to encourage industrial development, but only three industries made much progress: shoes, textiles and mining, and the latter was financed mainly from abroad as an important source of raw materials.

During the 1939–45 war there was very serious devastation, the third worst in scale in Europe (after USSR and Poland). Agriculture lost half its livestock and two-thirds of what little machinery it had. 40% of industrial capacity was destroyed.

The economy was restored by the end of 1946 with the aid of reparations from Germany and Hungary ($112m.) and $416m. from UNRRA.

During this period foreign-owned property was confiscated and the dominant foreign control of mining, industry and finance was eliminated.

In its rebuilding and prospective planning policies the government thus gained control of Yugoslavia's ample natural resources. Repayments on foreign loans were stopped, the huge debt of the peasantry was cancelled, incomes were levelled and saving enforced by restricting consumption.

In 1945 the government embarked on a rapid nationalization programme. By 1946 all banks and transport and 89% of industry were under state control. This was extended in 1947 to wholesale and finance institutions and in 1948 to small workshops, retailers and hotels.

An agrarian reform of 1945 limited private holdings to 35 hectares and limited the possibilities of capital expansion by taxation and credit policies. There were few large estates in Yugoslavia and the effect was to move 6% of agricultural land from landowners half into state farms, and half to poor and landless peasants. (There were 1,985,725 holdings in 1939 and 2,407,007 in 1946).

In 1946 a Federal Planning Commission was set up to prepare a plan in co-ordination with economic ministries and regional planning bodies. industrial production 394%, producer goods 552%, consumer goods 274%, agriculture 52% (over 1939). 41% of investment was to go to industry. 7% to agriculture (the latter never fully materialized).

The planners had abundant unskilled labour and natural resources. They lacked capital, skilled labour and managerial talent. The planners were politically motivated and it is highly likely that the plan was intrinsically unworkable. However, in 1948 Yugoslavia was expelled from the Cominform with its attendant withdrawal by Communist countries of aid[1] culminating in a veritable blockade, and was jolted on to its own 'road to socialism' which eventually led to the unique nature of the economy today.

The abandonment of the command economy did not take place until 1950.

---

[1] The USSR extended credits of $400m. for the five-year plan. Only $24m. had been taken before they were cancelled in 1948. (During later rapprochements with the USSR Soviet credits were made available but they were never fulfilled in full owing to subsequent political dissensions.)

Immediately after their expulsion the Yugoslavs continued with their plan with full vigour, and even began the collectivization of agriculture, in 1949.

GDP *per capita* (1970 estimate) £259.

BIBLIOGRAPHY

Allen, G. C., *British Industries and their Organization*, 4th ed. London, 1959
Bauchet, P., *La Planification Française. Vingt Ans d'Experience*. Paris, 1966
Baudhuin, Fernand, *Histoire économique de la Belgique, 1914–39*. Brussels, 1944
— *L'économie belge sous l'occupation 1940–44*. Brussels, 1945
Bernard, P. J., *Planning in the Soviet Union*. Oxford, 1966
Caire, G., *La Planification, Techniques et Problêmes*. Paris, 1967
Cairncross, A. K. (ed.), *The Scottish Economy*. Cambridge, 1954
Dobb, M., *Soviet Economic Development since 1917*. London, 1966
Friss, I. (ed.), *Reform of the Economic Mechanism in Hungary*. Budapest, 1968
Granick, D., *Management of the Industrial Firm in the USSR*. Columbia Univ. Press, 1954
Gutmann, G., and others, *Die Wirtschaftsverfassung der Bundesrepublik*. Stuttgart, 1964
Lutz, V., *Italy: A Study in Economic Development*. R. Inst. of Int. Affairs, 1962
Marione, E., *Les sociétés d'économie mixte en Belgique*. Brussels, 1947
Montias, J. M., *Economic Development in Communist Rumania*. Mass. Inst. of Technology, 1968
O'Mahony, David, *The Irish Economy*. Cork University Press, 1966
Pollard, S., *The Development of the British Economy, 1914–1950*. London, 1962
Pounds, N. J. G., *The Economic Pattern of modern Germany*. 2nd ed. London, 1966
Ravnholt, H., *The Danish Co-operative Movement*. Copenhagen, 1950
Rusinov, S., *Bulgaria: Land, Economy, Culture*. Sofia, 1965
Schwartz, H., *Russia's Postwar Economy*, 2nd ed. New York, 1954
Skrubbeltrang, F., *Agricultural Development and Rural Reform in Denmark*. Rome, 1953
Treize, A., *La Planification en Pratique*. Paris, 1971
Vicens Vives, J., *Historia Económica de España*. 5 vols. Barcelona, 1959
Worswick, G. D. N., and Ady, P. H. (ed.), *The British Economy, 1945–50*. OUP, 1952
— *The British Economy in the Nineteen-Fifties*. OUP, 1962

12 TRADE UNIONS

ALBANIA

The trade union structure is of the Soviet type (*see* page 315).

A few small workers' societies were formed in the 1920s. In 1920 also the Organization of United Workers was founded at Shkodër, comprising 16 trades. This was suppressed by the government in 1927. Other trade unions which grew up during strikes in 1929, 1930 and 1932 were suppressed by the Italian invaders.

On 31 Jan 45 the Communist Party initiated a workers' conference. This led to the formation of a trade union organization which held its first congress on 23 Oct 46.

There are 3 trade unions united in a Central Council (*Këshilli Qëendror i Bashkimeve Profesionale të Shqipërisë*) which has a Secretariat and is responsible for administration between the four-yearly congresses.
President: G. Nushi. Membership: 137,000 (1959).

AUSTRIA

Österreichischer Gewerkschaftsbund (Austrian Federation of Trade Unions)
f. 1945. President: Anton Benya. Membership: 1,512,405
16 Trade Unions.

(1) *Gewerkschaft der Metall- und Bergarbeiter* (Union of Metalworkers and Miners)
f. 1890 Chairman: Anton Benya. Membership: 290,000.

(2) *Gewerkschaft der Privatangestellen* (Union of Commercial, Clerical & Technical Employees)
Chairman: Rudolf Haüser. Membership: 262,225.

(3) *Gewerkschaft der Bau- und Holzarbeiter* (Union of Building and Woodworkers)
Chairman: Hans Böck. Membership: 197,206.

(4) *Gewerkschaft der Oeffentlich Bediensteten* (Union of Public Employees)
f. 1945. Chairmen: A. Gaspershutz, J. Seidl. Membership: 127,732.

(5) *Gewerkschaft der Gemeindebediensteten* (Union of Municipal Employees)
Chairman: R. Weisz. Membership: 122,515.

(6) *Gewerkschaft der Eisenbahner* (Union of Railwaymen)
Chairman: F. Prechtl. Membership: 119,000.

BELGIUM

Fédération Générale du Travail de Belgique/Algemeen Belgisch Vakerverbond (F.G.T.B.)
f. 1899. Secretary-General: Georges Debunne. Membership: 800,000.
15 Unions.

(1) *Centrale Générale du Bâtiment, du Bois, et des Industries diverses de Belgique* (Union of Building, Wood and General Workers).
President: E. Janssens. Membership: 192,000.

(2) *Centrale Générale des Services Publiques* (Public Service Workers).
f. 1945. President: E. Hamont. Membership: 180,000.

(3) *Centrale des Métallurgistes de Belgique* (Metal Workers).
f. 1887. Secretary-General: G. Wallaert. Membership: 150,000.

Confédération des Syndicats Chrétiens (C.S.C.) (Federation of Christian Trade Unions)
President: Auguste Cool. Membership: 904,672.
15 Unions.

(1) *Centrale Chrétienne des Travailleurs du Bois et du Bâtiment* (Wood and Building Workers)
President: K. Nuyts. Membership: 166,750.

(2) *Centrale Chrétienne des Métallurgistes de Belgique* (Metalworkers)
President: G. Heiremans. Membership: 149,095.

(3) *Centrale Chrétienne des Ouvriers du Textile et du Vêtement de Belgique* (Textile and Clothing Workers)
President: L. Fruru. Membership: 120,000.

Centrale Générale des Syndicats Libéraux de Belgique (C.G.S.L.B.) (General Federation Liberal Trade Unions of Belgium)
f. 1889. President: A. Colle. Membership: 120,000.

BULGARIA

The trade union structure is of the Soviet type (*see* page 315).

A printers' union was formed in Sophia in 1883. By 1904 there were 172 trade unions, and in that year both the Free Trade Union Federation and the

Marxist General Trade Union Federation were formed. These united in 1920 as the United General Workers' Trade Union Federation with 32,000 members. This was suppressed by the government after the *coup* of 1923. Independent unions which held a congress in 1927 were again suppressed after 1934, and a government-supervised Bulgarian Workers' Union was set up, forbidden to strike after 1936 (though strikes did occur), but benefiting from relatively progressive social legislation.

This was dissolved on the Communist takeover and the General Workers' Professional Union (ORPS) was set up in March 1945 with 263,742 members. The ORPS assumed its present name *Tsentraden Suvet na Profesionalnite Suyuzi*, Central Council of Trade Unions, in 1951.

The Central Council has an Executive Bureau and a Secretariat, and is responsible for administration between the four-yearly congresses.

President: P. Koritarova. Membership: 2,486,988 (1969).

CYPRUS

There are trade unions or branches of one in each of the 222 villages as well as the 6 main towns. 6 Federations of Trade Unions.

Total membership: 72,000.

Largest – *Pankypria Ergatiki Omospondia* (Pancyprian Federation of Labour) f. 1941. General Secretary: A. Ziartides. Membership: 34,000.

17 Unions.

CZECHOSLOVAKIA

The trade union structure is of the Soviet type (*see* page 315). During the reform period of 1968–9 the unions began to assume an active and independent role, but this tendency was reversed by the Soviet intervention.

A printers' union was formed in 1862. In 1897 the Czechoslovak Trade Union Federation was formed, affiliated to the Austrian Trade Union Commission.

Before the Communist takeover trade unionism developed along lines of deep national/political/religious cleavage. The National Socialist Party (*not* Nazis: *see* POLITICAL PARTIES: Czechoslovakia) dominated the trade union scene (National Socialist trade unions date from 1902). In 1902 also Christian trade unions were founded, and after independence (1918) a separate German organization was formed. In 1922 Communists were expelled from the central organization and formed their own 'Red Trade Unions'. By 1937 there were 699 unions in 18 federations.

These were suppressed during the Nazi occupation, towards the end of which works councils began to emerge which formed the basis of post-war trade union development. A national Trade Union Congress was held on 19 Apr 46.

After the Communist takeover all unions were compulsorily united in the Revolutionary Trade Union Movement (ROH) with 3,072,956 members.

There are now 18 unions united in the Central Council of Trade Unions (*Ústřední Rada Odborů*) which has a Presidium and is responsible for administration between the four-yearly congresses.

President: K. Poláček. In 1968 there were 5·5m. members.

DENMARK

Landsorganisationen i Danmark (Federation of Danish Trade Unions).
Chairman: Thomas Nielsen. Membership: 865,316.
60 affiliated unions.

(1) *Handels og Kontorfunktionoernes Forbund i Danmark* (Shop Assistants and Office Clerks)
f. 1900. Chairman: Max Harvøe. Membership: 140,000.

(2) *Dansk Smede- og Maskinarbejderforbund* (Blacksmiths and Ironworkers)
f. 1888. Chairman: H. Rasmussen. Membership: 89,000.

FINLAND

Suomen Ammattiliittojen Keskusjäjestö r.y. (S.A.K.) (Confederation of Finnish Trade Unions)
f. 1907. President: Niilo Hämäjäinen.
30 affiliated unions.

Suomen Metallityöväen Lütto r.y. (Metalworkers Union).
f. 1899. President: Sulo Penttilä. Membership: 92,887.

Rakennustyölaisten Lutto r.y. (Building Workers Union).
f. 1930. President: Aarno Aitamurto. Membership: 72,000.

Suomen Ammattijärjesto r.y. (S.A.J.) (Finnish Trade Federation)
f. 1960. Presidents: Jaahko Rantunen, Eero Lilyja. Membership: 96,108.
17 affiliated unions.

Suomen Merinues – Unioni r.y. (Finnish Seamen's Union).
f. 1916. President: Olavi Keitele. Membership: 12,304.

Toimi Henkilö – Ja Virkamiesjärjestöjen Keskusutto (T.V.K.) (Confederation of Salaried Employees)
f. 1944. Chairman: Oso Laakso. Membership: 2,000,000.
28 affiliated unions.

Virkamieslütto (Federation of Civil Servants)
f. 1917. Chairman: V. W. Heinstrom. Membership: 36,000.

FRANCE

Confédération Générale du Travail
f. 1895. President: Benoit Frachon. Membership: 2,400,000.
38 affiliated unions (one for each industry).

Force Ouvrière
f. 1947, by breakaway from *Confédération Générale du Travail.*
General Secretary: André Bergeron. Membership: 1,000,000.

Confédération Français Démocratique du Travail (C.F.D.T.)
f. 1919 as *Confédération Français des Travailleurs Chrétiens (C.F.T.C.)* 1964 –
C.F.D.T.
President: André Jeanson. Membership: 1,000,000.
Co-ordinates 4,425 trade unions, 35 professional federations and 102 departmental and overseas unions.

Fédération Nationale des Syndicats d̂Exploitants Agricoles F.N.S.E.A.
(National Federation Farmers Unions)
f. 1946. President: Gérard de Caffarelli. Membership: 750,000.

Fédération de l'Éducation Nationale (F.E.N.) (Federation of Teachers' unions)
Leaders: J. Marange, A. Drubay, A. Geismar. Membership: 450,000.

Confédération Générale des Cadres (Organization for supervisors, executive staff and technicians)
f. 1944. President: André Malterre. Membership: 250,000.

EAST GERMANY

Freier Deutscher Gewerkschaftsbund (Confederation of Free German Trade Unions)
f. 1945. Chairman: Herbert Warnke. Membership: 6,500,000.
15 specialized unions federated under *Freier Deutscher Gewerkschaftsbund.*

WEST GERMANY

Deutscher Gewerkschaftsbund (D.G.B.).
f. 1949. President: Heinz O. Vetter. Membership: 6,500,000.
16 unions affiliated.

(1) *Gewerkschaft Öffentliche Dientse, Transport und Verkehr* (Public Services, Transport and Communications)
Chairman: H. Kluncker. Membership: 978,078.

(2) *Industriegewerkschaft Chemie, Papier, Keramik* (Chemical, Paper and Ceramics)
f. 1947. President: K. Hauenschild. Membership: 542,768.

(3) *Industriegewerkschaft Bau, Steine, Erden* (Building and Stonework)
President: R. Sperner. Membership: 503,000.

(4) *Industriegewerkschaft Bergbau und Energie* (Mining)
President: W. Arendt. Membership: 435,152.

(5) *Gewerkschaft der Eisenbahner Deutschlands* (Railwaymen)
President: P. Seibert. Membership: 424,214.

(6) *Deutsche Postgewerkschaft* (Postal Union)
President: Carl Stenger. Membership: 356,000.

Non-affiliated unions:
Deutscher Beamtembund (Federation of Civil Servants and Public Officials)
f. 1949. President: A. Krause. Membership: 725,000.

Deutscher Angestellten-Gewerkschaft (D.A.G.) (Clerical, Technical and Administrative Workers)
f. 1945. Chairman: H. Brandt. Membership: 485,000.

GREECE

Greek General Confederation of Labour
f. 1918. General Secretary: Ioannis Kourmouzis. Membership: 389,000.

Pan-Hellenic Seamen's Federation
f. 1920. General Secretary: Sotirios Katsaros.

HUNGARY

The trade union structure is basically of the Soviet type (*see* page 315), but two areas of departure may be noted: (1) for a short time during the 1956 uprising unions organized themselves on a factory basis and independently of

the Communist Party, seceded from the World Federation of Trade Unions
and set up workers' councils. These were dissolved at the end of 1957 and
replaced by Factory Councils; (2) under the Labour Code of 1 Jan 68
promulgated in connexion with the introduction of the 'New Economic
Mechanism' trade unions have an increased role to play in economic
management, including a right of veto on managerial decisions which are
alleged to contravene the Code.

In 1862 a printers' union was formed. Union development then became
largely a matter of local craft unions, but a national trade union council was
instituted in 1898. Trade unions gained legal recognition only in 1916.

In the reaction following Béla Kun's Soviet Republic in 1919 the government came to an agreement with the unions (and the Social Democratic Party)
granting them limited toleration provided they abstained from political
activities and did not attempt to unionize agricultural and clerical workers.

After World War II the Communists eliminated the small craft unions and
likewise the influence of the Social Democratic Party, and had established a
Soviet model union hierarchy by 1949.

There are 19 unions in the Central Council of Hungarian Trade Unions
(*Magyar Szakszervezetek Orszagos Tanacsa*), which has a Presidium, and is
responsible for administration between the four-yearly congresses.
President: B. Blaha. In 1971 there were 3m. members.

ICELAND

Althydusamband Íslands (Icelandic Federation of Labour)
f. 1916. General Secretary: Óskar Snorri Jonsson. Membership: 34,940.

Landssamband Idnadarmanna (Federation of Icelandic Master Craftsmen)
f. 1932. Chairman: V. Sigurdsson. Membership: 3,000.

IRISH REPUBLIC

Irish Congress of Trade Unions
f. 1959. General Secretary: Ruaidhri Roberts. Membership: 5,000,000.
Affiliated unions from both N. Ireland and Eire.
Mostly small membership:
  (1) Transport and General Workers Union (Irish)
f. 1909. General Secretary: Michael Mullen. Membership: 150,000.
  (2) Workers Union of Ireland
f. 1924. General Secretary: James Larkin. Membership: 30,000.
  (3) Teachers Organization, Irish National
f. 1868. President: Thomas Warde. Membership: 13,900.

ITALY

12 national federations. Two largest:
C.G.I.L. (*Confederazione Generale Italiana del Lavoro*) (General Union Italian Workers)
General Secretary: Agostino Novella. Membership: 3,500,000.
38 affiliated unions.

C.I.S.L. (*Confederazione Italiana Sindecate Lavoratori*) 38 federated unions.
f. 1950. General Secretary: Bruno Storti. Membership: 2,450,523.

Some of largest affiliated unions:
(1) *Unione Italiana Lavoratori Dxlla Terra* (*U.I.L.T.*) (Handworkers Union)
Secretary: A. Rossi. Membership: 488,750.
(2) *Federazione Impiegate Operai Metallurgici* (*F.I.O.M. – C.G.I.L.*) (Metalworkers)
f. 1902. General Secretary: B. Trentin. Membership: 450,000.
(3) *Federazione Italiana Pensionate* (*F.I.P.*)
General Secretary: U. Fiore. Membership: 400,000.
(4) *Impiegati Agricoli* (*F.E.D.E.R. B.R.A.C.C.I.A.N.T.I.*) (National Federation Agricultural Workers)
Secretary: G. Caleffi. Membership: 400,000.
(5) *Federazione Nationale Lavoratori Edili Affini e del Legno* (*F.E.N.E.A.L.*) (Builders and Woodworkers)
Secretary: L. Rufino. Membership: 205,500.
(6) *Federazione Italiana Lavoratori Tessili e Abbigliamento* (*F.I.L.T.A. – C.I.S.L.*)
General Secretary: B. Fassina. Membership: 160,000.

LIECHTENSTEIN

Trades Union Secretariat
President: J. Frick.

Workers Union Secretariat
President: J. Beck.

LUXEMBOURG

Confédération Générale du Travail du Luxembourg (*C.G.T.*) (Luxembourg General Confederation of Labour)
f. 1919. President: M. Hinterschild. Membership: 31,500.

7 affiliated unions. Largest:
Letzburger Arbechter-Verband (Luxembourg Workers' Union)
f. 1916. President: B. Berg. Membership: 19,800.

MALTA

Confederation of Malta Trade Unions
f. 1958. General Secretary: G. Callus. Membership: 9,000.
21 affiliated small unions.

Non-affiliated: The General Workers Union
f. 1943. President: D. M. Cremona. Membership: 23,000.

THE NETHERLANDS

Nederlands Verbond Van Vakverenigingen (N.V.V.) (Netherlands Federation
of Trade Unions)
f. 1906. President: H. Ter Heide. Membership: 600,000.
16 affiliated unions.

Algemene Bond Van Ambtenaren (Civil Servants)
President: J. Hoogerwerf. Membership: 118,763.

Metaalbedrijfsbond N.V.V. (Metalworkers etc.)
f. 1886. President: M. Zondervan. Membership: 111,595.

Nederlands Katholiek Vakverbond (N.K.V.) (Catholic Trade Union Federation)
f. 1909. Chairman: P. Mertens. Membership: 400,000.
19 affiliated unions.

Nederlands Katholiek Bond Van Werknemers in de Bouwnijverheid (Building
Workers)
f. 1917. President: L. Brouwer. Membership: 79,000.

Christelijk National Vakverbond in Nederland (C.N.V.) (Christian National
Federation Trade Unions Netherlands – Protestant)
f. 1909. President: J. Lanser. Membership: 239,000.
24 affiliated unions.

Nederlandse Christelijk Bond van Overheidspersoneel (Government Personnel)
President: J. Ten Heuvelhof. Membership: 53,500.

NORWAY

Landsorganisasjonen I Norge (L.O.) (Norwegian Federation of Trade Unions)
f. 1899. President: Tor Aspengren. Membership: 588,000.
   (1) *Norsk Jern og Metallarbeiderforbund* (Union of Iron & Metalworkers)
f. 1891. President: L. Skau. Membership: 85,000.
   (2) *Norsk Kommuneforbund* (Municipal Employees)
f. 1920. President: Arne Born. Membership: 75,000.

POLAND

The trade union structure is of the Soviet type (*see* page 315). After the riots
and government changes in 1956 trade unions gained in independence and
power, but these gains have been largely eroded. During the demonstrations
and strikes which brought about the fall of Gomułka's government in Dec 70,
trade union buildings were attacked by workers, and demands for an
independent trade union organization were put forward.

Trade union movements had formed in all three zones of partitioned Poland
by the beginning of the twentieth century, and gained legal recognition in 1919
after independence. The movement developed along deep political/national-
ist/religious cleavages. By the 1930s there were 300 unions with some one
million members. Unions existed in the shadow of government persecution,
however, and under the Nazi occupation were banned completely.

With the Communist takeover the unions were restructured along Soviet
lines, a process formalized by the 1st Trade Union Congress in Nov 45. Craft
unions and anarcho-syndicalist tendencies were gradually eliminated.

There are 22 unions united in the Central Council of Trade Unions
(*Centralna Rada Związków Zawodowych, C.R.Z.Z.*), which has a Presidium
and Secretariat and is responsible for administration between the four-yearly
congresses.

In 1969 there were 9·7m. members. President: W. Kruczek.

PORTUGAL

No trade unions as such. Workers' and employers' interests are represented by
the voluntary *sindicatos* and *grémios* respectively. Each represents a particular
industry within a particular locality. *Corporações* (corporations) negotiate
collective contracts and arbitrate between the *grémios* and *sindicatos*.

ROMANIA

The trade union structure is of the Soviet type (*see* page 315).

Craft unions had formed (and been suppressed) in the 1880s. Industrial legislation at the turn of the century had obliged employers and employees to set up joint organizations. In 1906 there was a joint socialist-trade union conference. By 1914 there were 69 unions with 10,000 members; by 1920 there were 156 unions with 200,000. There were both Social Democratic and Communist unions, the latter illegal after 1929. Trade unions were banned under the corporatist legislation of 1938.

A Communist structure was set up after World War II with 500,000 members. All other union activity was suppressed by 1947.

There are 13 unions united in the General Trade Union Confederation administered by its Central Council (*Consiliul Central ale Sindicatelor*), which has a Presidium and Secretariat and is responsible for administration between the five-yearly congresses.

In 1968 there were 4·6m. members. President: C. Drăgan.

SPAIN

No trade unions as such. There are syndicates in which both employers and workers are represented. Independence limited by Act of 1969. A Cabinet Minister is President of each.

Largest:

(1) *Sindicato Nacional de Cereales* (Cereal Growers)
f. 1942. National Director: Antonio Reus Cid. Membership: 2,296,414.

(2) *Hermandad Syndical Nacional de Labradores y Ganaderos* (Brotherhood of National Syndicate for farmers, farmworkers and stockbreeders)
President: Luis Mambiedro de la Torre. Membership: 1,980,585.

(3) *Sindicato Nacional de la Construcción, Vidrio y Cerámuca* (Building, Glass, Ceramics)
f. 1942. President: P. G. Ormaechea y Casanovas. Membership: 843,000.

(4) *Sindicato Nacional de Transportes y Communicacionos* (Transport and Communications)
President: E. Villegas Girón. Membership: 689,000.

(5) *Sindicato Nacional de Actividades Diversas* (Miscellaneous Activities)
f. 1950. President: Dr Roberto Reyes Morales. Membership: 506,000.

(6) *Sindicato Nacional de la Madero y Corcho* (Wood and Cork)
President: E. de Pablos Gutiérrez. Membership: 300,000.

SWEDEN

Landsorganisationen I Sverige (Swedish Trade Union Confederation)
f. 1898. President: Arne Geyer. Membership: 1,659,729.
29 affiliated unions.

(1) *Svenska Metallindustriarbetareförbundet* (Metalworkers)
f. 1888. President: Ake Nilsson. Membership: 355,446.

(2) *Svenska Kommunalarbetareförbundet* (Municipal Workers)
President: G. Hallström. Membership: 214,816.

(3) *Svenska Byggnadsarbetareförbundet* (Building Workers)
Chairman: K. Johansson. Membership: 177,210.

(4) *Statsanställdas Förbund* (State Employers)
f. 1970. President: G. Kolare. Membership: 150,000.

Non-affiliated: Tjänstemanners Centralorganisation T.C.O. (Central Organization Salaried Employees)
President: L. Bodstrom. Membership: 670,000.

SWITZERLAND

Schweiserischer Gewerkschaftesbund (Swiss Federation of Trade Unions)
f. 1880. President: E. Wüthrich. Membership: 450,000.

(1) *Schweizerisches Metall- und Uhrenarbeiter-Verband* (Metal Workers and Watchmakers)
f. 1893. President: E. Wüthrich. Membership: 133,000.

(2) *Schweizerischer Bau- und Holzarbeiterverband* (Building and Woodworkers)
f. 1922. President: E. Canonica. Membership: 80,000.

Christlichnationaler Gewerkschaftsbund der Schweiz (Confederation of Christian Trade Unions)
f. 1907. President: H. Reido. membership: 92,924.

Christlicher Holz- und Banarbeiterverband de Schweiz (C.H.B.) (Building and Woodworkers)
f. 1899. President: J. Baltisberger. Membership: 29,106.

Non-affiliated: Fédération des Sociétés Suisses d'Employés (Salaried Employees)
f. 1918. President: R. Maier-Neff. Membership: 123,604.

TURKEY

Türkiye isçi Sendikauari Konfederas Yonu-Turk is (Turkish Trade Union Confederation)
f. 1952. Chairman: Seyfi Demirsöy. Membership: 800,000.
25 unions. 9 federations.
   (1) *Tüm Gida is* (Tobacco, Drink and Food)
f. 1957. President: Orhan Sorguc. Membership: 118,211.
   (2) *Teksif* (Textile)
f. 1951. President: S. Yilmaz. Membership: 100,000.

Devrimci Iscileri Sendikasi Konfederasyonu (Reformist Workers' Unions)
f. 1967. 17 member unions.

USSR

In contrast to the position in Western Europe, Soviet trade unions (*profsoyuzy*) do not represent the independent interests of the workers as against management or government. In official theory the USSR is a workers' state, and there can be no conflict between the working-class and its own organs of administration: the latter must by their very nature act in the interests of the former. Trade unions have been integrated into the economic administrative machinery, and are best regarded as departments of productivity and social and cultural welfare.

Unions are organized on the 'industrial principle': all the employees in one industry, whatever their status or job, are members of the same union. The unions are administered in accordance with 'democratic centralism'.

Collective farm peasants are not unionized.

Trade unions first appeared in 1905 in connection with the strikes and unrest of that year. From the start unions tended to grow up on the 'industrial principle' because industry in Tsarist Russia, though small in the overall sense, was organized in large-scale units.

Trade unions were by no means the only workers' organs. In 1905 the workers began to organize Soviets.

The first All-Russian Conference of Trade Unions was held in 1905, the second in 1906. By 1907 there were 652 unions with 245,355 members. After 1907 the unions were repressed and inactive till 1915, when there was a further wave of strikes. By May 1917 there were 2,000 unions with 1·5m. members. A trade union conference of June 17 founded the All-Russian Central Council of Trade Unions. At the first All-Russian Trade Union Congress (Jan 18) there were 4m. members.

In Bolshevik usage the term *tred-yunionizm* was pejorative. Unless inspired by the revolutionary party trade union demands would be sectional and narrow and lead not to a revolutionary transformation of society but to an accommodation with it.

In the early days of the Bolsheviks there was a movement towards workers' control by factory committees. The Bolshevik government interpreted 'workers' control' as centralized disciplined administration by the government organs of the workers' state. The trade unions shared this centralizing view, and were willing to accept responsibility for the administration of labour and social insurance legislation.

The issue of trade union autonomy was raised by the abortive left-wing 'Workers' Opposition' within the Communist Party 1920–1.

The 'New Economic Policy' re-introduced a market economy and with it the trade unions assumed a more traditional posture, relinquishing some of their administrative functions to the People's Commissariat (Ministry) for Labour (until 1933) and assuming wage-bargaining functions. In this situation the Communist Party made a point of establishing its hegemony at the 4th All-Russian Trade Union Congress in 1921.

From this position the real powers of the unions were steadily whittled away during the 1920s until the present pattern was established. In 1929 Stalin removed the union leader Tomskii, and the remainder of the independent leadership perished in the purges of 1936–38.

There are today 26 unions united in the monolithic All-Union Central Council of Trade Unions (*Vsesoyuznyi Tsentral'nyi Sovet Professional'nykh Soynzov*) which is responsible for administration between the four-yearly congresses, and which has a Presidium.

Union membership is not compulsory but it is usual.

In 1969 there were some 86m. members.

President: A. Shelepin.

UNITED KINGDOM

Trade Union Congress
f. 1868. General Secretary: Len Murray. Membership: 9,402,170. 150 unions. Largest:

(1) Transport & General Workers Union (T.G.W.U.)
General Secretary: Jack Jones. Membership: 1,475,556.

(2) Amalgamated Union of Engineering & Foundry Workers (A.E.U.)
f. 1967. President: Hugh Scanlon. Membership: 1,277,000.

(3) National Union of General & Municipal Workers
f. 1889. General Secretary: Lord Cooper. Membership: 830,000.

(4) Electrical, Electronic & Telecommunication Union/Plumbing Trades Union

f. 1889. General Secretary: Frank Chapple. Membership: 400,000.

(5) National & Local Government Officers Association (NALGO)

f. 1905. General Secretary: W. C. Anderson. Membership: 400,000.

(6) National Union of Mineworkers

Secretary: L. Daly. Membership: 344,030.

YUGOSLAVIA

Trade union activity began in the second half of the 19th century but was small in scale and unco-ordinated until the end of World War I.

The Communist-inspired Federation of Revolutionary Trade Unions set up in Apr 19 was banned in 1921 along with the Party itself. A law of 1922 forbade unions to have political affiliations. The United Workers Federation was set up in 1922. The crypto-Communist Organization of Independent Trade Unions was established in rivalry with this, but was banned in 1929.

After World War II and the Communist takeover a Soviet-type structure was established at a national trade union congress in Jan 45, uniting 30 unions on the 'industrial principle' with a total membership of 225,000.

After Yugoslavia's expulsion from the Communist comity of nations in 1948 trade unions developed in line with the general political evolution towards 'self-management' (*samonpravljanje*). The federation was renamed the League of Trade Unions of Yugoslavia (*Savez Sindikata Jugoslavije*), and was integrated into the machinery of Workers' Councils, retaining till 1958 the exclusive right of nominating Council candidates.

Since then the unions have come to represent the interests of workers in a real way, and strikes are not uncommon.

There are six unions in the SSJ. The supreme authority is the four-yearly congress. Between its sessions the Council (*Veće*) is responsible for administration, and elects a Presidium and Secretariat.

In 1964 there were 2·95m. members.

President: D. Petrović.

BIBLIOGRAPHY

Allen, V. L., *International Bibliography of Trade Unionism*. London, 1968
— *Trade Unions and the Government*. London, 1960
Binternagel, F., and Triesch, G. (eds.), *Die Gewerkschaften in der Bundesrepublik*. Cologne, 1951
Cole, G. D. H., *An Introduction to Trade Unionism*. London, 1953

Connolly, J., *Labour in Ireland.* Dublin, 1951

Deutscher, I., *Soviet Trade Unions: Their Place in Soviet Labour Policy.* London, 1950

Galenson, W., *Labor in Norway.* Harvard Univ. Press, 1949

— *The Danish System of Labor Relations. A Study in Industrial Peace.* Harvard Univ. Press, 1952

Harrison, M., *Trade Unions and the Labour Party since 1945.* London, 1960

Karlblom, T., *Die Svenska Fackföreningsrörelsen.* Stockholm, 1955

Klenner, F., *The Austrian Trade Union Movement.* Brussels, 1956

Knoellinger, C. E., *Labor in Finland.* Harvard Univ. Press, 1960

La Palombara, J. G., *The Italian Labour Movement; Problems and Prospects.* Cornell Univ. Press, 1957

Lorwin, V. R., *The French Labor Movement.* Harvard Univ. Press, 1955

Myers, C. A., *Industrial Relations in Sweden, Some Comparisons with American Experience.* Cambridge, Mass., 1951

Pelling, H., *A Short History of British Trade Unionism.* London, 1963

Philip, D., *Le Mouvement Ouvrier en Norvège.* Paris, 1958

Robbins, J. J., *The Government of Labor Relations in Sweden.* Univ. of North Carolina Press, 1942

Roberts, B. C., *Trade Union Government and Administration.* London, 1956

Schwarz, S. M., *Labor in the Soviet Union.* New York, 1951

— *Trade Unions in the U.S.S.R.* New York, 1953

Seidel, R., *Die Deutschen Gewerkschaften.* Stuttgart, 1948

Shillman, B., *Trade Unionism and Trade Disputes in Ireland.* Dublin, 1960

Vittorio, G. di, and others, *I Sindicatti in Italia.* Bari, 1955

The Trade Union Situation in Sweden. Intern. Labour Organization, Geneva, 1961

13 EDUCATION

ALBANIA

The Ministry of Education was formed in 1920. The education system at that time was mainly Moslem, but there were schools run by the Roman Catholic and Greek Orthodox churches and a school at Korytza for girls founded by Protestants. Schools were nationalized in 1933 and reorganized. Free elementary education was now obligatory for children between 4 and 13. After 13 they could go on to gymnasium or to town school. The gymnasia had eight-year courses on lower and advanced level, the town schools had four-year courses corresponding to the lower level. Pupils going to town schools could go on to commercial institutes; those going to gymnasia for the first four years only could go on to normal schools to train as teachers. There were technical schools with three five-year courses after town school. There were no universities. In 1936 nationalization was modified by the authorization of free schools. Those run by the Franciscan order and the Greek Orthodox church opened again under government control. In 1938 it was thought that illiteracy was still as high as 75%.

In 1930 the National Organization of Albanian Youth had been set up as a state organization directing the activities of all youth organizations for 'patriotic, moral and physical education' in and out of school. In 1946 the Communist regime passed a reform act laying down that all school text books must be prepared on the basis of Communist ideas.

Education is now on the Russian model, although the break with Russia in 1961 has deprived the country of help for higher education, especially at the University of Tirana (12,783 full-time pupils, 1969) which was founded with largely Russian assistance in 1957.

Elementary schools have four grades, seven-year schools have four corresponding grades and three more, secondary schools have four grades more than seven-year schools. Greek minority schools still exist but are largely Albanian staffed and government controlled. A two-year teachers' training college at Tirana opened as part of an increased emphasis on technical and professional training. In 1951 there were three High Institutes with courses in economics, sciences, technology and culture, and in 1952 one more. In 1963 a reorganization produced the 'incomplete secondary school' with compulsory courses of eight years from age 7 to age 16. Pupils might stay on for an extra 3–4 years;

the first four grades corresponded to the elementary school. Time allotted to humanities 42%, to science 34%, to handicrafts and labour training 17%, in the 8 year course; the later course divided time about equally.

All schools have a common curriculum and are centrally administered. They are all co-educational. Since 1946 they have worked a two-shift system to cope with the number of pupils. Every school has a patron – *e.g.* a factory or in the country a farm – which helps it with equipment and projects. The principles of education are laid down in the Party programme and directives are given by the Party central committee. Universities and higher institutions are entirely under the Council of Ministers. Central policy is carried out by local education bodies who are linked with central government and with local People's Councils. About 10% of the budget is allotted to education.

Year	Schools	Teachers	Pupils
1923	574	865	25,250
1938	677	1,551	58,717
1961	3,524	10,948	334,621
1964	4,000	15,000	405,000
1969	4,971	31,289	..

	1938–39			1970–71		
	Schools	Teachers	Pupils	Schools	Teachers	Pupils
Kinder-garten	23	40	2,434	1,423	2,460	47,500
Primary Education	649	1,477	55,404	1,374	18,944	260,645
Secondary and training	3	18	675	46	1,157	80,400
Higher Education	–	–	–	36	941	36,525

AUSTRIA

The present system has been developed through the Federal Constitution Act of 1929, the Federal Constitution Act of 1962 and the School Organization Act of 1962 as modified by supplements in 1965 and 1966. These acts have extended compulsory schooling from an eight to a nine years' course; the leaving age is now 15. The number of children in a class is laid down by a law, and must not exceed 36.

For children of compulsory school age there are general schools on three levels; primary schools (Volksschulen) entered at 6 for an eight years' course of four lower and four higher years of general education.

Upper primary schools (Hauptschulen) have two streams, and lead either to academic secondary schools and higher education, or to technical and vocational schools.

Polytechnics (begun in 1962) are compulsory for all who do not stay in upper primary school for the ninth year or go on to intermediate or secondary school. Secondary schools are entered at ten by children who have finished their fourth year in primary school and passed an examination. The Gymnasia have obligatory modern language from the first year and obligatory Latin from the third. They divide in the higher years into (1) humanities courses with one modern language, Latin and Greek, (2) Latin and two modern languages, (3) Geometry, Latin and one modern language. The Realgymnasia divide into (1) obligatory modern language and geometry, (2) Latin or a second modern language. Both types of school have a leaving examination which gives entrance to university. There are four universities maintained by the state, at Vienna, Graz, Innsbruck and Salzburg and two technical universities at Vienna and Graz. There are 14 schools of women's professions (secondary level) with 2,394 pupils.

All state education is organized and all private education inspected by the central Austrian Federal Ministry of Education, acting through nine provincial boards and their subsidiary district boards.

Year	Primary schools	Pupils	Universities	Students
1920	4,772	888,640	3	15,347
1923	5,420	818,795	3	16,000
1934	5,323	866,469	3	16,280
1951	5,227	856,554	3	12,767
1961	5,379	742,132	3	25,739
1970	5,217	963,579	4	36,366

BELGIUM

The position after World War I was the aftermath of religious differences in the nineteenth century: in 1879 a Liberal government had ordered each municipality to organize at least one school where religion was only taught out of hours. The State was to have a monopoly of teachers' training and appointments. Strong opposition arose; enrolment in the state schools diminished rapidly and hastily organized church schools had taken about 66% of the school population within a few years. The Catholics regained the majority in parliament in 1884 and kept it until World War I. They withdrew the state monopolies and allowed local authorities to keep the public non-sectarian schools or to replace them by independents. In 1918 a socialist ministry declared that teachers of both kinds of schools would be paid by the state, but there would be no subsidies for the independent schools.

From 1914 school attendance had been compulsory for age 6–14; illiteracy then was thought to be about 13%. After 14 children could go on to secondary schools, which were divided into lower and higher secondary, the former staffed from teacher-training colleges and the latter from universities. Higher secondary schools offered either a modern or a classical course. In 1920 each commune was obliged to maintain a primary school and pay for it with state subsidies.

In 1954–5 a Socialist-Liberal government undertook a reform programme. The independent primary schools, mostly Roman Catholic, are organized by private bodies, but some municipalities subsidized the independent primaries with heating, school meals and transport. Secondary or vocational schools might be run either by the state or by organizations, but all teachers should have state certificates and state pay. Independent schools must observe the language regulations concerning the use of French or Flemish. Parents might choose the type of religious instruction (Roman Catholic, Protestant or Jewish) offered to their children.

In 1958 it was decided to abolish tuition fees to all primary and secondary schools. The state would offer no more subsidies for the building of independent primaries.

Year	Elementary schools (public)	Pupils	Universities	Students
1920	7,959	960,819	4	9,329
1931	8,549	917,122	4	11,407
1938	8,712	955,038	4	10,775
1947	8,697	788,514	4	15,000
1961	9,279	918,822	4	28,346
1970	8,611	1,013,419	4	61,485

The universities are at Louvain, Brussels, Ghent (Flemish), and Liège. There are five royal academies of fine arts and five royal conservatoires at Brussels, Liège, Ghent, Antwerp and Mons.

In 1939 there were eight lycees for girls' higher education, 52 of the 154 higher grade schools were for girls, 5 of the 12 communal and provincial higher grade schools and 3 of the 5 private higher grade schools were also for girls. By 1955 there were 5,346 girl pupils in the athenaeums (classical course higher secondary schools) to 38,273 boys, 77 boys and 10,403 girls in the lycées; of the 152 state higher grade schools 29 were for boys, 52 for girls and 71 co-educational, the 488 independent higher grade schools had 52,821 boys and 18,547 girls.

BULGARIA

In 1920 education committees existed in all towns and villages, and a university had been established at Sofia with faculties of History and Philology, Medicine, Law. Physics and Mathematics. The state granted a yearly subsidy for half the cost of the schools and the towns and villages paid the rest. Education was free and obligatory (although this was difficult to enforce) for children of 7–12. At higher schools richer parents paid fees. Illiteracy was thought to be about the same (40%) in 1920 as in 1910.

Secondary education was divided between academic and vocational schools. By 1939 there were 5,325 elementary schools from which pupils could go on to 1,938 pro-gymnasia, 132 gymnasia and 358 professional and domestic economy schools. In 1950 education was reorganized on Soviet lines. The age limit for free and obligatory schooling was raised to 15; in 1969 the starting age was lowered to 6 and secondary schooling was made obligatory. Schooling is now divided into: elementary schools (first to fourth year), primary (first to seventh), preparatory (fifth to seventh), secondary (eighth to eleventh) and complete secondary (first to eleventh).

Year	Elementary schools	Pupils	Universities	Students
1910	3,786	430,011	1	2,260
1921	5,440	579,317	1	4,899
1926	5,685	461,971	2	5,091
1934	5,411	714,817	2	8,696
1946	9,238	889,854	9[1]	49,800
	(1946–47)			
1956	6,250	830,000	9[1]	37,451
1965	3,057	1,117,482	35[1]	98,394

[1] Includes all institutes of higher education which are now integrated with universities in one system.

CYPRUS

Central administration began with laws of 1920 and 1923 providing central payment of salaries for Moslem and Christian teachers. In 1929 all teaching was brought under government control. In 1933 a general act laid down a schools system which, with amendments, is still operating.

Elementary schools are mainly co-educational and have six classes. About three-quarters of them are one-teacher and two-teacher schools (one teacher to some 60 pupils). English is taught in the upper grades. Secondary schooling is either at Government schools, which are inter-communal, or communal schools. Greek children go on either to the Greek gymnasium or to the commercial schools, which are mainly private. Turkish children take academic courses at 'orta okul' for three years and then a further three years at lycée or college. Government schools have seven-year courses on English grammar school lines. There are also government technical schools which have academic and trade streams. Cyprus has provision for teacher-training and for vocational training, but no university. The government gives financial assistance to students studying at foreign universities.

CZECHOSLOVAKIA

In 1920 education followed a common European pattern; children went to national schools run by the state which were elementary, higher elementary or secondary. The secondary schools were either gymnasia, offering a classical education, or *Realschulen* with courses in modern subjects and the sciences. In Slovakia most of the schools were denominational, mainly Catholic, but this was not so in the rest of the state although there were sharp national divisions. In Bohemia there were 178 secondary schools of which 114 were Czech and 64 German. There were four universities, at Prague, Olomouc, Brno and Bratislava, the last two having been founded in 1919.

By the time of the German occupation in 1939, with the same system in force, there were over 15,000 elementary schools, 68% of them Czech, 21% German, 4% Ruthenian, 6% Magyar and 0·6% Polish. There were over 2,000 higher elementary schools of which 75% were Czech and 22% German. There were about 400 Gymnasia and *Realschulen*, of which about 370 were Czech and about 80 German. There were 212 state-aided commercial schools with about 41,000 pupils, three extra faculties not integrated into the universities, a Ukrainian University in Prague, four technical high schools in Prague and Brno (one Czech and one German in each city). There were also the higher veterinary academy, mining academy, higher agricultural college, academy of arts and high commercial school. The universities had about 20,000 students including 4,000 women. (Figures for elementary and higher elementary schools in 1937 give 868,000 girl pupils as against 860,000 boys and 214,000 girls as against 245,000 boys; but there were few girls in the technical high schools – 332 as against a total of 7,027).

In 1948 the system was reorganized by the Education Act of 21 Apr. By this the present uniform state system was instituted, with standard curricula and children, if possible staying at the same school for the whole period of their free and compulsory schooling, which is now from 6 to 15 (formerly 14). Secondary schools follow and are of one kind only, then training and vocational schools and university. There are 35 institutes of higher education altogether including 2 new universities and 12 technical universities. In 1970 political tests were re-introduced for all teachers and students.

Year	Elementary schools	Pupils	Universities	Students
1921	13,417	1,931,690	4	13,607
1930	15,064	1,793,356	4	20,444
1947	11,836	998,177	4	52,456
1961	12,580	2,220,781	6	88,564
1972	10,551	1,912,225	6	106,800

DENMARK

In 1920 education was compulsory for children from 7–14. Public schools were free with the exception of a few middle schools, and were largely supported by communal rates. The elementary grades included the grammar and middle schools; 13 of the grammar schools were government schools and 29 of them private. There were 121 private middle schools. Private schools received grants from the government, as did the 70 'popular high schools' – adult education schools with about 8,000 pupils. The university of Copenhagen had five faculties and admitted women equally with men.

In 1937, 34 of the elementary schools were maintained by the government, 3,899 were run by local communities and 565 were private. Students at the University of Copenhagen (1479), the University of Aarhus (1928) and the University of Odense (1964) numbered 35,413 in 1970.

Currently the school leaving age is 15. The primary and lower secondary schools take pupils from the first to the tenth grade; the latter have three final grades which are either voluntary non-examination forms or examination forms working for the Réal Examination. This is a leaving examination alternative to the Studentereksamen taken by pupils at the 108 upper secondary schools, which gives them access to university or to any other higher education institute. Only about 10% of schools are now private and they are under state or municipal supervision.

Year	Elementary schools	Pupils	Universities	Students
1911	3,422 (est.)	376,696	1	3,000 (est.)
1921	4,203	476,400	1	3,200 (est.)
1930	4,502	497,430	1	5,000 (est.)
1935	4,556	495,000	2	5,300 (est.)
1950	4,099	511,206	2	7,350 (est.)
1960	2,575	546,929	2	7,900
1970	2,455	527,401	3	35,413

FINLAND

Before World War II children attended obligatory day school for six years, beginning at 7. There was practically no illiteracy, but on the other hand very little interest in higher education. Some 10% of children went on to secondary schools and only 1% to university. The upper four grades of the elementary schools ran parallel with the lower four of the secondary schools, which elementary school children entered by examination at 11. At the end of secondary school a further examination gave entrance to university. Helsinki University was founded in 1640, Turku Swedish University in 1919 and Turku Finnish in 1922. There were also schools of economics in Helsinki (Finnish 1911, Swedish 1927) and Turku (Swedish 1927). The Institute of Technology in Helsinki had been founded in 1849 and the teachers' training college in Jyraskyla in 1934.

Currently children must attend school between 7 and 16. At 11 they take an examination for secondary school and must try again in the fifth or sixth grade if they have not passed. If they then succeed, they begin in the first grade of the grammar school. The elementary school has a six-year course standardized for all children; there is then a centralized two-year citizenship school with some pre-vocational training, some of them having a voluntary ninth grade. Elementary schools are mainly small – half the teaching population is employed in two-teacher schools and about 35% in bigger schools with 3, 4 or more teachers.

Grammar schools were originally based on German gymnasia and still follow this pattern except that languages take more time; Finnish children must learn Swedish as well as other modern languages. The grammar school is the only one offering entrance to higher academic education; other secondary schools only admit to vocational higher education. About half grammar school pupils are girls.

The state supports almost all schools, whether public or private. Elementary schools are run by local authorities, city councils etc., but the state pays 25% of costs in the city and 90% of salaries and 66% of other costs in the country. The state pays 80% of the operating costs of private grammars, and 70% of total costs of vocational schools and adult institutes. All schools are under the ultimate control of the Ministry of Education.

Year	Elementary schools	Pupils	Universities	Students
1912	..	237,107	1	3,030
1920	4,456+1,335 elem. grades in other schools	259,030	2	2,719
1930	9,885+1,396 grades	371,086	3	6,688

Year	Elementary schools	Pupils	Universities	Students
1950	5,965 sch. districts +220 schools in towns	488,307	3	9,273
1960	6,540 districts+ 421 schools	665,968	5	17,576
1970	4,626	416,966	6	45,775

FRANCE

In 1920 secondary education for boys was supplied by the state at lycées and by the communes and private organizations at colleges and independent schools. Secondary schooling consisted of a seven-year course which might be Latin and Greek, Latin and sciences, Latin and modern languages, science and modern languages. The lycees and colleges for girls were mainly private, state lycées and colleges did not offer the same curriculum as was available for boys. In 1925 government schools were allowed to offer it, which meant that from then on girls could follow the academic courses leading to university entrance. From 1930 they were also allowed to attend those lycées and colleges formerly only for boys.

(In 1917 lycées and colleges for boys had had 90,546 pupils, those for girls 37,677.)

Elementary education begins at 6, continuing until 13 (before 1936) then 14 (until 1947) 15 (until 1959) and now 16. After elementary schools there are five types of secondary course; elementary schooling ends with a two-year observation period from 11 to 13 during which it is decided which type of secondary schooling will suit the child.

The lycee offers a five-year general academic course, in classical, modern or technical streams, concluding with baccalauréat. Lycees and technical schools also have four- or five-year long professional courses; colleges have three-year short professional courses and three-year general courses in preparation for non-technical professions and teacher-training. There is also a three-year terminal course of general education and vocational training.

The universities have 17 law faculties, 6 medicine faculties, 4 pharmacy, 12 mixed medicine and pharmacy faculties, 23 science faculties and 21 faculties of letters. The law of Nov 1968 required re-organization within the universities so that courses could be run and research co-ordinated in line with the requirements for national diplomas.

Faculty work is re-organized in Education Research Units.

1970–71

Type of school		Schools	Pupils
Infant and elementary	state	65,679	6,326,288
	private	8,873	1,034,340

		Boys	Girls
General education	state	276,128	298,821
colleges	private	100,607	117,138
Secondary education colleges	state	613,195	624,610
Lycées	state	577,685	607,407
	private	242,725	262,404
Colleges of technical	state	262,939	175,269
education	private	51,208	117,562

Year	Elementary schools	Pupils[1]	Universities	Students
1911	82,488[2]	5,654,794[2]	17	41,190
1921	68,015[2]	3,835,816[2]	17	49,931
1931	80,346	4,635,435	17	78,674
1946	80,933	4,668,000	17	123,313
1954	80,857	5,282,500	17	151,215
1962	90,698	7,079,500	17	244,814
1971	74,552	7,360,622	23	647,918

[1] Enrolment figure greater than attendance because pupils changing schools are enrolled twice.
[2] Including Algeria.

GERMANY

In 1918 Germany had adopted the Prussian system of providing for elementary schools supported from the rates in every town and village, at which attendance was compulsory from age 6–14 for all children not attending other schools. Above elementary school were the middle schools which gave a professional or commercial education; continuation schools which provided similar but part-time courses; *Gymnasien* with classical courses of nine years in preparation for university; *Progymnasien* which did not have the highest classes of the *Gymnasien*; *Realgymnasien* giving more time to modern subjects; *Realschulen* and *Oberrealschulen* with modern languages instead of Latin. Girls attended the *Gymnasien* and special high schools. There were also technical high schools with about 12,000 students, about 10% of them women. There were 23 universities with faculties of theology, jurisprudence, medicine and philosophy. A law of 1920 laid down that children should attend the Foundation school for a four years' course before going to the *Volksschule*. Both kinds of elementary school were supported partly by the state and partly by local authorities. In the middle schools instruction was to be provided in modern languages, usually English and French. The *Realgymnasien* and the *Oberrealschulen* were abolished in 1938 and replaced by the German High School (*Deutsche Oberschule*) which gave most of its timetable to German culture and modern languages, and the *Aufbauschule* which gave an intensive academic education to the most intelligent pupils from elementary schools. Two more universities had been founded at Hamburg and Frankfurt.

In 1941 Latin script replaced the Gothic script in schools.

Year	Elementary schools	Pupils	Universities	Students
1911	61,557	10,309,949	23	56,428
1926	52,320	6,629,779	25	60,458
1932	52,961	7,590,073	25	68,148
1938	51,118	7,596,437	25	43,139

EAST GERMANY

In the German Democratic Republic (East Germany) a Soviet system has been adopted, in which children attend one school, either Polytechnic High School or Extended Polytechnic High School, for 10 or 12 grades.

Year	Elementary schools	Pupils	Universities	Students
1955	11,007	1,883,400	46[1]	60,148
1960	8,864	1,992,192	44[1]	75,205
1971	6,198	2,570,504	54[1]	152,315

[1] Includes institutions of university standard.

WEST GERMANY

In the German Federal Republic (West Germany) the present system comprises primary schools which have a nine years' course, intermediate schools, *Realschulen* with a six years' course and the *Gymnasien* with a nine years' course. Pupils attend from 6 years to 15. The final high school certificate gives access to any higher education institution.

Year	Elementary schools	Pupils	Universities	Students
1955	29,465	4,636,470	17	85,914
1961	30,346	5,003,652	17	163,863
1970	21,501	6,359,300	49[1]	555,564

[1] Includes institutions of university standard.

GIBRALTAR

Prior to 1939 the schools were mainly Roman Catholic schools assisted by government grants. A report in 1943 led to the establishment of the Education Department in 1944 and the appointment of a Director of Education. An Education Advisory Board prepared an ordnance on the school system which came into force in 1950.

Primary schools have infant departments which children may enter at five and where teaching is in English and Spanish; Spanish is no longer used by the time the children come to the junior section at seven. At eleven there is a selection examination for secondary schools and according to results the children go on to grammar school, secondary modern or technical school. Grammar schools and technical schools prepare children for the General Certificate of Education and for entrance to higher education, which they must get abroad. Gibraltar has no provision for higher education.

Year	Elementary schools	Pupils[3]
1911	13	2,656
1921	16	2,629
1931	13	2,700
1951	22[1]	3,400[2]
1961	24[1]	4,628
1970	23[1]	5,165

[1] All schools.
[2] Pupils in state schools.
[3] School age is 5–15.

GREECE

In 1920 the age for compulsory education was from 6 to 12, but in many districts this was difficult to enforce. Secondary education was divided between middle schools and high schools and was not free; the cost of primary education was paid by the state.

The secondary schools had about 51,000 boys and 5,000 girls. There were two universities with faculties of law, philosophy, theology and chemistry, and a polytechnic college. By 1939 the secondary schools had about 50,000 boys and 22,000 girls; the commercial schools had about 2,000 boys and 800 girls.

The conservatories for music and the arts had about 3,000 boys and 3,800 girls.

Since 1963 elementary education has been free at all levels. Following the primary schools there are gymnasia with courses divided into two three-year periods; in the latter period courses are divided between the classics and mathematics and sciences.

There are universities at Athens and at Patras. There are considerably fewer private gymnasia than public (197 to 739 in 1969) but more private technical and vocational schools (255 as against 49). Slightly less than half of elementary school pupils go on to secondary education (about 500,000) and of those about 35,000 go on to university and about 19,000 to higher education institutes of economics, agriculture, industry, political science and general technology.

Year	Elementary schools	Pupils	Universities	Students
1913	3,835[1]	–	2	3,250 (1912)
1920	7,224	532,103	2	–
1928	8,062	621,281	2	–
1940	8,339	985,018	3	6,269
1951	9,331	935,695	2	6,527
1961	9,995	895,887	2	15,218
1970	9,620	872,608	5	51,363

[1] 1911.

HUNGARY

Education at the end of World War I was on the German pattern; infant school was followed by elementary school, compulsory from 6 to 12, then middle schools, *Realschulen* and gymnasia. Every parish or commune was obliged to maintain an infant school. Parallel with the fourth grade of elementary school were the Burgher middle schools in which boys and girls separately began six-year and four-year courses respectively. Parallel with the sixth grade of elementary school were higher primary schools, also for boys and girls separately and with three- and two-year courses. Both types of school offered professional, commercial courses. Burgher schools were supported by the towns; the state supported high schools for girls and some of the gymnasia, which were otherwise maintained by larger communes or church organizations. The five universities each had four faculties (theology, law, medicine, philosophy) except for Agram which had no faculty of medicine.

There were a number of national schools; of the 16,000 elementaries 12,000 were Magyar, the rest Romanian, Croatian, Serb etc.

Between 1945 and 1946 the communist system was introduced, with one general school replacing the primary, elementary and lower grades of the middle schools and compulsory from 6–14. In 1948 the 4,322 denominational schools were nationalized, but in 1950 four of the teaching orders were allowed to go on staffing the eight licensed Roman Catholic schools. There are currently 6 technical universities, 4 medical, 3 arts and 1 economics university. There are 20 other institutes of higher education which have greater autonomy since the reforms of 1969.

Year	Elementary schools	Pupils	Universities	Students
1910 (includes Croatia and Slavonia)	19,339	2,938,091	3	10,162
1920 (Hungary proper)	6,162	856,941	4	9,719
1931 (Hungary proper)	6,856	966,347	4	11,184
1941 (Hungary proper)	8,103	1,104,916[1]	5	9,683[1]
1970 (Hungary proper)	5,626	1,177,887 (and 20 Higher Education Institutions)	18[2]	78,889

[1] 1939.
[2] Four universities proper and 14 specialist universities.

ICELAND

There is a central administration operating through 37 educational districts. Schooling is compulsory from 8–15 and all public schools are co-educational with a common curriculum. Children attend primary school at seven and go through the first and second stages to leave at twelve after a leaving examination. Primary education is general with one foreign language (Danish) taught from the 1st grade and a second (English) from the 2nd. From primary children go to intermediate secondary school for one year to take a standard examination admitting them to full secondary school, either grammar school or specialized school if they pass, or general secondary school otherwise. The general school leads to teacher-training school, vocational or technical school; grammar school leads to university entrance.

The University of Iceland in Reykjavik was established in 1909 and has faculties of law, philosophy, medicine, engineering and economics.

The first education act was passed in 1907 and revised in 1926, 1936 and 1946. The five laws passed in 1946 are the basis of the present system of compulsory schooling, primary and secondary school organization and teacher-training systems.

IRISH REPUBLIC

On the establishment of the Irish Free State the Irish language was included in all school curricula.

Elementary education was free. Secondary education was mainly under

332

private control, often church control, but all schools which received grants from the state were open to inspection by the Education Department. Technical schools were partly run by local authorities and partly by the state in that they were controlled by local authorities but maintained partly by state grants. The agricultural schools were run by the Department of Agriculture and ran residential courses in agriculture and domestic economy for farmers' sons and daughters; similar schools were run by the religious orders with state grants.

Technical and vocational schooling is currently controlled by local Vocational Education Committees and maintained partly by rates and partly by the state. Agriculture, rural sciences and other related subjects are still among the most important. There are three state agricultural colleges, 7 private colleges and numerous winter schools controlled by the County Committees of Agriculture. Separate elementary and secondary schools still provide for the majority of children, but there are 4 comprehensive schools so far (1971). There is also a policy of closing small one-teacher and two-teacher schools and bringing children to larger central schools.

Year	Elementary schools	Pupils	Universities	Students
1926	5,636[1]	493,380[1]	2	3,088
1936	5,243[1]	484,601	2	5,052
1941	5,114	464,108	2	5,431
1951	4,879	452,114	2	7,699
1966	4,685	496,516	2	14,686
1970	4,012	507,406	2	19,746

[1] Estimate.

ITALY

Schooling is compulsory for children from 6–14, in elementary schools which have two cycles. There are two grades in the lower and three grades in the higher cycle. The school week has 25 hours. Middle schools follow, still compulsory and free, with a three-years complementary course ending in diploma.

All schools are controlled by the Ministry of Public Education and teach a standardized curriculum which must also be followed in private schools. Secondary education begins with gymnasia courses. Children go on to a three-years *liceo* course for general education or to the *liceo scientifico* for five years or the *liceo artistico* for four years. Attendance in secondary and higher education is as follows. (The figures refer to government schools.)

333

1970	Schools	Boys	Girls
Junior secondary	8,755	(Total 2,064,762)	
Classical Liceo	722	101,333	103,441
Science Liceo	597	143,582	76,634
Teachers' schools	152	–	25,666
Teachers' Inst.	637	27,092	182,256
Tech. and Prof. Inst.	1,864	137,483	94,882
Agric. Inst.	71	14,537	1,020
Ind. Inst.	473	236,224	5,129
Comm. Inst.	683	117,654	111,302
Surveyors' Inst.	365	113,487	2,897
Managerial Inst.	87	1,859	9,786
Tech. girls' school	88	–	13,815
Art schools	123	(Total 21,625)	

In 1929 the Lateran Treaty included measures on the teaching of religion in state schools which have applied ever since. Religion was to be taught within school hours but was to be under the control of the church.

The chief reforms were made in 1923 onwards, following the political and philosophical ideas of the fascist academic Gentile. The main effect of this reform was in the spirit of education but some organizational changes were made. New Complementary Schools were founded to replace the former technical schools; the Gymnasia were preserved but the normal schools were reorganized as general vocational schools and new Science Lyceums replaced the science division of the gymnasium. Lower Technical Institutes were founded with four-year courses leading to Technical Institute.

Year	Elementary schools	Pupils	Universities	Students
1911	61,497[1]	3,002,168[1]	21	22,210
1921	125,542	3,930,367	21	41,176
1931	93,376	4,550,184	26	30,101
1936	105,136	4,875,344	26	72,944
1951	37,113	5,580,179	27	145,070
1961	41,044	4,339,500	28	174,989
1971	35,691	4,970,315	42	759,872

[1] 1908

LIECHTENSTEIN

The basic school law was passed in 1929 and amended in 1956. The curricula were established in 1948. The State Education Council lays down all curricula including those for private schools. Schooling is compulsory from 6–14. The

Volkschule course was originally followed by complementary courses in agriculture for boys and home management for girls, but these have been much expanded. After six years of primary schooling children go to *Realschule* for three years, to Girls' High School for four years (after the fifth year in primary) to gymnasium for five years or to technical middle-school for five years. There is an evening technical college at Vaduz but no other higher education. The state assists students to study abroad.

LUXEMBOURG

The school law of 1912 organized compulsory primary schooling; a decree of 1945 fixed the term of compulsory education at eight years, to be extended by discretion for a year or half a year. In primary school teaching is bilingual, German being taught in the first year and French in the second. Primary school is followed by two years in compulsory continuation schools. Secondary education is in lycées or technical schools; only the lycées lead to university. The boys' lycée course is either a Latin and Greek course or a modern course; for girls the classical course is Latin only. The classical courses are preparation for university entrance and the modern courses lead to specialized higher education outside the university. University courses must be taken abroad; there are post-secondary courses in Luxembourg for students going on to foreign universities.

MALTA

Prior to 1946 education had had no reform or reorganization since those inspired by the Kennan Report of 1876. Interest was mainly in primary education. In 1946 primary education was made compulsory from 6–14. There is a standard curriculum, but local variations are made at the discretion of local authorities. There is a permanent central administration under the Director of Education. Primary education is general, and is followed by grammar school, secondary technical school or vocational school. Secondary schooling is traditionally independent of government ruling in its curricula, but both grammar and technical secondaries prepare students for the General Certificate of Education and for higher education. Courses at secondary schools last from 5–7 years. The Royal University of Malta was formed in 1937 from former colleges and given its autonomy in 1947. It has faculties of theology, law, medicine and surgery, dental surgery, engineering and architecture, arts and science.

Year	Elementary schools	Pupils	Universities	Students
1911	172	21,983	1	149
1921	102	20,000	1	130
1931	165	30,134	1	120
1948	110	40,100	1	..
1957	113	55,515	1	..
1971	109	31,566	1	726

MONACO

The school system has a nineteenth-century basis, reformed in 1942 and 1945. Primary schooling lasts from 6–14, with five years' elementary and then supplementary or secondary schooling. Curricula are based on French models. There is a selection examination for secondary courses at eleven. Monaco has one general secondary school – the Lycée – which has a seven-year course for baccalauréat (the examining authority is the Académie d'Aix-en-Provence) which qualifies students for French university places, which they may take up with state assistance from Monaco.

THE NETHERLANDS

In 1917 a constitutional amendment stated that the government accepted all, and not just public, education as 'the object of (its) constant care'. In 1920 financial help for private primary education was made equal with help for state primaries. Education is still largely provided by and divided between the churches.

Administration is strongly centralized; however any corporation with legal status can ask a city government to establish an elementary school. If the corporation can guarantee adequate attendance then the city must comply. This does not apply to secondary schools; although they may still be requested the city is not bound to provide them.

Elementary education begins at 6 (7 before 1938) with the primary course. About 86% of children go on to advanced primary which has a three- or four-year course and a leaving certificate which admits to technical school. Of these, about 13% go on to gymnasium and lyceum which have five-year courses (in the case of the Latin grammar school, six years) and are streamed in the two upper grades for classics or science. These give access to university.

The universities have faculties of humanities, social sciences, natural sciences, technical sciences, medical sciences, agricultural sciences and are organized in 13 schools.

Year	Elementary schools	Pupils	Universities	Students
1911	5,363	916,594	4	–
1920	5,947	1,111,829	6	7,956
1930	8,328	1,268,724	8[1]	12,238
1938 (est.)	7,812	1,242,778	6	9,395
1947	7,936	1,293,269	10[1]	25,036
1960	8,039	1,460,819	11[1]	40,585
1970	8,125	1,438,831	13[1] [2]	93,594[2]

[1] Includes degree-giving institutions.
[2] 1969.

NORWAY

Children begin their schooling at 6 or 7, aording to whether they live in the town or in the country. At present compulsory schooling is for seven years, but from 1959 there has been a gradual introduction of a nine-year compulsory course, with an upper stage in the primary schools.

Schools are controlled and partly maintained by the municipalities, rural and urban. Primary school is followed by continuation school, general secondary schools with lower and higher stages, folk high schools, giving access to university, and vocational schools.

There are four universities, Oslo, Bergen, Trondheim – which consists of the State Institute of Technology and the State College for Teachers – and Tromsø which was founded in 1968. There are also the State Colleges of Agriculture, Sport and Architecture, the State Veterinary College and the Independent Theological College.

Year	Elementary schools	Pupils	Universities	Students
1910	5,941[1]	279,823	1	1,550 (1911)
1920	5,999	282,117	1	1,383
1930	5,802	304,462	1	3,615
1946	–	287,390	2	5,098[2]
1960	4,245	316,349	2	7,678
1971	3,579	555,367	4	32,989

[1] 1908.
[2] Bergen University was established in 1946 but not opened to students until 1948.

POLAND

In the first years of the republic the emphasis was mainly on primary education; secondary schools were comparatively few, most of them private and in the territory formerly occupied by Russia. The education law of 1932 provided a new basis for the system which lasted until reorganization under a decree of 1945 and a further one in 1956.

Primary education has a seven-year course, but it is not possible to build full seven-year schools in all areas. In country areas particularly the aim instead is to provide at least one central seven-year school to which pupils can go at the end of the four- and five-year courses provided in local schools. In 1953 there was a new standard curriculum for primary schools leading to a leaving certificate; pupils gaining the certificate go on to general secondary schools which have a four-year course as a continuation of primary school. The two frequently come together in one eleven-year school. There are also elementary vocational schools, technical schools, vocational secondary schools and various training schools.

In higher education, the universities are no longer seen as separate units; all institutions offering education at a certain level are seen as one conception.

Year	Elementary schools	Pupils	Universities	Students
1921	24,996	2,566,306	6	21,844
1931	26,939	4,245,626	6	32,694
1950	22,864	3,280,669	8	–
1960	26,152	4,827,600	7	–
1970	26,145	5,099,200	9 and 75 other institutions of higher education	322,100

PORTUGAL

Compulsory primary education has been in force since 1911; illiteracy in 1930 was still estimated at 32%, and in 1970 at 30%.

Public elementary education was supplemented by night-classes until World War II and by village learning centres in places where there were not sufficient children to fill a school. In 1936 there were 21,460 pupils at the evening course and 46,257 in the village learning centres; these figures are additional to the 448,587 pupils in public elementary school full-time courses. The number in secondary education was 17,956 and there were only 45 secondary schools and 5 schools for training teachers. There were four universities.

The proportion of secondary to elementary schools has since altered significantly; in 1970 there were 961,546 pupils in the elementary schools and 367,000 in the secondary and secondary-preparatory schools. Secondary education is divided between lycees and professional and technical schools.

Year	Elementary schools	Pupils	Universities	Students
1911	7,120	–	3	2,955
1920	7,007	170,415	3	–
1930	8,295	422,624	3	5,641
1940	8,021	467,997	3	5,071
1950	10,884	621,069	3	9,614
1960	18,086	887,235	3	16,185
1970	16,284	939,999	3	33,860

ROMANIA

The census of 1910 indicated 60% illiteracy. By 1918 there was free and compulsory elementary education, but insufficient schools for the law to be rigorously enforced. There were about 5,700 elementary schools with about 690,000 pupils. Secondary education was divided between lyceums, gymnasiums, seminaries and professional schools, with separate schools for boys and girls; about 29,000 boys attended and about 9,000 girls, the boys at 28 lyceums, 21 gymnasia and 7 seminaries, 12 normal schools, 61 professional schools and 23 agricultural schools; the girls at 11 high schools, 4 normal schools, 32 professional schools and 10 schools of domestic economy. There were two universities with faculties of law, philosophy, science and medicine and theology.

The elementary and secondary systems continued on similar lines until 1948 when a new system was introduced based on 'dialectical and historical materialism'. All church schools were placed under state control, and adult education was provided by Houses of Culture of which there were 11,500 in 1950. By then, illiteracy was estimated at 23%.

There are now general schools on the Russian model with ten-year courses from 6–15; secondary education is in general, technical or vocational schools, and lyceums were re-introduced in 1968, combining academic and vocational courses. There are 49 institutes of higher education in addition to the universities; the latest student figure of 151,705 includes students at these institutes.

Year	Elementary schools	Pupils	Universities	Students
1910	5,074	584,953	2	5,596[1]
1919	5,764	692,896	4	7,576[2]
1930	14,900	1,973,949	4	27,666
1942	11,041	1,607,879	4	..
1956	16,000	1,859,270	4	..
1966	15,513	3,327,856	5	136,948
1971	15,503	3,192,566	6	148,428

[1] 1915.   [2] Not including Cernarti.

SPAIN

Elementary education to reduce illiteracy has always been of prime importance. In 1910 illiteracy was 59·35%, in 1930, 45·46%, in 1947, 20·8% and in 1960, 14·24%.

Education has been compulsory since 1909 and free in the public elementary and primary schools. All schools, whether public or private, are under government control and inspection. There are twelve educational districts with the universities as centres. Secondary education is available at middle schools, of which there must be at least one in each province.

The constitution of the Republic which came into force in 1931 declared that Spain had no official religion. Education therefore was to be secular, but the churches had freedom to teach their doctrines in their own schools under state inspection. The Franco regime once again established Catholicism as the state religion and restored religious teaching to its former position. Administration was centralized.

Year	Elementary schools	Pupils	Universities	Students
1910	30,073	2,052,158	10	16,000 (est.)
1920	31,790	2,932,720	11	23,586[1]
1930	35,989	2,292,486	11	35,717
1941	44,572	2,375,911	12	34,669
1951	56,747	2,180,669	12	50,303
1960	96,734	3,751,469	12	86,873
1967	118,786	4,179,000	13	125,771[2]
1970	138,114	4,749,500	13[3]	..

[1] 1919.   [2] 1965.

[3] In 1972 4 new universities (Malaga, Cordoba, Santander and 'University of the Air') were created.

SWEDEN

In 1918 there were 16,821 public elementary schools in which education was free and compulsory. There were 77 public secondary schools, 49 people's high schools and 9 technical schools. There were 708,075 pupils at the elementary schools, of which 33,189 went on to the secondary schools and 3,768 to the two universities. By 1937 there were about 620,000 elementary school pupils of whom 55,000 went on to secondary schools and about 9,000 to the universities.

As well as the two universities at Uppsala (1477) and Lund (1668) there were private universities in Stockholm and Göteborg with faculties of philosophy and law (Stockholm) and of philosophy only (Göteborg), and a state faculty of medicine in Stockholm.

The school age was normally from 7–14, but in certain districts schooling was compulsory for seven, eight or nine years. Those not entering the eighth grade of an elementary school or going to any further school had to attend a continuation school for one day or evening course. Older secondary schools are still in use and have courses divided into lower and higher stages. Comprehensive schools offer elementary and secondary education in nine grades, after which the higher stage of secondary education is taken in vocational schools and 'people's colleges'. There are 6 state universities, including those once private.

Year	Pupils in elementary schools	Universities	Students
1910	791,545	4 (2 private)	3,528
1920	707,520	4 ,,	3,989[1]
1930	671,606	4 ,,	5,468
1940	548,682	4 ,,	4,567
1950	654,000	4 ,,	6,733
1960	843,000	4	25,535
1970	640,000	6	..

[1] 1921.

SWITZERLAND

The administration and pattern of schooling has remained virtually the same since 1918. There is no central authority since control is held by the cantons. Elementary schooling is free in all cantons, and in most there are secondary schools for boys aged 12–15 as an alternative to the normal secondary system. The elementary system was placed under the civil authority in 1874, and originally there was some difficulty in enforcing attendance in Roman Catholic communes.

The cost of schooling in some cantons falls entirely on the communes; in others it is divided between commune and canton. The secondary schools include gymnasia, high schools and vocational schools for girls and general professional and vocational schools. There are 7 universities where teaching is organized as: theology, law, economics and social sciences, medicine, arts and science. There are two Federal Institutes of Technology, at Zürich and at Lausanne, which had 7,175 students in 1970.

Year	Pupils in elementary schools	Universities	Students
1912	544,152	7	7,071
1921	536,219	7	6,510
1930	471,708	7	7,396
1941	452,506	7	10,121
1951	476,331	7	12,679
1960	571,548	7	16,576
1970	..	7	32,264

TURKEY

Before the establishment of the republic education was in theory compulsory for all children from 7–16 but might be given in state schools, private schools, community schools or – under inspection – at home. The state schools were directly controlled by the Ministry of Public Instruction, but there were large numbers of religious schools and seminaries. The middle schools took boys from 11–16 and in 1918 it was proposed to introduce similar schools for girls.

With the republic the state system incorporated primary schools for children from 7–12, secondary schools, 'preparatory' schools for children going on to higher education, lyceums and higher technical schools. Literacy was estimated at 11% in 1927, 29% in 1945 and 49% in 1970. The problem of illiteracy has been connected with the gradual introduction of the Latin alphabet which began in 1926; the publication of books in Arabic characters was forbidden after 1928 and the use of the new alphabet became general in 1930.

Children may still learn at home if certain conditions are satisfied, and all must receive primary education from 7–12. In 1970, of the 4,907,090 children in elementary schools, 1,189,136 went on to middle school, lycee, professional and technical schools.

The University of Istanbul was reorganized in 1933, having originally five faculties of arts, medicine, law, theology and science. A separate school of law was founded at Ankara in 1925 and separate faculties of history, geography and philology also at Ankara in 1934, and a college of medicine in 1938. There are now 2 universities in Istanbul and 3 in Ankara, including the Middle East Technical University. There are two other universities and a technical university in Trabzon. Religious instruction had been prohibited in state schools under the republic but was allowed in elementary and middle schools from 1948.

Year	Elementary schools	Pupils	Universities	Students
1918 (est.)	36,230	1,331,200	1	—
	(all schools)			
1940	9,417	905,139	1	6,739
1950	17,301	1,672,168	2	20,225
1960	22,011	2,548,927	6	44,368
1970	37,177	4,907,090	8	152,287

USSR

In 1917 the government secularized all schools and educational institutions; private schools which were not church schools were in many cases allowed to go on under government supervision. Elementary education was compulsory and co-educational. Secondary education followed the common pattern of real-school, progymnasium and gymnasium with separate gymnasia for girls. In 1934 schools were reorganized into three types, four-year, seven-year and ten-year, with factory schools and technical schools complementary to the elementary schools. In 1936 there were 164,081 ordinary elementary schools, 1,797 factory schools and 2,572 technical schools. The school age was from the age of 8 until 1944, when it was lowered to 7.

The labour reserve school for pupils between 14 and 17 was introduced in 1940, and in 1943 the co-education rule was altered to allow separate schools in urban areas. Co-education was re-introduced in 1954. From 1958, 'general polytechnic education' is to last until the age of 15 or 16 but at any rate for 8 years – the school-leaving age had been raised to 17 in large towns and industrial areas by 1956; the general course is to be followed by a two-year course in which school work is combined with production work for all children except those who go on to art schools. From 1959 the labour reserve schools were, with other schools, reorganized as town and rural professional and technical schools. There are also ten-year secondary courses for adults.

Figures issued in 1970 give universities as '800, including institutes and other places of higher education' and students as '4·5m. including 2·41m. taking correspondence or evening courses'.

Year	Elementary schools	Pupils	Universities	Students
1911	100,295	6,180,510	10	39,853
1926	108,424	9,903,000	23	–
1936	164,081	–	23	–
	All schools			
1950	220,000	37m.	–	–
1953	–	–	887 ('Higher educ. institutes')	1,527,000
1970	197,000	49·4 m.	800 ('Higher educ. institutes')	4·5m.

UNITED KINGDOM

The Education Act of 1918 required County Councils and County Borough Councils to provide 'for the progressive development and comprehensive organization' of education in their own areas. Funds should be made available to provide free secondary education for all under 18 who were capable of profiting from it; schemes must have central Education Board approval but were to be paid for by the local authorities from the rates, from taxation and from grants made to them. Elementary education was controlled by the Board, and administered by the local authorities. Attendance was obligatory and free for children from 5–14 until 1947 when the leaving age was raised to 15; from 1972 it was raised to 16. The Education Act of 1944 abolished all fees in secondary schools maintained by local authorities (including voluntary schools). In 1953 there were 6·2m. children in schools partly or wholly financed by local education authorities, 99,000 children in schools receiving a direct grant from the Ministry but otherwise independent, and 244,000 in schools inspected and recognized as efficient but receiving no state or local aid. Education was classified by the 1944 Act as primary (age 5–11), secondary (11–14, later 15) and further education. Secondary courses led to leaving examinations at two levels, the higher level admitting, with other entrance qualifications, to university. Currently children attend primary schools until 11; in some areas there is selection at 11 and pupils go on to grammar school or to secondary modern school according to fitness; in other areas there is no selection and all children go on to comprehensive schools. The largest group of secondary schools is the secondary modern group which provide a general education up to the minimum school leaving age; there are approximately 3,000 with 1·3m. pupils. There are academic grammar schools (about 1,100) with 605,000 pupils and many of them for boys or girls only, and about 1,200 comprehensive schools with about 950,000 pupils.

344

The universities are independent bodies which receive aid from the state; they are not the responsibility of any local education authority, although local authorities are obliged under the Education Act of 1962 to provide grants for students taking first-degree courses, most of them offered on the results of the General Certificate of Education examination and depending on the means of the student.

England and Wales

Year	Elementary schools	Pupils	Universities	Students
1918	20,983 (inc. 12,302 voluntary schools)	5,184,000	11	30,510
1938	20,916 (10,553 vol.)	4,526,701	12	43,379
	Primary and secondary			
1953	28,290	6,205,998	17	70,000
1970	28,500	8,500,000	34	184,304

Scotland

	Elementary schools			
1918	3,363	839,002	4	10,140
	Primary			
1938	2,900	630,425	4	10,364
1953	2,859	581,400	4	14,718
1970	2,587	622,647	8	35,202

Northern Ireland

1938	1,727	194,347	1	1,592
1953	1,626	198,390	1	2,733
1970	1,256	208,002	2	7,653

YUGOSLAVIA

In 1918 elementary education was compulsory and free; secondary schools were comparatively few. There was one university at Belgrade and another at Zagreb; a third was founded at Ljubljana in 1920.

Elementary courses lasted for eight years and were divided between elementary schools and continuation schools of four years each; children going on to secondary or technical schools did not go to the continuation course. All schools were controlled by the central Ministry of Education, but

345

there were schools provided for the national minorities under the Ministry's ultimate control – mainly elementary, secondary and teachers' training schools for Albanians, Magyars, Bulgarians, Czechs, Slovaks, Italians, Romanians, Turks and Ruthenians.

Elementary education currently consists of a four-year course with complementary schools offering six- and eight-year courses. Children go on to senior secondary schools, training and technical schools.

Year	Elementary schools	Pupils	Universities	Students
1921	5,974	800,868	3	11,686
1931	8,498	1,276,764	3	14,693
1953	13,781	1,382,843	82 faculties	56,935
1970	14,048	2,875,075	247 faculties	239,701

In 1918 there were still many different national systems within the new state. The law of 1929 provided a new single system for public schools; prior to this there was no general law and individual problems had been met by Ministry directives. The compulsory period was defined at eight years; in 1945 it was seven years and in 1949 eight. In 1948 an outline plan was drawn up for the seven-grade school with standard curricula and organization all over the state. Local governments in the different republics had always had some discretion in applying educational law; in 1955 a general law defined the powers of local government agencies in this respect.

Currently the primary schools have four elementary grades and four senior grades, the four senior having the same curriculum as the lower secondary schools, which pupils may go on to as an alternative. Higher secondary education is either in general schools leading on to university or in vocational schools. The organization of the system is based on the law of 1958.

BIBLIOGRAPHY

Baron, G., *Society, Schools and Progress in England.* Oxford, 1965
Dixon, C. W., *Society, Schools and Progress in Scandinavia.* Oxford, 1965
Fraser, W. R., *Education and Society in Modern France.* London, 1963
Grant, N., *Society, Schools and Progress in Eastern Europe.* Oxford, 1969
— *Soviet Education.* London, 1964
Huebener, T., *The Schools of West Germany.* New York, 1962
Idenburg, I. P., *Outline of the Dutch School System.* Groningen, 1964
Oittinen, R. H., *Education in Finland.* Helsinki, 1960
Scarangello, A., *Progress and Trends in Italian Education.* Washington, DC, 1964
Vodinsky, S., *Schools in Czechoslovakia.* Prague, 1965

14 PRESS

ALBANIA

There are 19 newspapers with an annual circulation of 45·5m. All papers are published in Tirana.

Major papers	Circulation	Politics	Founded
Zëri i Popullit, Voice of the People	57,000	The official organ of the Central Committee of the Albanian Workers Party	1942

ANDORRA

By agreement between France and Spain, no newspapers are published in Andorra, but each country supplies its national newspapers.

AUSTRIA

There are 30 daily newspapers (7 of them in Vienna) with a combined circulation of 2m. The most important are:

Major papers	Circulation	Politics	Founded
Kronen-Zeitung	466,000	Independent	1900
Kurier	426,000	Independent	1954
Express	320,000	Socialist	1958
Arbeiter-Zeitung	102,000	Socialist	1889
Die Presse	54,000	Independent/Business	1848

In addition, Austria boasts the *Wiener Zeitung*, founded in 1703, the oldest daily paper in the world.

BELGIUM

There are 45 daily newspapers, of which 29 are in French, 15 in Flemish and 1 in German. Freedom of the press is guaranteed by the constitution. The five papers with the highest circulations are:

Major papers	Circulation	Politics	Founded
De Standaard	322,000	Independent Flemish	
Het Laatse Nieuws	296,000	Liberal Flemish	1888
Le Soir	273,000	Independent French	1887
Het Volk	216,000	Christian Workers Movement, Flemish; published in Ghent	
Gazet von Antwerpen	189,000	Christian Democrat, Flemish; published in Antwerp	

BULGARIA

There are 17 daily newspapers with a circulation of 1·8m. Much the most important is the party newspaper, *Rabotnicheskoto Delo*, The Workers' Cause, with a circulation of 630,000. The theoretical organ of the party is *Novo Vrenie*.

CYPRUS

There are 1 English, 2 Turkish and 7 Greek daily newspapers. Three papers have a circulation over 10,000.

Major papers	Circulation	Politics	Founded
Haravghi, Dawn	13,570	Left-wing	1956
Eleftheria, Freedom	12,800	National Liberal	
Phileleftheros, Liberal	12,000	Independent; pro-Government	

CZECHOSLOVAKIA

Before the Russian invasion, there were 28 daily newspapers, 12 in Slovak. The party daily, *Rude Pravo*, founded 1920, has a circulation of over 1m.

DENMARK

There are 59 daily newspapers with a combined weekday circulation of 1·8m. Five daily papers have a circulation above 100,000. They are:

Major papers	Circulation	Politics	Founded
Berlingske Tidende	186,000	Conservative; midday	1916
Berlingske Tidende	167,000	Conservative; morning	1749
Ekstrabladet	165,000	Radical Liberal	1904
Politiken	140,000	Radical Liberal	1884
Aktuelt	100,100	Paper of the Social Democrat Party	1872

The first newspaper in Denmark was published in 1666. Freedom of the press was guaranteed in 1849.

FINLAND

There are 118 newspapers published more frequently than once a week. 102 are in Finnish, 15 in Swedish and one bilingual. The four papers with the largest circulations are:

Major papers	Circulation	Politics	Founded
Helsingin Sanoriat	265,000	Independent	1904
Aamulehti	128,000	Conservative	1881
Turun Sanomat	96,000	Independent	1904
Uusi Suomi	93,000	Conservative	1847

FRANCE

There are 167 daily papers with a circulation of 13·5m. Paris has 14 daily papers, whilst 14 provincial papers have a circulation above 200,000. The following Paris papers have a circulation above 250,000:

Major papers	Circulation	Politics	Founded
France Soir (including Paris-Presse)	1,200,000	Independent (but Paris-Presse pro-Gaullist)	
Le Parisien Libéré	775,000	Popular Independent	1944
Le Figaro	425,000	Moderate right	1826
Le Monde	352,000	Independent, left of centre	1944
L'Aurore	326,000	Conservative opposition	1944
Paris-Jour	252,000	Pro-Government	1957

The three largest provincial dailies are:

	Circulation
Ouest-France (Rennes)	655,000
Le Progrès de Lyon (Lyons)	450,000
Le Dauphiné Libéré (Grenoble)	405,000

EAST GERMANY

There are 40 daily newspapers with a combined circulation of 6·2m. The ruling Socialist Unity Party controls the great bulk of the press. The two papers with the highest circulation are *Neues Deutschland*, circulation 800,000 and *Berliner Zeitung*, circulation 500,000, founded 1945.

WEST GERMANY

There are 462 daily newspapers with a combined circulation of 23·5m. The five most popular daily papers are:

Major papers	Circulation	Politics	Founded
Bild Zeitung (Hamburg)	4,296,000	Popular tabloid	1952
Westdeutsche Allgemeine (Essen)	600,000	Independent	
Hamburger Morgenpost (Hamburg)	354,000	Pro-S.P.D.	
Hamburger Abendblatt (Hamburg)	325,000	Independent	
Frankfurter Allgemeine Zeitung (Frankfurt)	317,000	Independent	1949

Much the most popular weekly is *Der Spiegel*, published in Hamburg, with a circulation of 1,033,000.

GREECE

The *coup d'état* of Apr 67 considerably disrupted the Greek press. Six of Athens' 14 dailies subsequently ceased publication. The following three papers now operating have a circulation above 100,000:

Major papers	Circulation	Politics	Founded
Apoghevmatini	142,000	Conservative	1952
Ta Nea	131,000	Formerly Liberal	1931
Acropolis	101,000	Conservative	1881

The only newspaper to have increased circulation since 1967 is *Eleftheros Kosmos*.

HUNGARY

There are 25 daily newspapers with a circulation of 1·5m. The party daily is *Népszabadság* (People's Freedom), founded 1945, with a circulation of 750,000. The weekly *Szabad Föld*, circulation 414,000, is widely read in the countryside.

ICELAND

There are 5 daily newspapers published in Reykjavik with a circulation of 85,000. The three most popular are:

Major papers	Circulation	Politics	Founded
Morgunbladid, Morning News	38,000	Independence Party	1913
Timinn, The Times	18,500	Progressive	1917
Visir, The Bud	13,000	Independence Party	1910

IRISH REPUBLIC

There are 7 daily newspapers (all in English) with a combined circulation of 702,000. Five of these are published in Dublin. Those with a circulation over 100,000 are:

Major papers	Circulation	Politics	Founded
Irish Independent	174,200	*Fine Gael* organization	1905
Evening Press	150,000	*Fianna Fail* organization	1954
Evening Herald	139,300	*Fine Gael* organization	1891
Irish Press	128,400	Independent/*Fianna Fail*	1931

The *Cork Examiner*, founded 1841, has a circulation of 57,500 and is published in Cork.

ITALY

Italy has 83 daily papers, but with a combined circulation of only 5·8m.

Major papers	Circulation	Politics	Founded
Corriere della Sera (Milan)	550,000	Right-wing Conservative; owned by Crespi family	1876
La Stampa (Turin)	480,000	Centre-Left	1868
Il Giorno (Milan)	275,000	Independent	1956
Il Messaggero (Rome)	271,000	Centre; owned by Perrone family	1879
La Nazione (Florence)	215,000	Right-wing Conservative	1859
Il Resto del Carlino (Bologna)	213,000	Right-wing Conservative	1885
L'Unità (Rome)	200,000	Communist	1924

LIECHTENSTEIN

There are no daily newspapers. The Progressive Citizens' Party issues *Liechtenstein Volksblatt*, circulation 4,500, four times a week; *Liechtenstein Vaterland*, circulation 3,800, is issued thrice weekly by the Fatherland Union. The Christian Social Party produces the weekly *Der Liechtensteiner*, circulation 1,600. All are published in Vaduz.

LUXEMBOURG

There are 7 daily newspapers with a combinedcirculation of 140,000. Only three exceed 25,000. These are:

Major papers	Circulation	Politics	Founded
Luxemburger Wort	70,000	Christian Social Party organization (P.C.S.)	1848
Tageblatt	30,000	Socialist Workers Party organization (P.O.S.L.)	1912
Le Républicain Lorrain	25,000	Luxembourg edition; published in Metz	

MALTA

There are 6 daily newspapers, three in Maltese and three in English. The three major papers, all published in Valletta, are:

Major papers	Circulation	Politics	Founded
Times of Malta	10,000	Independent	1935
L'Orrizont	8,000	General Workers Union organization	1962
Malta News	5,000	General Workers Union organization	1964

MONACO

There are special editions for Monaco of *Nice-Matin* and *L'Espoir de Nice*, both published in Nice. There is an official weekly journal, *Journal de Monaco*, which publishes texts of laws, etc.

THE NETHERLANDS

There are 77 daily newspapers with a total circulation of over 3·9m. The four largest papers are:

Major papers	Circulation	Politics	Founded
De Telegraaf	396,000	Independent, conservative	1893
Het Vrije Volk	285,000	Labour-orientated	1931
Algemeen Dagblad	250,000	Neutral, published in Rotterdam	1946
De Volksrant	210,000	Roman Catholic	1920

NORWAY

There are 82 daily newspapers with a combined circulation of 1·5m. The five largest are:

Major papers	Circulation	Politics	Founded
Aftenposten	190,000	Conservative	1860
Dagbladet	103,200	Independent/Liberal	1869
Bergens Tidende	77,300	Liberal, published in Bergen	1868
Adresseavesen	74,000	Conservative, published in Trondheim	1767
Arbeiderbladet	71,300	Labour Party (A.P.) organization	1884

POLAND

The paper with the largest circulation is the Communist *Express Wieczorny*, circulation 550,000; the party organ, *Trybuna Ludu*, People's Tribune, founded 1948, has a circulation of 205,000. The Communist political weekly, *Polityka*, has a circulation of 195,000.

PORTUGAL

There are 32 daily newspapers with a combined circulation of 261,000; ten of these are in Lisbon. The three largest papers are:

Major papers	Circulation	Politics	Founded
Diario de Nóticias	160,000	Conservative, pro-Government	1864
Diario Popular	125,000	Republican	1942
O Século	90,000	Independent/Republican	1880

The chief Oporto paper is *O Primeiro de Janeiro*, founded 1868, circulation 80,000.

ROMANIA

There are 51 daily newspapers. The official organ is *Sćinteia*, founded 1931, with a circulation of 1m. Only papers controlled by, or affiliated to, the government exist. The monthly, theoretical organ of the Party is *Lupta de Clasa*.

SAN MARINO

There are no daily newspapers, but an edition of *Il Resto del Carlino* of Bologna gives special attention to San Marino.

SPAIN

There are 198 daily newspapers with a total daily circulation of 5·2m. The three main Madrid dailies are:

Major papers	Circulation	Politics	Founded
ABC	215,000	Monarchist	1905
Pueblo	202,500	National/Syndicalist organization	1940
Ya	142,000	Strongly Catholic	1935

Outside Madrid, the two most important dailies are the independent *La vanguardia Española*, published in Barcelona, with a circulation of 220,000 and *La Gaceta del Norte*, a Catholic Bilbao paper which sells 97,000.

SWEDEN

There are 148 daily newspapers with a total circulation of 4·42m. Four papers have a circulation above 250,000.

Major papers	Circulation	Politics	Founded
Expressen	522,500	Liberal, published in Stockholm	1944
Aftonbladet	443,900	Left-wing Social Democrat, published in Stockholm	1830
Dagens Nyheter	418,600	Liberal, published in Stockholm	1864
Göteborgs Posten	280,000	Liberal, published in Göteborg	1858

SWITZERLAND

There are 128 daily newspapers with a combined circulation of 2·1m. The five papers with the highest circulations are:

Major papers	Circulation	Politics	Founded
Tages-Anzeiger	180,500	Independent, published in Zürich (German)	1893
Neue Züricher Zeitung	92,100	Radical, published in Zürich (German)	1780
National Zeitung	74,600	Radical, published in Basle (German)	1842
La Suisse	63,000	Independent, published in Geneva (French)	1898
Tribune de Lausanne	57,400	Independent, published in Lausanne (French)	1862

TURKEY

In all, there are 338 daily newspapers, 24 of these in Istanbul and 22 in Ankara. Four have a circulation above 100,000.

Major papers	Circulation	Politics	Founded
Hürriyet	716,000	Independent	1948
Tercüman	213,000	Independent	1961
Milliyet	171,000	Independent	1950
Cumhuriyet	117,000	Independent	1924

USSR

In 1970 there were 8,694 newspapers with a total circulation of 141m., published in 57 languages.

Major papers	Circulation	Founded
Pravda, Truth	7,400,000	1912
Izvestiya, The News	8,000,000	1917
Trud, Labour	2,400,000	1921

There are two weekly periodicals with a circulation above 1m.: *Ogonyok* (2·1m.) published by *Pravda*, on sociology and politics; *Za Rubezhom* (1·1m.) reprints from foreign newspapers.

UNITED KINGDOM

The following daily newspapers have a circulation above 1m.:

Major papers	Politics	Founded
Daily Mirror	Independent/Pro-Labour	1903
Daily Express	Independent/Right-Wing	1900
Daily Mail	Independent	1896
Daily Telegraph	Conservative	1855
Evening News	Right-Wing	1881
Sun	Independent/Popular	1964

The Times, founded 1785, has a circulation of 401,000; the *Guardian*, founded 1821, has a circulation of 303,000.

YUGOSLAVIA

The major newspapers are:

Major papers	Circulation	Politics	Founded
Večernje Novosti	341,000	Organ of the SSRNJ; evening	
Politika	263,000	Principal pre-war journal; now organ of the Serbian SSRN	1901
Politika Ekspres	97,000	Evening paper of *Politika*	1963
Borba	86,000	The official Communist Party organ	1922

BIBLIOGRAPHY

Grannon, F. R., *The British Press and Germany, 1936–1939*. New York, 1972
Gronvik, A., *The Character of the Finnish Press*. Helsinki, 1953
Weber, K., *The Swiss Press: An Outline*. Berne, 1948

INDEX

Most of the chapters in this book run in alphabetical sequence and for this reason we have not attempted to produce a completely detailed index. The main aim has been to allow the reader to locate the country by page for any major subject included in this publication.